39256384

D1483790

AFRICAN AMERICAN
LEADERSHIP

SUNY series in Afro-American Studies
John H. Howard and Robert C. Smith, editors

AFRICAN AMERICAN LEADERSHIP

RONALD W. WALTERS
and
ROBERT C. SMITH

State University
of New York
Press

Published by
State University of New York Press, Albany

© 1999 State University of New York

Production by Susan Geraghty
Marketing by Nancy Farrell

Printed in the United States of America

For information, address State University of New York
Press, State University Plaza, Albany, N.Y., 12246

Library of Congress Cataloging-in-Publication Data

Walters, Ronald W.
    African American leadership / by Ronald W. Walters and Robert C.
Smith.
        p.   cm. — (SUNY series in Afro-American studies)
    Part I is a republication of Smith's 1983 Black leadership, with a
revised final chapter and an added postscript.
    Includes bibliographical references and index.
    ISBN 0-7914-4145-8 (alk. paper). — ISBN 0-7914-4146-6 (pbk. :
alk. paper)
    1. Afro-American leadership. 2. Afro-American clergy. 3. Afro
-American politicians. 4. Afro-Americans—Politics and government.
I. Smith, Robert Charles, 1947–   Black leadership. II. Title.
III. Series.
E185.615.W314 1999
303.3'4'08996073—dc21   98-26840
                                                                  CIP

10 9 8 7 6 5 4 3 2 1

To
Pat and Scottie

CONTENTS

TABLES

PREFACE

Any serious perusal of studies in the field of African American politics must conclude with the observation that studies of African American leadership have been neglected. The irony is that this lapse has taken place amidst significant signs of the growth in generic studies of leadership in American academia in general. Several programs of leadership studies have been established in various centers of higher education that have stimulated this trend: for example, the Leadership Program at Gettysburg College, the Leadership Research Program at the Wharton School at the University of Pennsylvania, the School of Leadership at Virginia Commonwealth, and many other leadership programs and curricula are in development as well.

In 1993, these centers and programs received funding from the Dwight D. Eisenhower Leadership Program of the U.S. Department of Education, funding twenty-nine separate programs devoted to various aspects of leadership. And although this program was eliminated from the budget of the Department of Education in the recent fervor to balance the budget, the program stimulated a considerable debate over the utility of leadership studies as a field of academic endeavor. The final assessment was that although such an initiative was in its infancy, it appeared that the issue of leadership, as such, was applicable across a broad range of social activities and research.

One recent study that attempted to summarize this thrust in higher education was by Helen and Alexander Astin, distinguished observers of trends in the general field of higher education.[1] This assessment, funded by the Eisenhower Program, entitled "A Social Change Model of Leadership Development," nevertheless has been typical in that it excluded any reference to studies of ethnic or African American leadership either in its concepts or selected bibliography, when the movements fostered by these groups have been the most powerful examples of social change in American history. Most important, *there was no indication that ethnic/racial leadership would encounter different challenges than mainstream majoritarian leadership and, as such, would warrant a special academic focus.*

AFRICAN AMERICAN LEADERSHIP

One of the real anomalies in the field of African American politics is the dearth of modern studies on leadership, even though the subject has been addressed historically in the literature of the field, as indicated in the more than half century of research reviewed in part I of this volume. There have, of course, been studies referencing important individual leaders—Black mayors such as Harold Washington and Coleman Young, presidential candidates such as Shirley Chisolm and especially Rev. Jesse Jackson, civil rights figures such as Martin Luther King Jr., Roy Wilkins, James Farmers, and others (see appendix B to part I). These studies, however, have focused on the political exploits of such individuals set in a wider context of political analysis or works of descriptive biography. Few have sought to take seriously the structure of African American leadership and its function as discrete categories of social relations and analysis.

Aside from the purely academic necessity for such studies, the case has been made by the authors for studies that focus specifically on African American leadership, because of the nature of the modern challenges faced by this racial group. Important questions need to be answered such as: What has been the historical development of Black leadership? What are the major sub-categories of Black leadership and how have they performed relative to each other? What is the primary function(s) of Black leadership and what resources do they utilize to perform such functions? What is the future of Black leadership?

The Black community, like any sizable community in America, has a rich legacy of leadership that has contributed much to the mobilization of that community. And like other aspects of the racial dynamic in America, while studies of the general phenomenon of leadership have proceeded from a majoritarian perspective, the value of a focus on Black leadership is that it takes into consideration the unique perspective of a subcommunity and a subordinate community as well, thus, correcting and, as such, complimenting the general picture.

However, scholars of the Black experience have also avoided the systematic study of leadership, for while there are many studies of the civil rights movement, as an example, there are few studies of the importance to its leadership as a class and the way in which it facilitated the objectives of that movement. It was as though the activity of this class and the way in which its members functioned as symbolic leaders, organizers, followers, and so on, was unimportant to the development of objective information on the way in which racial groups were mobilized, how the agenda-setting product of their mobilization was produced, or the social impact on society as a whole.

Beyond the civil rights generation, the emerging group of Black political and bureaucratic leaders have also made contributions to the Black community as a result of their incorporation into mainstream political arenas such as the cabinet and Congress. Nevertheless, a tension that will be evident throughout this volume is the conclusion of many scholars that the contributions that have resulted from Black incorporation into mainstream political arenas have been marginal at best because, these scholars argue, militant, protest strategies still need to be employed. Yet a study of this conclusion is important because it raises the question of whether the marginal contributions of Black political and bureaucratic leaders is inherent in the nature of such leadership positions, or in the specific contexts within which such leaders operate, or in the broader contexts of White supremacy, or in all of these factors.

It is obvious that one's conception of the function (and thus the structure) of leadership and leadership studies is based, at least in part, on one's expectations of a given leadership group in question, and on what status one wants the reference group to achieve—or what mission the group is to carry out. It also depends upon a realistic assessment of the general social context within which leadership is set, such as, whether one's vision of democracy permits the magnitude of such change in order to achieve the objectives of the group. In any case, this constitutes another important subject of study addressed in this book, one that calls forth, not only a narrow study of leadership, but a major analysis of the realistic possibilities of the performance of such leadership given the challenges it faces, the origin of those challenges in the nature of society, and the resources they have available to confront them.

This volume is the product of the collaboration of the authors over the years while we were on the faculty at Howard University, beginning with our co-editorship of a special issue of the *Urban League Review* on "Perspectives on African American Leadership."[2] More specifically, part I is a monograph by Smith, that summarizes the extant social science studies on Black leadership, and was originally published by the Institute of Urban Affairs and Research at Howard University in 1983.[3] Except for its last chapter and for minor editorial corrections, it is published here unchanged.[4] However, a postscript on research published since 1983 is included. The range and scope of this new literature does not easily fit the analytic categories used in the earlier studies. Thus, the postscript allows the reader to see both change and continuity in social science research on Black leadership from the 1930s to the 1960s, from the 1960s to the 1980s, and from the 1980s to the present. Part II presents a series of chapters by Walters, some of which—such as chapter 6 (A Paradigm of the Practice of Black Leadership), chapter 8 (The National Black Leadership Roundtable), and chapter 11 (Leadership toward What Ends?)—were written especially for this volume. The other chapters are revised and updated versions of articles originally written for other periodicals and books.[5] Part III consists of a final chapter where we attempt to specify the interactions or linkages between the theory and research on Black leadership and its praxis. We also in this chapter look at the future of Black leadership as the new century dawns, reflecting on the structural tension between accommodation and protest.

We hope that this modest volume at least performs the function of reaffirming many of the time-tested issues of Black leadership analyzed in earlier studies and sets forth, in a more modern context, what issues might supplement them and thus provide a richer, more textured perspective on this subject. In doing so, we also would hope that it contributes to the generic literature in the field of leadership studies and provides the increasing number of academic units and courses with a useful volume on the existing concept of "change-oriented" leadership, or "transformative" leadership, with respect to the unique experience of African Americans in politics.

We would like to acknowledge the cooperation of the Institute of Urban Affairs, Howard University, the National Urban League, and Lincoln University for initial publication of some chapters included here and for permission to reprint them here. The three anonymous reviewers selected by State University of New York Press provided comments that led to improvements in the manuscript's substance and organization. David Hopkins did a superb job of copyediting. We would also like to thank Scottie Gibson Smith for her assistance in the preparation of the manuscript.

ACKNOWLEDGMENTS

We are grateful to the National Urban League for permission to use in revised form material previously published in the *Urban League Review* and *The State of Black America,* and to the Black World Foundation for use in revised form of material previously published in *The Black Scholar.*

PART I

Theory and Research

INTRODUCTION

What is a Black leader? What part have Black leaders played in the changing status of the Black community in the United States? What objectives have they sought? What ideologies have they embraced? What are their methods and styles? Their organizations and offices? What is their relationship to the Black masses? To Whites? What is the role of the preacher and the church? The politician and the vote? How has Black leadership changed in the last fifty years? What are the factors that account for this change? To raise these questions and provide some answers based on the available research is the purpose of this monograph. To the extent that the research literature does not provide answers to these questions, then a second purpose of this study is to provide an informed basis for speculation and to suggest areas where further research is necessary.

Of course, to ask questions about Black leadership is to ask larger questions—to ask questions about the basic subjects of Black politics, the status and fate of Blacks in American society, the adaptability of the system, and about the possibility of racial justice. The requirements of scholarship make the answers to these basic questions tentative and limited. However, if on the basis of the literature I can supply a basis for informed debate and intelligent prescription, then perhaps this study can make a contribution to the practical problems faced by the leaders of Black America.

I am grateful to the students in my Black politics classes at Howard University, and to Dr. Lawrence Gary and the staff of the Institute for Urban Affairs and Research, for their contributions to the development of this study. Dianne Pinderhughes rendered a detailed critique of the manuscript, and Matthew Holden Jr. was extremely generous with his time and criticisms. Mack Jones, Ronald Walters, John Howard, and Milton Morris read the manuscript in whole or part and made suggestions that led to improvements. I should also like to thank my neighbor, Lorraine Huffaker, for her assistance in the preparation of the manuscript, and I am grateful to my wife, Scottie, for her suggestions and for typing several drafts of the manuscript.

CHAPTER 1

Social Science Theory and Research on Black Leadership

Most of the serious works dealing with the Black political experience in the United States are studies in leadership (Jones 1972:10; Morris 1975:9). Ladd (1966:114) writes that to ask questions about "Negro leadership" is to ask some basic questions not only about the nature of that leadership but also about the larger subject of Negro politics. Jones (1972:7) also argues that much of the research on Black leadership in America "proceeds in an atheoretical manner." Consequently, what is needed is the development of some fundamental categories of a theory of Black leadership and politics in America. While there are various meanings of theory (Stinchcombe 1968; Rapoport 1958), in general, empirical social science theory has three major functions: (1) it should serve as an aid to the inventory and codification of the existing knowledge of phenomena, (2) it should serve as a guide to areas where further research is required, and (3) it should contribute to the development of the capacity to invent explanations of phenomena in a series of interrelated verifiable propositions.

This study, of course, cannot purport to fulfill these functions adequately. Rather, it is an effort to formulate the categories that are fundamental to analysis and theory construction in Black leadership research. The procedure is to dichotomize the extant social science research—representing more than one hundred published and unpublished studies going back nearly fifty years—into the old "Negro" leadership literature, which dates roughly from 1930 to 1966, and the new "Black" leadership literature, dating roughly from 1966 to 1980. This dichotomy is based on the assumption, fundamental to this study, that a transformation in Black leadership occurred in the 1960s.

Given this dichotomy, in chapter 2, I inventory and codify the old literature of the Negro leadership group organized around the following major analytic categories: power structure, social background (including class, color, and ethnic origins), organization, leadership types, and whatever theoretical fragments may be gleaned from these categories. In addition to these basic categories of analysis, I also review the literature for facts and insights on the role of Whites, the masses, preachers, and politicians in understanding Negro leadership. After this review of the old Negro leadership literature, in chapter 3, I specify and analyze the factors affecting the transformation from "Negro" to "Black" leadership in the 1960s. Chapter 4 contains a review of the literature about the new "Black" leadership, organized around the categories used in the review of the old literature in chapter 2. Finally, in chapter 5, I attempt to pull together the existing knowledge, draw out the interconnections between the old and new leadership, and suggest directions for theory and research.

CHAPTER 2

The Negro Leadership Literature

In the scientific study of politics in the United States, the concept of leadership, despite its obvious centrality, has not been sharply defined. Indeed, in a major review of the political science literature on the concept, the author concludes that there is a lack of explicit focus on leadership as a core concept in the discipline's major journals and paradigms (Paige 1977:11–40). Indeed, Paige notes that Seligman's 1950 article titled "The Study of Political Leadership" was the first such article specifically devoted to the general subject of political leadership in the then forty-four year history of the *American Political Science Review*. In the general social science literature, the concept has been used in such diverse ways to characterize such varied phenomena that there is a lack of agreement regarding even the basic properties of leadership (Gibbs 1950:91; see also Burns 1978).

This ambiguity in the general concept of leadership is reflected specifically in the Negro leadership literature where there are a wide variety of definitions, implicit and explicit. Myrdal, for example, writes, "We should not start from an attempt on *a priori* grounds to define the principal concept. . . . We have only to settle that we are discussing the role and importance of individual persons in the sphere of social action" (1944, 1962:113). Similarly, Ladd (1966:4) writes that little effort was made at the outset to develop any full and precise definition of Negro leadership because "the study as a whole is centrally concerned with defining it."[4] However, in general, Ladd (1966:4) notes that Negro leaders are considered to be "persons able to make decisions affecting the choice of race objectives and/or the means utilized to attain them." Matthews and Protho (1966:178) use what they call an "operational definition" for Negro leaders, that is, "those persons most often thought of as Negro leaders by Negroes." Wilson (1960a:10) understands Negro leaders to be "civic leaders—persons who acted as if the interests of the race or community were their goal." Thompson (1963:5) uses what he calls a "functional approach to leadership" designating the individual actor as a leader who for some period of time overtly identifies with the Negro's effort to achieve stated social goals. In the most parsimonious definition, Burgess (1962:77) defines a leader as an individual whose

7

behavior affects the patterning of behavior within the Negro community at a given time.

While one might wish that the conceptual and terminological confusion in the literature about what constitutes leadership were less and that the theoretical basis for conceptualizing the term in a particular way were clearer, the varied definitions of the term are comprehensible and empirically relevant. And, while agreement on the meaning of Negro leadership is far from universal, a tendency can be discerned among the authors to agree that: (a) leadership involves affecting the attitudes and behavior of Negroes insofar as social and political goals and/or methods are concerned; and (b) Negro leadership is not limited to Negroes but may and indeed does include Whites. Perhaps Cox (1965), in his neo-Marxist historical analysis of the development of Negro leadership, makes this point most effectively: "But the common cause of Negroes in the United States is not fundamentally limited to Negroes. It is in fact an aspect of the wider phenomenon of political-class antagonism inseparably associated with capitalist culture. A principle involved in the process of democratic development is at the basis of the Negroes' cause, and for this reason leadership among Negroes is likely to be as effectively white as black" (1965:229). Given this understanding of the principal concept, I turn now to an inventory of the social science research on leadership among Negroes.

POWER STRUCTURE: SCHISM AND REALIGNMENT

Historical analysis of the development of Negro leadership in the United States records the emergence of the phenomenon during slavery and its coming to maturity roughly in the period 1890–1930 (Cox 1965; Huggins 1978; Meier 1968). To the extent that these historical studies are correct, we can date the development and consolidation of the modern Negro leadership group at about 1930. This is also an appropriate point of departure for a review of the social science literature on Negro leadership, because the first significant study of the phenomenon by a political scientist, Gosnell's *Negro Politicians: The Rise of Negro Politics in Chicago*, was published in 1935, and Myrdal's monumental classic appeared several years later. Thus, historical and methodological research fortunately converge; fortunate because, as Kerlinger (1964:700–701) points out, all too often methodological or scientific research proceeds in a vacuum, without adequate historiography, and consequently it lacks perspective.

The available research on leadership in local Negro communities in both the North and South during this early period (circa 1930–50) indicates that there existed reasonably well developed power structures and status hierarchies. In the South, the local power structures were usually constituted by a relatively small group of preachers, teachers, undertakers, lodge leaders, and those with light skin (Myrdal 1944, 1962:667–736; Dollard 1957:85–96). In the North, the leadership group was constituted by a handful of politicians, a smattering of business and professional men, gamblers and other underworld figures, and a larger group of teachers, postal workers, and other lower-level government employees (Gosnell 1935, 1967; Myrdal 1944, 1962:689–736). Nationally, the leadership was comprised of persons with a more pronounced middle-class character—that is, with considerable educational and professional achievements—and was disproportionately composed of what Myrdal called "Negro glamour personalities," for example, prominent athletes, entertainers, and others accorded status by the White community (Myrdal 1944, 1962:722–34; Huggins 1978:92; Bennett 1965:26; Bunche 1939).

The leadership of this period, especially in the South but in the North and on the national scene as well, tended to be "accommodationists" in Myrdal's classic formulation, unable or unwilling to challenge the system of caste segregation. The evidence in this regard is clear insofar as the South is concerned (Bunche 1973; Myrdal 1944, 1962:720–22; Dollard 1957:211, 230). However, in the North and on the national scene, there is evidence at this time of a "rising spirit of protest" (Myrdal 1944, 1962:744). A number of observers also characterize the northern wing of the leadership as "conservative" and "accommodationist" (Bunche 1939; Bennett 1965). Gosnell (1935, 1967), for example, in his description of Chicago politics in the 1930s, did not observe significant civil rights protest during that time.

The final phase of the civil rights movement—the mobilization of protest in the form of boycotts, sit-ins, and mass demonstrations—beginning roughly with the Montgomery bus boycott of 1955, was to have profound effects upon these traditional structures of power in Negro communities. Indeed, there is evidence that the civil rights movements of the fifties and early sixties occasioned an important transformation, and in some cases displacement, of the traditional status hierarchies and power structures of Negro America.

The research on power structures in the Negro subcommunity has largely been the province of sociologists, beginning with Hunter's (1953) formulation of the problem. Political scientists have taken theoretical, methodological and substantive exception to Hunter's "reputational" approach to the problem of locating power in the American community, preferring instead the "issue areas" approach developed by Dahl and his colleagues in the New Haven Study (Dahl 1961; Wolfinger 1976; Polsby

1963). It is beyond the scope of this study to review the merits of the tangle of issues raised by these two research approaches. However, to the extent that the issue areas approach seeks to "frame explanations that would identify participants in policy making and describe what they did" (Polsby 1963:70), then it was probably inappropriate to the study of power in the Negro subcommunity. This is true because by and large that community was, until the late 1960s, excluded from participation in the urban policy-making process through a variety of devices (Kilson 1971; Smith 1978a; Katznelson 1973). While students of power in the Negro subcommunity might have sought to identify and describe the behavior of participants in the issue areas internal to the subcommunity, none did. Thus, what little we know about structures of power in these communities derives from the reputational approach.

The following major studies of the power structure in Negro subcommunities are available: Hunter's (1953) study of Atlanta, Pfautz's (1962) study of Providence, Rhode Island, and Barth and Abu-Laban's (1959) study of Seattle. In Atlanta's Negro community, Hunter found a power structure of middle-aged, middle-class professional men operating through a relatively well-defined and stable structure of civil rights, religious, fraternal, business, and welfare organizations. Although the NAACP was rated the "top" organization in the subcommunity (followed by the YMCA), the Organized Voters Association was rated number three and apparently exercised some influence, especially in the larger community. The leadership of Negro Atlanta tended toward "closure"; 90 percent of the persons comprising this group knew each other "well" or "socially," often getting together in an exclusive social club.

The leadership was characterized generally as conservative in its approach to issues, engaged in what Hunter, quoting Cox, called "protest within the status quo" (Hunter 1953:128). Generally, leaders of the subcommunity never rated formal inclusion in the upper levels of Atlanta's decision-making process, but rather were approached informally to get their opinions. However, an important exception to this relatively fixed pattern was found in the realm of partisan politics "where top Negro leaders work with top white leaders" (Hunter 1953:132).

Although in terms of social background, organizational structure, and closure, Barth and Abu-Laban found certain common characteristics of the Negro leadership groups of Seattle and those of Atlanta, the most basic conclusion of their study is that the well-organized, stable structure of power discovered in Atlanta was missing in Seattle. This omission is attributed to the relatively small size of the subcommunity, which made it difficult to support large separate institutions; the rapid expansion of the Negro population, which disrupted the traditional leadership pattern; and the leadership's success in getting liberal civil rights legislation enacted, a position that it did not wish to jeopardize by supporting separate institutions (Barth and Abu-Laban 1959:75–76). Thus, while the leadership of Atlanta was to some extent inclined to maintain separate subcommunity institutions of power, in Seattle the leaders emphasized the larger community and did not seek to wield power within the subcommunity. Nevertheless, the Negro leaders of Seattle held few positions of importance in the larger institutional structure of the community, and their decisions had little impact on the city as a whole (Barth and Abu-Laban 1959:75).

By contrast, the power structure observed in the Negro subcommunity of Providence was remarkably similar to that in Atlanta. The leaders were male, middle-aged, and middle-class in their educational and occupational backgrounds, tended toward closure, and operated through a relatively stable organizational structure, although unlike Atlanta, the Urban League in Providence, rather than the NAACP, was rated the most influential local organization (Pfautz 1962:156–66). Pfautz also found, in a pattern similar to that in Atlanta, that Negro leadership was oriented more toward segregation than integration and tended to support "protest within the status quo" of Providence, a status quo characterized by residential segregation, economic deprivation, and considerable discrimination. Yet Pfautz observed an age-generation cleavage in the subcommunity between the younger integrationist-oriented leaders and the older segregationist-oriented leaders, and concluded that the Negro structure of power in Providence, like that of most of Negro America, was in the process of "schism and realignment" under the impact of the civil rights movement (1962:166).

I return to this problem of "schism and realignment" later, but, first, to summarize the outcome of our review of the power structure research, the power structures of the Negro subcommunities of America varied, depending on the size and demography of the community, and the attitudes and values of the leaders. In each of the communities noted above, a middle-class leadership was observed, and in two of the three communities, this leadership operated through fairly stable and institutionalized structures of power, characterized by a relatively high degree of closure. In all three communities the leadership was relatively conservative in its approach to issues regarding the status of Negroes, and it generally had little impact on the decision-making processes of the larger community.

In its final phase—the phase of direct action—the civil rights movement confronted not only an entrenched, conservative White power structure, but also in many communities an entrenched, relatively conservative Negro structure of power. Bennett (1965:26) reports that the national structure of Negro power—institutionalized in the executive boards and administrative offices of the leading civil rights organizations, and including the bishops and pastors of the largest and most influential churches; the editors and publishers of major Negro newspapers and periodicals; leading educators, businessmen, and professionals; and important White liberal, labor, religious and philanthropic allies— was also subject to challenge by the young activists of the civil rights movement because "down through the years, the Negro power structure has been more active in accommodating the masses to misery than in organizing them for an attack on the forces responsible for the misery" (Bennett 1965:36).

Killan and Smith (1960) document this challenge to the Negro power structure of a single city in their study of the Tallahassee bus boycott of the 1950s, which led to a displacement of the established accommodating leadership by one that was protest-oriented. The bus boycott was initiated and supported by a group of young Negro ministers affiliated with Dr. Martin Luther King Jr.'s Southern Christian Leadership Conference (SCLC) and opposed by both the Negro and White power structures. Eventually, by creating new organizations (such as the SCLC) and replacing the leadership of the old (such as the NAACP), these new leaders were able to secure mass support, obtain the recognition of the White power structure, and displace the established leadership. Killan and Smith suggested that the pattern observed in Tallahassee was becoming the trend for Negroes throughout the country (1960:257). Meier, in a historical essay on the significance of Dr. King, wrote that in the late 1950s and early 1960s "the leaders of SCLC affiliates became the race leaders in their communities, displacing the established local conservative leadership of teachers, old-line ministers and businessmen" (1965:58). Thus, the Negro leadership described and analyzed in the political science literature below is to some extent a leadership in a state of "schism and realignment."

COLOR, CLASS AND SOCIAL BACKGROUND

In his description and analysis of leadership among Negroes in the United States, Forsythe (1972:18) points out that the most "common and persistent" method of classification is in terms of the militancy construct, followed by color, ethnic origin, and class. In this section, the focus is on class, color, ethnic origins, and social background.

Except for the Myrdal (1944, 1962) study, there is little in the standard social science literature regarding class, color, and ethnic origins of Negro leaders. Rather, most of the analysis is in terms of standard social background variables such as sex, age, education, and occupation.

Thus, much of what we know about the nexus between class, color, and leadership in the Negro community results from Myrdal's inquiry.

The actual quantitative correlation between class and color is not known; however, it is probable that historically the Negro upper class was disproportionately mulatto. At the time of emancipation, Myrdal writes, "What there was in the Negro people of 'family background,' tradition of freedom, education and property ownership was mostly in the hands of mulattoes. . . . They became the political leaders of the freedmen during Reconstruction, as well as their teachers, professionals and business people" (Myrdal 1944, 1962:697). Specifically, Forsythe (1972:19) notes "of the 20 Congressmen and 2 Senators who represented blacks during Reconstruction, all but 3 were mulattoes." Furthermore, about 32 of the 39 leaders noted for their protest against slavery between 1831 and 1865 are usually described as persons of mixed blood (Forsythe 1972:19). Bennett (1965:40) describes the Negro leadership of the 1950s as the "Black Puritan Class," that is, the lineal and spiritual descendants of the antebellum and Reconstruction mulatto upper class.

Thus, leaders in the Black community have historically been disproportionately from the Negro upper class and, given the correlation between class and color in the community, these leaders have also tended to have a light skin color. However, Myrdal contends that color, independent of its relevance to class, is a minor factor for Negro leadership. In his analysis of the relationship between social class and leadership, color is relegated to a footnote because most upper-class Negroes are leaders by definition; because of the close correlation between class and color; because there is more lower-class leadership in the Negro community than there is in the White community; and in part because of the strong tradition of leadership activity by the lower-class preacher and lodge leader. Therefore, color is a tenuous basis for leadership analysis because "while it is plausible that a light skin color is often an asset to a Negro leader in his dealing with both whites and Negroes, it is also certain that a dark skin color is sometimes advantageous for a Negro leader. The two tendencies do not cancel each other since they occur in different types of leadership" (Myrdal 1944, 1966:1390). This may explain why much of the recent analysis of the concept of leadership ignores color as a variable.

Regarding ethnic origin, again there is little in the standard literature; however, Glazer and Moynihan (1963, 1970:35) and Cruse (1967:115–46) have noted the disproportionate influence of West Indians on leadership and politics in New York City. For example, Glazer and Moynihan (1963, 1970:35) quote Claude McKay, himself a Jamaican, on the fact that the "first Negro presidential elector in New

York state, the first elected Negro Democratic leader and one of the first two Negro municipal judges were West Indians." It is also often noted that Marcus Garvey was of West Indian origin, as are Stokely Carmichael, Congresswoman Shirley Chisholm, and Congressman Mervyn Dymally.

The research findings of this study are limited to New York. However, given the facts that New York City served as the headquarters for the major civil rights organizations and that Harlem has a central influence on Black thought (Cruse 1967:11–63), one might speculate that the West Indian influence extends beyond the boundaries of New York to impact on national Negro leadership. But this is speculation; what we know is that in New York—the nation's most ethnically diverse city— Negro leadership has been constituted to some extent by persons of West Indian background.

The social background and career patterns of political elites have long been of interest to political scientists and sociologists. Since political leaders are not randomly selected from the population at large, but rather are recruited from identifiable economic and social strata, students of politics are interested in the background characteristics of leaders for essentially two reasons: (1) it is thought that these characteristics in some measure provide insight into the nature of the community from which the leaders emerge, and (2) these characteristics are thought to influence the goals and resources that the leaders bring to the political process and thereby to influence the success or failure, in a broad sense, of the community's efforts to attain its goals (Matthews 1954).

In the discussion in the previous section on power structure in the Negro subcommunity, the sociological studies reviewed showed a leadership group that was disproportionately male, middle-aged, and middle-class in terms of the educational and occupational backgrounds of the group's members. Basically, the political science literature reveals a leadership of similar background, with some variation depending on the degree of militancy. For example, in Durham, North Carolina, Burgess (1962:79–81) found a leadership of largely male, middle-aged, well-educated professionals and businessmen, although the "radicals" tended to be younger than were the moderate or conservative leaders. Thompson (1963:25–57) found a similar pattern in New Orleans, as did Ladd (1966:223–27) in Winston-Salem, North Carolina and Greenville, South Carolina, and Matthews and Protho (1966:188) in the four southern communities they studied. Wilson (1960a:11–13) found that the leadership of Chicago was also largely male, middle-aged, and middle-class. Finally, in terms of religion, there appears to be a basic congruence between leadership and mass, although in Chicago, Wilson (1960a:12) found that the so-called "upper-class" faiths (i.e., Episcopalian, Presbyterian, Congregational, and so forth) were disproportionately represented among the leadership, and in New Orleans, Thompson (1963:31–32) found that Catholics were underrepresented among the leadership, given their proportion of that city's population.

In summary, in terms of social background the studies reveal essentially a middle-aged, middle-class leadership of men, although the "radical" or "militant" leaders have tended to be younger and less middle-class in terms of their education and occupations. Generally, in the South, preachers, undertakers, and other businessmen have been better represented in the leadership group than, for example, teachers have been. This is explained by Matthews and Protho (1966:185) in terms of the "vulnerability concept"—that is, leadership in the South has required that Blacks have relative economic independence from or invulnerability to Whites. Teachers who, because of their education, might have been natural leaders in southern communities have been relatively unrepresented in leadership groups because of their vulnerability to the imposition of sanctions by Whites, while the relatively economically independent preachers and businessmen have been disproportionately represented.

Finally, although men have been disproportionately represented in the Negro leadership strata, Negro women have nevertheless played a larger leadership role in the subcommunity than have White women in the larger community (Monohan and Monohan 1956:590–91). With this exception, Monohan and Monohan (1956) conclude their comparative analysis of the backgrounds of national Negro and White leaders with the judgment that the characteristics of Negro leaders in America do not differ significantly from those of the leaders in the larger community. Given the relative economic disadvantage of the Negro community in comparison to the White community, this is a significant finding. For it indicates that, in spite of its poverty, the subcommunity has been able to produce a leadership of "competence," which has been comparable to that of the more economically affluent larger community.

ORGANIZATION

Organization is indispensable to successful, sustained political leadership, especially in the interest-group process of bargaining and compromise, which is characteristic of aspects of politics in the United States (Truman 1951; Wilson 1973). Although the Negro community has historically been characterized by a high proportion of charismatic and what Myrdal (1944, 1962:734) calls "glamour personality"–type leadership, there is also evidence that Negroes, both lower and middle class, exhibit a tendency to form and participate in organizations at a greater rate than does even the organization-prone American in general (Myrdal 1944, 1962:952; Olsen 1970; Babchuck and Thompson 1962).

Although the political role of the church and its leadership will be considered later, it is clear that the church (and its spin-off organizations, such as lodges, burial associations, charitable clubs, and so forth) has historically been at the foundation of Black community life, bridging the transition from slavery to freedom and thereby providing "a feeling of continuity and stability to black society" (Hamilton 1972:18).

Apart from the church and the fraternal lodges, Negro leadership was exercised through a variety of "civic associations" including but not limited to the YWCA, the YMCA, the Pullman Car Porters, and especially the NAACP and the Urban League (Myrdal 1944, 1962:819–42; Hunter 1953:126; Pfautz 1962; Barth and Abu-Laban 1959). Toward the end of the 1950s and into the 1960s, Martin Luther King's SCLC began to emerge as an important leadership forum in the Black community, especially among younger activist ministers and professionals (Burgess 1962:185; Matthews and Protho 1966:185; Ladd 1966:192). Also in the 1960s, the Student Nonviolent Coordinating Committee (SNCC), and the Congress of Racial Equality (CORE) (Zinn 1964; Carson 1981; Meier and Rudwick 1973) were important organizations in the civil rights movement. However, the evidence suggests that, of the organizations devoted to "improvement and protest" in the Negro community, the NAACP and the Urban League were clearly the most influential, ranking either first or second in each of the local power structure studies.

The National Council of Negro Women, the Negro professional associations (bankers, doctors, lawyers, and so forth), and the Greek letter organizations have also engaged in lobbying and petitioning at both the national and local levels, and have generally worked to improve the status not only of their particular group but also the status of the race as a whole. However, Myrdal concluded that at the national level, as at the local level, the NAACP and the Urban League were "without question" the most important organizations in the Negro struggle against caste (1944, 1962:819).

There is little in the literature on organizations devoted to electoral politics, or about nationalist or leftist organizations among Negroes. Gosnell (1935, 1967:93–114) presents an essentially descriptive analysis of "parts of the Negro machine in Chicago," while Wilson (1960a:49) found that the Negro community of Chicago was most thoroughly organized by the Negro political machine. In the 1920s, the Citizens Liberty League was organized in order to mobilize the Black vote to gain elective and appointive office in St. Louis (Patterson 1974:44–45). Also,

Hunter (1953:126) found that the Organized Voters Association of Atlanta was among the most influential organizations in that community. But, in general, electoral-type organizations are not frequently observed in the subcommunity, except as part of the urban political machines (Walton 1972:56–69).

Regarding leftist and nationalist organizations, Myrdal (1944, 1962) discusses in passing some remnants of the Garvey movement, a back-to-Africa group called "The Peace Movement of Ethiopia," and the National Movement for the Establishment of a Forty-Ninth State, a group seeking a territorial state for Negroes in the United States. However, he dismisses these groups as "paper organizations" or as having "never amounted to much" (1944, 1962:813–14). Thompson (1963:59) excluded the Black Muslims from his study of New Orleans because "they are small and uninfluential," while Burgess (1962:177) concluded that the recently established Black Muslim chapter in Durham, North Carolina, was only potentially influential. In a reference to leftist groups, Hunter (1953:127) found that in Atlanta the Negro leadership sought to undermine quietly the influence of the leftist Progressive Party in the Negro subcommunity. Thus, the research literature leads one to conclude that effective political organization in the Negro community has tended to be nonelectoral and nonradical (that is, not leftist or nationalist) in character.

Of the politically active organizations in the community, when they are studied one by one and measured by their limited accomplishments, Myrdal (1944, 1962:816–17) writes, "It is possible to view (them) all . . . as futile and inconsequential"; however, he concludes that taken together they "mean Negroes are becoming increasingly organized for concerted social action and when seen in perspective this represents a basis for attempts at broader organization." This still seems to be the most sensible conclusion from the available research, one that is confirmed by the developments of the 1960s.

LEADERSHIP TYPES

As pointed out earlier, the most persistent and common basis of classifying Negro leaders has been in terms of some variation of the militancy concept. Yet this method of classification has also been the source of the most common and persistent criticisms of the literature. These criticisms are considered in chapter 5. But first, it should be noted that as far back as 1944, Myrdal typed Negro leaders in terms of accommodation and protest. This basic typology has persisted through the years in one form or another in studies of Negro leadership. Higham (1978:3–6) argues that in one way or another the choice between a leadership of protest and a leadership of accommodation has also been characteristic of nearly all other ethnic groups in the United States.

While the number of types of leaders has varied from Myrdal's (1944, 1962) basic twofold construct to Burgess's (1962) and Thompson's (1963) fourfold ones, the variables used in categorizing leaders have basically been structured in terms of acceptance or rejection of the extant race system, style or method of opposition to the race system, or style or method of race advancement activity.

Myrdal's classic formulation is based on the "extreme policies of behavior on behalf of the Negro as a subordinate caste: *accommodation or protest*" (1944, 1962:720). That is, because of their subordinate caste position, Negroes find all their power relations confined to the narrow orbit of accommodation or protest, or to some compromise between accommodation and protest" (1944, 1962:1133).[1] Thus, the typology is based on observed empirical regularities in the behavior of Negro leaders rather than on some abstract preconception.

Accommodation is described by Myrdal as historically the "natural," "normal," or "realistic" pattern of leadership behavior among Negroes, especially in the South. Accommodation requires acceptance of the caste system; thus, leaders "lead" only in that context. That is, they seek modifications in the life conditions of Negroes that do not affect the caste structure. Protest involves a rejection of the caste system. Behaviorally, the pattern consists of lobbying, litigation, and nonviolent protest in deference to law, the American creed, and the tenets of Christianity. The protest leader is most often observed in the North because the less rigid system of racial oppression in many northern communities provides the opportunity for protest to exist. This variable—the nature of the localized system of racial oppression—is often central to the classification of leaders in this literature.

Examining briefly the other typologies, Burgess (1962:181–86) developed a fourfold typological schema in her study of Durham:

1. The *conservatives* are defined as those persons who are least likely to voice opposition to caste, conforming closely to Myrdal's accommodation pattern of "pleading to whites."

2. The *liberals*, the largest of the types, are distinguished by their use of conventional political methods (for example, voting, lobbying, and litigating) to protest caste.

3. *Moderates* are characterized as functional leaders who subordinate their role as race leaders to their role as leaders in the community generally.

4. *Radicals* are distinguished on the basis of their identification with the masses, mass demonstrations, and the approach of Martin Luther King.

Thompson (1963:62–70) also identified four types of leaders in New Orleans:

1. *Uncle Toms*, who accept the caste system.
2. *Race men*, who militantly reject the caste system and engage in overt forms of nonviolent protest.
3. *Liberals*, who also reject the caste system, but who rely on moral suasion and appeals to the national government.
4. The *race diplomats*, who strike a middle ground between race men and Uncle Toms through reliance on education and persuasion to incrementally change the system.

Matthews and Protho (1966:186–90) in their study of four southern communities identified three types of leaders:

1. *Traditionalists*, that is, those persons who engage in meliorative action within the context of caste;
2. *Moderates*, who are defined as those persons who favor "welfare goals" and gradual change in the system through the use of conventional political methods;
3. *Militants*, who are characterized as those persons who favor "status goals"—that is, the immediate abolition of caste through direct action and mass protest.

Ladd (1966:150–92) identified the following types of leaders in Winston-Salem, North Carolina, and Greenville, South Carolina:

1. *Conservatives*, functional equivalents of Myrdal's accommodating leader, depending for success on access and acceptability to Whites;
2. *Militants*, who are followers of Martin Luther King's approach of seeking "status goals" (that is, the immediate abolition of caste) through mass protest;
3. *Moderates*, who are considered to be those persons who seek the middle ground between "status" and "welfare" goals, relying upon negative inducements effected through conventional political methods.

Finally, Wilson (1960a:214–54) labeled Negro leaders in Chicago as *moderate* or *militants* in terms of whether they sought "status" or "welfare" goals, whether they tended to seek racial explanations for apparent anti-Negro acts, whether they tended to agglomerate or disaggregate issues, and whether they relied upon mass protest and political-legal remedies or persuasion, education, and behind-the-scenes bargaining. In general, the moderates, the most numerous group in Chicago, preferred "welfare" to "status" goals (that is, immediate, tangible benefits rather than the more abstract goal of integration), tended to seek nonracial explanations for apparently anti-Negro acts, to disaggregate issues, and to have less confidence in mass protests or legal-political solutions.[2]

The foregoing brief sketch of the principal leadership typologies obviously cannot do justice to their subtleties and nuances. In trying here to summarize the various approaches, one should be aware that the typologies reviewed above were developed by scholars with different purposes and approaches. Thus, selecting commonalities among these typologies may do violence to the authors' original intents. Wilson, for example, is particularly adamant on this point. He writes that the labels militant and moderate were used "with the greatest misgiving," because of the tendency to "read substantive content into these words apart from the specific substantive material for which they are mere rubrics." However, in using them, he stresses that they "have no normative implications" and have "no connection with the kinds of leaders mentioned by other authors writing on Negro leadership" (1960a:214).

However, Wilson protests too much. There is a connection between his work and that of others writing on Negro leadership. This connection is, perhaps, clearest in Ladd's work, the last and most sophisticated of the Negro leadership studies. Fundamentally, the Negro leadership typologies appear to be based on a composite of goals, methods, and rhetoric. These variables are the explicit constituent elements of Ladd's leadership typology. The factor that determines the location of a particular type on what Ladd properly views as a leadership continuum is the degree of its acceptability to Whites (Ladd 1966:151). In other words, Ladd is saying that the goals, methods, and rhetoric of militants are less acceptable to the dominant group of Whites than are those of moderates. Consequently, the goals and so forth of moderates are less acceptable than are those of the conservatives. Or, put another way, in the literature leaders are more or less militant to the extent that their goals, methods, and rhetoric diverge from the conventional goals, methods, and rhetoric deemed appropriate by dominant-class Whites.

Ladd's leadership continuum thus allows us to see continuity in the literature because it enables one to compare the content of different styles in different times and places. As Ladd (1966:151) writes, "The limits and contents of the styles are determined by prevailing patterns of race relations which vary with time and place." The advantages and disadvantages of this approach to classifying Black leaders, then and now, are considered in chapter 5. Suffice it to say here that Ladd (1966:198) himself argued that the time-bound character of his construct might in a decade or so make it inadequate as an analytic tool.

PREACHERS, POLITICIANS, WHITES, AND THE MASSES

Because of their historical, structural, and synchronic importance to understanding Negro politics and leadership, I will briefly inventory the literature for data and insights on the roles of preachers, politicians, Whites, and the masses.

It is agreed that the Negro church and its leader, the preacher, play an important role in community leadership.[3] Many leaders during slavery and Reconstruction were ministers. "In practically all rural areas, and in many of the urban ones, the preacher stood out as the acknowledged local leader of the Negroes" (Myrdal 1944, 1962:861). Yet there is also general agreement that the Negro cleric—given the relatively extensive resources of the church—has failed to realize his potential as a race leader. For example, in the South, Myrdal found that the preacher was "the typical accommodating leader." While the preacher in the North was more politically and socially active, Myrdal concluded that "on the whole even the northern Negro church has remained a conservative institution with its interests directed upon other worldly matters, and has largely ignored the practical problems of the Negroes' fate in the world" (1944, 1962:861–63).

One finds in all the Negro leadership studies that, because of their mass following, the status of their profession, the facilities of the church, and the spiritualism of the race, a larger number of preachers in the subcommunity exercise leadership than do those in the larger community. However, in urban areas, only in Thompson's New Orleans did clerics "constitute the largest segment of the leadership class" (1963:34). Even in New Orleans "the vast majority of ministers are primarily interested in their pastoral role rather than political action" (Thompson 1963:35). There is evidence that Martin Luther King inspired a larger number of younger ministers to become involved in political action (Burgess 1962:185; Ladd 1966:192), but in general, ministers are typically classified in the literature as moderates, traditionalists, or conservatives.

Thus, while the evidence is clear that the Negro minister has been more politically active than his White counterpart—Matthews and Protho (1966:332–34), for example, report that 35 percent of the Negro respondents, compared to 18 percent of the White respondents, reported their ministers discussed elections, and 18 percent, compared to 5 percent, respectively, said their ministers endorse candidates. The evidence also showed that ministers have not been the dominant or most militant category of subcommunity leadership.

Politicians—elected or appointed—are conspicuous by their absence in the Negro leadership group. After the exclusion of Negroes from southern politics in the aftermath of the Compromise of 1877, a significant Negro politician group disappeared as an important segment of Negro leadership in the United States. Indeed, the reemergence of a significant Black politician class in the 1960s is one of the important transformations in Negro leadership examined below. But prior to that time, only in Gosnell (1935, 1967) and Wilson's (1960a) Chicago did politicians play a significant leadership role. Twenty percent of Wilson's sample of Negro leaders, for example, were either elected or appointed government officials (1960a:11).

The handful of Negro politicians have tended to be less middle-class in background than the other types of leaders (Myrdal 1944, 1962:733) and were moderate or conservative in their ideology. In terms of ideology, Reconstruction era politicians, whether in or out of office, "expressed a conservative viewpoint," according to Meier (1968:248). In Chicago, the machine politicians observed by Gosnell (1935, 1967) and Wilson (1960a) were generally cautious and conservative in their approach to racial issues. Ladd (1966) also found that politicians tended to be moderate. However, in an important generalization, he notes that politicians are more heterogeneous in social background and more difficult to type than are other leaders, because "the politician can be militant, moderate or conservative. The point is that he can do this in a way consonant with the demands of his leadership position and the expectations of his constituents (over the objection of whites)" (Ladd 1966:315). In spite of this capacity for greater ideological flexibility, Ladd nevertheless concludes that politicians tend to be moderate because: (a) the performance of their work requires compromise and bargaining; (b) the stuff of politics is "welfare"; (c) a number of political positions require the votes and money of Whites; and (d) organizational constraints on politicians lead to moderation. There is also evidence (Ladd 1966:315; Hunter 1953:140–41) that Negro politicians are more integrated into the dominant structures of power than are other categories of Negro leaders.

Finally, regarding the effectiveness of Negro politicians, Gosnell (1935, 1967:373) concludes, "under the existing political system, the Negroes secured about as many concrete benefits from the government as most other minority groups. However, because their needs were greater, these benefits were not sufficient. Inadequate as they were, these services came nearer to meeting their needs than in areas where the Negroes have not developed some political power."

In discussing the concept of leadership, it was concluded that leadership among Negroes that is provided by Whites may be as effective as that provided by Blacks. Several studies provide empirical support for this approach to defining the phenomenon. For example, Myrdal (1944, 1962:725) discussed the role of "white interracialists," generally upper-status White persons who "specialize in becoming fixers and pleaders for Negroes." Bennett (1965:26) noting that "The black establishment is not all black," identified important Whites in liberal, labor, religious, and philanthropic groups as part of the national structure of power in the Negro community. Thompson (1963:32) developed the category of "functional Negroes," that is, White persons "who identify so completely with Negroes that they are generally regarded as "Negro spokesmen." And Wilson (1960a:100) suggested that success in attaining Negro goals was related to the extent to which there existed powerful White liberal groups, the existence of which "means that it is possible to obtain action on behalf of Negro interests without having to organize Negroes."

But the role of Whites in Negro leadership has occasioned as much controversy as has the role of preachers, especially among the Black intelligentsia. Perhaps the most effective critique of the role of Whites in the Negro leadership group was rendered by Bunche in one of his memoranda for the Myrdal study. Bunche (1939) criticized the whole philosophy of interracial liberalism, arguing that White men exercised disproportionate influence in the selection of Negro leaders, and that Negro leaders in their quest for respectability showed too much concern for the opinion of Whites and as a result too little concern for the plight of the masses. The issue of the role of Whites is another factor in the leadership transformation of the 1960s and, as Bunche indicates, is related to the final topic of this section, the role of the masses.

The distance between the relatively small, active, middle-class Negro leadership stratum and the relatively inactive, desperately poor Negro lower class has been variously described as simply "class envy" (Myrdal 1944, 1962:731) or as Wilson (1960a:299) argued "a fundamental class antagonism" between the two groups. The relationship probably does not constitute a "fundamental class antagonism," but rather class-cultural suspiciousness and envy. The problem is two-pronged: (1) as Bunche (1939:550) and Myrdal (1944, 1962:731) pointed out, there is the lack of knowledge of and empathy with the mass of lower-class Negroes among some upper-class elements of the established leadership group, and (2) more importantly, there is a "more or less conscious repugnance on the part of the Negro lower classes to follow them" (Myrdal 1944, 1962:731). This latter factor is related to the failure of the leadership, in a proximate period of time, to meliorate the condition of the masses, which, in turn, leads to suspicions of "selling out" or what Drake and Cayton (1945:720–22) call "the ritualistic condemnation of Negro leaders." This failure is probably due to a lack of leadership power, rather than a lack of leadership interest or empathy. The result is an often sad and ironic relationship between Negro leaders and their mass followers, a relationship aptly summarized by Hunter (1953:140) as follows:

> Negro leaders maintain themselves in semi–power positions in some instances, by appealing to the fears of the general community concerning the unrest of their community, while on the other hand they appeal to their people on the basis that they are actively working out the problems which may be defined as causing the unrest they say they would assuage. They are apparently sincere in most instances, but it is also evident that the Negro leaders work under certain structural handicaps in attaining their goals.

The literature provides insight into another relationship between the masses and certain types of Negro leaders, namely, those variously described as race men, militants, or radicals. Burgess (1962:185), Wilson (1960a:224), and Ladd (1966:189) identify a younger, more activist leadership that is impatient with the pace of change and prefers direct action by the masses as a means to rapidly and radically change the racial status quo. Ladd (1966:188–89) provides a summary of the type: "Mass involvement is supported not only because it is seen as efficacious in advancing the race, but also because the militant finds continuous involvement with the masses in the political struggle desirable. . . . It increases political consciousness and serves to mobilize them. While conservative 'Haves' fear the 'Have-nots,' the militant does not for he considers himself one."

This type, emergent in the 1950s and early 1960s, came to maturity in the mid-1960s and, coinciding with the ghetto revolts, exerted a major influence on the transformation of Negro leadership that occurred in this period. We will turn to factors constituting this transformation after a brief discussion of theoretical formulations in the Negro leadership literature.

THEORETICAL FRAGMENTS

Although Jones (1972) has characterized much of the work on the Negro leadership group as atheoretical, some fragments of theory exist in the literature. The initial fragment was given classic formulation by Myrdal (1944, 1962). Simply stated, this theoretical fragment contends that Negro politics (and leadership) is a function of White politics and power. In a section of the first chapter of volume one titled "A White Man's Problem," Myrdal writes, "The more important fact, however, is that practically all the economic, social and political power is held by whites. . . . It is thus the white majority group that naturally determines the Negro's place. . . . The Negro's entire life, and consequently also his opinions on the Negro problem are, in the main, to be considered as secondary reactions to more primary pressures from the side of the dominant white majority" (1944, 1962:IXXV). On the basis of their observation of empirical regularities in Negro leadership behavior, Burgess (1962:186), Thompson (1963:58–59), and Ladd (1966:151) provide explicit support to the Myrdal formulation that the pattern of Negro leadership behavior is determined by the prevailing pattern of race relations.

Wilson (1960a) and the power structure scholars, to some extent, extend and specify the Myrdal formulation. Hunter (1953), Barth and Abu-Laban (1959), and Pfuatz (1962) emphasize the importance of the general community context in understanding power relations in the Negro subcommunity. They call attention to the fact that in varying degrees the patterns of race relations and race leadership vary by locality. Wilson (1960a) goes further. He accepts Myrdal's formulation that Black politics and leadership are a function of White dominance; however, he asserts that it is not an invariant nor the sole determinant. Wilson writes "Segregation is a great determinant of Negro life in the city but it is not an invariable determinant" (1960a:6). Rather, he suggests that consistent with the power structure scholars, "the structure and style of Negro politics reflect the politics of the city as a whole" (1960a:22). Finally, in a distinct contribution, Wilson contends that Negro leadership and civic action are a function of "constraints" inside the Negro community (1960a:6). In his chapter titled "The Negroes" in Banfield and Wilson's *City Politics*, Wilson identified the fundamental internal constraints on Negro politics as: (*a*) the existence of a large, economically depressed lower class and a small, isolated, underemployed middle class; and (*b*) the relative inability or unwillingness of the middle class to identify with the lower class and provide leadership for it (Banfield and Wilson 1963:297–98). In Wilson's view, Myrdal's formulation may be the "ultimate cause" of Negro politics; however, proximate explanations (or middle-range theory) require attention to local political structures and factors internal to the Negro community.

Thus, while the Negro leadership literature is certainly not theoretically robust, neither is it accurately described as atheoretical. Rather, three fragments of theory can be identified in explaining observed regularities in

Negro leadership behavior: (1) the ideology of White supremacy and the structure of White superordination and Black subordination in power relations, (2) the differential local patterns of White supremacy and dominance, and (3) the factors internal to the Black community, which are fundamentally class-based in character.

CHAPTER 3

Factors Affecting the Transformation from "Negro" to "Black" Leadership

It is obvious even to the casual observer that there has been an important transformation in Negro politics and leadership since 1966, based on the data from the last publication of the Negro leadership studies reviewed in chapter 2. Scoble (1968:329) has written that the events of the 1960s "essentially make obsolete all that political scientists thought they knew concerning Negro political leadership, politics and power prior to that time." This seems to be an overstatement, in that "one can observe important continuities with the past—as well as discontinuities" (Scoble 1968:330). Nevertheless, it is critical to understand that in some important respects there is today a new "Black" leadership formation. Factors constituting this transformation from "Negro" to "Black" leadership are the focus of this chapter.

Seven factors may be identified: (1) Population changes, (2) changes in the Negro class structure, (3) the civil rights revolution, (4) the community action program, (5) the ghetto revolts, (6) the Black power movement, and (7) changes in White attitudes toward Black people. In this chapter, the structural impact of these factors on the development of the new Black leadership are sketched.

The first factor is the migration of Negroes from the rural South to the cities. Between 1940 and 1970, the percentage of Negroes residing in urban areas increased from 49 percent to 81 percent. Between 1960 and 1970, the number of Negroes in central cities increased by 3.3 million, from 9.9 million to 13.2 million, while the number of Whites (48.9 million) remained the same. As a result, by 1974, 58 percent of the total Black population of the United States lived in the central cities (U.S. Bureau of the Census 1975, 1978). The general consequence of these changes was to increase the salience of Blacks in big city politics. Specifically, the larger percentage of Blacks in the cities expanded the local electoral base for Black elected officials.

The most basic change in the Black class structure relates to the growth and diversification of the Black middle class. As pointed out in the previous chapter, in the 1960s Wilson identified as an important weakness in Black politics the existence of a large, impoverished lower class and a small, underemployed middle class. While a large, impoverished lower class (variously estimated at one fourth to one third of the Black population) still exists, and the argument of Scammon and Wattenberg (1973) that more than half the Black population can be classified as middle class has been discredited, the evidence is nevertheless unmistakable that in the last decade or so there has been substantial upward mobility among Blacks in the United States (U.S. Bureau of the Census 1978:24, 42, 57, 83, 92; Wilson 1978; Freeman 1977). The growth and the development of a larger, more prosperous, educationally and occupationally diversified middle class means the Black community is able to recruit its leadership from a larger pool of skilled persons than was the case previously.

There is also evidence that today's Black middle class is more predisposed to align itself politically with the Black lower class than was the case earlier. Aside from the problems posed by the very existence of a large lower class and small middle class, Myrdal (1944, 1962), Wilson (1960a), and others also argued that the Negro middle class exhibited a relative inability or unwillingness to identify with the Negro lower class and to provide leadership for it. Banfield and Wilson (1963:298), for example, saw the Negro middle and lower classes separated by "difference of ethos and interests." But contrary to the recent findings of Bolce and Gray (1979), Hamilton reports that this divergence in interests between the classes has attenuated with the growth and development of the "new middle class." Hamilton argues that the pre-1960s Black middle class was largely based in the private sector and consequently it could develop "class interests antagonistic to those of the Black lower class." However, he argues that the new Black middle class is basically salaried from the public sector and "this circumstance largely determines the sort of hard, self-interest positions this class will take on certain public policy questions" (quoted in Poinsett 1973). While Hamilton's argument regarding the historical basis of the antagonistic class interests of the pre-1960s Black middle and lower classes may be disputed; since both the Black middle and lower classes today depend heavily upon the public sector, each has an objective interest, apart from considerations of ideology or race solidarity, in seeing the public sector expand. The interest of the Black middle class in the expansion of the public sector relates to the availability of employment opportunities (for example, the Urban League estimates that in 1980 more than half of all Black college graduates were employed in the public sector), while the interest of the Black lower class is due to the expansion of public assistance and various kinds of community services. Hamilton's research in Detroit, Atlanta, and Chicago shows that middle-class Blacks tend to support progressive issues and candidates and vote for the perceived conservative candidate less often than do Blacks of the lower socioeconomic classes (1976:244). Thus, there is emergent in the new Black politics what I call a kind of "structural liberalism" (Smith 1978a) that operates to bridge ethos and status differences between the Black lower and middle classes, and creates considerable cohesion in electoral choice and in public policy preference.

② The civil rights revolution—which included the passage of the Civil rights Act of 1964, the Voting Rights Act of 1965, and the Fair Housing Act of 1968—has, of course, had a profound impact upon Negro politics and leadership in the United states. The most basic consequence of these laws was the removal of the legal basis for racial dominance by Whites, thereby increasing the range of maneuverability of Blacks in the polity. More directly, in terms of political leadership, as a result of the Voting Rights Act, the percentage of eligible Black voters registered in the South increased from 28 percent in 1960 to 59 percent by 1973 (Campbell and Feagin 1975:133), and although proportionally the number of Black elected officials in the South and the nation remains small, there has been a substantial increase in their numbers as a result of the passage of the Voting Rights Act. For example, in 1966, there were approximately sixty Black elected officials in the South. By 1974, this number had increased to 1,314 (Campbell and Feagin 1975:141).

Thus, the civil rights revolution directly contributed to an increase in the size of the Black politician segment of the Black leadership group. Hamilton also suggests that the "status-welfare" cleavage observed by a number of students of Negro leadership and politics was "muted by the 1960s civil rights revolution which brought new status-granting legislation" (quoted in Poinsett 1973). That is, by removing the legal basis for the status inferiority of Blacks in this country, the civil rights revolution contributed to a decline in status concerns and an increase in interest in welfare goals.

④ The Economic Opportunity Act of 1964 included a variety of programs (for example, education, income support, health, and legal services) to combat the complex problems related to poverty in the United States, including "political poverty" or powerlessness. The legal basis for this attack on political powerlessness was the Community Action Program (CAP) with its call for the "maximum feasible participation" of the poor in community-based antipoverty programs. Although there is considerable dispute among specialists as to the origins of the phrase, there is general agreement with the "central thesis" of Peterson and Greenstone (1979:242) that, whatever its origins or purposes, in its evolution "community action was primarily an attack on the political exclusion of "black Americans" and that it proved "a far better mechanism for incorporating minority groups politically than for improving their economic and social position" (see also Fox Piven 1970; and Moynihan 1969).

As a result of CAP and the coincident emergence of community control, and the "black demand for participation in large American cities" (Altshuler 1970), Blacks began to take part in a wide variety of community-based boards, agencies, and organizations. These organizations—which in many instances were created through funding by the government—added an important new organizational structure to Black politics. In addition, the process of election to and service on the CAP boards probably provided a useful leadership socializing experience for a cadre of Blacks in both urban and rural politics. There is also evidence that the CAP experience served the leadership development function of identification, training, and recruitment. For example, in a nationwide sample of Black elected officials, Eisigner (1978a:6) reports that 20 percent of the respondents indicated that they had been involved in some capacity at a CAP agency.

According to Scoble (1968:330), the Watts "riot" and the several summers of ghetto revolt that followed in every large American city with a significant Black population (except the South) led to "an accelerated completion of an age-generational revolution peacefully initiated against 'traditional' Negro leadership during 1962–63 . . . in the form of a nationwide revolt of the lower class against middle class political leadership, superimposed upon the earlier age revolution." In addition, Scoble suggests the revolts led to an increase in militancy in the ghettos, a greater stress on welfare goals, an emphasis on exclusively Negro decision-making, and a rise in the influence of elected Negro leaders at the expense of the Negro business and civic leaders (1968:331–33).

The ghetto revolts had two other important effects on Negro leadership. First, they led to a marked increase in and intensification of the repression of Negro leaders by police, intelligence, and military authorities (U.S. Senate 1976; Button 1980). But they also probably increased the leverage of the established leadership in the policy process, because what the riots did was to make manifest the specter of mass violence often raised by the leadership. As a result, there was an element of stark reality in the leadership's frequently voiced alarms that "if you do not deal with us, there will be another long hot summer" or "the militants will take over."

To some extent the militants did take over or, as Allen (1969) argues, they were co-opted into the established Negro leadership. In the situation of uncertainty, tension, and disorder created by the revolts, the young militant wing of the leadership group erupted as a force in national Black politics with the articulation of the Black power symbol during the 1966 James Meredith March in Mississippi (Carson 1981:215–28). Coming one year after Watts, the propagandistic symbol gave added impetus to the incipient mass rebellion, and altered in important ways the symbolism and structure of Black leadership (Stone 1968:3–26; Killan 1968:125–46; McCormack 1973; Peterson 1979; and Smith 1981b).

First, the Black power symbol operated to further bridge the gap in interest and ethos between the middle and lower classes, and thereby to increase Black community solidarity. Aberbach and Walker (1970) present evidence that in the late 1960s a Black political culture emerged in urban Black communities. This culture cut across class lines to include Blacks "who have broken free from traditional moorings to become part of a Black community which includes persons from all social classes" (1970:379). Second, there is evidence that the Black power concept led to a more positive self-perception and a greater sense of psychological security and personal efficacy among a stratum of the Black population (MacDonald 1975; Shingles 1981; Hall, Cross, and Freedle 1972; Hraba and Grant 1970). Finally, the Black power concept stimulated the formation of a new structure of independent Black organizations and caucuses and, in conjunction with the ghetto revolts, facilitated the incipient incorporation of Blacks as constituent elements of the national regime (Smith 1976). In sum, with respect to leadership, what Black power represented was the emergence of what Wilson (1960a:278–79) called the "new Negro," militant and outspoken on racial issues. The new Negro, however, preferred to be called Black.

The final factor affecting the transformation of Black leadership is a change in the attitudes of the White elite and the masses toward race, racism, and the status of Blacks. In the post–World War II period, the liberal wing of the national White power structure committed itself to dismantling the legal basis of White supremacy (Myrdal 1944, 1962:iii–xxxiii; Martin 1979; Ellison 1973). This elite liberal consensus was symbolized by the U.S. Supreme Court's decision in *Brown v. Board of Education*, 1954 (Kluger 1975), and was given concrete expression in the civil rights legislation of the 1950s and 1960s. However, the liberal establishment was able to secure enactment of this legislation only as a result of the civil rights movement's mass protests and the accompanying violence and disorders (Wilson 1972a; Rogers 1981). In addition, there is evidence (Dye 1972:39–67) that, on the issue of civil rights, the opinion of the White masses followed that of the White elite. But, in spite of mass passivity and, in some instances, resistance to the demand of Blacks for civil rights, the data (Pettigrew 1971; National Conference of Christians and Jews 1978:13–21; Campbell 1971) are conclusive that the postwar opinion of Whites is less anti-Black and more racially accommodative than it was previously. This fact, of course, facilitates the participation of Blacks in the social system.

Given this identification and analysis of the factors affecting the transformation from Negro to Black leadership, and before reviewing the literature about the new Black leadership, it is possible to delineate empirically the structural impact of these factors through analysis of the changing composition of *Ebony*'s periodic listing of the "100 Most Influential Black Persons" in the United States. Since 1963, *Ebony*, the most influential of the mass-circulation Black periodicals, has published such a list annually.

According to the editors of *Ebony* (1975:46), each person on the list meets the following criteria: "The individual affects, in a decisive way, the lives, thinking and actions of large segments of the nation's black population. The individual commands widespread national influence among blacks and/or is unusually influential with those whites whose policies and practices significantly affect large numbers of blacks." These criteria (except for the racial exclusivity in terms of who is eligible for inclusion on the list) fit closely the definition of Negro leadership employed in the literature. However, the method of identification and selection of persons for the list is not manifestly scientific; thus, it is necessary to rely on the subjective judgment of the magazine's editors. Notwithstanding this fact, *Ebony*'s influential place in the nation's Black community—and especially the participation of *Ebony* senior editor Lerone Bennett, the distinguished historian, in the identification and selection process—gives credibility to the validity and reliability of the lists.

In table 3.1, the organizational or institutional affiliation of *Ebony*'s most influential Black persons is presented for the years 1963, 1971, 1975, and 1980. Clearly, the most striking change in the composition of Black leadership revealed by the table is the relative decline between 1963 and 1980 in the percentage of leaders of civil rights organizations and glamour personalities (that is, prominent athletes and entertainers), and a sharp increase in the percentage of persons who are elected or appointed government officials. In 1963, 18 percent of the *Ebony* leadership group were leaders of local or national civil rights organizations, and 10 percent were glamour personalities, but by 1980, these percentages were 7 and 2, respectively. In 1963, only 9 percent of the *Ebony* leaders were elected officials. By 1980, that figure had increased to 25 percent, after reaching a high of 31 percent in 1975. In addition, the number of appointed officials (including judges) increased from 15 to 20 percent between 1963 and 1980. Thus, the most basic change in the structure of Black leadership occasioned by the events of the 1960s is the decline in civil rights and glamour personality-type leaders, and the

TABLE 3.1
Institutional Affiliation, 100 Most Influential Negro Leaders,
1963, 1971, 1975, 1980

Affiliation	1963	1971	1975	1980
Elected Officials	9%*	23%	31%	25%
Appointed Officials	9	6	5	13
Judges	6	8	8	7
Church	5	3	5	7
Business	8	12	11	6
Labor	2	5	2	2
Professional Associations	0	1	4	4
Publishers	8	3	4	3
Civil Rights Organizations	18	11	8	7
Fraternal Association	1	6	9	12
Nationalists	2	5	2	0
Marxists	0	3	0	0
"Glamour" Personalities	10	5	2	2
Others†	12	10	7	10

SOURCES: *Ebony*, September 1963, pp. 228–32; April 1971, pp. 33–40; May 1975, pp. 45–52; and May 1980, pp. 63–72.

*The numbers represent percentage distributions for each year.
† Includes writers, journalists, educators, and military officers.

emergence of a leadership of elected officials. In 1975 elected officials constituted nearly a third of the Black leadership, compared to only 9 percent in 1963. This evidence of the often spoken of transformation from protest to politics is even more compelling if one combines the elected and appointed officials, because it shows that nearly half (41 percent) of Black leadership today is part of the official structure of government. This represents a major transformation in Negro leadership. For example, Huggins (1978:92) reports that in two surveys of "leading Negroes" in 1944 politicians were "conspicuous by their absence." This transformation in the Negro leadership group is reflected in the literature on the new Black leadership, which is largely a literature of Black elected officials, although Black appointed officials and judges are neglected.

Before examining this literature, further study of table 3.1 shows that the number of other types of leaders—for example, church, business, labor, and publishers—fluctuated during the period. However, the number of leaders who were affiliated with professional associations increased modestly from zero to 4 percent, and the number of leaders affiliated with fraternal organizations increased dramatically, from 1 percent in 1963 to 12 percent in 1980.

Finally, the table reveals that leaders of a nationalist or Marxist persuasion are relatively insignificant during the period, with their greatest number appearing in 1971—8 percent. However, by 1980, such persons disappear completely as influential persons in the Black community.[1] The inescapable conclusion of the *Ebony* data, then, is that the transformation from Negro to Black leadership in the 1960s did not lead to marked radicalization of the Black establishment (see also Henry 1981). The review of the new Black leadership literature in the next chapter further documents this conclusion.

However, before turning to this documentation, the structural consequences of the events of the 1960s for Black leadership are summarized below.

First, as a result of the civil rights revolution, racial domination in the polity has declined. This declining significance of race in the political system increases the range of maneuverability of Black leaders, because their thoughts and behavior on behalf of Blacks are no longer limited to what Myrdal called the "narrow orbit of accommodation or protest." Rather, Black leaders are now free to involve themselves in a variety of issues and problems beyond the traditional concerns of the civil rights leadership.

Second, the structure of Black organizations and decision-making is relatively more independent of Whites.

Third, Black leadership today is more integrated into dominant systems of governance and influence, including not only leading Blacks who are elected and appointed government officials but also persons in the prestigious media, corporate, and trade union hierarchies, the elite universities, and the philanthropic community.

CHAPTER 4

The Black Leadership Literature

We begin our review of the Black leadership literature with consideration of how students have defined the concept. Most have not. Holden (1973:4), following the Negro leadership scholars, first understands Black leadership generally to mean "those who seek (or claim to seek) the interests of the 'whole' black population." However, in a departure from the literature about the old Negro leadership, he adds that such persons purport to lead by "defining for blacks how they should relate to whites" (1973:4). More specifically, Holden suggests that it is appropriate to regard as a leader anyone who holds a key position in any of the "major black socioeconomic institutions" (1973:4). Thus, the leadership concept as developed by Holden concerns persons (Black or White) seeking or claiming to seek the interests of Blacks as a whole *in their relationship to Whites*. This latter notion is a departure from the traditional use of the concept in the literature. The rationale for this departure is not developed by Holden. Consequently, Holden's concept is dubious, for it ignores the fact that in Higham's view (1978:8), a large part—perhaps the greater part—of ethnic leadership has to do with internal processes of community development and symbolic expression.

Aside from Holden, the remainder of the new Black leadership literature largely ignores the problems of the leadership concept, probably because it is basically a literature about Black elected officials who are implicitly assumed to be leaders by virtue of their holding office. However, Hamilton (1981:8) points out that this implicit assumption regarding the Black leadership role of *Black* elected officials may be misleading. Defining a Black leader as "one who is racially black in a leadership role *and* who speaks and acts on matters of specific (but not necessarily exclusive) concern to Black people as a direct purpose of occupying that role," he argues, "if one were racially black and, say, mayor of an all-white town who never spoke or acted on issues of specific concern to blacks as such, it would not be proper to designate such a mayor as a 'black leader'." Similarly, regarding Black appointed officials, Smith (1981a:33) has raised the question of under what conditions and circumstances Black presidential appointees are to be viewed as leaders of the race. The important point here is that the race leadership of officials of the government (or other major American institutions, for example, the Ford Foundation) is a matter to be explicitly demonstrated rather than implicitly assumed.

POWER STRUCTURE: SCHISM AND REALIGNMENT

Since the early 1960s, there has been no systematic research on power structures as such in the Black community, either locally or nationally. However, nearly thirty years after his classic 1953 study, Floyd Hunter in *Community Power Succession: Atlanta's Policy Makers Revisited* (1980) reexamines Atlanta's power structure. The first thing to note about the power structure in Atlanta is that, despite the civil rights movement, the election of a Black governing coalition, and significant integration of the professional occupational structure, there still existed in 1980 a distinct superordinate White "community" power structure and a subordinate Black "subcommunity" power structure. The dominant power structure in Atlanta in 1980, as in 1950, was constituted by the major financial, industrial, and business leaders of the city, although a smattering of professionals and politicians existed at the periphery of the structure (Hunter 1980:43–49). Hunter writes that "a few blacks would also be included in Atlanta's overall power structure, particularly at the corporate board level." However, he adds that fundamentally the Atlanta power structure is White, and "the weight of the whole scheme veers unerringly toward the goals of business and the business-dominated technology" (1980:47, 49).

Atlanta's Black power structure in 1980, again as in 1950, was disproportionately male, middle-class, and middle-aged. Of the twenty-five top leaders identified by Hunter, only two were women. Businessmen remained at the top of the leadership structure, but by 1980 politicians had displaced preachers and professionals as the influential members of the "subcommunity" (1980:70–71). Finally, Hunter writes, "The black power structure is still powerful, in a real sense, only so far as its members are granted power, credit and social recognition by the white overlords of urban power in Atlanta" (1980:72–73).[1]

Holden, in his wide-ranging inquiry, interprets Black politics as occurring at both the local and national levels through a fairly well-defined and stable set of relationships that he calls the Black "quasi-government." Specifically, he argues that there is a "constant interplay" or interaction among the elites of the "major socioeconomic institutions" or organizations of the community that produces "a central tendency which becomes the judgment of the 'black community'" (1973:3–4). Such a judgment, he writes, has "substantial moral and political influence over some options available to anybody black living in the territorial ghetto and beyond." Thus, the structure of power in the Black community is held together by the "interdependent elites of the major Black socioeconomic institutions" and by a fairly stable leadership recruitment process that allows for the incorporation into the Black political world of such diverse personalities as Roy Wilkins and Stokely Carmichael. Specifically on the point of leadership schism and realignment, Holden contends that "there is a certain stability in the continuation of persons in leadership roles over very long times while—over the same times— new leadership personnel are constantly added as competitors, but seldom merely replace or displace their predecessors" (1973:7). As a result, there is a certain stability in the symbolism and ideological cleavages of Black politics.

In a partial test of the Holden thesis, Smith (1978b) found that among the Black political elites in Washington, D.C. (interest-group executives, members of Congress, presidential appointees, and journalists), there was empirical evidence of that "constant interplay" among the various leaders and anecdotal evidence that this interaction eventuates in a consensus as to the judgment of the Black community, at least insofar as issues in the federal policy-making process are concerned.

Regarding the leadership recruitment process, Salamon (1973) studied the impact on the traditional Black leadership structure in Mississippi of the opening of that state's political-electoral system to Blacks. He argued that the availability of elective offices to Blacks in Mississippi created the possibility of a host of new leadership roles that were relatively independent of Whites, and thus opened the possibility of a basic restructuring of the traditional leadership hierarchies.

Based on a questionnaire administered to the 336 Black candidates for elective office in Mississippi in 1970, Salamon concluded that by and large the persons who sought and won elective office in Mississippi resembled the traditional Black elite in terms of social background (1973:628). However, he also observed that while the traditional leaders were dominant, a new nonestablishment leadership also emerged to take advantage of the expanding political opportunities and to compete with the old leaders for influence among Mississippi Blacks.

But perhaps, Salamon's most important conclusion in terms of leadership recruitment/displacement is that "even the blacks with traditional backgrounds . . . evidence a change-oriented set of attitudes that distinguishes them markedly from the leaders of even a decade ago. In other words, while drawing substantially on existing Black elites, the movement has changed the character of Black political leadership infusing the old elite with fresh blood and new ideas" (1973:643). At the national level, Smith (1976:327–34) found a similar pattern. The old-line leadership of Black civil rights, professional, and elected officials in the late 1960s incorporated the younger, more militant (in terms of rhetoric and orientation to the masses) advocates of Black power and "caucus separatism" into the established leadership structure. Further, some established leaders also adopted the rhetoric and ideas of the young Black power rebels. Thus, the available research supports Holden's argument regarding the stability, continuity, and adaptability of the Black power structure.

CLASS, COLOR, AND SOCIAL BACKGROUND

Holden divides the Black community into two major classes—the bourgeois and the folk—each of whom is divided into subclasses. The bourgeois class is divided into the "gentry," that is, the color-conscious descendants of the free Negroes and mulattoes who exercised leadership during the Civil War and Reconstruction era, and the "solid middle class" (estimated at 25 percent of the Black population)—people whose middle-class status is defined in the same terms as the middle-class status of their White counterparts (1973:27–28). The "folk" are divided into the "working-class respectables," estimated at 30 percent of the Black population; the "striving poor," persons who work full-time but at poverty-level wages; and, the "immobile poor," the long-term unemployed and the welfare dependent (1973:29–30).

Historically, the gentry provided leadership for the Black community. However, Holden argues that because of its relatively small size and its "color snobbery" (1973:28, 31), leadership in the Black community has passed to the solid middle class. This tendency of disadvantaged ethnic groups (which has been observed throughout American history) to develop leaders who are marginal to the group—that is, persons of advanced economic and professional attainment—results in distrust of the Black bourgeoisie by the folk, and in class tensions that undermine the capacity for effective action (Holden 1973:31). Although Holden writes that the bourgeoisie has remained the prime source of Black leadership, "it has not been able to redeem the promises that—as a leadership group—it has overtly and implicitly made to produce racial change on a scale, and in a form, suitable to most of the Black population" (1973:36). As a result, there exists in the Black community a process Holden calls "centrifugalism"—a tendency toward severe internal conflict (1973:36). This tendency has been reported in the literature about the Negro leadership group. Thus, it appears that the transformation in leadership that occurred in the 1960s, while perhaps diminishing this phenomenon, did not eliminate it as a factor in subcommunity leadership.

The new literature provides no additional data on the ethnic origins of Black leaders. While there are, as Holden (1973) and Bennett (1965:42) suggest, some indications that the Black establishment is losing its caste-color flavor as a result of the events of the 1960s, there are no data available to establish this as conclusive fact.

A social background profile of the new Black leadership closely resembles the old Negro leadership of largely middle-aged, middle-class men. Salamon's (1973) description of Black candidates and office holders in Mississippi is an apt summary of the findings on the social background of Black elected officials nationally (Conyers and Wallace 1976:55–68; Cavanagh and Stockton 1982:10), and in two northern states, New Jersey (Cole 1976:37–55) and Michigan (Stone 1978:284–404). Salamon (1973:629) writes, "The typical candidate was male, well over 40 years old, at least a high school graduate, a white-collar professional or land-owning farmer, a home owner and farmer, and the recipient of a substantial middle class income by Mississippi standards. He was, therefore, hardly representative of Mississippi blacks."

Thus, in spite of the fact that today's Black leadership is disproportionately constituted by elected officials in comparison to the old Negro leadership, one does not observe significant differences in their social backgrounds. This is surprising since Myrdal (1944, 1962), Ladd (1966), and others have suggested that politicians were more likely to be representative of their communities (in terms of social background) than were nonelective leaders. However, this appears not to be the case. Indeed, Smith (1976:304–7) found that elected officials were more advantaged on most measures of social background than were their appointed counterparts in the national administration or the executives of the Washington offices of Black-interest organizations.

ORGANIZATION

The data from the *Ebony* survey reported in chapter 3 show that, in the last two decades or so, there has been a decline in individualistic "glamour personality"–type leadership and a rise in organizationally based leaders, especially leaders who are affiliated with fraternal and professional organizations. In addition, as a result of the Black power movement, a whole range of independent or caucus-type Black organizations have emerged. Smith (1981a:436–38) reports that between 1967 and 1969 (the peak period of Black power), seventy-three new national Black organizations were formed. These new organizations cover a range of Black community concerns and interests—for example, business/economic, educational, professional/occupational, and the explicitly political. In addition, as a result of the Community Action Program's doctrine of "maximum feasible participation," the availability of federal funds and organizers, and the effect of the ideologies of Black power and community control, a variety of grassroots, community-based organizations of the poor and lower middle class were formed in urban and rural Black communities (Peterson and Greenstone 1979; Bailis 1974). While a number of these organizations—notably the National Welfare Rights Organization—have withered away as a result of cutbacks in federal and philanthropic support, many persist as evidenced by the formation in 1980 of a national organization of community-based groups.

Thus, contrary to the often-heard lament that Blacks are unorganized, the evidence indicates that they may be overly organized and that the resultant intense competition over limited resources may contribute to a major problem in leadership effectiveness (Holden 1973:35).

This plethora of organizations in the Black community notwithstanding, Myrdal's conclusion of 1944 still appears to be valid. At the national and local levels, the NAACP and the Urban League are "without question" the most important organizations in the Black struggle for racial justice. As Wilson observes, numerous organizations have been formed in this century to advance Black interests; however, the NAACP and the Urban League have "almost alone among scores of organizational attempts succeeded in institutionalizing a concern over race relations" (1973:7).

Recent research on Black organizations focuses on their effectiveness in the policy-making process. Wolman and Thomas (1970) found in the middle 1960s that Blacks lacked effective access to centers of decision-making in housing and education, not because the system was closed to them, but because they lacked effective organization, and the limited organizational resources available were too narrowly focused on civil rights. More recently, Smith (1976:337–39) and Pinderhughes (1980) found that Black organizations have developed nominal access to most major federal policy areas, and have enlarged their focus to include the full range of domestic and foreign policy issue. However, they also found that this multiplicity of issues that are areas of concern to Black groups and the resource difficulties of the subordinate, dependent Black community "weaken their likelihood of being taken seriously within any of these arenas" (Pinderhughes 1980:36). Indeed, Pinderhughes (1980) and Bailey (1968) both conclude that the "middle-class" strategy of lobbying, litigating, and electioneering alone cannot be effective in meliorating the multiple problems of the Black community. Yet, in his study of more than twenty Washington-based Black organizations, Smith (1976:327) found that all except the welfare rights group and the nationalist-Marxist groups were committed to this middle-class model of political action.

Insofar as nationalist and leftist organizations are concerned, Smith (1976:65, 85) found that such groups as the All African Peoples' Revolutionary Party, the African Liberation Support Committee, and CORE were small and insignificant, and exercised little influence in the policymaking process. This lack of influence was due to the fact that these groups did not seek to play a policy-making role. Regarding this latter point, until the death of Elijah Muhammad, the Nation of Islam, the largest and most influential of the Black nationalist organizations, took what might be regarded as the ultimate nationalist position relative to efforts to influence government policy. Smith (1976:85) quotes Dr. Lonnie Shabazz, the minister of Washington Mosque No. 4, as saying, "We do not and will not lobby in any shape, form, or fashion because it would be attempting to advance our interests through the devil's system; it would be mixing two systems (ours and theirs) and there would be inevitable conflict." Since Mr. Muhammad's death, the Nation of Islam has split into an orthodox faction under Minister Louis Farrakhan, and a revisionist faction (called variously the World Community of Islam in the West or the American Muslim Mission) under Minister Wallace Muhammad. The revisionist faction is integrationist in its goals and practices (Muhammad 1980). However, because of the split, the revisionist and the orthodox factions are now only shadows of the organization the Nation of Islam was at the peak of its influence in the 1960s (Lincoln 1968).

In general, then, the evidence supports the conclusion that the nationalist and Marxist organizations in the Black community face nearly insurmountable difficulties in developing long-term viable organizations capable of sustained political activity (Geschwender 1977; Parenti 1964).

Since a significant proportion of the new Black leadership is constituted by elected officials, it is necessary to consider briefly their organizational base. Although the conventional wisdom is that the church is *a* principal, if not *the* principal, organizational base of Black electoral office seekers, the research indicates this is not the case. Rather, civil rights organizations (especially the NAACP) are as important as, if not more important than, the church. Salamon (1973:641) reports that 70 percent of the candidates seeking elective office in Mississippi in 1970 were recruited by church or civil rights organizations. Cole (1976:46) reports that civil rights organizations were the principal base for elected officials in New Jersey. Eisinger (1978a:9) reports that 74 percent of the elected officials in his national sample were drawn from civil rights organizations. The literature also indicates that party organizations play a minor role in Black electoral politics (Hadden, Massotti, and Thiessen 1968; Cole 1976:49). Further, Black elected officials are reluctant to build permanent community-wide electoral organizations. Instead, they prefer the freedom of personalized, entrepreneurial campaigns, using the traditional organizational structure of the community for the purpose of voter mobilization (Nelson 1978:65–67, 1977, 1972; Nelson and Meranto 1977; Murray and Vedlitz 1974).

Yet another emergent organizational form in Black politics is the convention movement. Efforts are currently being made to create a national Black political party, or what Holden (1973:172) calls a "mechanism of collective judgment, a regular conclave, so structured as to represent the widest possible range of opinions and circumstances— a kind of Afro-American general council." In essence, the leadership is seeking to develop a structure in Black politics to perform the interest aggregation function (Almond and Powell 1966:98–108). This effort is not new in Negro politics. Historically, there have been a number of Black political parties at the local, state, and national levels (Walton 1969; Walton 1972:121–31). As early as 1830, a National Negro Convention was launched as a permanent organization to discuss common problems and develop an overall national strategy to eliminate the problems then facing Blacks (Walton 1972:145; Bell 1957; Gross 1966). The national political parties in general have "disappeared almost as quickly as they have appeared" (Walton 1972:131). Although the Negro convention movement had a somewhat longer life (operating roughly from 1830 to 1860) than the national political parties have had, it too eventually disappeared, largely as a result of ideological conflict and internal strife (Bell 1957; Gross 1966). Again, in the 1930s a National Negro Congress embracing all of the major Negro socioeconomic, civic, and fraternal organizations was established. However, it also soon collapsed as a result of communist penetration and inadequate staff and financial resources (Myrdal 1944, 1962:817–19; Wittner 1968).

In 1972, yet another effort to develop such a structure of collective expression took shape at the National Black Political Convention in Gary, Indiana (Walters 1972; Strickland 1972; Clay 1972; Baraka 1972). The convention, which was broadly representative of the national Black community, was unable to successfully aggregate the various conflicting ideologies represented. As a result, the liberal integrationists eventually withdrew, leaving the convention a conclave of nationalists and Marxists. Although the convention continued as a movement, it lost much of its support from other major Black organizations and from Black elected officials, the groups that were the original basis of its strength.

The effort to develop a Black political party continues, however.

The Gary convention in 1972 voted not to set up a party, but rather to work to create the machinery for such a party. A conference of Black elected officials and national civil rights leaders meeting in Richmond, Virginia, in early 1980 issued a call for the establishment of a "task force" to study the feasibility of developing a Black party. However, at the National Black Political Convention held in Philadelphia in the fall of 1980, the National Black Independent Political Party was formally established. Ronald Walters, a leading academic advocate of a Black party and an activist in the convention movement, makes the case for such a party as a mechanism by which to: (1) organize and mobilize the Black community—in electoral and nonelectoral politics—around an agenda "commensurate with the needs" of the Black community; (2) hold Black elected officials accountable to the Black community; and (3) increase the leverage of the Black vote in presidential politics (Walters 1975, 1980).

Walters, as he might say, makes a good case, in Aristotelian fashion, for the party. However, the historical evidence and the experience at Gary and subsequent conventions indicate that, given the present level of organizational and ideological conflict in Black politics, the current effort at party building is likely to fail. The dominant integrationist wing of the leadership has already withdrawn from the effort. Given the factional and doctrinal splits between the various nationalist and Marxist ideologues observed at Philadelphia,[2] it is safe to conclude that the new National Independent Black Political Party, like its historical forerunners, will founder on the rocks of ideological diversity and factionalism.[3] Put simply, the Black community is too ideologically and organizationally diverse to function, even operationally (except in times of manifest crisis), as a united front, in a single, coherent political structure. The efforts of Black to create an all-encompassing party recalls the struggle of New York Jewry in the second decade of this century to establish a "Kehillah," a comprehensive communal structure that would unite the city's multifarious Jewish population. For nearly a decade the structure worked reasonably well. However, it too then foundered on the rocks of ideological, national, and religious diversity before its ultimate demise, thereby pointing to both the limits and possibilities of ethnic group life in the United States (Goren 1970:24–41).

In addition to the foregoing, Hamilton (1973b:88) argues that an independent Black party is "not advisable" because:

1. The resources in terms of manpower and money are simply not available on a broad enough scale to make an impact.

2. Blacks have invested considerable energy in gaining potential leverage and positions in the Democratic Party.

3. An independent party, while it may permit isolated Black candidates to win offices, does not permit "gaining an effective base of sustained power within the decision-making structure" of ongoing institutions of governance.

It also should be noted that a successful independent Black party might stimulate the formation of racist "White" parties of the right. This, in turn, would probably increase the rancorous debate on public policy with respect to race and deflect whatever leverage independent Black political action might have in legislative and executive elections, at least at the state and national levels where Blacks do not constitute a political majority. As Frye (1980:164) concludes in his case study of the National Democratic Party of Alabama, "third parties as an operationalization of the concept of 'black power' . . . are likely to be limited in success to minuscule areas of the American political arena."

Finally, a Black political party denies the fundamental exigency of the Black predicament in the United States. There can be no basic alteration in the political economy of Black America without structural change in the American economy, and structural change in the economy is not possible without an interdependent coalition of Black and White progressives.

Given the difficulties in creating a structure that would encompass the range of ideologies in the Black community, the dominant liberal integrationist leadership has sought to develop alternative mechanisms. There is first, the National Black Leadership Forum, a coalition of the executives of sixteen leading civil rights, civic, and political organizations. The Forum is supposed to meet regularly in an effort to develop a common Black agenda and strategy, and to share responsibilities in the articulation of Black interests in the federal policy-making process.

Second, there is the Congressional Black Caucus (CBC) (Barnett 1975, 1977, 1982; Henry 1977; Levy and Stoudinger 1976, 1978; Robeck 1974; Sheppard 1973; Smith 1981c, 1981d). Over the years, the Caucus has, in the words of former Congressman Walter Fauntroy, argued that "27 million blacks in this country view the members of the CBC as the elected government of the black nation." This is political hyperbole. However, there is evidence that in the development of its policy statements and legislative agendas, the Caucus does explicitly seek to aggregate the broadest range of opinion in the Black community (excluding nationalists and Marxists), and that it has had considerable success in this effort (Smith 1981d). Although the Caucus is not descriptively representative of the national Black community, and a number of its members are dependent upon White money and votes to retain their seats in Congress, the group is substantively representative of Blacks in that its voting record and official pronouncements closely reflect the liberal policy preferences of the Black community (Smith 1981d:220). As such, it is the organization that most nearly approximates a mechanism of collective judgment for the national Black community. As an extension of its aggregation capacity, the caucus has also created the Black Leadership Roundtable. Constituted by about 125 national Black organizations, this structure is supposed to serve both as a source of Black community input to the caucus and as a mobilization-community action network (Congressional Black Caucus 1982; on the Roundtable, see chapter 8 of this volume).

Finally, it should be noted that while organizational leaders have to some extent displaced charismatic ones, there is still in Black politics a place for the charismatic-individualistic leader. In some measure, the Rev. Jesse Jackson's leadership is based upon his personality (rather than on his organization, as is the case with the head of the NAACP, for example), and his ability to project an image as a leader who is able to communicate in the language of the masses. However, Jackson is only the best known of such charismatic leaders; they can also be observed at the local level among both establishment and nationalist/leftist leaders. Given the significance of oratorical skills in Black culture (Holden 1973:21; Hannerz 1968), such persons will probably continue to be a prominent feature of Black leadership.

LEADERSHIP: RHETORIC, GOALS, AND METHODS

None of the new Black leadership studies develop leadership typologies. Either the problem of typology is ignored (Salamon 1973; Conyers and Wallace 1976), or it is concluded that the typologies typically employed in the Negro leadership literature distort more than they illuminate about leadership beliefs, ideology, or style (Holden 1973:15–16; Smith 1976:332–33; Hamilton 1973a:xv–xvi; Cole 1976:81–82). However, if the standard typologies of Negro leadership are divided into their constituent elements—goals, methods, and rhetoric—then there are data in the Black leadership studies that permit the classification of leaders along these dimensions.

The attempt to classify the goals or beliefs of Black along the classical left-liberal, right-conservative abstraction is a mistake because:

> blacks have been the have-nots of the system. Abstract ideologies for "all mankind" mean less to them than filling voids created by oppression. How does one philosophically label Marcus Garvey who in the 1920s urged a "central nation" in Africa for all blacks? Was his movement as he alternately suggested, liberal... or conservative? Further nei-

ther black nationalism nor integration perch comfortably on a left–right spectrum. In much of the north black separatism is equated with radicalism; in the south the reverse. (Cole 1976:93)

Two other characteristics of Black thought are worthy of note. First, "in comparison with other groups in American society, Black communities produce inordinately large numbers of talented individuals and organized groups concerned with fundamental systemic change" (Barnett 1976:23). Second, the political thought of Black Americans has been largely problem-solving– and action-oriented; therefore, "one finds much of the thought produced by "activists" rather than by relatively unengaged observers" (Hamilton 1973a:xiii).

An examination of contemporary expressions of Black political thought shows the salience of the foregoing factors; Black thought bridges the left–right dichotomy, it evinces a concern for fundamental change, and it is largely the product of political activists.

LEADERSHIP BELIEFS

We begin our consideration of leadership beliefs and goals with a discussion of Black nationalism. There are a variety of Black nationalist goals or beliefs. The range of definitions of Black nationalism varies from simple racial solidarity to the complex ideologies of Pan Africanism and territorial separatism (Bracey, Meier, and Rudwick 1970:XXVI). While there may be some value as Walters (1973), among others, suggests, in terms of ideological unity in defining nationalism simply as racial solidarity, such a definition has little scientific value because it is too broad to discriminate among the variety of thought extant in the Black community. Thus, for purposes of scientific analysis the concept of nationalism should be restricted to a belief in some form of racial separateness, whether psychic or physical.

Using this more restrictive definition, one finds a variety of nationalist belief "systems." There are the cultural nationalists who seek to develop and consolidate a separate and distinct Black culture or way of life (Karenga 1977; Baraka 1969). There are the revolutionary nationalists who seek, ultimately through a "people's war," to force the U.S. government to negotiate the establishment of a separate Black state—the Republic of New Africa—in five Deep South states (Obadele 1971). There are the religious nationalists who seek ultimately through the intervention of divine providence, the establishment of a separate homeland for Blacks (Farrakhan 1980). And finally there are the Pan Africanists who seek, in unspecified ways, the ultimate liberation and unification of Africa under scientific socialism (Carmichael 1969). A number of these nationalist expressions are linked to Marxist or "communist" ideologies (Baraka 1975; Marable 1980). However, there are orthodox expressions of Marxist-Leninist thought as the "key to black liberation" (Ofari 1972; Davis 1974).

Finally, there is the integrationist approach, which also bridges the left–right continuum. First, there are the traditional liberal integrationists (Congressional Black Caucus 1971; National Urban League 1973). Second, there is the tradition of democratic socialism (Rustin 1971). Finally, in the aftermath of the election of Ronald Reagan, a small group of persons who describe themselves as conservatives have emerged, at least in the national media (Singer 1981; Watt 1981; Willingham 1981).

Before examining the research on leadership beliefs, it is perhaps appropriate first to examine what we know about mass attitudes toward these ideologies as a means to place leadership beliefs in some context. First, all the available survey data indicate that the majority of Blacks, whatever their sex, age, education, or place of residence, reject the separatist goal (Marx 1967:28–29; Brink and Harris 1963:119–20; Campbell 1970:15–17). Indeed, at the peak of nationalist agitation in the late 1960s, support for the ultimate nationalist goal of a separate Black state found support among only 7 percent of the national Black population, with the very young and the very old providing the highest levels of support at 10 percent (Campbell 1970:16, 18). No data are available regarding mass support for cultural nationalism, although there is reason to believe that support for it may be more widespread than is that for separatism, and is possibly growing (Holden 1973:64).[4]

Although there is a paucity of data on mass attitudes toward Marxism, what little we know suggests that Blacks support the major values and institutions of the society, including capitalism. Devine (1972:281), for example, found that, of those Blacks with an opinion, six out of ten believed that things like electric power and housing should be run by private business. Yankeiovich, in a 1974 survey of American college students, found that Black students were just as "capitalistic" in their value structure as were White students, manifesting strong beliefs in the sacredness of private property (72 percent), and in the right of business to make a profit (86 percent).

Finally, on liberalism–conservatism, the evidence is unambiguous. In their landmark study of American voting behavior and opinion, Nie, Verba, and Petrocik (1976:253–55) wrote:

> [B]lacks held predominantly liberal attitudes on the issues in the 1950s. Twenty-five percent were in the most extreme liberal decile, and a full 65 percent were to be found in the three most liberal deciles. Moreover, the remainder of the black population was moderately liberal, with less

than 7 percent of all blacks giving responses which placed them in any decile on the conservative side of the line. However, even with a predominantly liberal profile in the 1950s, the degree of change in political attitudes is greater for blacks than for any other group in the population. The extreme and homogenous liberal opinion profile of blacks in the early 1970s is striking. Where we found 25 percent of all blacks in the most liberal decile, we now find 62 percent of all blacks at this point. What is more, 85 percent of all black Americans now respond to the issues in a way which places them in the three most liberal deciles. . . . [And] the leftward movement of the black population has occurred not only on the issues of central importance to blacks—school integration and increased attention to black problems—but on issues of foreign policy and scope of government as well.

What is even more remarkable is that, while Blacks were becoming more liberal during this period, all other population groups except Jews were becoming increasingly conservative. Thus, the data are clear: the so-called new Black conservative leadership finds less support among the masses than do even the nationalists and Marxists.[5]

Turning now to leadership beliefs, the studies show that Black leadership, like Black followership, is liberal and integrationist but committed also to the idea of racial solidarity. Salamon (1973:636) found that more than 95 percent of the Black candidates for office in Mississippi expressed strong support for such liberal policies as guaranteed jobs, national health insurance, and reductions in military spending; 90 percent expressed a strong sense of racial solidarity; and 60 percent supported the Black power principle of independent Black organization and political action. In New Jersey, Cole (1976:94), using a self-placement ideology scale, found that 16 percent of the Black elected officials described themselves as radical, 52 percent as liberal, 7 percent as middle-of-the-road, and none as conservative (the remaining 25 percent responded as "other" or "none"). In comparison, none of the White elected officials in Cole's sample described themselves as radical, 42 percent as middle-of-the-road, 14 percent as conservative, and 34 percent as liberal (the remaining 10 percent were classified as "other" or "none").[6] Cole also found that 61 percent of the Black elected officials supported Black power as a slogan to bring Black people together and as a means to achieve the group's "fair share of society's benefits" (1976:101).

Conyers and Wallace, in their study involving a national sample of Black and White elected officials, found a "consistently stronger liberal tendency on the part of Black officials than on the part of White officials" (1976:30). For example, 76 percent of the Black officials but only 30 percent of the White officials, believed it was the responsibility of the "entire society" to guarantee "adequate housing, income and leisure"

(1976:31). Although there was majority support among the Black officials for independent Black businesses and universities, only a minority (24 percent) favored an independent all-Black party. In general, then, the Conyers and Wallace data show that Black elected officials who are liberal integrationists favor racial solidarity and independent Black institutions in business and education but not in politics, where "working through the established party structure" is preferred to an independent Black party (1976:27).

Smith (1976)—on the basis of a series of loosely structured interviews with Blacks who were members of Congress, executives of Black interest organizations, presidential appointees, journalists, and staff members of congressional representatives—classified the Black leadership in Washington as both conservative and integrationist. The former classification was based upon their "acceptance of, or more precisely, accommodation to the capitalist, free market, welfare state characteristics of the present day U.S. political economy" (Smith 1976:313). Their classification as integrationists was based upon their goal of seeking, incrementally, equal access for Blacks to societal economic and political opportunities (Smith 1976:318, 332). There were Black nationalists and Marxists present among Washington's Black elites and groups, but they were small or insignificant in number.

Although Smith labels the dominant ideology of the members of the Washington Black establishment as conservative, he points out that they nevertheless are probably the most progressive of all organized lobbies in the federal policy-making process (Smith 1976:316). They are labeled conservative because they reject in principle or as "unrealistic" socialist alternatives to the present organization of the economy. But several members of the Congressional Black Caucus were labeled by members of their staffs as "closet socialists." That is, they were considered to be persons who support socialist principles as requisite to resolving the problems of the ghetto poor but, because of the perceived limitations of American politics, are unwilling "to go public" with proposals based upon explicit socialist principles.[7] Recently, however, Ronald Dellums of California reportedly publicly announced his membership in the Socialist Party (Pinderhughes 1979:21). Further, Congressman Parren Mitchell of Maryland has called for the nationalization of certain basic U.S. industries (specifically petroleum) as a means by which to resolve the problem of ghetto joblessness (Dorfman 1980). Thus, within the Black establishment, the socialists may be "coming out of the closet."[8]

In his revisit to Atlanta, Hunter also describes the ideology of the members of that city's Black establishment as conservative for several reasons. First, he states, "As the top leaders have prospered, their values resemble more and more the prevailing values of the city and nation."

Second, Hunter considers Atlanta's Black leaders to be conservative because they seek "systematic integration, not separatism," and "the general maintenance of the larger American system." Finally, he notes that they "keep order in the ethnic quarter" (1980:71, 73). Hunter also notes that there are underlying policy differences between the Black and White leadership in Atlanta. These differences reflect the liberalism–conservatism axis in American politics and policy. For example, the White leadership in Atlanta "wanted more and more building—of huge central city projects, rapid transit, airport improvement, Omni-International and expanded higher income housing in outlying areas," while Blacks sought solutions to problems of ghetto housing, unemployment, crime, and drug addiction (1980:151–52). Because Black leadership, in seeking solutions to these problems, fails to take account of the "oligarchical" management of the economy and propose a "democratic" alternative, Hunter believes it plays a basically conservative role in the city's politics.

Holden classifies Black leadership beliefs as clientage, opposition, and withdrawal. *Clientage*, which is akin to Myrdal's accommodation type, rejects direct challenges to White supremacy, relying instead on powerful Whites to effect change. *Opposition*, which is akin to Myrdal's protest type, relies on appeals to the universalistic norms of democracy and protest within the framework of constitutionalism to change the behavior of Whites. *Withdrawal*, which is akin to Black nationalism, rejects the norms and values of White society and calls for physical or psychological withdrawal from American society (Holden 1973:42–43). Holden argues that, while the opposition type is dominant in the Black leadership group, all types can be found, and that the advocates of withdrawal increased in influence between 1966–67 (1973:43).

If one includes as forms of withdrawal the organizational consequences of the Black power ideology and the movement for community control in the ghetto as Holden does, labeling them respectively "caucus separatism" and "street-level populism" (1973:70–73), then it is true that the advocates of withdrawal have increased in influence in the Black leadership group. However, to include Black power organizations such as the Congressional Black Caucus and the variety of community-based organizations in the category of withdrawal is an analytical error. These groups have not "withdrawn" from the confrontation with White supremacy, as to some extent have the various nationalist ideologies reviewed above. Rather, they represent an important effort to construct an ideological and organizational base for a more effective challenge to the system of White supremacy.

Holden's book is more than description and analysis; it also involves prescription. Indeed, the book may be viewed as an academic manifesto of the integrationist wing of the Black leadership group in the

United States. As such, it is probably the most systematic and cogent defense of integration extant. Holden argues that there is an "inescapable interdependence" between Blacks and Whites in the United States. As a result, he argues that integration is the only realistic objective for Blacks in the United States, because the nationalist goal of territorial separatism and the Marxist goal of armed rebellion and revolution are "nothing short of romanticism" (1973:96–130).

Holden defines integration as the "result which exists when two or more diverse parties are brought together in what is a common political enterprise and a common structure of respect, even though each of the parties may also have certain additional structures (self-development) peculiar to itself" (1973:137). In the context of contemporary Black politics, this coming together of the two diverse parties, one Black and the other White, in a common enterprise, could easily be interpreted as a loss of "Black identity" in order to fit into the larger American structure. Consequently, Holden adds that integration is desirable even though each of the parties may also have additional enterprises peculiar to itself. By this careful modification, he cuts at the core of the argument of the opponents of integration; he argues for integration without the loss of Black identity.

Specifically, Holden argues that the goal is an integrated society where there would be "substantial evidence that race would not predict the distribution of either material benefits or psychic esteem in any significant degree" (1973:137). The fact that race substantially predicts the distribution of material benefits in the United States is amply documented (U.S. Bureau of the Census 1978). Also, in spite of the progress occasioned by the civil rights and Black power movements, there is still substantial evidence that race predicts the distribution of psychic esteem as well. That is, Blacks continue to suffer from negative racial stereotypes and have lower self-esteem than do Whites (Sussman and Denton 1981; Clark and Clark 1980). Nevertheless, it is the core belief and dream of the integrationist belief "system" that a society without these racial differentials in material and psychic well-being is both desirable and possible.

In sum, the evidence is clear that the dominant belief or ideology among Black leaders is liberal integrationist, and that they are representative of the broad masses of Blacks in holding this belief. The findings regarding leadership methods and rhetoric that follow complete our discussion of the constituent elements of the leadership typology.

GOALS AND METHODS

In their nationwide survey of Black elected officials, Conyers and Wallace (1976:20) found that 90 percent of the respondents indicated that conventional political methods (including litigation and petitioning) were "very important" or "fairly important" in achieving progress for Blacks in America; 55 percent gave these responses for mass demonstrations and protests, and 21 percent said that they subscribed to violence, when peaceful methods failed to achieve progress. Smith (1976:324–27) classified leadership political methods as moderate (voting, litigation, and lobbying) and militant (mass demonstrations and protest), and found that moderate methods clearly predominated among Black elites and groups in Washington. In fact, Smith writes that "data suggest an even higher degree of convergence among Black elites and groups in terms of political style than political beliefs such that even nationalist groups like CORE . . . pursue their goals through moderate methods" (1976:327). Of the twenty Black groups surveyed by Smith, all save two—the African Liberation Support Committee and the National Welfare Rights Organization—indicated that moderate methods were the preferred means of gaining access to and influencing policy-makers.

Thus, the preferred political style of the Black leadership group today emphasizes moderate or conventional methods at the expense of militant or unconventional methods. This preference is in spite of the fact that there is a considerable body of evidence and argument that a racially stigmatized and historically poor and oppressed minority cannot rely on such methods alone to achieve economic and social progress (Pinderhughes 1980; Wilson 1966; Keech 1968; Hechter 1972; Bailey 1968). This preference is also in spite of the fact that there exists a kind of "protest ethos" in the Black community (Eisinger 1974), predisposing the masses to favor the use by the leadership of more militant political methods. In a poll by Louis Harris for the National Conference of Christians and Jews (1978:98), a sample of the Black public and the national Black leadership was asked to agree or disagree with the following statement: "The only time blacks make real progress is when they hold protests and non-violent demonstrations." Forty-nine percent of the mass sample agreed, but only 29 percent of the leadership sample agreed with that statement. Harris writes, "it is fair to conclude that the black public is seeking a leadership which will more forcefully implement a strategy for black equality" (National Conference of Christians and Jews 1978:98).

Harris explains the leadership's reluctance to endorse militant political methods in terms of its fear of a "severe backlash by Whites in the event of such overt street activity." While the fear of White backlash may be a factor, it is also probable that the leadership fears failure in the effort to mobilize a substantial protest movement in terms of meaningful payoffs (that is, policy outputs), even if a successful mass protest movement could be revitalized.

The leadership is in all likelihood correct.[9] The success of the protest movement in the 1960s can probably be accounted for in terms of a peculiar set of circumstances: the issues were localized and clear (discrimination in public places, denial of the right to vote, and so forth); protest techniques were relatively new and newsworthy; and important White groups (for example, the church, labor, and Jews) formed a part of the civil rights coalition. The issues today (such as affirmative action, welfare, and full employment) are murkier, and national rather than regional; former allies are now rivals; there are fewer Bull Connors or Jim Clarks; the media are less attentive; and the kind of young Black who provided cadre leadership in the 1960s is now more likely to be on the executive ladder in government or corporate bureaucracies. Stokely Carmichael starting out today, for example, would probably end up with a law degree from Yale and a GS-16 at the Department of Housing and Urban Development.

Thus, there appears to be a mass-elite cleavage on appropriate political methods to achieve the goal of integration. Fundamentally, the argument of the dominant leadership group is that protest is a limited resource in the post–civil rights era[10] and that, while it is not clear that conventional methods produce dramatic policy benefits, it is probably nevertheless true that the lack of conventional participation (especially voting and lobbying) is associated with a systematic exclusion of Blacks from public goods, for example, appointed office, food stamps, regular garbage collection, or less police harassment.

In terms of the final element of the leadership typology, Smith (1976:26–32) found that associated with moderate political methods is moderate or conciliatory rhetoric (with an emphasis on law, morality, and the American democratic, constitutional ethos of equality, freedom, and justice), while the rhetoric of the militant tends toward confrontation with an emphasis on liberation, the Third World, anti-imperialism, corruption, and decadence of the American society and polity.

PREACHERS, POLITICIANS, WHITES, AND THE MASSES

It is not the church as an institution per se, but rather a certain number and type of individual ministers that have provided leadership for Black America (Holden 1973:12). Based upon a review of local leadership patterns, Hamilton (1972:127–29) classifies the political activism of the Black preacher into three role types: *church-based*, where the minister's influence is due to his leadership of a large congregation, and he is active in the community in the sense that he is consulted on local issues by public and private decision-makers; *community-based*, where the minister is active in both electoral and pressure group politics, although an effort is made to keep separate the political and church activities; and *church-based programmatic*, which is a combination of the two, where the minister uses his church power base to attain economic and political goals for his followers.

Hamilton provides classification but no data on the frequency of occurrence of each type or their empirical correlates.[11] In general, despite their presumptive importance, there is a lack of systematic, empirical research on the political behavior of the Black clergy. An exception is the work of Berenson, Elifson, and Tollerson (1976) on the correlates of political activism among the Black ministry. On the basis of a 1970 questionnaire administered to a nonprobability sample of 154 Black ministers from a universe of 184 in Nashville, Tennessee, it was found that political activism among the Black clergy was correlated with age, education, monetary strength of the church, and Black identification. Specifically, the study concludes that young, highly educated preachers with a strong sense of Black identification and from financially secure congregations are the most politically active (Berenson, Elifson, and Tollerson 1976:338). Thus, it appears that political activism among the Black clergy is not as widespread as is often thought. Indeed, it is probable that a majority of preachers and churches are a conservative force in Black politics "working against the widespread radicalization of the Negro" (Marx 1967:105).[12]

The data available on the extent to which Black preachers hold elective office indicate that, compared to Whites, they are more active but not markedly so. Cole (1976:43) found that 7 percent of the Black elected officials in New Jersey were preachers, compared to none of the Whites. Smith (1981b:210) found that 12 percent of the Black congressional delegation were clerics, compared to only 1 percent of their White colleagues.

The literature on the new Black leadership is almost wholly a literature about elected officials, with a few exceptions. These exceptions include Jackson's (1977) work on Black judges; as well as that of Smith (1981a) and Mock (1981, 1982) on Black presidential appointees; and Henderson (1978a and 1978b) on Black urban administrators. Regarding presidential appointees, the research evidence indicates that in the Kennedy-Johnson administrations, Blacks constituted approximately 2 percent of the senior level appointees, while they comprised 4 percent of such appointees in the Nixon-Ford administration, and 12 percent in the Carter administration;[13] they tend to be from middle-class backgrounds. Other characteristics are: they tend to be selected on a partisan basis; they tend to come from the fields of law and business in Republican administrations and from education, civil rights, and community service in Democratic administrations; they tend to exhibit racial solidarity in terms of intercommunications and policy focus; and their impact on public policy depends heavily upon the electoral support Blacks give to the candidacy of the president who appoints them (Mock 1982; Smith 1981a).

Henderson (1978a) concludes that urban Black administrators tend to be: relatively young compared to their White counterparts; well-educated (although they are less educated than are their White colleagues); likely to have worked for community, nonprofit, or educational institutions prior to their government career, while their White colleagues were more likely to have come from the business or corporate sector; and, they are more likely to advocate community, civic, and professional interests than are White administrators, although the majority of both Black and White administrators were generally not advocacy prone. Finally, Jackson (1977) shows that the "typical" Black judge is similar to his White counterpart in terms of age, religious affiliation, place of birth, and education, but is dissimilar in that the typical Black judge grew up in less comfortable circumstances than did his White colleagues, was more politically active prior to his appointment, and came to the bench with more prior judicial experience than did his White colleagues.

Insofar as Black elected officials are concerned, there has been a dramatic increase in their number since the mid-sixties. It was only recently that the Joint Center for Political Studies reported for the first time that Blacks now constitute 1 percent of the 490,200 elected officials in the United States (Williams 1982). The vast majority of these Black officials are elected at the local level; approximately 90 percent are either municipal, county, or local educational or law enforcement officials.

The research evidence shows that the electoral process tends to act as a screening mechanism that systematically filters out nonestablishment type Black candidates (Salamon 1973:644); that Black candidates tend to be elected by majority or near-majority Black constituencies (Hadden, Massotti, and Thiessen 1968; Bullock 1975; Smith 1981b);[14] that equitable representation depends upon the level of Black resources, for example, educational and income levels, and on the method by which local governing bodies are elected (Latimer 1979; Karnig 1976; Karnig and Welch 1981; Engstrom and McDonald 1981); that Black office-holders tend not to aspire to offices beyond the local and congressional levels (Stone 1980); and that the electorates tend to be racially polarized (Murray and Vedlitz 1978; McCormick 1979; Hadden, Massotti, and Thiessen 1968). While it is probably true that Blacks in cities where there are Black mayors receive more equitable urban service delivery, have a more equitable share of city employment and contracts, and are less victimized by the police than are Blacks in other cities, the research indicates that Black mayors have had little success in reordering urban priorities or changing city expenditure patterns (Keller 1978; Hamilton 1978; Levine 1974, 1976; Jones 1978; Preston 1976; Watson 1980).[15] Black elected officials on rural southern governing boards have had "at best a negligible impact" in general with respect to Black interests (Jones 1976). Yet Black elected officials win reelection fairly consistently.

In a "pilot study" exploring the conditions of the electoral success of Black incumbents, Keller (1979) focused on the tenure of Mayor Richard Hatcher in Gary, Indiana. He found that despite rapidly increasing crime, rising unemployment, and the deterioration of business, Hatcher, although he lost some support from his Black constituency, nevertheless was able to win a third term. Keller (1979:61) suggests that Hatcher won because of his superior political organization and his satisfactory policy performance in the eyes of the majority of the Black electorate. Apparently, the Black citizens of Gary accepted Hatcher's explanation that the problems of the city were beyond his control and that he had done the best job possible, given the circumstances. Thus, it appears that the increasing demands and expectations occasioned by the initial election of Black mayors can be accommodated without fundamental shifts in urban priorities and policies that objectively meliorate mass misery.[16]

As a result of the development of the sixties, there has been increased participation by the masses (lower-middle-class and lower-class persons) in Black community leadership (Holden 1973:71). However, there is disagreement in the literature regarding the efficacy of the participation of the lower classes in Black leadership. Ellis (1969) argues that the participation of such persons represents the emergence of a more authentic leadership. On the other hand, Holden (1973:115) argues that, although such persons certainly can contribute to Black leadership, in a "modern complex society" middle-class leadership must play the dominant role. This scholarly dispute is also reflected in the leadership stratum, where there is a debate between the moderate integrationists, the militant leftists, and the nationalists as to the possibility and efficacy of mass involvement in leadership. And, as we noted in the previous section, there is a leadership–mass cleavage regarding the extent to which mass protests and demonstrations are an effective political method. While dominant leadership is reluctant to attempt to organize mass action, it nevertheless continues to raise the specter of spontaneous mass violence in the form of "summer blowups" in major U.S. cities as a means to gain leverage in the policy-making process.

The role of Whites in Black leadership has probably declined in recent years as a result of the emergence of Black power with its emphasis on "caucus separatism," and independent Black organization and decision-making. Whites, however, still play a role in Black leadership. The two principal civil rights organizations—the NAACP and the Urban League—remain interracial in governance, and the Urban League remains peculiarly dependent upon the "holders and managers of white capital" (Holden 1973:5). The NAACP Legal Defense Fund is headed by a White man;[17] the Black congressional delegation is to some degree dependent upon White institutions and individuals for campaign support (Smith 1981b:209). Smith (1976:55) found that half of the Washington-based Black interest organizations were dependent upon White corporations, foundations, labor unions, or the federal government for a "major source of their support." Thus, much of the leadership of Black America is to some degree dependent upon White America. In his development of the clientage concept, Holden (1973) seems to suggest that such dependence—or as he prefers "interdependence"—is an invariant characteristic of Black leadership. He writes, "the fact is that there are almost no institutions within the black population which have the objective capacity to operate free of some form of clientage, whatever their moral preferences. . . . Many varieties of overtly militant politics—from Black caucuses in white churches to the Panthers . . . depend[s] on being able to secure and retain white allies" (Holden 1973:15; on clientage in Black politics, see also Kilson 1971).

THEORETICAL FRAGMENTS

If the literature on the old Negro leadership is not theoretically robust, then the new Black leadership literature is by design unconcerned with formulating generalizations of a theoretical nature. Most of the studies of Black elected officials are exploratory or descriptive in design and purpose. Three exceptions may be identified. Jones, in his case study of the emergence of the first governing group of Black elected officials in Atlanta, argues that "it is theoretically useful to conceptualize black politics as a power struggle between Whites bent on maintaining their position of dominance and blacks struggling to escape this dominance" (1978:92). Salamon (1973:619–22) applies the "modernization perspective" to his study of the transformation of elite recruitment patterns in Mississippi that resulted from the opening of the electoral system to Blacks, arguing that transformation of elite recruitment patterns is the central feature of the modernization process. Holden (1973) argues that the distinguishing and determinative feature of Black politics is White supremacy. However, two other variables internal to the Black community are also considered by Holden to be of theoretical significance: (1) certain aspects of Afro-American culture that inhibit the leadership coordination required by scarce resources (1973:16–26); and (2) "class tensions" between the Black middle class and the masses that hinder leadership effectiveness (1973:30–34).

Except for Salamon's (1973) modernization perspective and Holden's (1973) culture construct, the theoretical approaches of the new literature are wholly consistent with the fragments of theory gleaned from the old literature. This suggests continuity in the Negro-to-Black leadership transformation, and forms a basis for a coherent effort at theory building in the subfield.

CHAPTER 5

Leadership in Negro and Black: Problems in Theory and Research

The purpose of this monograph is to contribute to the knowledge and understanding of Black leadership in America. This is accomplished by reviewing the literature on Black leadership in order to inventory and codify existing knowledge, identifying gaps in the literature as a means of suggesting research problems and hypotheses, and facilitating the development and use of theoretical references appropriate to research in the subfield.

In the foregoing parts of this study what we know about leadership in Negro and Black America was codified under five categories of analysis. A recapitulation or summary of what has been learned will not be attempted here. Rather, I shall discuss some of the strengths and weaknesses of the two bodies of knowledge as a means by which to evaluate their reliability and validity.

THE NEGRO LEADERSHIP LITERATURE

Perhaps the most basic weakness of the old literature on Negro leadership is its reliance on the case method. In a day of systematic quantitative research, the case study approach in the discipline is less favored as a tool of inquiry. The major shortcomings of the case study are its limited and static character (Froman 1948; Kaufman 1958). First, under the canons of modern science, one cannot make reliable generalizations on the basis of a single case or even several cases—logical inference requires information from a random sample of all cases. Second, case studies are almost always static, dealing with only a single point in time. Finally, the case method makes it difficult to check the reliability of the findings, because it is extremely problematic and time-consuming to replicate a case study precisely.

Thus, the initial limitation of the Negro leadership literature is its reliance on the case method, and its essentially descriptive use of the case materials. Although the studies are not atheoretical, as Jones (1972) contends, the fragments of theory discernible are not generally systematically used by the authors to develop hypotheses or to formulate empirical regularities.

The most frequent criticism of the Negro leadership literature, however, is in terms of its use of the militancy construct. In one variation or another, this concept has been basic to discussions of the leadership phenomenon among Negroes. In one way or another, critics (Cole 1976:81; Scoble 1968:345; Smith 1976:332; Holden 973:15; Hamilton 1973a:xv; Forsythe 1972:18) have contended that the concept is so characterized by ambiguities that it is rendered invalid as a tool of inquiry. In an empirical study investigating the utility of militancy as an "analytic concept and as a practical way to react to Black politicians," Harrigan (1971:5) found in an examination of community leaders in Washington, D.C., in 1968–69 that it was extraordinarily difficult to apply the concept consistently. This was due to the fact that the definition is dependent upon one's frame of reference; that is, one cannot be militant in isolation. Rather, one has to be militant in relation to something. Because of these conceptual problems and its often value-laden characteristics, Harrigan concluded that militancy as an analytic concept was almost useless.

Such limitations do not mean, however, that these studies do not constitute a useful body of knowledge. First, they provide historical material on past patterns of Negro leadership. As pointed out earlier, all too often modern behavioral research proceeds in a historical vacuum (in some cases because adequate historiography is not available) without a sufficient appreciation of the influence of history on today's "measurable behavior." These studies, going back nearly fifty years, thus provide scientific data that are useful to an appreciation of the proximate historical context of the new Black leadership.

Although the studies are limited by their narrow data bases—only one was national in scope and just two were based upon research in a northern city, Chicago—they do provide detailed analysis of the leadership groups and are useful for purposes of hypothesis formation, if nothing else. In addition, the studies use fundamentally the same types of methods and data sources, and reach essentially the same conclusions concerning the nature and types of Negro leaders. Thus, the reliability, validity, and generality of the findings are enhanced. In some small degree, the bias inherent in a single case study is to some extent avoided because each study in a sense is a replication (although not a precise replication) of the other.

Finally, for purposes of analysis, it is possible to preserve the militancy concept by disaggregating its constituent elements. The major problem with the concept is its "focus on means rather than ends" (Forsythe 1972:18) or its failure to capture the reality that leadership types can "best be understood only when their stated goals are examined" (Hamilton 1973a:xvi). Of course, to a considerable extent the militancy concept was more often tied to means or methods rather than goals or beliefs, because much of the cleavage observed in the Negro leadership stratum (1935–65) revolved around methods rather than goals. That is, the basic belief or goal of Negro leadership—elimination of the system of caste segregation—was by and large accepted by all leadership types. Thus, leaders were empirically distinguishable, not in terms of their goals, but in terms of their means, methods, or styles of pursuing the generally accepted goal of eliminating caste.[1] Militants, moderates, conservatives, Uncle Toms, race men, and so forth were thus typed on the basis of their methods and styles of opposition to the caste system because this generally was the observed empirical regularity.

However, the critics make an important point when they argue that, in classifying leaders, means should be subordinate to ends. Unless political methods determine political beliefs (which to some extent may be the case for Black leadership), then in political praxis as in political science a preoccupation with methods narrows rather than enlarges our understanding of the political world. For political scientists and political leaders, methods should be the tools of one's work and should not be substituted for substantive goals. Thus, to be a viable concept the ends-means components of militancy must be specified.

This was done in the review of the Black leadership literature. The leadership typology was disaggregated into its three constituent elements—beliefs, methods, and rhetoric—and applied fruitfully to the available data on Black leaders, thereby permitting the distinguishing of leadership militancy on the basis of each of the elements. Leaders are classifiable as militant or moderate in terms of their goals, methods, and rhetoric, or some combination thereof. Militancy is defined as the extent to which a leader's beliefs, methods, or rhetoric depart, at any given time or place, from the beliefs, methods, and rhetoric of dominant Whites.

THE BLACK LEADERSHIP LITERATURE

Looking at what can be learned from the new literature on Black leadership compared with the old Negro leadership, one is disappointed. While the case study approach is generally avoided, there are really few studies of the new Black leadership that are of the depth and sophistication of studies pertaining to the old Negro leadership. Rather, there is almost an exclusive preoccupation with descriptive research on various phenomena associated with Black elected officials to the exclusion of Black appointed officials, community-based leaders, preachers, Black caucus-type organizations, and especially nationalist and leftist leadership. There is also little effort to develop formal leadership typologies or to put the research findings in even the most elementary of theoretical constructs. Thus, one learns relatively more from the old Negro leadership studies in spite of their limitations than one does from the most recent research on Black leaders.[2]

Putting these bodies of research together, one notes the emergence of a sizeable number of Black elected officials (and leading Blacks in the executive branch, the judiciary, and other societal control institutions such as corporations, universities, and foundations); a decline in glamour personality–type leadership, and the emergence of new caucus and community-based organizations. However, aside from—and perhaps in spite of—these important changes of the 1960s, there appears to be more continuity than discontinuity in Negro to Black leadership in terms of social background, organization, power structure, ideology, and the roles of preachers, Whites, and the masses. For example, the evidence shows continuity in terms of the militancy-moderate cleavage. Contemporary moderates tend to adhere to liberal, integrationist belief, conventional methods and rhetoric, while militants tend toward socialist or nationalist beliefs and unconventional methods and rhetoric. Militants also tend to be more predisposed toward involvement with and support of mass action than do moderates. There is, of course, some overlap. Some leaders who are moderate in their beliefs favor militant methods and mass action, and some leaders who are militant in their beliefs are moderate in their methods if not also in their rhetoric. However, these are exceptions. In general, the pattern is one of consistency along all three dimensions of the typology, and a profile of the leadership types today resembles in many ways the profile drawn by Myrdal nearly forty years ago. Looking back on the important transformations of the 1960s, one might say that in Black leadership the more things change the more they seem to remain the same.

DIRECTIONS FOR FUTURE RESEARCH

A number of gaps in the knowledge about Black leaders and directions for future research emerged from this review. First, students of Black leadership need to go beyond research on Black elected officials and civil rights organizations. While there is a small and growing body of research on Black persons in elective offices, we know next to nothing about Blacks in appointive positions at the local, state, and federal levels, nor has there been much research on the increasing number of Black leaders or, more precisely, leading Blacks in other official positions.

Additional study is needed on the leadership role of Blacks in fraternal, professional, the new caucus organizations, especially the "mechanisms of collective judgement" and the leftist and nationalist organizations. For example, what accounts for the apparent increasing influence of fraternal organizations in Black politics, or what are the social backgrounds and political organizing behavior of Black nationalist and Marxist leaders and organizations? What has been their impact on mass thought and behavior? On each of these questions, we do not know enough to engage even in intelligent speculation.

Further research on the role of the church and clergy in Black politics is also in order. According to the conventional wisdom, the church is the important organizational base in Black electoral politics. However, the available research shows that the church may not play as important a role in the mobilization of the Black electorate as do civil rights organizations. The research of Berenson, Elifson, and Tollerson (1976) offers some suggestive lines of inquiry, and Hamilton's (1972) typology of church roles in Black politics is potentially useful in organizing field research on the subject.

Research on the power structure of the Black community—both nationally and locally—should be undertaken. This research should use both the reputational and decision-making approaches to identify both the external and internal dynamics of the distribution of power in the Black community. Regarding the internal dynamics of community power, we need studies of the sanctions (if any) that various leadership elements are able to use vis-à-vis their followers, and of the influences that followers exert over leaders. Finally, an important question here is the relationship of the emerging Black elected officials' stratum to the more traditional institutions and bases of power in Black America.

The ethnicity, class origins (including skin color), and the structure of leadership beliefs and their relationship to mass attitudes also ought to be investigated. Regarding the latter, scattered survey data are available on Black elite and mass attitudes toward integration, nationalism, and socialism. But what is needed is a systematically developed schedule to identify the core values, beliefs, attitudes, and policy preferences of each ideology; a specification of their internal consistency (or lack thereof); and their relationship to each other, to leadership, and to mass behavior. Students should also investigate the extent to which available or feasible political methods shape, constrain, or even determine leadership beliefs.

Finally, research on leadership at the grassroots level—or what Higham (1978) calls the "small community" level—is needed. Above the visible structure of "large community" leadership, organization, and external relations, there is an infrastructure of churches, bars, street corner cliques, beauty and barber shops, and small group associations that together constitute the community. The characteristics of leadership at this level are not well understood. But as Higham (1978:18) writes, "it is clear that the large community ordinarily handles the external relations of the group. . . . The small community, on the other hand, creates and sustains the web of daily life." The small community deserves attention in its own right, but we also need to know the relationship between the two leadership types (small and large) in the setting of the external agenda of the community. An example of the former kind of research that might be interesting is what Holden (1973) calls "church politics," the often talked of but never researched struggle for positions of leadership in the church hierarchy (bishops and pastors, deacons, members of boards of trustees, and so forth). One would want to know, for example, the impact of this internal church politics on the role of the church and clergy in external relations. Finally, closely related to the phenomenon of small community leadership are those sometimes competitive campaigns for leadership in local NAACP chapters, or the processes by which local Urban League executives are selected.

There are other items for a Black leadership research agenda that might be derived from this study. The foregoing, however, constitute areas requiring immediate attention if the subfield is to move rapidly toward the advancement of a series of interrelated verifiable propositions about the leadership phenomenon in Black America.

Theory

The consensus that clearly emerges from the literature reviewed here, both the old and new but especially the old, is that the most appropriate general theory for the study of Black politics and leadership is some variant of the race dominance/power approach. In one form or another, nearly all the students who sought to explain Black leadership theoretically did so in terms of the subordinate power position of Blacks relative to Whites.

Salamon (1973) satisfactorily demonstrated the utility of the "modernization perspective" in his study of the emergence of a Black politician stratum in Mississippi. But, in general, the modernization approach lacks the grounded specificity of the race-dominance framework, and isomorphism with the political experience of the peoples of the Black world (Jones 1972:7). And "although the process of modernization, particularly industrialization, has implications for race relations, the evidence suggests that its role is at best indirect. It creates some conditions that are conducive to securing changes in race relations, but does not independently alter highly developed patterns of race relations" (Morris

1975:19). Thus, the modernization approach is probably less appropriate as a general theory than is the race-dominance framework.

Jones (1972) has made the most clear-cut contribution toward developing the basic concepts and hypotheses of the power/race dominance approach as a systematic framework to order inquiry on Black leadership. His most basic assumption is that "a frame of reference for Black politics should not begin with superficial comparison of Blacks and other ethnic minorities . . . [but rather] it should begin by searching for those factors which are unique to the Black political experience, for this is the information which will facilitate our understanding of blacks in the American political system" (Jones 1972:7–8).[3]

Given this assumption, Jones, building on the earlier work of Roucek (1956), argues that Black politics should be conceptualized as "essentially a power struggle between blacks and whites, with the latter trying to maintain their superordinate position vis-à-vis the former" (1972:9). But in order to clearly distinguish "black political phenomena" from other extensions of the "universal power struggle," the stipulation that the "ideological justification for the superordination of Whites is the institutionalized belief in the inherent superiority of that group" (Jones 1972:9) is added as a necessary specifying condition. Finally, Jones presents five Black "goal-directed patterns" of activity (integration, accommodation, Black consciousness, Black nationalism, and revolution) that can, with modifications, be usefully applied to "advance explanatory propositions" regarding Black leadership (Jones 1972:12–17). Although Jones in this initial formulation develops only the basic concepts of the framework, in a subsequent case study he applies it with modest success to an analysis of the emergence of the first Black-led governing coalition in Atlanta (Jones 1978).[4]

In addition to Jones, Katznelson (1971) has also argued that power must be the central construct in the reformulation of race relations research in the discipline. More recently, Greenberg (1980) in a cross-cultural study case uses the concept "racial domination" to order his research findings on race politics in the United States and three other advanced capitalist societies. Thus, from the Negro leadership literature and from the more recent work of students of race politics, the racial domination approach emerges as the most *basic*—but not the sole—frame of reference for the study of leadership and politics in racially stratified societies.

A number of students of Negro leadership have argued that, in addition to racial domination, a secondary factor in explaining patterns of leadership in Black politics in the United States is the structure of particular racial environments. Walton (1972:11–12) has, perhaps, been clearest on the theoretical import of this factor:

> Basically speaking, Black politics springs from the particular brand of segregation practices found in different environments in which Black people find themselves. In other words, the nature of segregation and the manner in which it differs not only in different localities but within a locality have caused Black people to employ political activities, methods, devices and techniques that would advance their policy preferences. In *short, Black politics is a function of the particular brand of segregation found in different environments in which Black people find themselves.* And the politics of Blacks differs significantly from locality to locality. Although there are many striking similarities between the political activities of Black Americans in different localities, there are differences far greater than geography can explain. Basically, the differences lie in the variety of forms that segregation and discrimination have taken in this country. (emphasis in original)

It should be clear that Walton does not deny the central theoretical importance of racial domination. Instead, Walton suggests that racial domination in the United States has been particularized, and that this particularity has to be taken into consideration in understanding and explaining Black politics and leadership.

The foregoing factors, which are essentially exogenous, suggest that fundamentally Black leadership behavior is a function of factors external to the community. Two endogenous factors—class and culture—are also theoretically suggestive.

Class is thought to be theoretically significant because of two factors. The first pertains to the Black class structure itself—the relatively large lower class, or as it is called today, the underclass, a stratum increasingly isolated from the opportunities of modern society (Glasgow 1980; Wilson 1978). The second factor is the largely middle-class leadership's unwillingness or inability to make rapid and sustained progress toward melioration of the terrible problems of the underprivileged. These two factors give rise to what are variously referred to in the literature as class "tensions," "conflicts," or even "antagonisms" between the Black leadership and masses.

Evidence and arguments were presented earlier in this review showing that class conflict in the Black community declined in the 1960s as a result of the civil rights revolution, the growth and diversification of the middle class and the Black power movement. Yet one reads today in both the popular and scholarly media of an unprecedented class conflict between the relatively secure new Black middle-class and the marginal Black underclass (Bolce and Gray 1979; Delaney 1978). However, when viewed in the light of the pertinent data, such assertions appear to be without scientific foundation. There is some evidence of a leadership–mass cleavage on political methods, with the masses favoring more militant actions. But in terms of basic beliefs and policy preferences, one finds fundamental unity in the Black community at all class levels, and between the leadership and the masses in support of the ideology and policies of liberal integration.

Thus, the theoretical significance of class in Black politics is limited. This is not to deny that there are differences of sentiment, ethos, and opinion in Black America between the leadership and the masses. Rather, it is to suggest that these differences do not constitute class "antagonisms." Indeed, the class factor in studies of Black leadership may be best construed as an aspect of culture. While specialists disagree as to whether the Black community constitutes a separate and distinct political subculture (Morris 1975:119–23), the data are unmistakable that there are significant differences between Black and White Americans in terms of their level of support for the system, their level of trust in the system, and political knowledge and efficacy (Morris 1975:123–34). These aspects of the Black "subculture," together with the reality of continued racial oppression, powerlessness, and economic deprivation give rise to a series of characteristics identified by Holden (1973:17–26) as creating a culture adverse to effective leadership because it results in very high demands on the leadership but relatively low support.

These cultural characteristics take the form of class tensions manifested in the ritualistic condemnation of Negro leaders as "Uncle Toms" or "sell-outs" who have lost touch with the masses. These rituals of Black culture have always been and, in the nature of the Black person's lot in this country, probably always will be an aspect of the relationship between Black leadership and followership. This is in spite of the fact that "it would be difficult to document a belief that any major Black leadership group purposefully sought to retard the advance of the race as a whole" (Hamilton 1981:8–9). Yet, because the masses are understandably disappointed with the pace of improvement in their life chances, there is extant in the community a relatively low level of trust in the leadership and a tendency to blame the leadership for the society's failure to respond to demands for racial justice. This is a cultural rather than a class phenomenon.

To conclude, contrary to the often stated allegation, the literature on Black leadership is not atheoretical. Rather, a basic frame of reference and two useful subconstructs of theoretical value are present in the literature. At this point, these fragments of theory cannot be regarded as a coherent set of propositions from which hypotheses for empirical research can be deduced. Yet the recent research on Black elected officials has tended to ignore even these fragments in favor of descriptive or exploratory research. While exploratory research is appropriate in an emergent subfield as a means by which to lay the groundwork for theoretical exegesis, we now have enough historical and scientific research about the Black leadership phenomenon to begin to translate available theoretical schema into testable propositions to guide and structure inquiry in the subfield. To encourage students to do so has been a principal aim of this monograph.

POSTSCRIPT

The purpose of this postscript is to review the political science and related social science literature on Black leadership since 1983, the year of publication of the initial monograph. This essay is brief since there have been relatively few systematic studies of African American leadership in the last fifteen years. While studies in leadership dominated the field of Black politics for decades, today there are a "plethora of approaches and topics covered under the rubric of black politics" (McClain and Garcia 1993:255) and systematic studies in leadership have virtually disappeared.

For example, a recent review of the political science literature on Black politics classifies the recent research into such varied categories as urban politics, voting rights and public policy, presidential politics, Congress and the courts, political socialization and attitudes, and Black women and gender issues, but nothing on Black leadership (see McClain and Garcia 1993; see also Walton 1989).

There are, however, a few studies that deal with aspects of the phenomenon of African American leadership. I first review these studies.[1] Then, I examine several recent developments concerning African American leadership, including its continued institutionalization, the emergence and consolidation of an alternative Black conservative leadership formation as well as the emergence of the category of so-called public intellectuals who seek to play a leadership role. I also discuss the lack of utility now of *Ebony*'s annual lists of the 100 most influential Black Americans as a tool to analyze Black leadership. Finally, as a suggestion for further research I discuss use of the growing number of biographies and memoirs about and by Black leaders as a "data" source. While there is certainly a need for a series of carefully designed empirical studies of local and national Black leadership patterns and practices, biographical analysis might also be helpful in understanding and assessing Black leadership.

RECENT STUDIES IN
AFRICAN AMERICAN LEADERSHIP

Recent studies in Black leadership have focused on the evolution and the effectiveness and influence of the Congressional Black Caucus; on patterns of mayoral leadership; and on the idea of a new style of African American leader categorized under the rubric of deracialization. They include a small body of studies on African American women as leaders; the "Jesse Jackson literature"; a few studies of Black organizations; and several overview articles and books that provide a kind of overall assessment—generally critical—of modern Black leadership.

The Congressional Black Caucus

The Black congressional delegation and the Congressional Black Caucus (CBC) continue to be a major foci of research on Black leadership. When the Black Caucus was formed in 1969 the Black congressional delegation was constituted by nine members of the House and one member of the Senate, Republican Edward Brooke of Massachusetts. In the thirty years since, the size of the Black House delegation has more than quadrupled (38 in 1998) but there is still only one African American senator, Carol Mosley Braun, a Democrat elected from Illinois in 1992 (Senator Brooke was defeated in 1978 after serving two terms). The delegation is not likely to increase much beyond its present size and indeed may decline, perhaps sharply, after the reapportionment and redistricting processes in 2001. This is because of the Supreme Court's decision in *Shaw v. Reno*[2] and related cases suggesting that the purposeful drawing of majority Black legislative districts violates the Constitution's equal protection clause. Such purposefully drawn districts with Black majorities have been critical to the growth in the size of the Black House delegation, since relatively few Blacks have been able to win elections in majority White districts.

Except for an increase in the number of southern (and to some extent rural) representatives, the Black congressional delegation in the 1990s, despite its larger size, resembles on most relevant characteristics the delegation of the 1970s. It is constituted by mostly middle-aged, middle-class men (although women are 20 percent of the Black delegation compared to 9 percent of the House as a whole);[3] is overwhelmingly liberal in ideology and Democratic in partisanship; disproportionately dependent on political action committees (PACs) (particularly labor-connected ones) for campaign finance support; and because of the financial and other advantages of incumbency members find it relatively easy to win reelection. (For a comparison of the 1970s and 1990s delegations along these dimensions see Smith 1981b and Bositis 1994.) Except for size, the major difference between the 1970s and 1990s delegation is that in the latter, Blacks are more widely represented in the formal arenas of power in the House—the major committees and the Democratic Party leadership (again compare Smith 1981b:213–18; Bositis 1994:19–21).

Research on the Black Caucus as an African American leadership collectivity presents a somewhat mixed picture, in terms of its influence as a force inside the House as well as its leadership effectiveness in the larger processes of Black politics.[4] Swain (1993) in a controversial study argues, in effect, that Black representation in Congress and the Black Caucus itself are unnecessary because White members of the House represent the interests of Blacks as well as and, in some cases, perhaps better than Blacks. Whitby (1997) challenges Swain's findings on methodological grounds, contending that she examined too few cases (nine Black and four White members of the House) in too short a time period (1987–89). Looking at a larger number of cases over a longer time span Whitby finds a distinctive dimension of substantive representation by Black members, compared to Whites.

Until the election of a Republican House majority in 1994 scholarly assessments of the effectiveness of the Congressional Black Caucus as a leadership institution in the House and beyond was mixed. Several observers (Jones 1987; Harris 1994; Bositis 1994; and Champagne and Rieselbach 1995) viewed the group as an increasingly influential bloc in the House and in national politics generally. Jones, for example, wrote "the CBC does indeed constitute a viable force in Congress . . . [and] by and large the future appears bright" (1994:237–38). Campagne and Rieselbach concluded that in 1993 the CBC "emerged as a major player" in Congress (1995:154). And Bositis wrote "The future influence of the Congressional Black Caucus and its individual members in the U.S. House of Representatives in the 104th Congress and beyond will be very great, providing the Democrats retain a controlling majority" (1994:68).

Other observers assessing the caucus during the period prior to the Republican takeover were less sanguine. Assessing the group after the first year of the Clinton administration, Smith (1996:222) described the caucus as "an isolated, frustrated relatively inconsequential force in the House." Similar assessments were reached by Berg (1994) and Singh (1996): that because of its left liberal agenda and the institutional constraints of Congress and the American political system, it is virtually impossible for the caucus to wield anything more than symbolic power in the Congress.

Smith and Berg reach their pessimistic conclusions partly on the basis of a detailed study of the alternative federal budgets prepared by the caucus since 1981 (see Berg 1987, 1994:122–36; Smith 1996:224–25; see also Thornton 1983). While proposing a projected balanced budget over a five-year period (earlier than either the Reagan administration or the Democratic majority in the House), the caucus budgets proposed major cuts in defense spending, major increases in social welfare spending, and substantial increases in taxes on corporations and the wealthy. Comprehensive and controversial, it is not surprising that these budgets were soundly defeated year after year. Rather, it is not their defeat but the manner in which they were defeated. Smith (1996:216) writes, "what is more revealing about the status of the black agenda in the House than the outcome of the roll call votes on the budgets is the sense of isolation, anger and bitterness by Blacks in the House as they are routinely ignored by party colleagues and leaders." And Berg writes that the budget debate and vote by 1987 had "become an empty routine, a symbol of the exact mixture of respect and disdain in which the Democratic party hold its African American members" (1994:131).

In part because of this sense of disdain and disrespect and the resulting isolation and frustration increasing numbers of senior Blacks have voluntarily left the House since 1980. Since 1982 thirteen senior members of the House have retired or resigned, including many who were important party and committee leaders. The isolation of Blacks in the House and their sense of frustration is exacerbated by Republican control of the body and their pursuit of a conservative agenda on race-related and social welfare policies.

As members of the House Democratic majority, the caucus since its inception was able to exercise some leverage, however modest, on congressional decision-making, given its size as a Democratic voting bloc in the party caucus and on the floor, and the centrality of the Black electorate to the Party's electoral coalition. The control of the House by the conservative Republican majority—in which the Black vote plays no role and with but a single Black Republican in the House—to the extent that it endures, means more so than ever that Blacks in Congress are simply a presence, not a power.

While scholars differ in their assessments of the effectiveness of the caucus as a force in the House and national politics, there is a consensus on its near-term future. Given its adherence to a liberal agenda (which it should be said reflects the opinions—overwhelmingly—of the African American community), the caucus faces a major dilemma. This is because in the near term both elite and White mass opinion are likely to be hostile to liberal initiatives, especially on race. Thus, the caucus might abandon liberalism (and thus its representation of Black opinion) or turn to various forms of protest in the Congress and movement politics beyond. It is likely to do neither. Some observers of the caucus advocate a turn toward protest and popular mobilization (Berg 1994:136; Smith 1996:224–25), but they do not see it as likely. Rather, in agreement with most students of the caucus, they see the resolution of the dilemma in a turn toward patronage-based accommodation rather than protest. Champagne and Riselbach write, "The passage of time, the increase in the number of CBC members, and changed congressional circumstances have increased the incentives for the former course, and these incentives can be expected to increase further in the years ahead" (1995:152). Berg, however, has a cautionary word about this likely turn to accomodationism rather than protest. He writes:

> Members who turn to the accommodationist strategy also find themselves in a double bind. They may have chosen to concentrate their efforts on obtaining jobs and contracts for their constituents because the path to more basic changes are blocked; but once they make this choice, they may be portrayed as petty, parochial, and corrupt. Indeed, once they begin to live and work in the world of patronage politics they may well slip into actual corruption. Hence the turn to accommodationism may contribute further to the negative political climate that brought it about in the first place. (1994:136)

Mayoral Leadership

Although African Americans have served as leaders of most of America's major cities including several with relatively small Black populations (see appendix A), there is relatively little research on Black mayoral leadership styles or patterns or how they may have changed since the election of the first Black mayors in 1967. This in spite of the fact that it is widely recognized that the extant models of mayoral leadership in the United States are clearly deficient in their ability to capture the dynamics of social change in Black-led cities (Persons 1985). This deficiency in the extant models (on the extant social science models of mayoral leadership, see Pressman 1972) was vividly demonstrated by the "anomaly" of the Philadelphia Move incident, which violated prevailing assumptions regarding Black mayoral leadership when a Black mayor supported a bureaucratic decision to bomb a Black neighborhood (Persons 1987).

Reed (1988) in a theoretical essay delineates the structural constraints that have prevented Black mayors from using their leadership positions to challenge the web of economic interests and privileges that have effectively kept the problems of poverty and the urban underclass off the agenda of Black-led cities. Several case studies (Jones 1990; Persons and Henderson 1990; Perry 1990b; Starks and Preston 1990; Jackson 1990; Rich 1990; Ransom 1990) have shown that "Black mayors tend to govern by virtue of their personality, not by the use of political organization" (Preston 1990:133).[5] Although the style of Black mayoral personality-centered leadership varies from city to city, in no city has a Black mayor developed a vision of urban reform centered on the urban poor or developed any ideology or organization that challenges the dominance of the business community in limiting the urban reform agenda

(Nelson 1990; Stone, Imbroscio, and Orr 1991). Similarly, Rich (1996) studied Black mayoral leadership in school-reform politics in Gary, Newark, and Detroit, finding that Black mayors are reluctant to lead and generally were not very effective in school-reform leadership not because of business dominance, but because to do so "risks alienating one of the most powerful interest groups in city politics, teachers unions" (1996:204).

Most of the research on Black mayors focuses on big city mayors, but of the more than two hundred Black mayors in the United States the overwhelming majority govern small towns in the rural South. Morrison (1987) presents an innovative comparative analysis of the leadership styles of Black mayors in three small Mississippi towns. He found a relatively close leadership-constituency linkage in these towns and, at least in the immediate aftermath of their elections, and improvement in the living conditions of African Americans (on elected Black leaders in the rural South, see also Hanks 1987).

Overall, however, mayoral specific leadership studies are in short supply, especially comparative ones. Rather most of the research continues to focus on the conditions and coalitions that facilitate the election of Black mayors or the impact of their policies on the African American community (Browning, Marshall, and Tabb 1990, 1997).

Deracialization and a New Category of African American Leadership

With the election in 1989 of Douglas Wilder as the first elected Black governor in the United States (Yancey 1990; Jones and Clemons 1993; Edds 1990), David Dinkins as New York City's first Black mayor, and African American mayors in Seattle and New Haven (both cities with relatively small Black populations) political scientists employed the concept of deracialization to capture the dynamics of what they saw as a new development in Black politics and Black leadership (Perry 1990a, 1991; McCormick and Jones 1993; Persons 1993).[6] Stated succinctly, deracialization is a strategy for African Americans to become what Kilson (1994) calls "transracial leaders"; that is, African American leaders of non–African American constituencies and institutions. As an electoral strategy it refers to efforts by Black candidates to deemphasize their race and race-related issues while emphasizing issues that appeal across racial lines in order to win elections in and represent the interests of multi-ethnic constituencies.

Although the development of the new concept of deracialization after the 1989 elections suggests that something new was occurring in African American politics and leadership, with rare exceptions most

Black mayoral candidates and many Black candidates for legislative offices have appealed to and often attracted some White support by emphasizing transracial issues and coalitions. Even Jesse Jackson, the preeminent race leader of the post–civil rights era, subordinated the strategies and issues of his second presidential campaign to a deracialized quest for inclusion and recognition as a Democratic Party leader rather than as a mere "Black" leader (Smith 1990). And after the Nixon administration, most African Americans who have served in high-level executive branch posts have viewed themselves as leaders of America who just happen to be Black (Smith 1996: chaps. 4–5). Colin Powell is emblematic of this phenomenon, in his role as national security advisor under Reagan, as Joint Chiefs Chair under Bush, and as Republican party leader and prospective presidential candidate.

While most political scientists, African American as well as White, applaud the emergence of a transracial or deracialized category of African American leader, several have cautioned that this development may bode ill for the future of Black *group* progress (Smith 1989; Starks 1991; Walters 1992). Starks, for example, writes that such leadership "detracts from the substance of black politics" (1991:216). This trend, however, is likely to continue in part because it represents the logic of system incorporation and the electoral opportunity structure and because of the inevitable opportunism of politicians. Thus, in the future we are likely to see an increasing bifurcation between "leading Blacks" (leaders of American institutions and constituencies who just happen to be Black) and "Black leaders," those individuals who seek to lead the race by representing Black constituencies and the Black community in terms of its internal institutions and processes or in its relationship to the larger American society and polity.

Women in African American Leadership

The historian Kevin Gaines writes:

> The male-dominated gender politics of uplift posed difficulties for black women as race leaders. . . . Black women are thus placed in the subordinate position of sacrificing gender consciousness and their reproductive self-determination in the name of race unity. In other ways, this male orientation affected how black oppression was theorized, emphasizing the victimization of black men through lynching or economic exclusion and silencing the particular victimizations of black women. (1996:13)

Gaines' "theorizing" or "historicizing" of the relationship between gender and African American leadership is a controversial and contested one (see also James 1997). The dominance of men in African American leadership is clear; however, historically Black women have always played a more important role in their community's leadership than have White women in American leadership.

Today Black women continue to play a more prominent leadership role, constituting for example about 20 percent of all Black elected officials and almost a fourth of the Black congressional delegation. In spite of this there is relatively little research on the leadership work of Black women. As Walton writes, "The literature on black female activism, whether in civil rights or the political struggle, tends to be biographical, descriptive and more historical than analytical. These studies offer little theory and few generalizations" (1994b:252; on this point see also Braxton 1994b). Beverly Allen states the problem this way: "leadership theories are rarely generalizable to women and minorities. . . . The result has been an unfortunate lack of understanding of the importance and role of female networks for community leadership" (1997:61).

Research on African American women as leaders is therefore an area ripe for theoretical and empirical work. First and foremost, we must determine whether there are gender-based differences in terms of issues or leadership styles. We know there is not as much of a gender gap in African American mass opinion or voting behavior as there is in the White community, but this may not hold at the leadership level. But, as things stand now, we simply do not know and this is an area clearly in need of study, ideally from a variety of disciplinary and methodological perspectives.

The body of research that does exists on African American female political leaders is in an embryonic state. There are historical studies of the important and neglected role of women activists in the civil rights movement (Crawford et al. 1990), studies of the differential recruitment and socialization of Black women elected officials (Harmon-Martin 1994), and interpretative studies on the relative success of African American women leaders (Darcy and Hadley 1988; Prestage 1991). There are also scattered descriptive studies, including Prestage's (1987) work on Black judges and Gill's (1997) study of Black congresswomen; several studies of grassroots or community level Black female leaders (Sack 1981; Giles 1988; Ardey 1994); Walton's (1994a) analysis of biographical and related material on Black female presidential candidates, and his study of Black women delegates to the United Nations (Walton 1995b).

But, again these studies are largely descriptive without theoretical analysis or analytic generalizations. Research on women as a category of African American leadership, therefore, should be high on the social science research agenda.[7]

African American Organization

In general, effective leadership—even by charismatic individuals—requires effective organization. Relatively little work has been done on the organizational infrastructure or underpinnings of African American leadership. Several studies have focused on the continuing decline in organizational efficacy and programmatic relevance of the old-line civil rights organizations (Cruse 1987; Lusane 1994:23–36; Smith 1996:87–126). Pinderhughes (1992, 1995) has an ongoing research project focusing on the civil rights groups and the Leadership Conference on Civil Rights, and on their adjustments to the tensions occasioned by the changing composition of the civil rights coalition and the emergence of new civil rights claimants and issues. There is also an impressive body of survey-based research on the continuing important role of religion and the church in Black politics and leadership. These studies indicate that the church and religion are important incubators of political activism and race-group identity and solidarity, as well as a major institution for political leadership and resource mobilization (Dawson, Brown, and Allen, 1990; Brown and Wofford 1994; Reese and Brown 1995; Harris 1994: see also Lincoln and Mamiya 1990 and Taylor 1994). There are also several studies of the Nation of Islam since the death of Elijah Muhammad, analyzing the radical changes undertaken by Wallace Dean Muhammad, the subsequent factionalization of the group into several sects, and the revitalization of a "new" Nation of Islam under the leadership of Louis Farrakhan (see Mamiya 1992; Smith 1996:100–105; Magida 1996; Singh 1997; Gardell 1997; see also Lincoln's 1994 revision of his classic study).

We still, however, know hardly anything about "small community" or "grassroots" leadership and organization—for example, about local NAACP and Urban League chapters,[8] or the community problem-solving organizations that deal with children, schools, drugs, and so on. There is a little research on local community activism by Black nationalists, radicals, and more mainstream local organizing groups (see Bush 1984; Jennings 1990, 1992; Timoner 1996; Covin 1997; and chapter 9 in this volume).[9] Local leaders were critically important in the mobilization of resources during the civil rights movement, laying the foundations and establishing base camps that facilitated the successes of national organizations and leaders (Dittmer 1995; Payne 1995). And in a fine case study comparing Black and White 1960s student civil rights activists, Fendrich (1993) shows that these activists—especially the Blacks—have remained politically active and committed to the ideals of the movement, although they feel relatively powerless in the contemporary era of political conservatism.

The Jesse Jackson Campaign Literature

Jesse Jackson's 1984 and 1988 presidential campaigns generated a modest literature in their own right. The first of these studies was Reed's (1986) harshly critical broadside in which he argued that it was inappropriate for Jackson to run for president (because he was a preacher and civil rights leader and not an elected official), and that Jackson's campaigns retarded the development of a viable Black political movement. Barker and Walters's (1989) edited collection was more sympathetic to Jackson and more optimistic about the 1984 campaign's contribution to Black politics.[10] The eleven chapters in this volume analyze the political context out of which the campaign emerged, Jackson's leadership and campaign styles, the constituents and voters, the impact of the campaign on the Democratic convention, and its impact on the Democratic Party. In another edited collection on the 1984 campaign Morris (1990) presents a thorough assessment, with especially good papers on the historical and political contexts, the political mobilization process, and a concluding chapter contrasting the insurgent, protest character of the 1984 campaign with the more routine, institutionalized 1988 campaign.

Other treatments of the campaigns by academics include Smith and McCormick (1985); Henry (1986); Frye (1986); Cavanagh and Foster (1989); Tate (1992); and Hertze (1993). In addition to these studies by academics, there are also accounts by journalists (Faw and Skelton 1986; Collins 1986) and a critical, insider account by Colton (1989), Jackson's 1988 campaign press secretary. Finally, in addition to these campaign-specific studies, Stanford (1997) has written a thorough, historically informed and balanced analysis of Jackson's leadership behavior in international affairs, focusing on his "citizen diplomacy" in the Middle East, Africa, and the Caribbean.

While there is a fair amount of work assessing the Jackson campaigns for president, they offer few new generalizations about Jackson's leadership style; nor is there a consensus on the significance of the campaigns or their impact on African Americans and the party system. His campaigns, however, by all these accounts were symbolically significant and important in elevating Jackson's status as the leading race leader of the post–civil rights era.

Critical Studies

Since the work of Ralph Bunche—the first African American academic political scientist—critical analysis—sometimes harshly critical—has been a staple of scholarly work on Black leaders. Given the status and condition of the race at any given historical moment and the systemic constraints under which Black leaders must operate to alter this status and condition, such criticism is inevitable. This critical stance of African American intellectuals toward African American leaders is not likely to change until the status of the race radically improves. This puts Black leaders in a near impossible position, given the resources of the Black community and constraints imposed by the ever evolving system of race domination in the United States.

In the tradition of Bunche's 1930s critiques of Black leadership,[11] in the last several years a number of studies although differing in approach and method have arrived at essentially the same analytic generalizations regarding African American leadership in the post–civil rights era. That conclusion, variously stated, is that the leadership has failed to mobilize the limited resources of the Black community as part of a strategy and program to extract from society the resources necessary to reconstruct urban African American communities. (Relatively little attention is paid to the necessity to redevelop rural Black America, although conditions there are not unlike those in the cities, reflecting perhaps the urban backgrounds and biases of modern African American leadership, intellectual as well as political.)

Cruse (1987) in a historical analysis argues that the African American leadership is wedded to an outmoded civil rights–social welfare ideology, when in fact "civil rights justice, for all intents and purposes has been won; there are no more frontiers to conquer, no horizons in view that are not mirages that vanish over the hill of the next Supreme Court decision on the meaning of equal protection" (1987:385). And Cruse (1987:385) writes, *"The truth is, however, there exists in black America no such organized black leadership consensus that is either willing or able to replace, oppose or simply ignore and bypass the organized remains of the old, civil rights–welfare leadership"* (emphasis in original).

Covin (1993), in what he calls a "discourse on African American leadership" based on a series of "conversations" with members of the California Legislative Black Caucus, concludes "black leaders have no leadership theory specific to their condition that directs them" (1993:34). The veteran members of the California legislature that Covin talked to in 1989 told him that they recognized that passing laws—at least the kinds they are able to pass—would not deal with the conditions of the race. But they had no alternatives (except one member's suggestion that Black leaders should move into their inner city communities and live among their constituents), leading Covin to conclude, "That leaves them at loose ends about what should be done to obtain solutions to problems upon which they are agreed. Within the context of the United States perhaps the most difficult problem for black leaders is conceptualizing a way in which they can be effective" (1993:29).[12]

Lusanne (1994) analyzed the situation of Black leadership after the election of a neoconservative Democratic president in 1992: "Black leadership confronts a deleterious social situation in the United States under which it has virtually no control. The economic and social salvos by the Reagan and Bush administrations and changes in the political economy of U.S. capitalism has profoundly impacted and limited the options available to Black leaders and activists in their efforts to address the conditions of the Black community" (1990:4).

Jones (1994) in an interpretative essay argues that Black leadership is becoming increasingly irrelevant because it is functionally integrated into the state apparatus and, in part because of this integration, it lacks the capacity to deal with the increasingly permanent character of Black poverty. Reed (1996) in a theoretical essay argues in a vein similar to Jones that this functional integration into the state apparatus, what he calls "political incorporation," has resulted in the "demobilization" of the African American community. In his 1996 work Smith provides empirical documentation for the interpretative and theoretical analyses of Jones and Reed. Based on a detailed study of Black political incorporation in the post–civil rights era (focusing on the civil rights lobby and Black participation in national political institutions—Congress, the executive branch and the Democratic Party). Smith concludes: "This book provides dismal, detailed evidence of the irrelevancy of black politics in producing in the last twenty-five years benefits for most blacks, especially the imperative to reconstruct and integrate the ghettos into the mainstream of American society" (1996:277).

These critical studies suggest that there is a consensus in the African American scholarly community that African American leadership is, to use the subtitle of Lusanne's book "At the Crossroads" (on this point, see also McClain 1996). While there is a scholarly consensus on this point, there is no consensus among these scholars about the appropriate direction for the Black community and its leadership in the next century. Cruse and Smith favor some variant of Black nationalism. Cruse (1987:371–91), for example, calls for the establishment of a Black political party as a first step in the development of a new Black leadership and the mobilization of the Black community. Yet Smith (1996:84), after detailed study of the efforts to form a Black political party in the 1970s and early 1980s, writes: "It is very unlikely . . . that blacks will be able to overcome the institutional, ideological and structural barriers to party formation."

Meanwhile Lusanne and Reed seem to favor a black-white left-labor coalition, but Jones (1994:355) contends that "the extent to which black leadership assumes that white allies or support are necessary to achieve its goals, it of necessity brings to the battlefield its own Trojan horse."

Covin does not attempt to propose an ideology or strategy for the Black leadership conundrum that he analyzes. Perhaps because he knows that Black scholarly critics of Black leaders, like the leaders themselves, have no leadership theory specific to the modern conditions of the race that might guide their intellectual work.

RECENT DEVELOPMENTS IN AFRICAN AMERICAN LEADERSHIP

Since the initial publication of this monograph, there have been two recent developments in African American leadership that require scholarly attention. The first is the consolidation of a new African American conservative leadership group. Second, is the emergence of a group of scholars, referred to as "public intellectuals," who also seek to provide an alternative to the liberal/civil rights leadership establishment.

Black Conservative Leadership

When Ronald Reagan was elected president in 1980 the conservative movement in the United States deliberately sought to create a new Black conservative leadership group as an alternative to the left-liberal Black leadership establishment (Saloma 1984:130–37; Jones 1987). This effort to create an alternative Black leadership was part of a larger effort by the conservative movement to bring about a revolution in the contextual basis of political and policy debate in the United States (Walton 1997).

The conservative movement's first objective was to discredit liberalism and delegitimatize the role of the government in the society and the economy and, through its economic program, to cripple the capacity of the government to act on social problems by destroying its revenue base. This general attack on liberalism had specifically racial motives: (1) to delegitimatize the Black quest for racial and social justice through recurrent attacks on affirmative action, the welfare state, and the "failed" Great Society programs of the 1960s; and (2) to change the context of the policy debate on the so-called Black underclass from an emphasis on the responsibilities of government to a focus on the shortcomings of Blacks themselves in terms of the absence of individual responsibility, "family values," and community self-help. In order to accomplish these race-specific objectives, White conservatives understood from the beginning that they would have to discredit the liberal Black leadership establishment and create a visible alternative. This process got under way in the early 1980s and by the mid-1990s it was complete—complete in the sense that a full-fledged Black conservative leadership network had been consolidated and this network has had considerable influence in reshaping the policy debate on race (Conti and Stetson 1989).

This network consists of a number of well-publicized intellectuals (Thomas Sowell, Walter Williams, Glenn Loury, and Shelby Steele) and several think tanks, journals, radio talk shows, and political forums. While there have been relatively few conservative elected officials (all elected from majority White constituencies), the Reagan and Bush administrations skillfully used the appointment process to create and sustain a Black conservative leadership of government officials, the most notable example being Supreme Court Justice Clarence Thomas.

Critics contend that these Black conservatives are "manufactured" leaders, without significant support in African American mass opinion or any organizational presence in the community (Jones 1987; Kilson 1993; Smith and Walton 1993).[13] While these criticisms are largely correct, this does not mean these individuals have not been influential in helping to move the debate on race and public policy in a conservative direction.

For example, a principal line of argument of conservative theorists, Black and White, is that the problems of the Black underclass are not structural or systemic but individual and communal, reflecting a lack of morality and individual responsibility.[14] By the time that President Clinton ran successfully for the presidency in 1992, this view was the dominant one in Washington political and policy circles. Thus, President Clinton campaigned on the theme of "personal responsibility" (implying that poor Black people lacked such responsibility) and a promise to "end welfare as we know it." Then, in the midst of his 1996 reelection campaign the president signed a conservative, Republican-crafted welfare reform bill that indeed ended welfare by abolishing the sixty-year-old New Deal guarantee of income support for poor women and their children.[15] This radical legislation was opposed by virtually the entire Black leadership establishment, yet the president felt politically free to sign it without fear of sanctions by that establishment. This is partly because the political and policy contexts for debate on the issue had been so radically altered since 1980, thanks in part to Black conservative advocacy.

Black conservatives in America do not have a mass constituency in the Black community or linkages with institutions indigenous to Black America. Nor have they sought to build such a constituency or such linkages. Rather, their role is not to lead Black people but to lead White opinion about Black people.

"Public Intellectuals" as African American Leaders

A similar leadership role is also sought by a group of relatively young scholars referred to as public intellectuals (see Berube 1995). The Reagan administration sought to discredit liberal Black leadership and develop a conservative alternative as part of its attempt to move the context of political and policy debate in a conservative direction. A similar strategy was followed by the Clinton administration in its efforts to discredit and disempower the liberal wing of the Democratic Party and move it (the party) in a centrist, neoconservative direction (see Walton1997:373–76).

In his first term in office, Clinton offered no new initiatives in civil rights or urban reform and by and large kept his distance from the Black leadership establishment,[16] preferring to rely instead on the informal advice of well-known (in elite circles) public intellectuals such as Harvard English Professor Henry Louis Gates and former University of Chicago (now at Harvard) sociologist William Wilson (although he declined to follow Wilson's advice that he veto the welfare reform bill).

This group of intellectuals, like their conservative counterparts, have been promoted by Whites into positions of prominence by the publication of their work and publicity in the elite media (the *New York Times*, the *New Yorker*, the *New Republic*, PBS/National Public Radio, the *Atlantic*, etc.). The ideological orientation of this group (it also includes such persons as Harvard theologian Cornell West and the writer Stanley Crouch) ranges from left-liberalism to Clinton-style centrism. What they have in common is hostility to the Black leadership establishment (Gates [1994] argues that the very notion of Black leadership is a myth), and hostility to Black nationalism (what they refer to as "identity" politics). In their writings they tend to focus not on politics or public policy per se but rather on cultural issues (especially popular culture) in writings that tend to be theoretically esoteric and empirically divorced from concern with issues of racism and poverty or the internal dynamics of Black politics.

Like their conservative counterparts, they tend to have no base of support in African American mass opinion or linkages to indigenous African American institutions. Nor do they seek such support or linkages. Rather, they too seek to lead by shaping the climate of elite opinion and debate on "race matters" in the United States. Or as one observer writes, "Black public intellectuals . . . speak to the white elite about the black problem in America" (Hill 1996:67).

Public intellectuals as a putative new Black leadership formation in the DuBoisian talented tenth tradition (see Gates and West 1996) is a relatively new phenomenon. Whether this group will be able to emerge as an alternative to the Black leadership establishment and exercise the kind of influence on public debate and policy on race as have their conservative counterparts at this writing cannot be known.

METHODOLOGICAL NOTES:
EBONY 100+, AND BIOGRAPHY AS A TOOL FOR
RESEARCH ON AFRICAN AMERICAN LEADERSHIP

Ebony 100+

In addition to my use of *Ebony*'s list of the 100 most influential African Americans as an analytic device, other scholars have employed it in the study of Black leadership (see Henry 1981; Gates 1994; Lusanne 1994:23–36). The *Ebony* lists were always at best a crude device, a suggestive indicator since the criteria of selection were not objective or replicable but rather were based on the subjective, perhaps idiosyncratic decisions of the magazine's editors. Nevertheless, the annual lists did provide an accessible tool to study Black leadership and make some inferences about its changing composition since 1963.

Now, however, the lists are nearly useless for even this modest purpose. First, the editors of *Ebony* have slightly modified the original 1963 criteria (see pp. 53–54) for inclusion on the lists. The new criteria (*Ebony* 1996:119–20) ask: (1) Does the individual transcend his or her position and command widespread national influence? and (2) Does the individual affect in a decisive way the beliefs, thinking, and actions of large segments of the Black population, either by his or her position in a key group or by his or her personal reach and influence? (Interestingly—and inexplicably—by neither of these criteria did Justice Clarence Thomas in 1997 qualify as an influential individual.) Second, the authors have added a new category of organizational leaders with the following qualifying criteria: (1) the individual should be the chief executive officer of an independent organization that commands widespread influence in Black America, (2) the organization must be a broad-based national group with a mass membership, a national headquarters, and a full-time staff, and (3) the individual and his or her organization must transcend a particular field, occupation, or specialty, and must have an ongoing program affecting the vital interests of African Americans (*Ebony* 1996:130). This new category of organizational leaders in particular makes comparison over the years especially difficult.

In addition, in part because of the new category of organizational leaders, the lists have been enlarged from 100 to "100+" (in 1996, 126). This means that it is no longer possible to analyze the relative influence of categories of leaders over time, since there is no fixed benchmark or measuring point.

Therefore, students in trying to ascertain the relative influence of elected or appointed officials, civil rights or religious leaders, glamour personalities or Black nationalists in the leadership of Black America will have to look elsewhere for data; perhaps employing Bennett's (1964:chap. 2) definition and some modifications of Dye's (1973, 1982) empirical methodology.

Biography as a Tool for Research on African American Leadership

In recent years there has been a kind of flowering of biographies and memoirs by African American leaders. While there is still much work to be done in this area,[17] as the "Selected Bibliography of Biographies and Memoirs of African American Leaders" in appendix B shows, there is already a substantial body of materials spanning several decades and covering a broad range of categories of leaders. As research material, first these biographies and memoirs might be classified into categories of leaders (civil rights, elected officials, Black radicals/nationalists, etc.). And then they might be analyzed in terms of such analytic categories as social background, recruitment, socialization, ideology, leadership styles, and the constraints, internal and external, on leadership effectiveness. These categories could then be used to compare leadership by types and over time. This should produce generalizations, perhaps testable propositions, and a rich contextualized and dynamic body of studies in Black leadership (see Denzin 1989).[18]

CONCLUSION

Since the 1960s the social science community in general and political scientists in particular have largely abandoned the *systematic* study of African American leadership, although there has been a remarkable increase in interest in leadership as a generic phenomenon.[19] Most of the research that has appeared in the last ten years has been published in books and edited works rather than the more accessible and rigorous journals. And these studies have sometimes tended to be historical, descriptive, and occasionally hortatory and polemical, rather than systematically designed in the tradition of the rigorous leadership studies of the 1950s and 1960s. The conclusion that emerges is a limited body of research that is ad hoc, atheoretical, methodologically diffuse, and hence noncumulative—in other words, a confused series of unrelated and disjointed articles and books instead of a cumulative body of knowledge. There are also a number of critical studies that tend to call attention, appropriately, to the deficiencies of modern Black leadership, but often without sufficient attention to the structural constraints and contextual factors under which it operates.

This means that the study of African American leadership, like the phenomenon itself, is at a crossroads, with no clear theoretical or methodological guideposts. This means the scholarly community has little to say to itself as a community of scholars and even less to say to the leaders of Black America. This means also that there is much work to be done.

APPENDIX A

African American Mayors, Selected U.S. Cities,
With Percent Black Population 1960–1990
and Year of Election of Black Mayor

	1960	1970	1980	1990	Year of Election of Black Mayor
Atlanta, Ga.	38.3%	51.3%	66.2%	67.1%	1973
New York City*	14	21.1	25.2	28.7	1989
Baltimore, Md.	34.7	51.3	54.8	59.2	1984
Gary, Ind.*	39	53	71	80.6	1964
Birmingham, Ala.	39.6	44.6	55.2	63.3	1974
Detroit, Mich.	29	43	63	75.7	1973
Chicago, Ill.*	22.9	32.7	39.8	39.1	1983
Newark, N.J.	34	54	58	58.5	1970
St. Louis, Mo.	28.6	40.9	45.5	47.5	1995
Richmond, Va.	34.2	42.4	52	55.2	1977
Oakland, Calif.	22.8	34.5	46.9	43.9	1948
Washington, D.C.	53.9	71.1	70.2	65.8	1975
New Orleans, La.	34.2	45	55.3	61.9	1977
Denver, Colo.	6.1	9.1	12	12.8	1991
Seattle, Wash.	4.8	12.6	9.4	9.5	1989
Dallas, Tex.	19	25.4	29.3	29.5	1995
Philadelphia, Pa.*	26.4	24.2	37.8	39.9	1983
Los Angeles, Calif.*	13.5	17.9	12.6	14	1973
San Francisco, Calif.	10	13.4	12.7	19.9	1995
Cleveland, Ohio	21.6	38.3	43.7	46.6	1967
Minneapolis, Minn.	2.4	6.3	7.8	13	1993
Houston, Tex.	9.1	16.3	22.4	25.6	1997

*An asterisk indicates that at this writing the city no longer has a Black mayor.
Except for Cleveland and Gary, all other cities that have Black mayors have had
them continuously since the first was elected.

SOURCE: *City and County Data Book, Statistical Supplement* (Washington,
D.C.: Government Printing Office, 1967, 1977, 1983, and 1993).

APPENDIX B

Selected Bibliography of Memoirs and Biographies of African American Leaders, By a Leadership Typology

This bibliography is selective and suggestive of the types of materials available. It is by no means exhaustive.

CIVIL RIGHTS

Jervis Anderson. *Bayard Rustin: Troubles I've Seen* (New York: HarperCollins, 1977). A major strategist in the civil rights movement.

Taylor Branch. *Parting the Waters: America in the King Years, 1954–63* (New York: Simon & Schuster, 1988). The most comprehensive King study and his *Pillar of Fire: America in the King Years 1963–65* (New York: Simon & Schuster, 1997). A third volume covering the period 1965 to 1968 is planned.

Eric Burner. *And Gently He Shall Lead Them: Robert Parris Moses and Civil Rights in Mississippi* (New York: Oxford University Press, 1994).

James Farmer. *Lay Bare the Heart: An Autobiography of the Civil Rights Movement* (New York: Arbor House, 1985). The memoir of the leader of CORE during the 1960s.

Marshall Frady. *Jesse: The Life and Pilgrimage of Jesse Jackson* (New York: Random House, 1996).

David Garrow. *Bearing the Cross: Martin Luther King and the Southern Christian Leadership Conference* (New York: William Morrow, 1986).

David Garrow (ed.). *The Montgomery Bus Boycott and the Women Who Started It: The Memoir of Jo Ann Gibson Robinson* (Knoxville: University of Tennesse Press, 1987). A memoir of Robinson but generally a fascinating study of the role of women in the success of the boycott.

David Lewis. *W.E.B. DuBois: Autobiography of a Race, 1868–1919* (New York: Henry Holt, 1993). The definitive biography, covering his early career. A second volume is forthcoming.

Richard Lischer. *The Preacher King: Martin Luther King, Jr. and the Word That Moved America* (New York: Oxford University Press, 1995).

Kay Mills. *This Little Light of Mine: The Life of Fannie Lou Hamer* (New York: Dutton, 1993). A true grassroots leader.

Barbara Reynolds. *Jesse Jackson: The Man, the Movement, the Myth* (Chicago: Nelson Hall, 1975), republished as *America's David* in 1985 with the same text but a new introduction.

Cleveland Sellers (with Robert Terrell). *The River of No Return: The Autobiography of a Black Militant and the Life and Death of SNCC* (New York: Morrow, 1973).

Denton Watson. *Lion in the Lobby: Clarence Mitchell's Struggle to Pass Civil Rights Laws* (New York: Morrow, 1990). Known as the 101st senator, the head of the NAACP's Washington office during the civil rights era.

Nancy Weiss. *Whitney M. Young and the Struggle for Civil Rights* (Princeton: Princeton University Press, 1989). The head of the Urban League during the civil rights era.

Roy Wilkins (with Tom Matthews). *Standing Fast: The Autobiography of Roy Wilkins* (New York: Viking Press, 1982). The memoir of the longtime head of the NAACP.

Andrew Young. *An Easy Burden: The Civil Rights Movement and the Transformation of America* (New York: HarperCollins, 1996).

RADICAL ACTIVISTS

Imamu Amiri Baraka. *The Autobiography of Leroi Jones/Amiri Baraka* (New York: Freundlich Books, 1984). Memoir of an important Black nationalist leader who during the 1970s embraced communism.

Claude Clegg, III. *An Original Man: The Life and Times of Elijah Mahammad* (New York: St. Martin's Press, 1997).

Angela Davis. *Angela Davis: An Autobiography* (New York: Random House, 1974).

Benjamin Davis. *Communist Councilman from Harlem* (New York: International Publishers, 1969). A memoir.

Martin Duberman. *Paul Robeson* (New York: Knopf, 1988).

Gerald Horne. *Black & Red: W.E.B. DuBois and the Afro-American Response to the Cold War, 1944–1963* (Albany: State University of New York Press, 1986). Focuses on DuBois' last years as he moved toward an embrace of communism.

Gerald Horne. *Black Liberation/Red Scare: Ben Davis and the Communist Party* (Newark: University of Delaware Press, 1992). The Harlem Republican turned communist in the 1930s.

Mel King. *Chain of Change: Struggles for Black Community Development* (Boston: South End Press, 1981). The Boston political activist.

Arthur Magida. *A Prophet of Rage: A Life of Louis Farrakhan and His Nation* (New York: Basic Books, 1996). The only full-length biography of the most important Black nationalist leader of the post–civil rights era.

Bruce Perry. *Malcolm: The Life of the Man Who Changed Black America* (Barrytown, N.Y.: Station Hill, 1991). Controversial in its interpretations but still the most comprehensive biography of Malcolm.

Al Sharpton and Anthony Walton. *Go and Tell Pharaoh: The Autobiography of the Reverend Al Sharpton* (Garden City, N.Y.: Doubleday, 1996). The New York City political activist.

ELECTED OFFICIALS

Legislators

Edward Brooke. *Challenge of Change* (Boston: Little, Brown, 1966). The first Black elected to the U.S. Senate since Reconstruction.

Shirley Chisholm. *Unbought and Unbossed* (Boston: Houghton Mifflin, 1970). The first Black woman elected to Congress.

Shirley Chisholm. *The Good Fight* (New York: Harper & Row, 1973). A memoir of her campaign for president.

Wil Hapgood. *King of the Cats: The Life and Times of Adam Clayton Powell* (Boston: Houghton Mifflin, 1993).

Charles Hamilton, *Adam Clayton Powell: The Political Biography of An American Dilemma* (New York: Atheneum, 1991).

Barbara Jordan and Shelby Hearon. *Barbara Jordan: A Self Portrait* (Garden City, N.Y.: Doubleday, 1979).

Adam Clayton Powell Jr. *Adam by Adam: The Autobiography of Adam Clayton Powell, Jr.* (New York: Dell, 1971). The legendary Harlem preacher-politician.

James Richardson. *Willie Brown: A Biography* (Berkeley: University of California Press, 1996). The longtime Speaker of the California Assembly and subsequently mayor of San Francisco.

Mayors

Wilbur Rich. *Coleman Young and Detroit Politics: From Social Activist to Power Broker* (Detroit: Wayne State University Press, 1989).

Carl Stokes. *Promises of Power: A Political Biography* (New York: Simon & Shuster, 1973). The first Black mayor of a major American city.

Coleman Young. *Hard Stuff: The Autobiography of Coleman Young* (New York: Viking, 1994).

Others

Hulan Jack. *Fifty Years a Democrat: The Autobiography of Hulan E. Jack* (New York: Benjamin Franklin House, 1982). The longtime Democratic Party activist and first Black president of the borough of Manhattan.

John C. Walter. *The Harlem Fox: J. Raymond Jones and Tammany Hall* (Albany: State University of New York Press, 1989). A memoir of the first Black head of Tammany Hall, the New York County Democratic Party organization.

Bruce Wright. *Black Robes, White Justice* (Secaucus, N.J.: Lyle Stuart, 1987). A memoir by a controversial New York City judge.

Appointed Officials

Carl Gardner. *Andrew Young: A Biography* (New York: Drake, 1978). Superficial but the only thing available.

E. Fredric Murrow. *Black Man in the White House* (New York: Coward-McCann, 1963). Eisenhower's lone Black White House staff aide, the first in history.

Alex Poinsett. *Walking with Presidents: Louis Martin and the Rise of Black Political Power* (Washington, D.C.: Joint Center for Political Studies/Madison Books, 1997). The veteran newspaperman and advisor to presidents.

Colin Powell. *My American Journey* (New York: Random House, 1996). The national security advisor and chairman of the Joint Chiefs of Staff.

Carl Rowan. *Breaking Barriers: A Memoir* (New York: Harper Perennial, 1991). Journalist, diplomat and first Black to serve on the National Security Council.

Louis Sullivan. *Healing America's Wounds: One Man's Journey Through Race, Health Care, and Politics* (Lanham, Md.: Rowman & Littlefield, 1997). The first memoir by an African American cabinet officer, the health secretary in the Bush administration.

Bob Woodward. *The Commanders* (New York: Simon & Schuster, 1991). Good material on General Powell's role in the Persian Gulf War.

PART II

Theory and Praxis

INTRODUCTION

In this part, we intend to elaborate upon the review of the literature of African American leadership described in part I, describing the context within which it behaves. The basic context addresses the arena of the local community, where the function of leadership is to help maintain the stability and growth of community in its normal social and institutional modes. The leadership often has a representative function where it has to represent the interests of Blacks to the larger White majority community and where there is conflict to mobilize the Black community to articulate its interests.

On the national level, Black leadership has much the same profile. It attempts to organize the national interests of the Black community with respect to many discrete specialties of interests for the purpose of further developing those interests among the community membership through the benefits of national resource mobilization. However, the mobilization of national organizational resources also works to provide the basis for the legitimacy of Black national interests and the politics of claims upon national institutions for various policy and other resource outcomes.

We will, therefore, utilize this descriptive framework as the basic context for further describing the political behavior of Black leadership. Chapter 6 is devoted to filling out the contextual description; chapter 7 will present a historical summary of Black national leadership highlighting periods of "strategy shift"; chapter 8 will present a case study of the National Black Leadership Roundtable; chapter 9 provides examples of the utilization of militant popular Black struggle at the local and national levels; chapter 10 analyzes the critical issues of the unity and accountability of Black leadership; and chapter 11 will summarize the previous chapters in this part and include a section on the relevance of the leadership literature to Black political leadership.

The intent of part II is to describe and to restate in more modern terms the function of leadership as it relates to the politics of the Black community and update previous works, and to refer to problems and areas of study where there is a continuing need for the development of theory, empirical research, and strategic approaches. part II, then, takes a "ground-up" approach to Black leadership in the modern era by building a framework, presenting some cases, and providing the raw material that may suggest fertile areas of research to be subsequently pursued.

CHAPTER 6

A Paradigm of the Practice of Black Leadership

Conceptualizing the practice of Black leadership requires an appreciation of the way in which Blacks in general have used power—or Black politics—within American society in order to penetrate the racially stratified, White-dominant social system. This model of American society has remained remarkably constant over the years. Thus, it is important to address at the outset the basic challenge that Black leadership has to confront in the performance of its tasks, which colors most areas of the life of African Americans.

This discussion suggests a basic concern with *political* leadership, since obviously "leadership" takes place in many fields of endeavor such as the arts, medicine, technology, the professions, and so on. Our interest is in leadership that seeks to directly remove the physical and institutional impediments to the achievement of Black progress both individually and collectively. As such, it is devoted to an assessment of those active and passive conflicts that nonetheless have the capacity to influence the quality of African American life through more traditionally defined "political behaviors and decisions." Thus, we will analyze the political character of Black leadership in challenging and overcoming these impediments and the conflicts they engender.

Here, we take the position that as the end of the twentieth-century approaches, it is still the case, as determined by a wide variety of measures, that racism constitutes the major impediment to the forward progress of African Americans in the United States. And although other powerful factors impinge on Black life-chances—such as the changes in the nature of the American economy with the rapid impact of technology on the process of production and thus, on fitness for the labor force and the globalization of the availability of productive work—the most damaging factor that compounds the effect of these is racism (Feagin 1988; Feagin and Vera 1995; Hacker 1995; Smith 1995).

MODERN RACISM

On June 29, 1981, the Joint Center for Political Studies sponsored a meeting of thirty African American academics and university administrators to consider priority issues in the wake of the initiation of the conservative era of Ronald Reagan. The proceedings of this meeting were reviewed by the Black Leadership Forum, a coalition of fifteen national Black organizations, the following year, and in 1983, the center published, "A Policy Framework for Racial Justice." The introduction to the framework begins with the following thought:

> [N]ow that the drive for civil rights of the 50s, 60s, and 70s has been blunted, the fundamental question is squarely before us: Is America willing to support equitable social policies? The present answer to that question is a resounding "no." That answer is stimulated by a powerful and continuing climate of racism, and it has been given force and virulence by the nation's experience with the worst economic conditions since the Great Depression and by long-term economic uncertainties. (Joint Center for Political and Economic Studies 1983:1)

This statement indicated that the economic problems of the country are material to the condition of Blacks and that they are being exacerbated by the virulence of racism. As such, the forum concluded that three issues involving Blacks are of emergency concern: *the economy, the family,* and *education.* However, while they asserted that racism is the central problem, unfortunately the analysis that addresses each of the priority areas they cite is either absent altogether or largely deficient. We will attempt to rectify this by describing some of the racial contours of this problem below.

The Economy

The importance of the transition in the nature of the American economy for Blacks from an industrial-based economy to a service-oriented system and its globalization is found in both the declining presence of Blacks in the labor force and the impact of these factors upon their wages. Much of this is due to the nature of the higher-technological-skill-base requirements of jobs that challenge Blacks who disproportionately have held jobs, for historical reasons in the industrial economy, that could be performed by physical labor. The evidence for this is being discovered in studies that show considerable disparities between Blacks and Whites in the number of days worked, and the impact of their lesser presence in the labor force on the decline in their average wage ("Buirg Study"). The impact of racism has exacerbated this problem by the tendency to either exclude Blacks from the labor force disproportionally, or to distribute to them lower-level jobs in any case.

Support for this view is found in a 1990 analysis of the economic status of Blacks by Professor David Swinton, who concluded that there were two main causes of Black income inequality: (1) the fundamental inequality in wealth as a result of limited wealth and business ownership as a contributor to overall income, and (2) the disadvantaged status of Blacks in the labor market (Swinton 1990). Swinton's finding, however, raises the question of why the causes that he identified, especially the labor market status problem, persist.

Swinton and other economists have produced studies that illustrate the role of history in the presence of Blacks in the labor market and the role that race plays in their tendency to hold lower-status occupations. However, current indications are that the residual racism continues to play its part and although there are many sources of confirmation for this view, one important study will illustrate the point.

Between 1989 and 1992, a study was conducted by the Employment Council of Greater Washington D.C., the Urban Institute, and the University of Colorado that administered 1,532 tests to employers in four metropolitan labor markets: Chicago, Denver, San Diego, and Washington, D.C. In the tests, discrimination in employment was detected by the use of Black and White testers of equal education and experience for job vacancies in a variety of industries using mail, telephone, and face-to-face interviews. The study found a substantial pattern of discrimination against African American testers compared with their White counterparts. It revealed that Whites obtained job interviews at a rate 22 percent higher than Blacks and job offers at a rate of 415 percent higher than Blacks (Fix and Struk 1993).

Although the above evidence of racism in the labor market is convincing, it is even more insidious, according to other researchers who have assessed the data. They suggest, first, that the study implies the strong possibility that every nonprofessional minority participant in the labor force who performs multiple job searches is likely to experience discrimination. Second, inequality rises in the process of the acceptance of a job, since differential entry-level salaries were offered to Black and White testers at considerable rates of disparity. The average starting wage offered to Whites was $5.45 an hour where both Black and White applicants were accepted, but where only Whites were accepted the average starting wage was $7.13 per hour. Lastly, testers are most effective as a tool of assessment where jobs are publicly posted, but where personal referrals are common in some industries, the inability of minorities to have access to the system of job interview and hiring poses a significant problem that is often not taken into account in any data (Bendick, Jackson, and Reinoso 1997:86–87).

The Family

A weakness of the policy framework referred to above is that it attributes the failure of the Black family essentially to the Moynihan-like thesis of the prevalence and growth of female-headed households.[1] From that assumption, it proceeds to offer policy prescriptions based almost solely on the enhancement of the social position of Black single mothers. However, it does not mention the condition of the Black male, nor the role that he plays in family stability and thus, the necessity to focus on this problem from a policy standpoint. This is a serious flaw inasmuch as economists Darity and Myers argue: "the marginalization of black males has caused the rise in female-headed families and contributed to the fall in labor force participation of otherwise higher-earning family heads. This, in turn, has resulted in a widening of racial earnings differentials" (Darity and Myers 1992:122).

Thus, many of the social disabilities that render the Black family unstable is related to the negative condition of the Black male in the labor force. This is significant inasmuch as Darity and Myers show that stable employment is related to improvements in education and thus, human capital, and that, "black males incarcerated or deeply scarred by arrest records and criminal involvement . . . saw no educational gains" (Darity and Myers 1992:136). Therefore, the increasing incarceration rate of Black males, they would cite as a major factor in earnings inequality, and in the resulting impact upon family stability. This finding sheds light on another conclusion of one scholar that the impact of these collective factors upon the structure of the Black family, even two-parent households, was exacerbated by the policies of the Reagan administration, which led to the loss of an average of $2,000 in income in the period 1980–1984 alone (Mullings 1986:15).

Education

The evidence for racial discrimination in education is often difficult to assess directly because the contributing factors are indirect. Such factors are: the out-migration of Whites who have transferred personal economic resources to other school districts in the suburbs; the deprivation of financial resources to cities by virtue of the decline of federal financial contributions; and the inequality in the funding mechanism for education through local property taxes with the result that higher-income White districts produce greater revenue for schools than lower-income Black areas.

These issues have led to the consolidation of districts where Blacks constitute a predominant share of the school district population, and with the defeat of busing by White parents as a remedy for racial integration, the issue of Black education falls increasingly into the predictable paradigm where national racial issues are being fought out. Although there are serious problems with the original assumptions of integration as a tool for educational excellence, still the attitude of society is illustrated by the elimination of methods for school-based racial integration. Indeed, the Harvard Project on School Desegregation released a report in March 1997 finding that school segregation has increased over the past fifteen years to a level greater than when the 1971 decision in *Swann v. Charlotte-Mecklenburg* ushered in the era of busing. On the strength of this finding, other observers immediately declared the "death of integration."[2]

A concrete example will suffice. In February 1997, the administration of Gov. Christy Whitman of New Jersey refused to order the desegregation of a 92 percent Black and Hispanic high school in Englewood. Her ruling was ultimately an acknowledgment of the racial hostility that existed toward "forced" busing among the citizens of Englewood Cliffs and Tenafly, both of which were party to a ten-year, multimillion dollar legal proceeding with Englewood in opposition to further mandated school integration. And while attention has been given to the prevalence of private schools developed in the South as a way of resisting racial integration, it is significant that most White teenagers in Englewood attend private schools (Hanley 1997:B4). The timid handling of this case by the court—as well as the 1995 decision of the Supreme Court in *Missouri v. Jenkins*, which nullified a lower court judge's attempt to provide revenue-enhancement strategies for attracting White students to integrated charter schools—illustrates that the courts are not the citadel of racial justice in education that they appeared to be a generation ago.

Although it has been suggested that some of the most damaging evidence of racial discrimination in education remains indirect, direct evidence also exists, such as the racial drop-out rate and "push-out" rate in integrated schools, and the treatment of minority students within the school setting. For example, a study assessing the direct effect of racism was conducted by the ACORN organization, which used Black and Hispanic testers in various schools in New York City, and found that minority parents were treated differently than White parents (Cose 1996:26). Study results also indicate that "Whites were offered information (often without prompting) on programs for the gifted. Blacks and Latinos sometimes found even getting into the buildings to be 'difficult'; when they did get in, they were generally told only about 'regular' classes."

One could describe at considerable length the maltreatment of Blacks and other minorities, and the racial impediments to normal access to the social resources that would allow normal societal interaction within American culture. As indicated above, it is toward the removal of the impediments that Black leadership is directed. Black leadership, like any leadership, contributes to the maintenance of community in a number of areas of social life, as well as taking responsibility for group advancement. Black leadership assumes the role of the maintenance of progress, but since the social life of Blacks is heavily colored by such impediments, its role—and thus its unique function—is complicated by the prevalence of racism in both sets of responsibilities.

The Issue of Leadership Context

A summary of the above discussion of racist impediments should suggest to the keen observer a truism—Whites have more to do with the leadership of Blacks than Black leadership does as a general proposition of the conduct of daily life. This fact flows from the reality of the preponderant power Whites exercise over society in general and in particular, the control over specific social activities that shape Black opportunity structure such as jobs, housing, finance, the production of consumer goods, the management of the processes of law and political leadership, and other activities.[3]

Thus, our discussion, indeed, any discussion of Black leadership, should not be conducted based on the assumption that Blacks *absolutely determine* the course of their own existence. Rather, Blacks have exercised significant relative influence over their lives and livelihood episodically, a fact that Martin Luther King Jr. lamented at one point as a deficiency in Black leadership and a rationale for either chaos or inactivity (Washington 1992:178). This leaves open the question of whether or not Blacks *could* determine the course of their daily lives if they were organized differently or operated on different philosophical or political assumptions.

Therefore, the political debate between the races is often over (1) the nature of the agenda of importance to Blacks, and (2) who will exercise the leadership over that agenda and in what arena. The forceful demands made by Black leaders on presidents in the process of "agenda-setting"—for political inclusion and an end to segregation made by W.E.B. DuBois to Woodrow Wilson, for jobs in the war industry that A. Philip Randolph made to Franklin D.Roosevelt, for the desegregation of the military that Randolph made to Harry Truman, for civil rights social justice that the civil rights movement made to Presidents Kennedy and Lyndon Johnson—have raised the question of whether the demands would be resolved in favor of one or the other force.[4]

Normally, such questions are resolved in favor of the "white power structure," which includes those Blacks who have been selected as community leaders. Martin Luther King Jr. noted this when he said at one point:

> The majority of Negro political leaders do not ascend to prominence on the shoulders of mass support. Although genuinely popular leaders are now emerging, most are still selected by white leadership, elevated to positions, supplied with resources and inevitably subjected to white control. The mass of Negroes nurtures a healthy suspicion toward this manufactured leader. (Washington 1992:308)

Contrast this with the plea he made elsewhere for the primacy of leadership and the urgency of the development of leaders addressed to the new period of mobilization:

> There is a dire need for leaders who are calm and yet positive, leaders who avoid the extremes of 'hot-headedness' and 'Uncle Tomism.' The urgency of the hour calls for leaders of wise judgment and sound integrity—leaders not in love with money, but in love with justice; leaders not in love with publicity, but in love with humanity; leaders who can subject their particular egos to the greatness of the cause. (Ibid.,143)

Our focus on the situations faced by Blacks dictates a perspective based on what is or has been possible, given the history of events and their probable impact on current events, and the sum of that perspective presents no other view but that Whites shape the essential context for Black leadership. This fact was recognized early in the study of Black leadership by Daniel Thompson, who asserted that "insofar as the formulation or execution of policies and practices governing the civic, political, economic, educational, professional, and cultural life of the community is concerned, Negroes are powerless" (Thompson 1963:163). Conversely, Black leadership, lacking the necessary power to determine the fate of the Black community, operates consistently within a relatively narrow "zone of influence" that is marginal in its daily effect, but on given issues may bring important influence to bear.

INTERNAL LEADERSHIP

Black politics takes place both within the Black community and the White community in a way that was described above, as a two-level process and therefore, as Harold Cruse once observed: "The Negro intellectual must deal intimately with the White power structure and cultural apparatus, and the inner realities of the Black world at one and the same time" (Cruse 1967:451). We will now describe the manner in which the dynamics of Black leadership functions in this two-level process.

Community Maintenance

The form and function of Black leadership at the community level was a natural outgrowth of the unique resistance context of their relationship with America, which began at the very moment that African slaves organized to obtain their freedom, by whatever means available (Franklin 1984:71–102). To the extent that organization was necessary—which implied the construction of leadership, a process of decision-making, and goal setting—politics was at the heart of the enterprise, regardless of whether it was to organize slave rebellions on boats or on plantations, or to manage the daily challenge of living as slaves on plantations or as "free" Blacks.

Originally, in the plantation society, authoritative decision-making was performed by the White master and, to some extent, his overseers, who in some cases were Black. This was the dominant system within which the slaves worked and lived. Slowly, as it became fashionable to "Christianize" slaves as a method of legitimizing slavery, Black ministers became figures of moral authority; and as the Christian religion was used also as a tool of the socialization of slaves into English culture, Black churches were permitted and the role of the Black minister expanded (Frazier 1964:1–19).

Thus, the church emerged as the first social organization of Blacks in America and it also was the strongest because it performed a multiplicity of leadership roles in the practical life of the African American. It directed "community maintenance" activities such as the rituals of spiritual celebration that encompassed such practical aspects of life as birth, marriage, moral living, financial support, and death. And although there were no political clubs, even in the so-called "freed" Black communities, the church provided a source of internal organization for the Black community and, as such, a vehicle for the representation of Black interests to the larger White community.

Education was also a route to leadership, as the slaves understood very quickly the power of English culture and its relationship to their emancipation. The English settlers understood this also, thus they prohibited the slave from learning to read and write the English language. Frederick Douglass details in his autobiography the tension between Blacks on his plantation who took every opportunity to learn to read and the Whites who understood the danger of the power this would give them and therefore prohibited them from being educated, often violently (Douglass 1962:70–87). Notwithstanding these prohibitions, free Blacks and slaves alike became educated and as they did so, their community organizational structure expanded itself to accommodate new roles. There were elite Black organizations that mirrored those in the

White community, comprised of social clubs, professional groups, educational clubs, secret societies, civic clubs, and the like. Most of these groups did not adopt overt political roles, but because residents in the typical Black community were all members of the same churches, the church came to express a collective sentiment of many social organizations.

Small wonder, then, that many of the leaders of the Black community have been ministers. In the nineteenth century, they abounded: Nat Turner, who led one of the major slave rebellions in the 1830s, was a minister whose visions led him to take up arms against the White masters; Rev. Henry Highland Garnett, fiery abolitionist and diplomat; Bishop Henry McNeill Turner, an early Pan Africanist; and many others.

However, the Black class structure also began to diversify in the nineteenth century, as the first Black lawyer was admitted to the bar in 1845, and other professionals began to develop. The most important fact was that this pattern of diversification continued into the twentieth century, as government bureaucrats, labor leaders, college presidents, magazine publishers, and scientists all came to fruition. However, the opportunities for dedicated political leadership were severely restricted in the first quarter of the twentieth century as Blacks in the South were still largely prohibited from electoral participation and Blacks in the North, who were relatively fewer in number, had just begun to make their presence felt.

The substance of Black politics was characterized by grappling with the issues of the survival and development of the Black community. Those community-maintenance issues more often dealt with subjects such as work, education, and nondiscriminatory treatment, but since these activities were ultimately regulated by the dominant community, the nature of Black leadership was to fashion the demands for these resources. Thus, much of the internal work of leaders involved the "sorting process" with respect to these demands and the way in which the community might be mobilized to achieve them within the limitations of its own resources. Once achieved or not, the task was to monitor the results, and to participate, insofar as possible, in the administration of community affairs.

In any case, many of the problems of the Black community were addressed, increasingly using a variety of tactics and strategies as the leadership cadre grew in many arenas of life.

The Resulting Paradigm

Professor Matthew Holden's conceptualization of over twenty-five years ago remains exceedingly accurate because he assumed: first, that the structure of the leadership class is remarkably stable over time; second, that those individuals who accede to positions of leadership do so by virtue of various organizational interactions through networks that comprise a political system; and, third, that the major functions of Black leaders are service (political and cultural uplift), mutual aid (social service), and self-interested pursuits (such as business leaders). He observed that the necessities referred to above created the evolution of the "black quasi-government" as the leadership structure to manage the internal or "centrifugal" affairs of the Black community.[5]

Holden suggested that

> the "quasi-government" is held together by the interdependent elites of the major Black socioeconomic institutions. It would thus be quite realistic to regard anyone holding a key role in such an institutions as a "black leader." As a term of art, however, it referred to men and women who have, at various times, been regarded, or have sought to have themselves regarded, as conscious architects of some definite strategy for "race uplift," "redemption," "race advancement," "equality," "civil rights," or . . . "liberation." (Holden 1973:4)

The collective action of these leaders constituted a system of influence as the power resource of the political system.

In this work we admittedly concentrate on the first kind of leader, whose conscious effort was to provide political service, though we understand the necessity for a more comprehensive treatment of the entire leadership class. Nevertheless, the following discussion divides the first of Holden's categories into a framework of individual and collective leaders for a descriptive analysis as the basic leadership dichotomy.

The Basic Leadership Dichotomy

Individual Leaders.   The emergence of individual African American leaders was difficult, in that the social context within which they emerged did not recognize Black leadership—or Black expressions of power or control—as legitimate because of the subordinate position of Blacks in society. Rather, the White majority did come to recognize Black leaders as a marginal aspect of their own control over the entire society and thus over Black life.

This is why an individual such as Frederick Douglass came to prominence outside of the prevailing political system, as a prominent dissident, supported by other Black and White dissidents. Then, slowly, by sheer force of his eloquence in opposing slavery and the lack of franchise for Blacks, he was recognized by the wider society, but only after the scourge of official slavery had ended with the Civil War. It was then possible for him to be accorded the status of a "Black leader" who was acknowledged generally in society, by presidents and others. His prominence was legitimized by the award of various official positions and by his role as an unofficial adviser to the government on Black affairs.

This paradigm of the individual Black leader was passed on to Booker T. Washington, who came into prominence with the death of Douglass and he, too, was legitimized by prominent Whites in business and government and as such came to be enshrined as a national leader of Black people. The national status of Douglass' leadership did not have to depend upon a South that was controlled by a recalcitrant, anti-Black, and even dangerous White majority until late in the nineteenth century and thus, very late in his own career. Nevertheless, Booker T. Washington's claim to national leadership was shaped by this factor, which conservatized his ideology and strategies of race advancement. Thus, his claim to leadership of Blacks in both the North and South was contested by northern Blacks such as William Monroe Trotter and W. E. B. DuBois (Franklin 1967:397).

The idea of a single, national Black leader was also contested in the twentieth century by the progress of Blacks in various sectors of society, for prominent men such as Marcus Mosiah Garvey, DuBois, A. Philip Randolph, and Paul Robeson were forceful, charismatic, and purposeful men, and were also mostly contemporaries. The emergence of Black men and women of accomplishment in so many areas of life complicated the single Black leader model, as a natural process of the diversification of Black professional growth through education was realized. However, what has most often created the appearance that there was only one dominant Black figure on the scene in any era of history has been the political drama by those leaders involved in the public struggle to achieve civil rights. Nevertheless, as Smith shows in part I of this volume, as the civil rights sector was truncated in the late 1960s and thereafter, other categories such as elected politicians, business leaders, media personalities, and others have expanded.

Collective Leadership. The Black community has had a long history of attempting to fashion collective leadership, the origin of which might have officially begun on a national scale as early as the Negro Convention Movement in the 1830s when Black men came together in a convention to address urgent problems facing their people. Indeed, the first resolution of the convention, which met in February of 1830 to consider the propriety of Blacks fleeing into Canada, expressed the following sentiment: "Resolved: That we do most cordially rejoice the bond of brotherhood, which rivets a nation together in one indissoluble chain, has collected so large a portion of our people together to sympathize and commiserate the condition of our brethren recently from Ohio, now in

Canada."[6] One observer remarked about the convention that "although the convention movement failed to secure mass support for any one strategy—cooperation with whites, independent action or emigrationism—or to achieve black political, social or economic equality, it provided forums, at the state and national levels, for developing a free black leadership class" (White 1985:16). From that period to the present, the struggle for collective Black leadership has taken various forms. However, through it all, the underlying assumption has been that political strategies would be stronger and success more probable with it than without it.

Then, the civil rights movement of the 1960s is well known for having been conducted by the "Big Five" civil rights organizations (the NAACP, the National Urban League, the Congress of Racial Equality, the Student Non-Violent Coordinating Committee, and the Southern Christian Leadership Conference) but this group was often augmented by the National Welfare Rights Organizations, the A. Philip Randolph Institute, and other such organizations. Although there were admitted tensions among these organizations, the strength of the human resources they brought to the coalition were of such decisive value that they endured as a unit. A most insightful observation about the way in which they worked together was made by psychologist, Kenneth Clark, who said:

> The civil rights groups vary in organizational efficiency as well as in philosophy, approach, and methods. The rank and file of liberal or religious whites might be more responsive to the seemingly non-threatening, Christian approach of Martin Luther King, Jr. More rough-minded and pragmatic business and governmental leaders might find a greater point of contact with the appeals and approaches of the NAACP and the Urban League. The more passionate Negroes and whites who seek immediate and concrete forms of justice will probably gravitate toward CORE and SNCC. . . . The variety of organizations and "leaders" among Negroes may be viewed as . . . the present strength of the movement rather than as a symptom of weakness. . . . Each organization influences the momentum and pace of the others. The inevitable interaction among them demands from each a level of effectiveness and relevance above the minimum possible for any single organization. (Clark 1982:155)

Clark's description of the individual organizations and how they behaved collectively would probably find few who would object. What we take from this illustration is the validation of the effectiveness of collective leadership within the Black community within a movement setting that strongly complements its effectiveness in other arenas as well.

Elaboration of the Leadership Class in the Twentieth Century

Thus, there existed a strong leadership structure within the Black community throughout most of the twentieth century that changed according to the development of the Black class structure and according to the demands of its attempt to assert itself within the larger social system through fostering political movements. The leadership structure will typically include the ministers of the largest churches, the heads of the civil rights organization, the heads of business and civic organizations and the press, and perhaps an educator or two (Holden 1973). However, in larger localities where Blacks are prominent, this structure is augmented by the members of the city council, the mayor, school board members, members of Congress, union leaders, and other figures who form the top of the leadership structure pyramid.

This group manages the processing of resources, messages, and other aspects of the relationship between the Black community and the city establishment leadership within the entire civic culture. In fact, the modern civic culture in most American cities has some element of Black participation, according to the strength of the population and the leadership cadre.

What are examples of such activities? A brief example taken from two Black newspapers in May 1997 shows that the Black community leaders have routinely sponsored events to reward the academic achievement of Black youth who have excelled. The pictures of the youth were presented in the pages of the local newspapers, and the stories carried news of the events that honored them. Moreover, some of the events carried evidence that the community organizations, such as the churches and other social clubs, mobilized to raise funds to defray some of the college expenses of the Black high school graduates, especially for those whose performance had been particularly outstanding. This is a community-maintenance activity, because it helps to ensure that many youth will have the necessary start in higher education and, thus, will contribute to the further expansion of the Black middle class. And it is a characteristic "self-help" activity that achieved little notice or recognition from sources external to the Black community ("21 Outstanding" 1997:1; also "Youth Recognition" 1997:7-A).

The above is an example of a social function, however; internal political function of leadership is illustrated by the appointment of a new executive director for the Ohio Legislative Black Caucus ("Ohio" 1997:1). The Ohio Legislative Black Caucus, founded in 1967, is one of a number of such caucuses in several states where the organizational structure is in the hands of Black state legislative officials. The executive director, as in many other states, is chosen by the executive committee of the caucus, and the director is primarily responsible for functions such as strategic planning, fund-raising, recruitment of Black candidates for various offices, preparation of the organizations' annual budget, and organization of the annual convention. The caucus organization acts as a resource for campaigns led by various members of the caucus, with the priority issues decided by the organization and implemented by its executive committee. Thus, where Black state legislative officials have gained the seniority to allow them to serve in critical posts in a given legislature, the internal caucus decision-making on various legislative issues takes on special significance.

Decisions such as those made above are generally made away from the glare of public view in informal settings and often involve a wide variety of categories of leadership consultation. However, as the body of elected officials has grown, such decisions have tended to be made more often by elected officials as the dominant political leaders of a community or state.

On the national and local level, then, as the civil rights protests and legal battles opened up opportunities for Blacks to vote and hold office in the major political institutions in the 1970s, the national leader status of ministers and civil rights leaders declined. Smith, in part I, describes the nature and causes of changes in the Black leadership structure using the database of the "100 Most Influential Negroes," an annual listing composed by *Ebony* magazine. Between 1963 and 1980, the categories of leaders exhibiting the most significant declines were civil rights leaders (18% to 7%) and glamour personalities (10% to 2%), while the number of appointed government officials, grew strongly (9% to 13%) and elected officials (9% to 25%), increased strongest of all. The changes among the various categories have continued into the 1990s, as the growth of the Black middle class, and the expansion of the opportunities to serve in both appointed and elected office have increased.

Having observed that the *categories* of leadership have expanded, it should be said that this has had a concomitant affect upon the characteristics of national leadership.

Characteristics

It is interesting that on the death of Frederick Douglass, Rev. F. J. Grimke, called for "the Black race to . . . stand up for a pure leadership; honor the men, and the men only, whose character you can respect, and whose example you can commend to your children." Then, he launched into the words of Holland, the poet:

Give us men,—Men whom the lust of office does not kill;
Men whom the spoils of office cannot buy;
Men who have honor, men who will not lie;
Tall men, sun-crowned, who live above the fog
In public duty, and in private thinking. (Gregory 1971:278)

The question of what characteristics Black leaders should have occasionally attracted commentary by Martin Luther King Jr. Thus, King recast the above poem as follows:

God give us leaders! A time like this demands strong minds,
  great hearts, true faith and ready hands;
Leaders whom the lust of office does not kill;
Leaders whom the spoils of life cannot buy;
Leaders who possess opinions and a will;
Leaders who have honor;
Leaders who will not lie;
Leaders who can stand before a demagogue and his
  treacherous flatteries without winking!
Tall leaders, sun crowned, who live above the fog in public
  duty and private thinking. (Washington 1992:148)

It is possible to see in King's embellishments the characteristics he valued in leaders. Nevertheless, this wish for "pure Black leadership" is reminiscent of the wish fulfillment or hopes that Blacks in slavery had for a deliverer, a Jeremiah, who was unspoiled, incorruptible, and strong. This sentiment is echoed by Congressman Ronald Dellums, who in an essay on Black leadership wrote: "I believe it is imperative that we dedicate ourselves to a higher morality than we presently witness, and that we come to believe in ourselves as a people with such strength that we can lead the movement toward a higher public morality and a recognition of new rights" (Dellums 1993:183). Dellums, like other leaders, believed that in order to use the moral capital of America to address socially progressive issues facing poor people and discrimination against non-Whites one would have to come to the table with clean hands.

The moral basis of Black leadership has been a source of the political currency of Black politics. However, such individuals have also been described as progressive, pragmatic, conservative, or radical.

MOBILIZING MODE OF INTERNAL LEADERSHIP

In the section on Black leadership in his expansive study of Black life, Gunnar Myrdal shows that the pattern of Black leadership originated at the very inception of Black/White contact (Myrdal 1962, 2:711–12). From this he infers that one of the strains in the Black leadership has been the dual pattern of having to utilize resources for the maintenance function of the Black community while, at the same time, performing the mobilizing role of the community in the achievement of resources from the larger White community. In short, the task of providing internal leadership in the normal community activities of social life, such as promoting positive family and community values and organization, labor force opportunities, educational opportunities and quality, compete constantly with the demands of mobilizing the community to develop the pressure on the majority for obtaining the resources necessary to achieve these goals.

Nevertheless, one of the major roles is the representative function of Black leadership, where it mobilizes the interests of the Black community and presents them to the larger political structure. In doing so, the assumption that Blacks should lead other Blacks is a natural concept, as indicated, the only issue being the scope of that "leadership" and its autonomy. Mary McLeod Bethune once expressed to the National Advisory Committee of the federal agency she headed, the National Youth Authority, the following: "May I advise the committee that it does not matter how equipped your white supervision might be, or your white leadership, it is impossible for you to enter as sympathetically and understandingly, into the program of the Negro, as the Negro can do" (Franklin and Meier 1982:196). This was one of the first such expressions of the strongly held view of the basis of the representative functions of Black leadership. In order to mobilize this interest effectively, it first had to be organized internally and in that task, there has always been a cadre of organizers who performed such tasks.

Black Organizers

Professor Aldon Morris' work is relevant here. It suggests that Black social movements were successful, in part, because they relied upon the community resources base provided by organizations and institutions that were already in place exercising the community-maintenance function (Morris 1984). However, when the mobilization occurred, normal patterns were disrupted: workers in normal social pursuits transferred their activities to the movement, some lawyers had to take on cases of those involved in the movement, businessmen had to finance some of the activities of the movement, and so on. In fact, the disruptive pattern of movement activities as well as the strain on resources, together with the oppositional direction of the movement toward the White community, often eliminated the majority of the leadership class from active participation; and although the movement called forth a considerable redirection of resources, much of it was important, though passive. These resources were utilized by the active sector to promote the aims of the movement within the larger set of majority-controlled institutions. Thus, these leaders often lived a precarious existence because of the demands of system-challenging projects, the personal courage and other family sacrifices required, and the reluctance of established organizations to lend their support to radical causes and approaches on a long-term basis.

Individuals have often arisen with the unique talent or the will to mobilize people to overcome such obstacles within the community and to use their human power to bring pressure to bear upon those with the resources in order to change oppressive systems or to open up new avenues for advancement. In some cases, the function of organizer was often combined in the leadership function, but in many other cases it was separate, which is to say that more often than not, leaders utilized the skills of organizers to accomplish tasks, who themselves just as often went unheralded. While the media has focused on these leaders, their exploits, and their personalities almost exclusively, their staff infrastructure has garnered little if any attention, as if their exploits came to fruition single-handedly, as if by sheer force of will.

In the scholarly literature, the Black organizer has most often been either omitted altogether or written about from the perspective of his or her engagement with one or the other civil rights organizations. Individuals such as George Wiley, founder and head of the National Welfare Rights Organization in 1967, was a leader organizer; Bayard Rustin was an activist and organizer who was employed by A. Phillip Randolph to organize the famous March on Washington of 1963, and he later advised Martin Luther King Jr. on tactics and strategies. Martin Luther King Jr. was a leader, and relied on a cadre of such organizers as Wyatt T. Walker, Andrew Young, Jesse Jackson, James Bevel, and others. The Student Non-Violent Coordinating Committee had a leader/chairman, but relied on local organizers in field situations throughout the South and the same could be said for the remaining "Big Five" civil rights organizations such as the Congress of Racial Equality, the NAACP, and the National Urban League. The fact that many of the organizers were younger or as young as their leaders was noted by Martin Luther King Jr., who noted the reason for this: "A consciousness of leadership, and a sense of destiny have given maturity and dedication to this generation of Negro students which have few precedents" (Washington 1992:161).

Typically, in any Black community, as in other communities, leadership has arisen both autonomously according to the urgency of the issues to be addressed and out of preexisting institutional structures with ongoing programs of action. One of the most important functions of mobilizing the interests of Blacks historically has been performed by the volunteer organizer who functioned at the neighborhood level and who may or may not have been associated with a local chapter of a major national organization. Volunteers most often ran the campaigns on local issues: stopping the highways from coming through the Black communities, which were vulnerable because of their lack of institutional power; fighting rate increases on buses; mobilizing pressure on city hall in the latest incident of police brutality; fighting to acquire much-needed neighborhood facilities such as street lights, recreation facilities, or paved roads. These individuals, few of whom had any formal training as organizers, learned how to campaign: to go door-to-door talking to neighbors, to put together a press conference, to get out leaflets or flyers on issues, or to do any one of the hundreds of mundane organizing tasks that make campaigns work. Examples include the work of E. D. Nixon, who organized the Montgomery Bus boycott, drawing on his skills as an organizer for the Brotherhood of Sleeping Car Porters, to William Lucy and Jerry Wirth of the American Federation of State, County and Municipal Employees (AFSCME), who assisted King in the Memphis garbage workers' movement, to the more recent emergence of the Coalition of Black Trade Unions, where Black unionists, with their formal organizational skills, were a unique group within the Black community.

Perhaps the Black organizer has not been as salient a figure in the studies of leadership because of the fluctuations in his or her roles, which have often arisen and disappeared with organizations that were formed in order to address the various causes that came about. In any case, it is demonstrable that in many cities, a predictable group of individuals have often been involved in "floating coalitions" of activity, especially where the larger, more stable organizations have not been anxious to assume responsibility for highly charged issues.

This was especially true during the 1960s innovation of the Community Action Programs in many cities, where community organizers gained quasi-official status and a mandate to organize neighborhoods and individual citizens to participate in the decision-making process at the city government level—and were paid to do so. So effective were many of these organizers that they often intervened in the system of official decision-making, alienating mayors and members of city councils who felt that this was their private preserve. As such, these organizers often went beyond the simple task of informing citizens, to mobilizing them against city hall through protest demonstrations. As a result, opposition developed in the Congress, and funding for their function was eliminated from the budget. Eventually, the concept of "citizen participation" itself was also killed.[7]

Finally, it is important to note that the practice of Black organizing has changed from a period of high mobilization in the mid-1960s to mid-1970s, when such mobilization was a key dimension to the exercise of Black power, to a low period of such mobilizations in the 1990s when it is assumed that institutional politics should be the main methodology of leadership. Nevertheless, some renowned organizers have made the transition and are still active, such as Ron Daniels, head of the Center for Constitutional Rights in New York City, who had previously been involved in a number of other movement activities; Professors Adul Alkalimat of Chicago and Sam Anderson of New York City, Marxist organizers who have continued to sponsor meetings and exercise intellectual leadership of this wing of the movement; Sokoni Karanja in Chicago with the Center for New Horizons; and others.

A modern example of effective organizing has been the work of Joe Reed in Alabama. Reed has risen through the ranks of the Democratic Party in Alabama from the days when it was tightly segregated in the 1960s to become the leader of the Alabama Democratic Conference in the 1990s. In this role, as a nonelected official, he has had extraordinary influence in the political affairs of the State of Alabama, stemming not only from his role in the Democratic Party, but also from his leadership since 1964 as associate executive secretary of the Alabama Education Association and his membership on the Montgomery City Council.

Reed worked intimately with Black elected officials and the political leaders of the state to recruit candidates for the legislature, and he has participated in critical political issues such as congressional and state redistricting. One result of his efforts is that the largest cadre of Black elected officials in the nation exist in a state that was a bastion of the Confederacy, with 442 elected officials overall and 24 Black state legislators, the third largest number in the nation.[8]

Because of their position closest to the grassroots, Black organizers often manifest an oppositional stance to established national Black leaders. Thus, it was possible to hear Black organizers in the South being critical of Martin Luther King Jr., whom they often called "De Lawd" and whom they derided for showing up to be a momentary symbol of the movement while they were left with whatever hard work or errors the Southern Christian Leadership Conference (SCLC) made in the process. More recently, this negative critique has continued and has followed Jesse Jackson, for example, whom his detractors suggest often shows up for the pictures and leaves them to follow through on organizing people to achieve the goals of his rhetoric. I reject this is as a valid critique of any national leadership (*a*) because it is the function of national leaders to act as symbols of movements and causes and, thus, to suggest that national leaders must follow through on issues they espouse from a national platform at the local level is not characteristic of *any* truly national leadership; and (*b*) because it is not possible without a formidable national organizational apparatus in any case.

Otherwise, one might see the nature of Black leadership as existing on a continuum where, because of the peculiar nature of the Black experience, the struggle dimension undergirds the "normal" functions of community maintenance and thus, one deals with activities that are colored by the Black/White conflict dynamic incessantly in a variety of manifestations. Therefore, the larger and more dynamic mobilizations of the national Black leader to claim rights and resources is merely part of a continuum of both the underlying constant race tensions that shape the problem, and the tactics used to deal with it.

NATIONAL LEADERSHIP

National Political Institutions

Here, it will be necessary to operationalize the theory discussed above, utilizing more concrete examples in which the Black community and the majority White community exhibited patterns of conflict and cooperation in the achievement of the political objectives of the Black community's status rights, socioeconomic rights, and resources.

Thus, the second major arena of Black leadership was characterized by the participation of Blacks in the wider society. Historically, the White majority has not easily accommodated the entry of Black Americans into political participation. Thus, the character of Black leadership has been defined, on the one hand, by an accommodationist imperative where leaders such as Booker T. Washington were faced with the clear challenge of providing direction for Blacks in an environment of White hostility. There any semblance of equality would be rejected with the force of preponderant power.

On the other hand, Black leadership has had an oppositional character, opposing those attempts to subjugate the Black community through repressive laws or social practices, and attempting to implement an offensive program of social change. This mandate has often found Blacks responding, at one time in history, to the resistance of the dominant system to Black participation, a resistance that impeded forward progress and enhanced the process of racial subordination and oppression. Whereas at other times, there would be less resistance from the dominant system, and this facilitated the forward movement made by the initiative of Blacks, bringing some accommodation and inclusion into social, economic, and political institutions.

So, the leadership strategy has been to utilize Black politics, first, to obtain the right to participate, which called for the use of a *tactic* of integration at one level, but which also was a *strategy* to define or redefine the character of American society altogether. This often called for such tactics as individual or collective protest, legal representation in the courts, or legislative strategies in order to acquire the necessary public policies that were important to empowerment.

The second objective, once such a right to participate was obtained, was to utilize it for the benefit of the Black community primarily. Exercising societal leadership in either the private sphere, for example, as head of major foundations, or in the public sphere as a publicly elected representative carried the responsibility to manage the interests of both the African American community and other groups as well. This concept, which might be regarded as a theory of Black politics, was embraced by the Black leadership cadre.

Thus, one of the most important resources has been human power and this has required a concentration on the tactics and strategy of mass leadership, designed to effectively target the power of Blacks as a group to certain social objectives.

The emphasis on group action was also critical because of the power arrayed against Blacks and their need to change their socioeconomic status. Indeed political scientist Robert Dahl, a theorist of the democratic process, suggests that the effective use of the political system for individuals depended upon the amount of change required:

> [Y]our chances of gaining a favorable action from the government depends on still another factor: how much change you require in the behavior of other people in order for government to do what you want it to do. The greater the amount of change required, the less your chances of success—other things being equal of course. (Dahl 1972:389)

The logic of his observation is that in order for individuals to make a substantial amount of change, they must develop modes of behavior that yield them more power to operate strategies. This has been the great goal of the practice of Blacks in politics and a major problem of theorists of Black politics as well. Below, I will address the two arenas of Black politics as the environment for the exercise of leadership and as a platform for a discussion of the phenomenon.

National Leadership Structure

Nationally, a variety of organized national groups dominate the Black leadership structure. At the top are the heads of recognized national Black organizations such as the Congressional Black Caucus (CBC), the NAACP, the National Urban League, the Southern Christian Leadership Conference, the National Council of Negro Women, the National Rainbow Coalition/PUSH and others. These organizations have an interlocking membership of individuals who sit on the boards of several organizations at one time. Furthermore, each organization has its own local chapters and resource networks. However, very little of the contribution of local chapters of these organizations has an impact on the performance of the national office. In fact, in most cases, there are two streams of activity, one local and another national, with intersections being made at the point of administration, such as the management of funds and at critical programmatic junctures where local resources or support may be required.

Then, there are the coalition organizations formed by the heads of these organizations, such as the National Black Leadership Forum, which includes leaders of thirteen top organizations, including the Joint Center for Political and Economic Studies, heads of Black fraternities and sororities, executives of national political organizations such as the CBC and the National Conference of Black Mayors, and other local officials.

There has also been a considerable elaboration of various types of political organizations, an indication of the growth of their power. In addition to the CBC and the National Conference of Black Mayors, there is the National Black Caucus of Local Elected Officials (of the National League of Cities), the International Conference of Black Mayors, Black School Board Officials, and the National Association of Black County Officials. Other organizations of nonelected officials exist such as the Black political party caucuses, the National Political Caucus of Black Women, and the National Coalition of Black Voter Participation. The status among these organizations, of course, complies with their relationship to the various levels of government.

There is also a considerable degree of overlap among these organizations in their individual membership, as a member of one is likely to be a member of another. This means that the effective leadership class of the Black community has a high degree of coherence and integrated membership.

Leadership in the Electoral Arena

It is now well known that despite the passage of the Fifteenth Amendment to the Constitution ensuring the right to vote, Blacks were, in practice, prohibited from voting, especially in the South, for a period extending up to the mid-1960s. It became an important aspect of the civil rights movement to enforce that amendment, clearly evident in the words of Martin Luther King Jr., in a speech on May 17, 1957, at a mass rally at the Lincoln Memorial that commemorated the third anniversary of the *Brown* decision of 1954:

> Give us the ballot and we will no longer plead to the federal government for passage of an anti-lynching law; we will by the power of our vote write the law on the statute books of the southern states and bring an end to the dastardly acts of the hooded perpetrators of violence. Give us the ballot and we will transform the salient misdeeds of bloodthirsty mobs into the calculated good deeds of orderly citizens. Give us the ballot and we will fill our legislative halls with men of good will, and send to the sacred halls of Congress men who will not sign a Southern Manifesto, because of their devotion to the manifesto of justice. Give us the ballot and we will place judges on the benches of the South who will "do justly and love mercy," and we will place at the head of the southern states governors who have felt not only the pang of the human, but the glow of the divine. Give us the ballot and we will quietly and nonviolently, without rancor or bitterness, implement the Supreme Court decisions of May 17, 1954. (Washington 1992:198)

It is worth citing the long passage from Dr. King's speech above because it conveys to the reader the expansive expectations of the civil rights movement and the actions that were being taken to sacrifice lives and resources for justice. The Voting Rights Act was won on the battlefield of "Bloody Sunday" in Selma, Alabama, on March 6, 1965, when televisions in the living rooms of America showed peaceful civil rights marchers being beaten unmercifully by mounted policemen. The public outcry jolted President Lyndon Johnson and the Congress into action, and the bill was signed on August 6, 1965.

One significant long-term trend has been the growth in the number of Black elected officials. Before the Voting Rights Act was passed in 1965, there were an estimated three hundred Black elected officials at all levels of government. As is indicated in table 6.1, the growth since that time has been dramatic. By 1994, there were nearly 8,000 Black elected officials in office, and although the *number* of officials continues to grow, the *rate* at which they are growing has slowed dramatically from the early 1970s, when the annual increases were sometimes quite striking. The slower rate of growth at 2% and 3% per year in the 1990s is an indication that while many areas with a Black majority have elected Blacks, Blacks will have to run for office in nonmajority Black political jurisdictions. This will likely change the nature of the agenda of Black candidates because they will not be able to pursue purely Black politics.

TABLE 6.1
Growth in BLack Elected Officials

Year	Total	U.S.	State	City & County	Law Enforcement	Education
1970	1,469	10	169	715	213	362
1980	4,890	18	308	2,832	526	1,206
1985	6,016	17	390	3,517	661	1,431
1990	7,335	20	416	4,485	769	1,645
1991	7,445	26	447	4,496	847	1,629
1992	7,517	25	474	4,557	847	1,614
1994	7,984	41	520	4,819	922	1,682

SOURCE: Report, Elections, Statistical Data, Bureau of the Census, Department of Commerce, Section 9, Table no. 452, p. 284, 1996.

Issues Mobilization in the National Arena

The mobilization of Black leadership traditionally has been directed toward the attainment of concrete objectives as represented by the original threat of the March on Washington by Black labor leader A. Philip Randolph in 1941. In short, as Everett Carl Ladd Jr. has said, "Negro political leadership in the urban South is issue leadership. The issue [is] race advancement" (Ladd 1966:135). Indeed, the mere fact that so much of the Black leadership was willing to mobilize their organizations to follow A. Philip Randolph to fight for fair employment in the 1940s was proof of the high salience of this issue within the Black community.

The same point might be made of the decade of the 1960s. Emboldened by the success of the 1954 Supreme Court decision of *Brown v. Board of Education of Topeka, Kansas*, mandating integrated education, and the Montgomery, Alabama bus boycott, Blacks in both the North and South launched a series of physical challenges to all forms of racial segregation that have not, as yet, ended. Fueled by the student movement of the late 1950s and early 1960s, protesting segregated eating facilities, the adults began to protest against segregation in employment and public accommodations, and for the right to vote and participate in the southern society at large. One major high point of the civil rights movement was the 1963 March on Washington, organized by A. Philip Randolph. This massive protest demonstration provided an opportunity for all Americans to witness the broad cross-racial consensus that the civil rights movement enjoyed at that moment in history.

Black protests, however, grew violent in the 1960s, as the temper of the northern movement became expressed in an urgency that was incomparable to the more defensive tactics utilized by Martin Luther King Jr. in the South. By 1967, a "Black Power movement" was born with Stokeley Carmichael as its leader, and by 1969, five hundred cities were burning in an exorcism of violence. The impact of the more militant politics, spawned a renewed appreciation of African culture and the push for Black studies became a political objective of Black students and faculty members on White college campuses all over the country. Thus, many major colleges and universities were politicized as the struggle for Black studies was joined by the struggle for women's rights and protests against the Vietnam War.

Other protest demonstrations by Black organizations have occurred since the 1970s with the objectives of seeking to commemorate the goals of the 1963 March on Washington, or to signal the public objection of Blacks and others to the anti–civil rights Supreme Court decisions of the 1980s. However, the largest demonstration in American history was the Million Man March, held in October 1995, which was organized by Minister Louis Farrakhan, head of the Nation of Islam. This march, which brought more than a million Black men to Washington, D.C., on October 12, 1995, was not a traditional protest demonstration, but carried the theme of "atonement and reconciliation," as a way of seeking the recommitment of African American males to their basic responsibilities to their families and their communities ("Million Man March" 1995).

CONCLUSION

What Makes Leadership Black? Or the Question of Ideology

Since Black leaders assume the task of attempting to mobilize the interests of the Black community by the use of their political power in various arenas, the major conclusion that can be drawn is that what makes Black leadership "Black" is the same set of factors that makes politics "Black." In the first instance, definition of Black leadership entailed the community function and thus, an emphasis on the group and its culture and the social well-being of that cultural group as an absolute value. In this sense, the view that Black leaders were "race men," as suggested by Myrdal, is evident at an early time in the evolution of their activity. Professor Kevin Gaines finds that "uplift ideology's argument for black humanity was not an argument for equality. Indeed, the shift from race to culture, stressing self-help and seemingly progressive in its contention that blacks, like immigrants, were assimilable into the American body politic, represented a limited, conditional claim to equality, citizenship and human rights for African Americans" (Gaines 1996:4). However, it is not necessarily the color of those involved, since color is not an absolute of race, but the experiences of those involved that define the nature of their use of power and the objectives toward which power is directed.

Elsewhere, I attempted to suggest what make politics Black, that is to say, what constitutes the normative and behavioral difference between the conceptions of "Black" politics and the "politics" of Black America (Walters 1992:202). In the latter sense, the politics of Black America might be structured so as to conform to the historical eras or key events in the nation; it might be structured so as to conform to analysis of the dominant institutions of the nation both public and private; it might be structured to conform to the dominant ideological tenets of various groups within the majority; and it may be structured to assess the behavior of Blacks with respect to normal strategies of political participation.

However, any casual perusal of the content of African American life would render such an approach useful but, if viewed only from the dominant majority perspective, wholly insufficient, in that it would lose the coherence and credibility that comes from the essential meaning and context of those who defined it and, thus, who are its actors and agents of history. To this extent, a cultural explanation of Black leadership would be roughly congruent with the definition of Black politics:

1. Leadership has been exercised by people of African descent.

2. Leadership has proceeded from the collective interests and concerns of people of African descent—including involvement in historical events defined by a "racial uplift" tradition, and leadership to overcome the impediments to the full enjoyment of every aspect of American life (such as slavery, prejudice and discrimination, institutional racism, and any pattern of exclusion or racial inferiorization of Black humanity).

3. Leadership has relied on social rather than economic resources because of the transfer of Black capital to Whites in the process of slavery.

4. The leadership of a minority within a majority has implied the use of strategies of leverage and coalition rather than outright power.

5. Leadership has diversified into many different professions, political institutions, and arenas.

Therefore, these variables define "Black leadership" as a distinctive social category in relationship to American society. Beyond the task confronted in this chapter of defining the rough terrain of Black leadership in both its cultural setting and within the larger society, we move on to describe and assess the practical manifestations—or praxis—of Black leadership in the various arenas suggested above.

CHAPTER 7

Black Leadership and the Problem of Strategy Shift

The successful achievement of goals by any group in society rarely occurs by accident but rather by a conscious concern with strategy. Political strategies that Blacks have directed toward the policy system have been utilized in an effort to achieve more favorable public policy addressed to the problems faced by their community. The fact that government is heavily involved in the solution to the problems of Black Americans is directly rooted in a history of government implication in the subjugation and continued denial of basic civil and human rights. In more recent times, governmental as well as major private economic and social institutions have also been responsive to Black initiatives in the amelioration of the plight of the underclasses, but as resources, national moods, and issues change, the strategies of Black leadership have likewise had to adjust. Today, a new period of adjustment is necessary because of the growing estrangement of major American institutions from the Black agenda and, at the same time, the continued need for that agenda to be vigorously pursued. In this respect, the comment that "we don't need to go back to the (strategies of the) sixties" suggests an implicit use of a "stage theory," that is, the use of strategies according to the presumed level of Black advancement in society.

Strategies, however, should be tailored to the objective situation, and in addressing which to utilize, a comprehensive view of the history of strategies should be undertaken with a view to using the best combination. Likewise, the notion that a back-to-the-sixties approach is inappropriate suggests further that Blacks are able to utilize the same strategies that other groups have used successfully and in the same ways. Such a conception may not be congruent with the special role of Blacks in U.S. history. A brief typology of such strategies might include the following.

STRATEGIES

At a forum of the Congressional Black Caucus featuring several Black leaders, Rev. Jesse Jackson suggested that "some combination of registration, legislation, demonstration, and litigation" will be necessary to move issues forward as the major political strategies. If this is accepted, then voting, public policy formation, civic pressure, and court suits are the major political strategies through which the Black community mobilizes its power to levy influence upon institutions and issues in the political system. What follows is an illustration of selected cases in each category.

Voting

As the two presidential campaigns of Jesse Jackson illustrated, the issue increasingly involved in using voting to obtain political resources is not only the encouragement of a strong turnout and voting so that a suitable representative can be elected to office; it is also the fact that such support creates strategic leverage for leaders in the political process (Walters 1988:110–38). Jackson was not elected to office, but support for his candidacy enabled him to deliver a clear expression of the progressive agenda directly to the American public rather than indirectly; the general mobilization for his candidacy caused some to be elected at other levels of government; and the legitimacy of his campaign enabled him to bargain to include progressive items on the agenda of the Democratic Party. Increasingly, strategic voting should provide leaders with even more flexibility to leverage issues.

Public Policy

Leaders are involved in a process of what has been called "agenda setting" when they seek to establish priorities for community or national consideration (Cobb and Elder 1983). Perhaps the greatest public policy consensus among Black leadership is with respect to the importance of jobs. In fact, the 1993 March on Washington decried the high level of unemployment and launched a strong challenge to the North American Free Trade Agreement, widely held to eventually reduce high-wage jobs in the United States by putting low-wage workers in the United States in competition with low-wage workers in Mexico. March leaders said: "We demand that the basic standards of American and international law be upheld, both in our country and by those with whom we trade. These rights include a minimum age for the employment of children and acceptable conditions of work with respect to wages, hours, working conditions, and occupational safety and health for every worker" (New Coalition of Conscience 1993:3).

Civic Pressure

In Miami, Florida, leaders of the Black community initiated an economic boycott of tourism when the city rescinded a key to the city for

South African leader Nelson Mandela, who had spoken out in support of Cuban leader Fidel Castro on his 1990 visit to the United States. The boycott was continued for three years, during which it cost Miami more than $20 million in direct tourism from the cancellation of an estimated twenty-four meetings involving 46,000 delegates. The leaders of the protest negotiated a twenty-point agenda for change that contained demands for greater representation of Black-owned convention-quality hotels on Miami Beach, 125 visitor industry scholarships for Blacks, and single-member voting districts for Miami, Dade County, and the school board, among other concerns. The boycott ended on May 12, 1993, when an agreement, which will be monitored by Miami Partners for Progress, was signed between Black leaders and city officials. One observer said of the agreement: "Their ambitious blueprint for change . . . will test not only the commitment of the local business community, but also the credibility of the handful of boycott leaders who acted on behalf of the Black community" ("Biracial Blueprint," 1993:1A).

Litigation

The next major litigation battle over the legitimacy of the Voting Rights Act was precipitated by the *Shaw v. Reno* decision of the Supreme Court in the spring of 1993. The five-to-four decision, supported by Justices William Rheinquist, Antonio Scalia, Anthony Kennedy, and Clarence Thomas, was delivered by Justice Sandra Day O'Connor, who deprecated districts based solely on race and that dismissed so-called traditional standards of redistricting such as "compactness" and "contiguity." The Court stated that the five White plaintiffs were allowed to raise questions of "equal protection" since the 12th Congressional district of North Carolina, which precipitated the case, was "so irrational on its face the it can be understood only as an effort to segregate voters into separate voting districts because of their race, and that the separation lacks sufficient justification" (Kaplan 1993:1762).

The district, represented by African American Mel Watt, was created by the application of Section 5 of the 1982 Amendments to the Voting Rights Act, and this action, by implication, challenges the legitimacy of that section. If not overturned, it could also challenge some of the other fifty-two majority Black and Hispanic congressional districts. The stakes here are that the size of the Congressional Black Caucus, Black state legislative delegations, and Blacks representing other jurisdictions are under attack with this ruling; it will take a significant political effort (including in all likelihood a change in the Court's composition) in support of litigation to reverse this challenge.

If there is any shift that is endemic to the focus of such strategies outlined above, it is the fact that in the long struggle for racial equality—which essentially positioned Black civil rights leaders against the system—that integration as the standard of race advancement should be refocused toward the internal problems of development faced by the community where they exist. It is a logic that says, for example, that in a 90 to 95 percent Black school district, the strategies for achieving quality education should not continue to emphasize busing and school integration at the expense of acquiring quality resources and performance for that system the way it exists.[1]

Mass Demonstrations

The mass demonstrations have also been a major part of Black strategy from the early days of this century, when the NAACP led marches down the streets of Harlem protesting against lynching and other atrocities against Blacks, to the March on Washington Movement that was threatened by A. Philip Randolph in 1941 but not consummated, and especially the famous 1963 March on Washington that featured Martin Luther King Jr. and his "I Have A Dream" speech, to the fabulously successful (in terms of the size of the turnout) Million Man March of 1995.

The 1963 march in particular has kept the tradition of mass marches alive because participants in the civil rights movement have sought to commemorate this march every ten years with occasions at which they not only celebrate the 1963 march, but utilize it as a forum to raise current issues. These marches, however, have been largely ceremonial and lacked the timing and the urgency of the 1963 march inasmuch as they were not held in an atmosphere of social movement, and thus they also lacked the force of that march, being essentially one-day affairs that direct policy demands toward the political system with little follow-through.

STRATEGY SHIFT

Nevertheless, it is an established fact that periods of strategy-shift are part of the traditional Black experience. More recently, there have been three distinct periods of such shifts; the first of these occurred in the 1957–60 period with the civil rights movement, the second in 1966–67 with the Black Liberation/Pan African Movement, and the third, in 1970–72, with the move toward Black electoral politics. In each of these periods the seeds of various movements existed simultaneously, although one would emerge as the dominant force in Black political strategy and ultimately gain prominence over that which preceded it.

What accounted for these shifts most fundamentally were factors such as the existence of a favorable national mood, the death of a popular president, a growing economy, a predominantly liberal Congress, or other important elements. However, the strategies of Blacks, when examined independently, were a key ingredient in the outcome of their struggles and as such require continuous analysis for the greatest understanding of their role. In addressing this problem, because the current mood in the Black community may presage a return to noninstitutional strategies, only a brief reference to the strategies of the 1960s is made with references to the limits of an institutional political strategy alone.

THE STRATEGY OF CIVIL RIGHTS

The shift into a more aggressive strategy of massive mobilization of people into activities demonstrating their resistance to the denial of the right to public accommodations, jobs, voting, housing, and other civil and human rights was designed to express dissatisfaction with the status quo and provoke the appropriate authorities to change systems and behaviors that supported this oppression. Without going into a lengthy review of this well-known history, it is enough to say that the movement accomplished the objective of developing the kind of pressures necessary to move its prime issues to national priorities, and contrary to some opinions, it produced widespread and concrete results.

What was initially striking about the civil rights mobilization was the rapidity with which it attracted recruits who expanded the range of activities designed to oppose institutions practicing racism and segregation. Such activities had been conducted in the Midwest and South since the late 1950s but did not gain national exposure until 1960 with the sit-in movement (see, e.g., Morris 1984). Very quickly there were all varieties of sit-ins, and the activity escalated from the most benign forms of protest to expressive violence in 1963, as the movement reached a plateau with the famous March on Washington. The emergence of Dr. Martin Luther King Jr. was important, not only because the movement had a charismatic catalyst but because his organization, SCLC, became the center of strategic planning involving a cadre of committed and astute young Black ministers. They knew, for example, that just as they were dedicated to the use of nonviolent civil disobedience as a system challenging strategy in places such as Albany, Georgia, and Selma, Alabama, the counterviolence of the White authorities would create the drama that ultimately gained national exposure. Just as important, although other groups such as the Congress of Racial Equality, the National Association for the Advancement of Colored People, the Student Non-Violent Coordinating Committee and others, served as shock troops in many of the toughest places in the movement together with SCLC, coordinated planning did become necessary (see, e.g., Garrow 1978:212–36). This planned strategy, together with the general atmosphere of urgency created by the sporadic violent rebellions occurring in the cities, created the ultimate pressure for the agenda-setting movement to be effective at securing legislation.

The legislation passed as a result of the civil rights movement had a favorable impact on the average Black family. First, median income of Black families rose most sharply in the period 1964 to 1969, from a level of $5,921 to $7,978 (U. S. Bureau of Census 1980:483). At the same time, the largest one-year increase of $778 in this decade occurred in the 1965–66 period. Second, such increases in income were a reflection of heavy annual increases in labor force participation by Blacks, as the most significant increases in this category occurred in the same period, 1964–69. While the actual increase in the Black employed grew from 7.4 million workers in 1964 to 8.4 million in 1969, the largest annual increase occurred in 1965, 260,000 workers. As a consequence of the improved overall employment picture, rates of unemployment dropped most sharply in 1968 (6.7%) and 1969 (6.4%), from a high in 1960 (10.8%). Finally, improvement in the economic status of Black families contributed to large increases in college enrollment, with the sharpest increases occurring between 1966 and 1970.

While it would be far too simplistic to suggest that these changes came about only in response to the strategy of the movement, it would be equally simplistic to suggest that they happened as a result of the natural workings of the economy, even though GNP in the decade of the sixties grew by 40 percent, and Black median family income grew by 35 percent. An important contribution to the increases in Black median family income may be traced to the economic policies of the Johnson administration, specifically the Economic Opportunity Act of 1964, and Title VII of the 1964 Civil Rights Act, which established the affirmative action machinery.

Lyndon Johnson sought to set an example of federal leadership by including in his January 1964 proposal to Congress funding of $970 million—one percent of the federal budget—for the Economic Opportunity Act (Weisbord 1965). In doing so, he was being responsive to the fact that so much of the inequality Blacks faced was rooted in their low economic status in society. In fact, their overwhelming representation in the statistics on poverty revealed that about 40 percent of the non-White population in 1964 was classified as poor. While he anticipated a role in this effort for the private sector, he was prepared to exercise federal initiative for the first two years. This policy did not materialize, however, from the benevolence of Johnson, but rather, as one analysis put it:

Black groups now demand that social and economic impoverishment
be recognized. They are no longer willing to wait for the benefits of
increased economic prosperity to trickle down to them as future productive components in the economic system. Society is no longer able
to ignore poverty and economic disparity. (Henderson and Lewdebur 1972:33)

At the same time, in an environment of a growing economy, which had
produced 5.3 million jobs between 1960 and 1965, 7.7 percent of them
in the manufacturing and 10 percent in durable goods industries where
Blacks had the skills to be employed, the Johnson administration also
began to put pressure on public and private employers through the
establishment of the Equal Employment Opportunity Commission (Bardolph 1970:5–6). These twin developments were largely responsible for
the overall improvement in the economic status of Black families, a
result traceable also to the various pressures generated by movement
strategies.

ELECTORAL STRATEGY SHIFT

The next great shift of strategy on the policy system occurred in the
1970–72 period, when it became clear that electoral politics had gained
priority over the civil rights movement. Actually, the civil rights movement had achieved one of its objectives in the 1965 Voting Rights Act,
which sparked massive increases in registration and voting. This mobilization was influenced by the alienating politics of the 1960s, such that
rates of voting dropped slightly from a high of 58.6 percent in 1964 to
57.9 percent in 1968 and even to 52.1 percent by 1972, and 48.7 percent by 1976 (U.S. Bureau of the Census 1973:27). However, it was perceived that the yield of rapid increases in the number of Black elected
officials (BEOs) more than off set this decline in participation, as Blacks
suddenly captured the governing machinery of cities and many other
political bodies, from sheriffs to congresspersons. Actually, there had
been 200 BEOs in 1964 and 400 by 1968, but by 1973 phenomenal
annual increases of 24 percent (1970), 27 percent (1971), and 22 percent (1972), respectively, brought the number to 4,311 by 1977 and
over 5,000 by 1983 (Joint Center for Political Studies 1979:xii). This
indeed represented substantial movement, which also brought with it an
ideology, a strategy, and social support.

With regard to securing the vote as an object of strategy during the
civil rights movement, a full-blown theory of political power was seldom
articulated. But there was an understanding, especially among the more
political groups such as the SNCC, for example, that the purpose of

establishing the Lowndnes County Freedom Organization was to have an organization into which the power of the vote could be invested, so that issues faced by its members would be addressed either by outright control of the political system or by their ability to influence its decisions. Carmichael and Hamilton make this point: "SNCC believed that in order to break through the racist Mississippi society, Black people must awaken their potential political power. Organizing around the vote was a key to this, as were demonstrations to desegregate public facilities" (Carmichael and Hamilton 1967:87). Very quickly, however, Bayard Rustin of the A. Philip Randolph Institute urged the leaders of the civil rights movement to change strategies and move from "protest to politics," suggesting an institutional relationship with the Democratic Party as the key to the achievement of policy goals (Rustin 1965:25–31). Thus, from the 1964 convention and the political support given to Lyndon Johnson, the logic of an electoral-oriented strategy became a major factor in the arsenal of Black leadership.

By the early 1970s, slogans that gave evidence of an institutionalized political strategy became prominent; for it was now believed that it was necessary to "learn the rules of the system" in order to be successful in the new institutions, that there were no more "Black issues," that "politics (electoral) is the cutting edge of the civil rights movement," and that "it's not the rap, it's the map, it's not the man, it's the plan."[2] Without suggesting that any of these comments are necessarily inaccurate, the force of this new pragmatic ideology was itself evidence of the extent to which Black leadership had become institutionalized.

Black government officials had grown into a self-conscious class, and the masses had accorded them the legitimacy of leadership. From their seats on school boards, city councils, county councils, state legislatures, and the Congress, elected officials began to form themselves into organizations such as the Southern Conference of Black Mayors (1971), the National Black Caucus of Local Elected Officials (1972), the Congressional Black Caucus (1969), and others. In addition, the Black appointed official (BAO) constituted an important adjunct in perhaps a more important way, that is, to the degree to which Black leadership (and thus the Black movement) had become institutionalized. By January 1980, it was observed that there were 275 Black senior-level appointees in the Carter administration, and while the presence of such officials was not new, their expansion was indeed striking (Martin 1978). This led Robert Smith, in a systematic study of Black political appointees, to suggest:

> In sum, in the twenty years since the "historic firsts" of the Kennedy-Johnson Administration, blacks have made substantial aggregate gains

in appointive federal office. The gains are observed under both Democratic and Republican Administrations, but the most dramatic increases occur in the Carter Administration such that at its end one can conclude that blacks had been successfully integrated into the executive policy making apparatus of the federal government. (Smith 1984:376)

This phenomenon was replicated, of course, at the state level; however, at the national level, it was an impressive display of institutionalized Black leadership that now focused its energies and strategies on wrestling with the institutions of which they were now a part in an effort to exercise influence.

THE NEW LEADERSHIP CLASS

A major reason for the legitimacy accorded this new Black leadership was the arrival of a formidable support base in the Black middle class, which had taken advantage of the occupational and educational opportunities of the 1960s and 1970s and had achieved a degree of socioeconomic mobility. They were more often than not also employed by one of the major political, social, or economic institutions, and were faced with the companion task of attempting to make the relationship viable. Evidence of the new class is found in the fact that while only 25 percent of Black families made over $15,000 in 1964, by 1980, 30 percent made over $20,000 (Bureau of the Census 1980). Thus, although there is a growing "underclass" of poor Blacks (Glasgow 1980), there is a concomitant rise in middle-income Blacks whose lifestyle is more conducive to the strategies adopted by the new leadership class. It is worth observing that in the past, it was probably the distance of most Blacks from the policy system, as well as from the direct control of their leadership by major institutions, that gave legitimacy to noninstitutional strategies as well.

At the same time, it should be noted that Black leaders are still not as directly attached to the economic system as Whites are, due to the far fewer representatives of economic institutions in the leadership pool. Professor Charles Henry, for example, has made an analysis of the *Ebony* magazine annual listing of the "100 Most Influential Blacks" in the period 1971–79 (and including the 1963 listing) (Henry 1981). From his study of this pool, which is reasonably representative of the leadership in the Black community, it is possible to determine the changes in the various categories of persons who are perceived to be leaders (see table 7.1).

Given the large increase in government officials and the decreases in professional, labor, and civil rights leaders, our previous analysis finds

TABLE 7.1
Percent Increase or Decrease of Categories of Black Leaders, 1971–1979

Category	Percent
Business	–2%
Government	11
elected	9
appointed	2
Professional/Labor/Civil Rights	–18
Religion	5
Media	1

SOURCE: Charles Henry, "Ebony's Elite," *Phylon* 42 (1981): 120–32.

some confirmation. However, the relative low level of business representation cast a very different profile from that of the White leadership pool, where Henry says that approximately 60 percent of the pool of influential leaders are from the business sector (Henry 1981:125). The low level of representation of this sector in the Black community is continuing testimony to either the low level of economic growth or the fact that those who have become business leaders are not substantially involved in the overall leadership of the Black community.

In addition, the evidence from the *Black Enterprise* annual surveys of the top 100 Black businesses suggests that the economically able Blacks are in the nonpolitical fields of entertainment and construction, followed by automobile dealerships, publishing firms, and cosmetics firms.[3] By and large, the profile of economically able Blacks in business does not appear to suggest that they would have the same investment in political leadership questions to the same degree as corporate heads in the White community. The impact of this factor on Black leadership is to leave it without a major economic resource, but free from direct ties to the dominant forces of the economic system. For instance, one would have to calculate seriously what additional constraints would be operative on Black strategies if the principal officer of a major U.S. corporation was part of the leadership group. Given the cumulative effect of the arrival of new strategies, by a new class of leaders, what has been the effect upon issues?

IMPACT OF INSTITUTIONAL STRATEGIES

Among the various political roles, I will select that of mayor to illustrate an important leadership dilemma. Because Black mayors have been one of the more visible category of the new political leadership, particularly of those who have become stewards of many major metropolitan cities, "what difference has it made?" While it is possible for many Black mayors to suggest, and analyses support them,[4] that they have spent somewhat more in their cities on social service delivery, housing, and employed more Blacks than other, White mayors, perhaps the reality such claims have produced in answer to the question is that their efforts have resulted in marginal contributions to the overall survival of Blacks. One of the perspectives gained in the past two decades is that mayors do not *control* major productive resources, they can only *broker* them. Thus, they cannot intervene effectively into the cycles of despair experienced by urban Blacks. This suggests a considerable distance between the institutional function of Black mayors and the reward expectation of their Black constituents, which are expressed more often in racial institutional rather than just institutional terms.

This fact was illustrated rather poignantly in the 1984 campaign of Rev. Jesse Jackson when some mayors acted to preserve their access to the White House by supporting the candidate they perceived to be the best potential occupant, and other Black mayors supported Reverend Jackson's candidacy. The question here was addressed by Professor Smith in an important footnote to the study referred to above: "Are all black appointees automatically black leaders? If not, what are the conditions that make some appointees race leaders and other not? And of those who are, what is the implication of this for their work as government officials, that is, what is their proper relationship to the government and the black community?" (Smith 1984:386). This question, which he no doubt posed as a theoretical one, requiring empirical verification, is, in fact, a highly practical question suitable to be asked of the Black mayors to whom I refer. For it is obvious that some mayors both with regard to the campaign of Reverend Jackson and in other visible circumstances act as institutional heads rather than as race leaders; that is to say, they have weighted their roles on the side of their institutional responsibility, rationalizing this act by believing that if they are "good" (professionals in their institutional roles) officials, they will automatically serve their racial interests.

Because this contradiction emerged to a very public level in the Jackson campaign and occurs daily in practical situations where the interests of Blacks are lodged in political institutions, one could logically conclude that Blacks will increasingly evaluate leadership on these two dimensions and occasionally force a leader to choose which role they are exercising as a fundamental definition of their mission in office. Ultimately, however, this dilemma is not so much a comment upon the absence of presence of the "free will" of Black mayors and other elected

officials, but upon the institutional constraints within which they operate and the incremental production of benefits to less powerful groups
that such institutions normally produce.

Institutional constraints have, in general, placed severe limitations
on the ability of Black leaders to affect significant policy changes, especially from within the institution itself. In this regard, the Humphrey-
Hawkins bill, the major Black public policy focus of the 1970s, stands
as a poignant illustration as seen in the detailed analysis of Professor
Smith in his *We Have No Leaders* (Smith 1996:187–210). After a considerable period of mobilization by the Congressional Black Caucus,
which sponsored the legislation initially in 1978, a severely emasculated
bill was signed into law by President Carter. In 1979, he formally de-
activated its provisions (which the legislation allowed him to do), pleading the priority of the fight against inflation, while ignoring the infla-
tion-fighting provisions of the Humphrey-Hawkins bill, and set it on the
shelf of history. What was responsible for this outcome?

First, I have argued elsewhere that one reason lay in the initial process of obtaining political commitments from presidential candidates
(Walters 1983:IV, 5). Blacks cannot secure firm policy commitments as
long as they do not have a strategy of political sanctions against Democratic presidential candidates, in an effort to counter the automatic
expectation that the Black vote will be Democratic without any commitments. In short, Carter made no substantial commitment to
Humphrey-Hawkins because he did not have to.

The other reason resides in the political strategies of he postpresi-
dential election period, and here one could say that the overriding reason why the Humphrey-Hawkins bill failed was neither the president
nor the Congress felt it to be a national priority. Nevertheless, to the
extent that the actions of pressure groups are important in developing
national agenda priorities, the Congressional Black Caucus, which initiated this bill, did not effectively mobilize the weight of Congress. Furthermore, it is even possible to argue that its institutional role was not
sufficient to allow it to develop the necessary mobilizational capacity to
raise this issue to a national priority. At this point the caucus had not
developed a strategy for widening its base beyond its fifteen or so members by influencing over eighty congressional districts with more that 20
percent Black population, and it had no viable field organization that it
controlled to produce the communication with Congress and the White
House to turn this issue into one of national scope. Lastly, the style of
mobilization for the bill depended essentially upon elite mobilization at
special meetings sponsored by the Congressional Black Caucus. Symbolic gatherings of leaders on the steps of the Capitol building substituted for genuine national demonstrations, thus the scale of mass sup-

port was severely limited. To this extent, the caucus has shown that it can mobilize elites, and was successful in mass mobilization with regard to the Martin Luther King Jr. Holiday bill. But perhaps one critical difference here is that the King bill was presented as a simple, popular piece of legislation, while the Hawkins bill was packaged as a rather complicated policy issue of appeal to a policy-oriented elite, rather than a simpler organizing issue more suited to mass mobilization.

Finally, Black institutional leadership has found that the ability to conduct successful confrontation over issues *within* an institution is not only limited by its formal rules, but by the superior political resources adversary groups can bring to bear, both by virtue of their tenure in the institution, their familiarity with its rules, and their degree of organization outside of the institution. Generally speaking, politics supersedes expertise on issues or in the use of institutional rules (even these can also be highly political resources), such that the degree to which individuals or groups have established ties to influential actors both inside and outside of a variety of institutions and with the White House will be to their advantage in the pursuit of their policy goals. This knowledge places a great deal of emphasis on the linkage of Black institutional actors with salient individuals and groups outside of their institutions, and especially the effectiveness with which the external groups are able to mobilize political resources. It also extends the range of political resources sought—depending upon the issue, considerably outside of the Black community—to other ethnic and issue-oriented mobilization groups, a fact that often results in the necessity to make temporary coalitions.[5] Information is also a political resource, and while some institutional leaders often use intellectual resources from within the Black community, others seldom do so. The profile of political resources used by institutional leaders often determines both their legitimacy and, in many cases, their effectiveness in achieving goals.

IMPLICATIONS FOR STRATEGY

Given our analysis of the potential of both noninstitutional and institutional political strategies, how do we describe the relationship between the two? To begin with, we assume that whatever the relationship Blacks have with institutions, the political history of Blacks suggests that *political strategies designed to produce large changes should be system-challenging.*[6] It was, of course, easier to conceptualize and implement such system-challenging strategies when the Black leadership was largely excluded from participation in institutions, but large-issue changes are rarely possible within institutions, and have generally come as a result of political realignment or some other such external power shift. Substantial focus should, then, be placed on generating the kind of mobilization outside institutions that makes it inescapable for institutional leadership to address large issue change as part of their priority agenda. In this regard, two suggestions are offered: (1) the adoption of a comprehensive concept of leadership function or the employment of strategies designed for large social change, and (2) the need for rationalization of the Black leadership structure in accordance with these objectives.

STRATEGIES FOR "LARGE CHANGES"

There are two schools of thought concerning the kind of mobilization that has the capacity to bring about social change that benefits people who do not possess the standard variety of power resources. One school of thought is represented by Piven and Cloward, who suggest that "whatever influence lower-class groups occasionally exert in American politics does not result from organization, but from mass protest and disruptive consequences of protest" (Fox Piven and Cloward 1977:36). This strategy essentially exploits the power inherent in alienated mass groups that have the capability to act out their frustration, often in collective ways that are threatening to systems of organized authority-institutions. Although government as a whole acted "with all deliberated speed"—that is, slowly or not at all—to rebuild damaged urban neighborhoods after the destruction of the Black rebellions of the 1960s, even those violent actions contributed to the perceived urgency of the civil rights legislative policy agenda. Nevertheless, since a major weakness of disruptive strategy is often its "disconnectness"[7] from policy issues or from organic relations with the policy system, other focused methods of change are required.

INCREMENTAL STRATEGIES

The second school of thought is that represented by Browning, Marshall, and Tabb, who argue, in a study of urban politics, that "protest is not enough," that the key to changes in policy is the process of "ethnic incorporation," which is a result of electoral mobilization where protest-demand strategies can be the catalyst. Specifically, they say that "the basic resources relevant to incorporation are size of minority population (the number and percent Black and Hispanic), supportive white population, and minority demand-protest and electoral mobilization. These resources facilitate the formation and success of multi-ethnic liberal challenging coalitions" (Browning, Marshall, and Tabb 1984:256).

In fact, if these criteria work on a local level, then they should also be viable in the arena of national politics. On the national level there was a major reinvestment in electoral strategies within the context of the Jackson campaigns of 1984 and 1988 that initiated a process of incorporation (Rainbow Coalition 1984). The coalitions of Blacks, White liberals, labor, and religious organizations, which were formed during the Jackson campaigns, set the stage for later political victories of such individuals as David Dinkins, who became mayor of New York City, and Doug Wilder, who won election as the governor of Virginia in 1989. These examples of incorporation, however, either did not last long enough to manage the issues at hand—each having lasted only four years—or in any case, their power would not have been sufficient to do so. In the case of Virginia, the size question was determinative since Blacks were only 17 percent of the population, but were nearly twice that in New York City and in neither instance of incorporation could they determine the agenda of the leader whom they helped to elect.

While most of the Browning, Marshall, and Tabb conditions are satisfied in the extent to which Blacks have invested their resources in institutional politics and electoral mobilization in the past two decades, it has been left to protest strategies to mount the requisite pressure on institutions that might cause them to take the African American agenda seriously. However, ironically, the availability of protest strategies may diminish with respect to whether or not both the race and issues of the candidate are presumed to be in favor of the constituent group. Blacks are not as disposed to launch protest demonstrations where they perceive that there may be an opportunity to have their agenda adopted through the normal course of politics, especially given the fact that individuals who look like them and share their issue concerns are in positions of influence. However, this checking factor on militant action may be just that which those who place racial minorities into ostensible positions of authority count upon in helping to arrange the peaceful processing of issues on an otherwise volatile front of politics.

The final element recommended by Browning, Marshall, and Tabb is the "supportive white population" and both locally and nationally in the 1990s such sentiment has all but disappeared, except when the non-White minorities are elected or appointed to administer an agenda that is essentially formed for the advantage of the White majority. Otherwise, the tensions are so great among the White majority, that there has been little room for a residual support of measures that have a clear benefit to non-White minorities.

The major difference between these two approaches appears to be the open question regarding the degree of change accomplished either by the process of ethnic incorporation or mass disruptive demonstrations.

In any case, it would appear that large changes at the national level must also utilize a variety of strategies in a deliberate process of interactive relationships. Any one process might include a combination of activities such as (1) protest demonstrations, (2) more effective congressional lobbying, and (3) a strategy of electoral sanction that Browning, Marshall, and Tabb do not consider. Put simply, the conceptualization of Black political strategies designed to achieve favorable public policy must be comprehensive in character by utilizing both institutional and noninstitutional methods. In addition, the use of political strategies should also be versatile and potent enough to conform to the requirement of heightening selected issues to the level of public policy priority. The comprehensive conception of political strategies would also allow more aggressive, noninstitutional strategies to be operationalized in response to objective situations that call for them.

The above conceptualization of the function of political strategy requires the rationalization of Black leadership into roles and structures that would make the operation of strategies more efficient. With regard to roles, since much of this chapter has been concerned with the limitations of institutional leadership, perhaps it should be said that the analysis here is meant as a constructive effort to gain some perspective on the practical expectations possible from major institutions and therefore the persons who are a part of them. The historic gains from the development of a class of Black institutional leaders is that when issues that affect the Black community become a part of institutional agendas, there are those in position to provide the necessary leadership. Thus, where previously Blacks were totally dependent upon the good will and leadership of others, today, at least it is a question of relative dependence. One of the logical conclusions of this point is that larger yields from the policy system are dependent upon larger actions that traditionally have been initiated by outside institutions, led by noninstitutional leaders. At least, this would appear to require a substantial reinvestment in the role of such relatively more independent and powerful leadership and organizations. But it would also mean that institutional and noninstitutional leaders should be involved in a common structure of decision-making.

There are existing leadership organizations in the Black community that are oriented toward business, religion, fraternal association, family and youth affairs, academics, civil rights, politics, and many other categories of activity. There are also more comprehensive organizations such as the National Black Leadership forum. However, the forum, an organization of thirteen of the heads of a much larger number of national Black organizations, is not well known in the Black community at large. Nevertheless, it is attempting to function in a national leadership capacity with an uncertain basis of legitimacy, which will only be acquired as it becomes further institutionalized and presents a program of leadership to the Black community for its acceptance or rejection.

The Black community urgently needs a forum for *legitimate decision-making* with an inclusive structure of membership, since without such a structure, the effective operation of a more potent strategy to achieve public policy or (more importantly) community development goals is impossible. Rationalization of the leadership structure also requires that organizations determine with greater accuracy their capability to perform certain specified roles such as mass mobilization, public policy formation and monitoring, elite mobilization, fund-raising, and so on. Given the ascendancy of institutional leaders over noninstitutional ones, and the marginal output of institutional strategies, it is important that the value of traditional, noninstitutional leadership be recognized in that the adoption of system-challenging strategies has always required a leadership as independent as possible from institutional sanction.

The elections of 1980 and 1994, more than electing Republicans to the presidency and to control of the House of Representatives and the Senate, gave continuing evidence of a profound and widening racial cleavage in society between Black and Whites (Walters 1985). This is occurring within an atmosphere perceived to be conservative and racist by most Blacks, and there are signs of real retrogression for the group in general, to the extent that 36 percent of Blacks are in officially regarded poverty (an increase of 7% since 1970) and even the middle class has lost $2,000 in average family income since the advent of the Reagan administration (Center on Budget 1984).

Whether or not there is a strategy shift at this moment in history will be largely dependent upon the actions of elements in the Black masses and the middle classes that have traditionally led them. However, it would appear that an unprecedented crisis might be created by the juxtaposition of an increasingly institutionalized Black middle class and their support for noninstitutional political strategies. However, indications in the presidential election of 1984 found that most of the Black middle class voting in support of lower-class interests continues an important trend in cohesive Black political behavior. This cohesiveness has been important in shaping the actions of a leadership class that has typically responded slowly to strategy shifts, as Louis Lomax suggested during the 1960s:

> The demonstrators have shifted the desegregation battle from the courtroom to the market place, and have shifted the main issue to one of individual dignity, rather than civil rights. This revolt, swelling under ground for the past two decades, means the end of the traditional Negro leadership class. Local organization leaders were caught

flat-footed by the demonstration; the parade had moved off without them. In a series of almost frantic moves this spring, they lunged to the front and shouted loud, but they were scarcely more than a cheering section—leaders no more. (Lomax 1970:502)

Already with the elections referred to above and the growing evidence of the exercise of power by conservative Republicans and Democrats with a punitive edge directed toward the Black community, there has still not arisen a leadership sufficient to challenge the trend in the mid-1990s. Whether or not this scenario will be played out again by the year 2000, by a leadership reluctant to accept the inevitable necessity for periodic strategy shifts, will be determined by how much they have learned about the limits of sole reliance upon institutional strategies in the pursuit of large changes in policy for the Black community. In fact, strategy shift is needed at both the national and local levels.

STRATEGY-SHIFT AT THE NATIONAL LEVEL

One model of strategy direction is related to the national level wherein the highest Black political formation, the Congressional Black Caucus (CBC), is conceived to play a basic role in ordering the participation of other national Black organizations, especially where the attempt to either enact or protect policies important to the Black community is at stake. In offering a direction, it is important to note the fundamental change in the political environment brought about by the shift from Democratic to Republican control of the dominant political institutions in the country, especially the U. S. Congress.

In the wake of the 1994 accession of the Republican Party to the control of the Congress, the power of the CBC in the House of Representatives was eclipsed. After the 1990 census' redistricting, the CBC reached forty members of the 103rd Congress, in 1992. The caucus had achieved the chairmanship of three standing committees of the House and thirteen subcommittees, and in the 103rd Congress had reached forty members, with Sen. Carol Moseley Braun, and thirty-nine members of the House, including one Republican and thirty-eight Democrats. Thus, the strength of the Caucus was based on the Democratic control of the House. In that position, it comprised 14.4 percent of the House Democratic Caucus (Bositis 1993).

However, in 1994 with the Democrats out of power, although the CBC grew to forty-one members with the addition of Republican J. C. Watts of Oklahoma, it posed the strategic dilemma of how the CBC might continue to wield power. To begin with, the numbers dropped by one, as another Republican was elected and Black Democrat Alan

Wheat left the House in order to campaign in a losing bid for a Senate seat from Missouri. Then, with the party change-over, CBC members lost three standing committee and eighteen subcommittee chairmanships as well as seats on the powerful committees on Ways and Means, Appropriations, and Rules.

SOME BASIC PROPOSITIONS

Since the committee chairmanships of the CBC were lost, the residual power of the group shifted to focus on organizing the voting power of the CBC to intervene strategically in the House Democratic Caucus, in the committees, and on the floor. In this regard some basic propositions would appear to be requisite to the continuing exercise of whatever power is possible:

1. *Unity*: Although, in the study cited above by the Joint Center for Political and Economic Studies, much was made of the thirty-eight Democratic votes in the 103rd Congress and calculations of the Joint Center show that members of CBC voted together a high percentage of the time, the group will have to exercise an even higher level of cohesion in order to maintain any influence whatsoever in the House Democratic Caucus and occasionally on the House floor.

2. *Leverage*: Second, the power of any cohesive small group lies in its independence and in its ability to become a "swing vote." *President Clinton has given every indication that he intends to move farther to the "center"—to the right in our terms. This means that the CBC votes stand in danger of being isolated, unless they become both more cohesive and more unpredictable.*

3. *Coalition Politics*: Although the thirty-eight votes of the CBC are important, the CBC should become *the true basis of a progressive coalition of votes* in the House, combining its thirty-eight votes with those of as many of the Hispanic Caucus as possible, White associate members of the CBC, Women's Caucus, and other progressives. This could amount to a number between 80 and 90 votes, large enough to be have to be consulted by both the White House and the Republican leadership and the Democrats on most issues.

4. *A Moral Voice*: After the 1994 elections, not only did the CBC lose power in the Congress, including having its funding denied as a public service caucus by the House Republican leadership, it also bore the brunt of some of the racist rage that ushered in the conservative tide. The CBC chairman, Kweisi Mfume, was reported to had said:

"While the power of the Caucus grew, so did the voices of our critics. . . . We have received literally thousands of racist threats and buckets of hate mail." Nevertheless, he asserted, "Our moral leadership will be more crucial in the months ahead of us than ever before. We have always been a voice for the most vulnerable members of our society." (Cooper 1994:A21)

ARENAS OF STRUGGLE

In the House Democratic Caucus, ironically the power of the CBC was enhanced because of the loss of other, mostly conservative Democrats. Whereas the percentage of the CBC was 14% in the 103rd, in the 104th it approached 18 percent, a substantial factor in the Democratic Caucus with nearly 20% of its members. Such a bloc of votes will have to contest for a role in deciding the agenda of the Caucus as in the past with a co-equal group of conservative Democrats who are now re-energized with conservative Republicans in control of the House.

In several subcommittees where the treatment of legislation will be most critical, the CBC itself has a membership that approached a significant level in the 103rd Congress. For example, the Joint Center study of the CBC in the 103rd Congress, referred to in table 7.2, illustrates that Blacks constituted large proportions of the representatives on several full and subcommittees. On a considerable number of subcommittees, the CBC members constituted more than 50 percent of Democratic members as shown in table 7.3.

After the 1994 elections, the ratios of Democrats to Republicans changed dramatically on most committees in order to reflect Republican dominance, but, regardless, Blacks still retained some residual influence on some votes in the full committees and some subcommittees. Therefore, the key to influence is to maximize the coherence of legislative approach both as members of the CBC and in coalition with members of the Progressive Caucus, both in joint action with the Democratic Caucus and as an independent factor.

On the floor, the key to the exercise of influence lies in being the margin of difference between blocs of votes, a process that places a premium on the development of an efficient CBC whip system. For example, in the 103rd Congress, the margin of votes between the parties in the House was 37; in the 104th Congress, it began as 27 votes (with 1 Independent and 1 vacancy) and ended up as 39 because of the shifts from Democrat to Republican by several members. By the 105th Congress, the margin was 21 votes (1 Independent and 1 vacancy), which means that theoretically, the CBC, with 37 votes could exercise

TABLE 7.2
Percent Blacks of Democratic Members,
Selected House Standing Committees 103rd Congress

Standing Committees	Percent
District of Columbia	62.5*
Post Office and Civil Service	46.7*
Government Operations	40.0
Small Business	33.3
Banking, Finance, and Urban Affairs	23.3
Ways and Means	20.8

*These two full committees were abolished by the Republicans when they took over the House in 1995.

TABLE 7.3
Percent Blacks of Democratic Members,
Selected House Subcommittees of the 103rd Congress

Subcommittee	Percent
Judiciary and Education	50
Select Education and Civil Rights	60
Human Resources and Inter-Government Affairs	60
Postal Operations and Service	100
Minority Enterprise, Finance, and Urban Development	75
Oversight (Ways and Means)	57

powerful influence over straight party votes if it signaled that it would break with the Democratic Party. However, the fact that the Democratic Party is already fractured into groups such as the progressives, moderates, and the "Blue Dog" conservative wing reduces the influence of the CBC on most votes.

CAUCUS ORGANIZATION

Expanded Committee Structure

One of the positive features of the CBC has been the maintenance of its own committee structure, apart from whatever formal committee assignments were maintained by its members. In this atmosphere, this alternative structure of committee organization may be vital. Nevertheless, it is important to devise a more elaborate structure of committees within the framework of the CBC in order for the traditional allies and policy constituencies of the CBC to have a structure through which they are able to continue to communicate and assist in the process of policy mobilization.

Remobilization of the Brain Trust

In the current conservative atmosphere, the CBC will need to mobilize an external constituency to provide the kind of pressure on the political system that it may not be able to generate internally. It is anticipated that the nature of the conflicts will be intense and the stakes vital, and therefore the larger Black community must be included in the struggle to retain aspects of their quality of life where the federal government has been responsible for providing resources. Therefore:

1. *The Brain Trusts* (informal advisors to CBC committttees) may provide a mechanism for expanded outreach to the Black and other communities where policy expertise and mobilization of resources are necessary. Members of some of the various Brain trusts have played such a role as individuals and in small groups, but this situation dictates an expanded and more aggressive utilization of their potential contribution. Increasingly, however, the brain trust should take on an economic support mobilization, especially among Black professionals in their sphere of operations in order to finance campaigns to protect and enhance legislation.

2. *The Black Leadership Roundtable (NBLR)* was a workable form of organization that included over two hundred heads of Black national organizations that were helpful in policy mobilization during the Reagan administration. This group should be revived as an external arm of the CBC that will assist with the process of information dissemination and contact with local political officials with respect to current legislative initiatives. I will discuss the value of the NBLR in the next chapter.

3. *The CBC Foundation*: It is obvious that in this more conservative era in the Congress, the CBC Foundation will have to play a much more vigorous role as a separate organization involved in research and policy development. The advent of the CBC Research Institute in 1990 was a significant undertaking, but needs to be revived in order to mobilize the substantial research infrastructure of scholars nationally who are located in universities and other research orga-

nizations. It will also need sophisticated communications capability to be able to access such individuals and computerized sources of information, and to disseminate information as well.

STRATEGY SHIFT AND COMMUNITY DEVELOPMENT

If the thesis is accepted that the impact of the rise of institutional leadership in the Black community in the 1970s was powerful in that it oriented strategies toward grappling successfully with external institutions, then perhaps it will also be accepted that for the past two decades, the focus on the use of external mechanisms of power in order to affect policy and institutional positions have overbalanced the Black agenda in that direction.

A strategy shift, however, toward more direct involvement in local leadership should be immediately undertaken in light of the fact that the most urgent and primary task of Black leadership is the *internal* reconstruction of the Black community through strengthening its *common frame of reference* to enable it to achieve control over those factors vital to its survival and development. What is meant by "common frame of reference?"

To begin with, every kind of community has a common social, economic, political, and cultural frame of reference that, in fact, defines it as a unique collectivity rather than isolated individuals. However, if we take the definitions provided by Professor Andrew Billingsley, the Black community is a social system where people share norms, expectations, and sentiments, and where the members are held together by shared values and goals. The coherence of the Black community in particular is held together both by the forces of racial oppression as well as a history of common experiences and the evolution of a distinct shared culture. Most people who live together share a set of common institutions and behave toward the outside world in a similar fashion (Billingsley 1992:65–74).

Billingsley also suggests that in a significant segment of the Black community, Black families are in crisis from a "cluster of conditions with devastating consequences" such as poverty, teen pregnancy, homicide, crime, stress, divorce, unemployment, and the like (Billingsley 1992:69). This view is generally supported in a national survey on African American life by Professor James Jackson of the University of Michigan. He calls these "grim" data that are part of the pattern of persistent exclusion from American life that affects African Americans in many ways (Jackson 1991:264–73).

The primary aspect of this proposition is not unique to Blacks but is found in all ethnic or racial leadership as a normal aspect of their function in protecting the integrity of their group. New initiatives should begin with the understanding that the common frame of reference of the Black community has been weakened to the point of destruction in some cases. It has been weakened by such factors, or examples, as:

1. Dependence upon external social agencies for needed support (for whatever reason) reoriented dependence outside of the community and developed external authority figures.
2. Integrated public accommodations and services have been beneficial, but have also destroyed Black businesses and other institutions by the decision of Blacks not to patronize them for one reason or another.
3. The physical destruction of the Black community in the rebellions of the 1960s was often not repaired and many services were not resumed.
4. Affluence enabled many middle-income Blacks to move out of the inner city, taking skills, economic resources, and leadership with them.
5. Gentrification has attacked the lower-income spectrum of the community, uprooting and scattering Blacks to other neighborhoods.
6. Competition for the mind and energies of Blacks is taking place in the invitations to become involved in drugs, cults, gangs, negative consumerism, television-level information consumption, and other nonpositive activities.

These illustrative factors and many others are responsible for creating the cancer eating away at the body of the Black community, making it too ill to provide the support and protection needed by its members in difficult periods. Perhaps, one day, when the thoroughly integrated middle-class millennium arrives, such an emphasis upon community will not be necessary, but given the common resources available, even in an unorganized state, the community should be utilized for more than a mere place of residence and psychosocializing. Thus, the resulting damage to the common frame of reference is important, since it is this reference that provides the perspective that indeed there is a community of interests among a certain people, with a shared history, culture, and objectives and a way of responding to the world that, while it is not the same for all Blacks, may nevertheless be widely understood by them.

Thus, the urgency to assume the purported tasks is created by the deterioration in the status of the general Black community as a direct result of federal government policy and the failure to adopt internal strategies leading to increased self-reliance. With regard to the former, we have already mentioned that budget and tax policies of the "Reagan Revolution" have provoked considerable decline in the Black standard of living.

Moreover, in the 1990s, there is the passage of welfare reform, a reform that has actually eliminated welfare as an entitlement, replacing it with a five-year limitation on benefits and a work requirement and other measures. This new program has also been "devolved" to the states, in that the funding and authority to manage the new social program has been passed to state governments. However, the inadequacy of the funding for day-care and other factors that would make work a viable option for many, the limitations of the duration on public assistance, and the possibility that racially motivated intentions may visit the impact of the punitive aspects of the new programs upon the Black community disproportionally, may lead to a substantial growth in poverty and lack of income among Blacks (see, e.g., Edelman 1997).

Thus, the "devolution" of many social programs, such as welfare and some housing programs, may present many more challenges to local government and to the vulnerable communities in those areas. This presents a logical focus of leadership to shift strategies to shore up such communities by giving far more attention to politics and policies of state governments and their impact on localities.

The requirement, therefore, is to limit the damage by mounting new initiatives that stabilize the community and provide new resources for advancement, with a balanced approach that continues to direct strategies toward major local institutions, but that also develops strategies that organize internal community resources and utilizes them toward common, achievable objectives.

LOCAL ACTIONS

At the local level around the country, leadership organizations are active in attempting to initiate action on behalf of the Black community and here we will only refer to them as suggestive of a much wider pattern of activity. For example, a "Leadership Summit" was held in Suitland, Maryland, a suburb of Washington, D.C., in early May 1997, for the purpose of attracting community leaders, local council members, and state officials to devise a long-term strategy to establish programs to assist businesses in the areas and priorities for services needed by the community around the "Suitland Action Plan" ("Leadership Summit" 1997:A6). The result of the meeting was similar to that in Buffalo, New York, where on April 5, more than two hundred people attended a meeting of grassroots organizations to express their concerns to Mayor Masiello about many of the most pressing problems facing the inner city of Buffalo around the theme of "A Grassroots Agenda for Buffalo's Future" ("Grassroots" 1997:3). And the names of the organizations present at the meeting was an indication of what kind of units are active in the community; they included: the Hamlin Park Taxpayers Association, the Afro-American Police Association, Men of Color Helping All (Black firefighters), the League of Muslim Women, the Masten Neighborhood Advisory Council, the Delavan/Grider Block Club Association, the Masten Block Club Coalition, and the Concerned Citizens. Moreover the meeting voiced concerns about leadership accountability in both the public and private sectors with respect to issues of race, questionable racial hiring practices by the city, the closing of street-level open-air drug markets, the addition of police patrols and detectives to high-crime areas, and the resolution of the high number of unsolved homicides. Finally, in the space of one week, community activists, led by the Richmond, Virginia NAACP chapter, protested against Governor George Allen at a mid-day rally for having issued a proclamation making April Confederate History and Heritage Month, to honor Confederates who fought between 1861 to 1865 (to preserve slavery) ("Anti-Allen Protest" 1997:A1). A few days later, local activists picketed the Richmond Convention Center when former President George Bush came to speak, alleging that as vice president and titular head of the "Drug War" in the mid-1980s, Bush allowed the massive distribution of drugs into the poor and minority communities by the CIA (ibid., A3).

These are some brief indications of community activism in selected areas in the spring of 1997, and although it is a random selection, and the sample is small, still it gives some evidence that vital aspects of leadership responsibility are still occurring at the local level, even more vital than at the national level, where it is often difficult to experience strong concerted action for reasons I will continue to explore in later chapters.

CONCLUSION

I have attempted to present both an analysis of the historical evolution of strategy shifts and a model of an agenda for future strategies addressed to the local and national arenas that answers the question of which direction might be suggested as fruitful for the Black community. In that regard, it assumes that through the consistent attention of leaders to the problems that arise in such arenas and their effective use of strategies, the deleterious effects upon the Black community of the current policies or any future such policies would be considerably softened.

In this regard, it is possible to suggest, on the basis of the barest of evidence presented above, that the argument for the *necessity of a strategy shift at the national level* is a sign that it has not occurred, at least not sufficiently, while there is considerable evidence that in localities there is growing leadership activity with respect to a number of issues.

In subsequent chapters I will seek to elaborate in greater detail the responsibilities of Black leaders to shift to new models of strategies, addressing both the local and national arenas and considering such issues as the National Black Leadership Roundtable in Chapter 8 and militant Black leadership in Chapter 9.

CHAPTER 8

The National Black Leadership Roundtable

One of the more significant, yet less well-known experiments, in devising a national leadership structure for African Americans was expressed in the tenure of the National Black Leadership Roundtable (NBLR 1977–91). An outgrowth of the activists' period early in the development of the Congressional Black Caucus, the roundtable sought to devise a framework for the incorporation of national Black organizations into the task of mobilizing as many Blacks as possible through the mechanism of their membership to support the caucus policy agenda. I will describe the evolution, structure and mobilizing activities of the NBLR and provide a critique of the organization's existence and the reasons for its demise.

THE DISTRICT OF COLUMBIA HOME RULE CASE

One of the earlier successes of the Congressional Black Caucus members was the role they played in obtaining home rule for the District of Columbia. In January of 1973, Charles Diggs became chairman of the House Committee on the District of Columbia and promptly introduced a bill (H.R. 9682) to provide home rule for the District of Columbia in February. Shortly after the bill was voted out of committee in July, a plan was formulated for obtaining the necessary votes for passage. It included Diggs, as the manager of the internal House lobbying effort, through liaison with the White House and the congressional leadership; Brock Adams (D-WA) as floor manager in the House; and Congressman Walter Fauntroy, Delegate from the District of Columbia, as the person to mobilize external support for the measure in key congressional districts. It was this latter activity that was most important for the formation of the NBLR.[1]

A whip list was developed that contained the congresspersons most likely to support the bill and immediately it revealed a sizeable number of congressmen from southern and border states who had made no commitment to support it and many of these districts contained a significant number of Black voters. The Joint Center for Political Studies released a listing in 1973 showing that there were 58 congressional districts with 25 percent or more Black population and 37 were in the South. Some of these districts were in Deep South states such as Mississippi, where considerable civil rights activity had taken place and where the Black vote was swiftly increasing.[2]

By the end of August, Congressman Fauntroy had developed a strategy designed to influence reluctant southern and border state congresspersons to vote for the bill, the essence of which was a classic lobbying activity. His staff would contact as many organizations as possible in those districts of recalcitrant members and ask them to contact their member and urge them to support the pending Home Rule bill. The strategy contained the following measures:

1. Lists of contacts of national Black organizations such as Black elected officials, clergy, civil rights activists, and others was developed and the membership broken down into congressional districts, conforming to the target list of forty-two Congressional districts in fifteen southern and border states.

2. Then, a profile of each district was developed to reveal the Black voting strength compared to the representative's margin of electoral victory and the president's margin of victory in the 1972 national elections. This helped to yield information concerning the member's vulnerability to appeals for support.

3. Letters were sent by Congressman Fauntroy to all Black elected officials and other members in the identified coalition organizations that explained the issue and asked the recipient to write his or her Congressman requesting them to support home rule for the District of Columbia and to send a copy of the letter to his office in Washington, D.C.

4. Volunteers were assigned to make follow-up calls to those to whom letters were sent, asking if they had received the letter and reminding them to send copies to Washington. This way, corrections could be made for erroneous addresses, telephone numbers, and other content. Using this method, more than five hundred responses were generated in the fifteen-state area.

5. Tallies of the replies were kept daily and fed into the congressional whip system that had been established for action on the bill. By prompt tallying, members of the CBC would, then, know which votes had moved into category of "firm," "wavering," and so on, and consequently which votes had to be pursued next.

One example of the success of the lobbying was David Bowen, whose 2nd Congressional District in Mississippi was 45.9% Black with a 39% Black voting-age population. However, he previously had voted against the caucus 66% of the time on issues of importance to Blacks and as of late September, he had also not indicated his position on home rule.

Congressman Fauntroy sent letters to thirty-two Black elected officials in Bowen's district and achieved a response from eight or 25 percent and Fauntroy received copies of the letters that illustrated that some effective communication had taken place and that Bowen had responded to each letter. The result was that when the bill was voted on Bowen voted for it.

The bill passed in the House (343-74) and eventually was signed into law by President Nixon. However, the large margin of victory may indicate that other factors played a role other than the lobbying strategy. Whether the lobbying was decisive or not, it provided a model of leadership that could be effective and that required the cooperation of national organizations. On the other hand, this lobbying activity, which was formalized as the "Action Alert Network," was deeply resented by some House members as having violated the collegial rules of the House against campaigning or lobbying by House members in each other's districts, and rules of the House were passed that forbade such activity. This meant that an "outside" organization would have to perform such a task in the future.

STARTING THE NBLR

A major innovation in the early development of the Congressional Black Caucus was the formation by Congressman Parren Mitchell of "brain trusts" on a variety of issues. This became a mechanism for mobilizing the ideas and involvement of the new professional class of Blacks, many of whom, like Congressman Mitchell of Baltimore, were interested in Black business development. This became a standard way for the caucus to interact with Blacks outside of the Congress and to claim a mass following that enhanced their legitimacy. Thus, following the precedent of Mitchell's business brain trust, thirteen other such groups were created in relatively quick succession.

Congressman Fauntroy created a "Political Participation Brain Trust" and by 1974 this group, together with that directed by Mitchell were, what Congressman William Clay called, "the most significant programmatic strategy embraced by the CBC" at that time, which "gave the Caucus a level of parity with other political powers in the House of Representatives" (Clay 1992:269). By July 1977, brain trust meetings had been held in four areas: (1) Black voter participation; (2) aged, health, education; (3) communication, criminal justice; (4) international affairs (Political Participation Brain Trust 1977).

It was the 1976 meeting of the Political Participation Brain Trust of about a hundred persons in Washington, D.C., during the annual CBC weekend where Fauntroy raised the question of replicating the success of the home rule legislative case by bringing together a much larger group of national Black organizations to operate not just in the area of political participation, but in other policy areas as well.

The NBLR was authorized by the Political Participation Brain Trust in 1976 and on September 24, 1977, the Voter Participation Brain Trust of the CBC accepted the responsibility to draft a specific proposal for the structure and function of the NBLR ("Preview" 1976). Subsequently, a meeting was held in December of 1977, and its first formal structure was adopted.[3] The theory for operation of the NBLR was based on the model of the District of Columbia home rule fight, which Fauntroy called the "arithmetic of power." This theory held that where Blacks constituted either the majority or a significant impact on the electoral fortunes of a member of Congress, there was potential policy influence that could be marshaled to discipline the member to be accountable to the interests of the Black constituency. Fauntroy used the term as follows:

> The nation witnessed the impact of Black political strength when it saw Black voters deliver the margin of victory to Jimmy Carter last year. We mastered the *arithmetic of power* in the 1976 presidential election; let us further develop and refine the power as a tool in local, state and national elections; let's use it also here on Capitol Hill and in the state houses to protect the gains we've made thus far, as well as secure new strategies to meet the social and economic needs of the people of our country.[4]

In fact, the theory could also have been regarded as the "geometry of power" because it depended upon the interaction of three diagrammatic variables. The vehicle for this was the "Action Alert Network," a CBC staff operation that developed a computerized listing of names of influential Blacks by congressional district, many of whom were members of large national Black organizations. They would constitute a support network on key legislative issues. Thus, either through direct contact between the managers of the network or through the national organizations, or both, such groups could be mobilized to impact on legislation. In fact, the CBC did develop an activity known as the "Action Alert Network" as a part of its staff responsibilities.

The meeting of July 18, 1977 was critical inasmuch as it laid the foundation for an attempt by the Congressional Black Caucus to exercise more activist strategies that would involve many thousands of Black people outside of the Congress in its effort to initiate a policy agenda. Some key results of this meeting were commitments to maintain the Action Alert Network, the development of a "Black political plan" as well as journalist and former congressional aide Chuck Stone's recommendation for a National Black Leadership Summit on the crisis in Black America. Both the ideas of the summit and the "plan" would be crucial to the development of the NBLR.

In any case, preparations for the initiation of the Black Leadership Roundtable were begun in January of 1978 and the first meeting was held on March 11 and the primary policy mobilization became H.R. 50, the Humphrey-Hawkins Bill on Full Employment and Balanced Growth ("CBC Staff" 1978). This had been the main item on the agenda of the CBC since May 20, 1975, when the CBC held an important hearing on full employment—"Toward Full Employment: A Viable Economic Goal"—which initiated this policy campaign ("Congressional Black Caucus" 1975).

The second major meeting of 1978, however, was held on July 15, and the fact that caucus chairman, Parren Mitchell, played such a prominent role in initiating the call for Black leaders to meet and in setting the agenda was an important indicator of its intended prominence in caucus affairs. The first item on the agenda was the roundtable structure, and various forms of organization were considered; however, the model of the business roundtable was chosen on a recommendation by Ken Amos a Washington, D.C. former IBM business executive who had been a member of that group. The idea evolved to invite the CEOs of 300–400 heads of major Black organizations to become members and to organize them into the various issues—areas on the CBC agenda.[5]

On February 24, 1979, the National Black Leadership Roundtable held a meeting of two hundred heads of organizations in Washington, D.C., to discuss the president's proposed budget reductions in the Comprehensive Education and Training Act (CETA), a job training program (−15.2%), low-income housing (−18%), social security benefits (−3%), nutrition programs, health programs, and others. A subsequent emergency meeting of the NBLR together with other organizations was held on April 23–24 to stimulate opposition to President Carter's budget cuts ("For the People" 1979). On this occasion, the traditional methods were utilized, such as office visitations; however, Fauntroy earlier had urged all participants, by letter, to "write, phone and send telegrams to your representative and senators in opposition to the domestic budget cuts which the President had recommended" (Fauntroy 1979). Other suggested strategies included:

- Meetings by community leaders with each U.S. representative and senator from the area to express opposition to the budget cuts;

- Meetings with mayors, county officials and governors to determine the local impact of budget cuts;

- Statements to the press in opposition to the budget cuts. ("Suggested" 1979)

In 1979, the CBC hired a full-time director of Action Alert Network development who spearheaded a southern regional conference in June of that year. This was predicated on the fact that the strength of the Black population was concentrated most in many southern congressional districts and that, if the recalcitrance of southern legislators could be broken, the caucus agenda would have much broader support. Therefore, one hundred of these districts with White representatives and high Black populations were targeted for action in eleven southern states. Attendance at the conference was substantial, since the 150 National Black organizations were asked to designate delegates and one thousand attended, most coming, however, from Alabama.

The primary objective of this meeting was to institute the National Action Alert Communications Network in the southern congressional districts, and in this, the NBLR emerged as the key mobilizing agent. The overall strategy of the CBC was operationalizing its agenda by utilizing the dynamic ingredient of national organizations with a grassroots base, which drew wide support from the delegates. In a subsequent report on the Southern Regional Forum, Walter Fauntroy defined the purpose of the network as follows:

> The purpose of this network will be to assist Black organizations and individuals in following the actions of the public officials whom they elect, and to alert Black people when those elected officials need to hear from their Black constituents before they vote or otherwise take actions that affect the quality of life in Black America.

The mechanical task of the national Black organizations was to break down their membership into the relevant congressional districts and designate a "point-person" for the organization in the said district to mobilize others when called upon to do so. He further indicated that the network had been most effective in defeating an antibusing amendment in the summer of 1979. This amendment would have prohibited the assignment of pupils to schools farther than the nearest school to their home for any reason ("Working" 1979).

A survey of the delegates was taken at the Southern Regional Forum and the 30 percent of the conferees who responded felt that Congress was doing only a fair (54.7%) job on the whole, that

Congress was doing a poor job (63.2%) for Blacks, that President Carter was doing fair (56.2%) on the whole, that President Carter was doing a poor (47.2%) job for Black Americans, and that the Congressional Black Caucus was doing an excellent (25.8%) or good (45.1%) job ("A Report" 1979).

The NBLR response to the *Bakke* decision of the Supreme Court was testimony to the growing conception of the vital role it could play. By the July meeting, the *Bakke* case had been decided and it was a primary item on the NBLR agenda, as well as other issues such as the Proposition 13 California ballot initiative on taxes, Black College Financial Assistance, the firing of UN Ambassador Andrew Young, the Human Rights of the "Wilmington Ten" (civil rights activists imprisoned in Wilmington, North Carolina), and Black participation in the Democratic National Committee. To these issues were added updates on the CBC Legislative issues of Humphrey-Hawkins, urban policy, minority enterprise, and African developments.

The NBLR continued in 1980 to develop into a formidable network of communication and policy strength for the caucus. The Democratic National Committee held an Issues Forum Convention in the summer of 1980 and an NBLR meeting was organized at that meeting to continue to mobilize organizations. Evidence of the growth of NBLR was undeniable. In the spring of 1979 there were only 31 network volunteers, but by contrast there were 8,000 by the end of 1980, having a potential reach of 1.9 million Black voters in 96 Congressional districts with 15 percent or more Black population who constituted the potential margin of victory in congressional elections. Nevertheless, the September meeting of the NBLR was focused on mobilization for both the 1982 budget and "get out the vote" activities for the fall national elections ("For the People" 1980). Moreover, in December, Walter Fauntroy, head of the NBLR, had also become the elected chairman of the Congressional Black Caucus itself.

THE REAGAN ERA

As it became clear that the policies of the new administration of President Ronald Reagan would further threaten Black interests, the Congressional Black Caucus would accordingly intensify its policy mobilization to protect policies that it advocated. One major theme of the CBC in the early 1980s became that of "the Black Leadership Family"; however, it was a theme without an ideology until Walter Fauntroy conceived of "The Black Leadership Family Plan." It was clear from earlier sessions of the NBLR, Fauntroy intended to respond directly to the admonition of Ossie Davis, keynote speaker at the inaugural dinner of the caucus in 1971. Davis' remarks on that occasion were entitled, "The Plan, Not the Man," and in his speech, he appealed to the CBC to

> give us a plan of action. . . . A Ten Black Commandments, simple, strong, that we can carry in our hearts and incur memories no matter where we are and reach out and touch and feel the reassurance that there is behind everything we do a simple, moral, intelligent plan that must be fulfilled in the course of time even if all of our leaders, one by one, fall in battle. Somebody will rise and say "Brother! Our leader died while we were on page three of the plan. Now that the funeral is over, let us proceed to page four." (Clay 1992:167)

This powerfully evocative thought was the basis for the development of the "Black Leadership Family Program for the Survival and Progress of the Black Nation," which was constructed by a subcommittee of the NBLR headed by Washington, D.C. businessman Theodore Adams. The first draft was completed in November 1981 and the final document was issued in February 1982 ("Black Leadership" 1982). The document embodied a variety of purposes, as a summary of the ideology of the caucus, an overall blueprint of the political objectives of the Black community, a description of some enabling tactics, and a guide to programmatic operations of Black organizations in public policy. As such, its stated purpose was to:

1. Develop a basic set of rules by which Black Americans can live.
2. Establish a Black development fund.
3. Provide a set of instructions for implementation of the plan.
4. Establish an Action Alert Communications Network for Black people throughout the nation.

Twelve goals or rules were set forth that included such items as: Protect the elderly and support the youth; register and vote; support the religion of your choice; report crime; contribute to the Black Defense Fund; buy and bank Black; know your elected officials; boycott negative media; support Black family and community life; support Black defense organizations; support Mother Africa; excel in education. These rules were theoretically assigned to various categories of "Receiving Organizations" such as labor, religious, and so on, according to the content of the rule to implement with a stated mission.

The plan was to be funded by a Black Development Fund and administered by an Implementation Council. The fund would be created by individual contributions from each Black person who would be asked to contribute one dollar to any of the twelve categories of work outlined in the Black Family Plan. Fauntroy believed that if Blacks would contribute just one percent of their income per year, it would yield the fund $1.4 billion to fund the various activities of the organization. His view of the product of such funding was that:

> Five or six years down the road we would be functioning as an extended family. Leadership would be working together on a number of overriding issues that can best be addressed by all of our various institutions working in concert. As a result of that kind of leadership and cooperation at the state and local level, the various institutions would be cooperating more on projects and activities that improve the quality of life for Blacks. (Raspberry 1982:11)

The redesigned structure of the NBLR anticipated this by its designation of a Vice President for Implementation, whose function was to give programmatic direction to the national and local projects adopted by the organization. Indeed, the implementation of the work of network development extended to interaction with state and local groups.

At the local level, a number of cities developed citywide leadership structures in the 1970s. For example, the Detroit Association of Black Organizations (DABO) was founded in 1979, and, thus, provided both an affiliate structure and base for the sponsorship of the Third Annual Roundtable Conference in 1987. In any case, there were other such local groups affiliated with the NBLR. One such group was the Columbus (Ohio) Black Convention. The first convention took place in 1980, sponsored by ten community organizations that became the Federation of Community Organizations, headed by Khari Enaharo ("The 1982 Black Convention"). The disseminated Program of the Convention contained the Rules of the Black Family Plan and the Operational Instructions, and the keynote speaker was Walter Fauntroy, who had taken on the role of distributing the plan as widely as possible.

The Columbus Black convention became a citywide organization designed to implement the resolution adopted in the conventions. For this reason, the method of the limiting the number of priority goals, assigning responsibility for their implementation to specific groups, and attempting to achieve measurable success was similar to the design set forth in the Black Family Plan.

Several state organizations eventually became affiliated with the NBLR and some, such as the Illinois and the Kansas Black Leadership Roundtables, adopted the structure of the national organization and the plan as their basic working document. Other organizations evolved their own statewide leadership structure, closely patterned on the NBLR but unique to their own requirements. One of the most important was the New Jersey Black Issues Convention (NJBIC). Newark City Councilman Donald

Tucker, president of the National Black Caucus of Local Elected Officials, and a member of the NBLR, responded to the network and the organizational implications of the NBLR thrust in forming the convention:

> The Convention is designed to be a forum for the exchange of information among the Black organizations, the Black elected officials to establish an ongoing dialogue with Black professionals, civic, social and economic organizations around issues critically effecting the Black community. (Tucker 1983)

The convention addressed issues of both local and national importance and in the newsletter prepared for it, one finds displayed the purpose and rules of the Black Leadership Family Plan and a statement that the NJBIC "had adopted the goals for implementing the Plan" ("UPDATE" 1983). Donald Payne, then a member of the Newark City Council and an important actor in the formation of NJBIC was an early member of the CBC International Affairs Brain Trust and was elected to Congress in November 1988 and became CBC chairman in 1994. Thus, the NJBIC, which still exists at this writing and has been an effective communication vehicle between Black political organizations at the state level in New Jersey, has a legacy that extends to the NBLR.

REORGANIZATION OF THE NBLR

The NBLR was reorganized in 1983 as an independent organization separate from the CBC, with its own by-Laws and elected board of directors. The officers included:

President

Vice President for Public Policy

Vice President for Political Participation

Vice President for Finance

Vice President for Implementation of the Black Leadership Family Plan

Secretary

Treasurer

This structure reflected the fact that the key activities of the organization would be focused on policy, political participation, and fundraising, with the plan as a general guide to the organization's activities. The Implementation Council had also been created for the purpose of operationalizing the plan and as the reorganization team for the entire

NBLR structure. It decided upon a dues structure, staff needs, and regional workshops to focus on Black leadership, and proposed a close relationship to the Black Leadership Forum (BLF). This latter organization of thirteen top Black organizational leaders in various fields (such as civil rights, mayors, CBC head, local elected officials, fraternal, religious and labor leaders, etc.) had come into existence in the Carter administration to push for policy at the White House level largely behind the scenes. In the debate over the relationship between the two organizations, a proposal was made that the NBLR would relate to the BLF as its mobilizing organization with the BLF as the executive committee and the acknowledged "parent" leadership (Fauntroy 1983). However, this proposal was rejected by the forum and the two organizations remained separate entities.

Strengthening the NBLR would be important, since several crucial events in 1983 would underscore the need for a national leadership organization. The Reorganization Report was finally adopted on June 11 and issues were considered such as the People's Platform, the NBLR Voter Registration Program, the Black presidential candidacy, and the 20-year anniversary of the March on Washington. Several of these political issues would involve the NBLR directly.

First, the mobilization for the twenty-year anniversary of the March on Washington was being planned with the creation of a "People's Platform" document of priority issues to accompany it and to be the guiding policy document for the following year's electoral activities. In order to facilitate this, Fauntroy called into existence a new "Coalition of Conscience" as the organizing force for the march, set for August 27, which constructed the theme of "Jobs, Peace and Freedom." The NBLR was a part of this mobilization, however, as its own coalition of Black organizations had reached 150, it wanted to participate in the shaping of the People's Platform more fundamentally and this eventually occurred. Eventually the platform became a joint statement of the Black Coalition for 1984 (the Black Leadership Forum) and the National Black Leadership Roundtable.

Second, there was the nascent activity with respect to the emergence of Rev. Jesse Jackson as a candidate for the Democratic nomination for president in 1984. The Black Leadership Forum took the leadership on the issue of a Black presidential candidacy for 1984 and held a series of meetings. At the decisive meeting held in Chicago on April 30, 1983, Congressman Fauntroy was present and this writer, secretary of the NBLR, reported that a survey of the organization revealed that over 80 percent of the organizations supported the idea of a Black presidential candidacy.[6] The result of the meeting was revealed in the following consensus statement:

> We reaffirm our position that a Black seeking the Democratic nomina-
> tion for the presidency of the United States is a viable option. We
> affirm the necessity of a candidacy for the Presidency which focuses the
> Nation's attention on the urgent needs of our cities as well as our
> depressed rural areas, our poor, our ailing economy, and the erosion
> of our rights.
>
> We find no reason why competent, dedicated leaders should elim-
> inate themselves from consideration because they happen to be Black.
>
> We now accelerate the process of voter registration, issue forma-
> tion, and delegate organization in pursuing such a candidacy.
>
> Finally, in the process, we shall consult with other Black business,
> political, religious, civic and fraternal leaders as well as with Hispanic,
> women, and labor leaders in order to insure broad and representative
> participation in this process. ("Statement" 1983)

Subsequently, the NBLR and the Political Science Department at
Howard University sponsored a forum, "The Black Presidential Candidacy: Issues and Strategies," chaired by Congressman Fauntroy, which
facilitated a vigorous public airing of the idea of a Black presidential
candidacy.[7] Thus, the NBLR was one of the vehicles for the mobilization
of support for the eventual candidacy of Rev. Jesse Jackson in the early
phase of this movement.

Third, as the statement above indicates, there was the full realiza-
tion of the depth of the impact the conservative movement was making
on legislation in the Congress. In a communication that went out to a
number of leaders requesting that they sponsor a statewide Black leadership meeting, Congressman Fauntroy said that one of the goals of such
meetings was to evaluate the draft of the "People's Platform" in light of
"actions that an administration would be expected to take to reverse the
'Heritage Foundation' type executive actions that the Reagan Administration has taken designed to 'defang' civil rights enforcement and to
'de-fund' the left" (Fauntroy 1983).

To respond to the Reagan administration's elimination of CETA,
the CBC, led by Congressman August Hawkins, formulated H.R. 1036,
the Community Renewal Employment Act, which called for spending
$3.5 billion on jobs. The bill recognized the national unemployment rate
stood at 9%, but to this constituted nearly 20% in the Black community, and whereas in 1979, the unemployment rate was 5.8% and those
unemployed for fifteen weeks or more constituted 1.2 million, by 1983,
it was 10% and 4.4 million (CBC Fact Sheet 1983). And although at a
press conference with the Democratic leadership in the House and Senate, Hawkins indicated that there were two hundred firm votes for passage in the House, it ultimately went down to defeat ("Democratic
Leaders" 1983:A4).

A "NATIONAL BLACK PARLIAMENT"

The Implementation Council of the NBLR continued to promote an activist set of programs for the coalition of Black organizations it led, such that in 1984, virtually the entire set of officers and staff and many of its key state leaders became pivotal figures in the campaign of Rev. Jesse Jackson for president. Nevertheless, the council sponsored a new model of operation in 1984 that consisted of its aim that the NBLR become the "national Black parliament," a representative assembly composed of the heads of major Black organizations who would come together annually to discuss critical issues and, according to the plan, adopt resolutions and programmatic ideas by consensus, and take responsibility for achieving measurable progress until the next meeting. The form of the annual conference consisted of plenary sessions where the issues were presented; this dissolved into "interfaces" where, according to the categories of organizations in the plan, leaders debated issues and devised solutions. These solutions were then presented to a final plenary and adopted. As this model was operationalized, the 1985 and 1986 conferences clearly became the high point in the organization and leadership of the NBLR.

The first conference with the new format was held March 14–16, 1985, and drew over three hundred leaders, doubling the previous base of 150 organizations of the roundtable. And without a review of the myriad recommendations presented by each of the "interface" sessions, it is clear that one theme running through most of them was the urgency created by the assault of the Reagan administration on most of the agenda of the NBLR, from policy resource programs in housing and urban development, employment, health, education, and minority business development, to the complex of civil rights issues represented by affirmative action and minority business set-asides. Thus, the resolutions and plans of action cited the actions of the administration in these fields and proposed action to protect existing programs or initiate new ones.

The character of the NBLR, as it emerged from the CBC, should naturally be conceived to have a strong public policy orientation. However, an equal portion of its activities were directed toward the enhancement of the coherence of the Black community goals and the quality of Black leadership. Indeed, Fauntroy had issued a memorandum to the NBLR board before the conference and, in suggesting the themes that should guide the thinking about the meeting, he posed a vital question to be addressed: "What can we do for ourselves?" His view was expressed as follows: "We must make a historical covenant with ourselves that the freedom and dignity of our people, while recognizing the responsibilities of other institutions, rest essentially upon what we do ourselves, and how seriously we have taken the mantle of leadership and self-determination" (Fauntroy 1985).

What was also clear from the March 1986 meeting was that the NBLR had adopted a more sophisticated set of conference rules that allowed for debate within the interfaces and the development of reports to the plenary body of two types: those recommendations the interface members would carry out among themselves, and those they would recommend for action by the entire roundtable. The latter category were debated in plenary session and adopted by vote of the roundtable members. The adopted recommendations would then be passed on to the board of directors for implementation. At the board level, a "sorting" process would occur that would assign the recommendations on to the relevant vice president or to the staff.

Finally, it was clear that the roundtable had grown in the organizational strength of its coalition and in the extension of its reach. By 1985, the goal was adopted of convening six new roundtables by the end of the year in such states as Illinois, California, Louisiana, Massachusetts, Missouri, and Ohio. In fact, concrete steps had been taken in most of these states, which would join New Jersey and North Carolina, which had already submitted their requests for charter membership (NBLR 1985/86:10).

KEY INTERFACE ISSUES

In this connection, an important recommendation that was also not directed toward government policies originated in the Professional Affairs Interface and was concerned with leadership development. The proposal, which marked the beginning of the debate about mentorship among Black professionals, was as follows:

> Many of our youth are in need of professionals as role models with which to pattern their lives. Lacking such models, they turn to those who earn their living in the streets as examples of persons to emulate. We as professional organizations and members thereof must develop "mentor" or "role model" programs on the local level to counter the negative models and images that our youth are exposed to and to encourage the growth of our future Black leaders. Intra- and interorganizational programs must be developed to serve this purpose. Our organizations should seek to work with local school systems and community groups to implement these programs. (Black Professional Interface 1985).

A written proposal accompanied this recommendation for a Leadership Institute, modeled along the lines of the recommendations that were aimed at high school and college age youth.

One of the most active of the interface leadership groups was International Affairs, which was particularly active in 1985 and 1986. The most critical issue was American response to South African apartheid, which had been brought to a decisive level by the further exclusion of Blacks from citizenship by the adoption of a new constitution and the incarceration of Black leaders inside the country. The response to this was the initiation of demonstrations, led by the Free South Africa Movement, a coalition of organizations headed by TransAfrica, a Black American lobby organization chaired by Randall Robinson. These demonstrations were begun by the refusal of Robinson, Fauntroy, and Dr. Mary Berry, distinguished professor and member of the U.S. Civil Rights Commission, to leave the South African embassy after demanding of the ambassador that apartheid be ended. The spectacle of these three leaders being led away in handcuffs, sparked additional demonstrations at the site of the South African embassy and its consulates in several cities, and it prompted the call for legislative action. As the movement became popular among all segments of the American people, Congress was forced to act, and twenty pieces of legislation, led by Congressman Ronald Dellums' bill to cut off all U.S. relations with South Africa, and H.R. 1460 by William Gray and S. 635 by Edward Kennedy to halt any new economic relations with South Africa. The latter bill became the operative proposal that drew support from many organizations.

The NBLR was supportive of this thrust and on May 14, 1985, a special meeting was called by the International Affairs Interface of all 350 organizations in the roundtable to support this legislation. This meeting recommended (1) that the policy of the Reagan administration of "constructive engagement" with South Africa be opposed and that, instead, (2) American citizens support a policy of economic sanctions against the South African government. The interface also recommended that (3) all organizations lobby to support the Dellums and Gray/Kennedy legislation, that (4) they adopt a specific day for their organization to demonstrate at the South African Embassy, and (5) that Black organizations should increase the pressure on local governments to divest their economic resources from companies that were economically involved the South Africa. These organizations would lend support to the activity which resulted in the passage of the Anti-Apartheid Act of 1986.

Another perennial problem in the Black community has been how to construct an economic development mechanism that is controlled and directed by Blacks. One answer was proposed at the annual NBLR Summit on September 28, 1985, at the CBC Weekend, which consisted of a national minority investment vehicle known as "The U.S. Investment Company." Intended to be responsive to the plan's emphasis on a development fund, it was engineered by Congressman Parren Mitchell and a team of Black businesspersons. The model was that investment would take the form of a public corporation registered on the New York Stock Exchange as a profit-making company. Blacks (and any other investors) in America or abroad would be able to invest in the company with the expectation of making a return. The main objective, however, would be for the company to remain viable and a small portion of its profits would form a capital fund with which to make loans to other Black businesses at rates of interest below the prevailing rates.

The main requirement for the registration of the company was that it raise $200,000 for the public offering of stock in order to capitalize it, a task that was managed by the minority law firm of Hart, Caroll & Chavers, P.C. The initial securities offering was expected to raise $20 million, which would be placed in minority financial institutions that were federally insured. The appeal for the funds was made through the NBLR with the above-named law firm putting all funds collected in escrow until the target of $200,000 was reached.

At the inauguration of the appeal for the funding, Mitchell, an expert on minority business development, said that one reason that made the investment company idea a natural one, in addition to its obvious mandate in the plan, was that federal programs that were meant to enhance the status of minority businesses, such as Executive Order 11246 and Public Law 95–507 on minority set-asides, were never meant to supplant private programs of Black economic self-help. Moreover, he averred that there was a "visible decline in all areas within Black and minority communities over the past few years" of the Reagan administration that acted as incentive "to bring a minority venture capital fund to the front burner" ("America's" 1985).

The campaign began with much auspicious fanfare and hope that this audaciously ambitious project would succeed. Congressmen Fauntroy and Mitchell spoke before many groups in support of contributing to the investment company throughout 1986. Flyers sent out announced that the creation of the vehicle would: "be an investment pool contributed by Blacks and other minorities for minority businesses; tap the public capital markets; [and thereby] multiply our resources" (Futuregram 1985). However, the necessary funding for the stock offering did not materialize by the 1987 deadline, the managers of the effort having raised only half of the required amount a year later. Therefore, amounts contributed at $1,000 or more were returned to donors and lesser amounts remained with the NBLR unless there were individual request for refunds.

This effort revealed serious flaws in the NBLR structure and function, including the lack of sufficient staff to organize a serious campaign to support and follow up appeals by the leadership. Thus, the economic weakness of the organizations in the coalition, and the fundamental lack of confidence in such an appeal by a significant segment of Black America who were exposed to it caused the project to fail.

THE HIGH POINT

In many ways the 1986–87 period was the height of the NBLR operations in terms of its strength and influence, frequency of meetings, and general legitimacy among Black leaders nationwide. For example, the March 1986 spring conference was held with a full agenda of issues, but as much as anything with a focus on the 1986 Congressional elections. During this year, the NBLR leadership traveled to over thirty conferences of Black organizations to spread the message of the Black Leadership Family Plan, the priority recommendations of the interface, and the program to get out the vote for the elections.

The project to get out the vote focused on nationalizing the campaign through the NBLR organizations to go into selected districts and assist with fund-raising and other campaign activities. This entailed the distribution of over ten thousand Campaign Workers Assistance Project (CWAP) cards and flyers to member organizations for further dissemination to their volunteers. The cards were filled out by local organizers to indicate when they would campaign for a candidate favored by the mobilization. Information included names of key contact persons, estimated numbers of workers, and other pertinent information. The result was that the November 6 NBLR press briefing on the election could report that five new members of the CBC had been elected and that in particular, the national fund-raising activities of the NBLR assisted Mike Espy in his winning campaign for the first seat from a Black majority district in Mississippi since Reconstruction. The second goal, to affect the Senate races, targeted ten senators with the result that seven of the ten were elected, including: Shelby of Alabama; Cranston of California; Graham of Florida; Fowler of Georgia; Breaux of Louisiana; Mikulski of Maryland; and Sanford of North Carolina ("Roundup" 1986). The last objective, to catapult CBC member Charles Rangel (D-NY) into the post of Democratic Whip in the House, was not realized, despite an elaborate national campaign.

The priorities for 1987, as outlined at the Tenth Anniversary Black Leadership Summit, held on March 13–15, contained the usual plethora of issues such as: supporting a Telethon for Aid to Africa sponsored by Richard Griffey, a California businessman who was head of Coalition for a Free Africa; continuing to support the Invest America Fund of

Travers Bell, an African American investment banker, as an alternative to the previous investment vehicle; supporting the National Alliance of Postal and Federal Employees (NAPFE) Health Benefit Plan, in exchange for a NAPFE pledge of $5,000 of support for NBLR for each policy; support of the National Urban Coalition "ABC" program in Science, Math, and Technology for Children; and statehood for the District of Columbia (Baskerville, September 26, 1987). CWAP was also activated for Harold Washington's reelection campaign for mayor of Chicago in 1987 and for Margaret Morton's bid for Connecticut's 4th Congressional District, which she lost.

The most galvanizing activity, however, was for the 1988 campaign of Rev. Jesse Jackson for president. The preparation for getting out the vote for Jackson played heavily upon the fact that there was a 4 percent increase in voter turnout in the 1986 elections, some of which was contributed to by the activity of the organizations in the NBLR network. Working with Richard Hatcher, Jackson's campaign chairman, a mobilizing meeting was held on June 28, 1987, for the purpose of organizing a national structure. This was characterized by each CBC member taking responsibility for 138 congressional districts and 34 states where either Blacks were a significant portion of the population or the Jackson campaign needed assistance. The NBLR organizations reactivated CWAP to constitute the basis of the African American mobilization, which would work under the Jackson campaign state coordinators at the local level. In addition, a fund-raising strategy for the campaign was outlined with maximum targets for each category of organizations under the plan. This structure was further solidified by the fact that, again, NBLR leaders became key actors in the Jackson campaign structure and, from that vantage point, traveled the country in support of the campaign by mobilizing the NBLR organizational structure or worked to include it in the vital operations of the campaign itself.

COMING DOWN FROM THE MOUNTAINTOP

It is ironic in that one of the strains in the organizational resources of the NBLR was the mobilization of the Jackson campaign, because the NBLR was increasingly becoming financially troubled as fewer than 100 of the organization's 300 members were contributing financially as of the beginning of the year.

The financial crisis was evident in the increasing demands on two paid staff persons with the crushing responsibilities of managing the various meetings and conferences, responding to state and local affiliate duties, and becoming involved as directors in projects the NBLR interfaces had assumed. The issue of finances emerged at the March 1987 summit and was responded to by the Economic Empowerment Interface, which pledged to raise $3 million for staff and project support. Nevertheless, the state of the finances were declared an emergency by the staff, which presented a report on cash flow amounting to an estimated $100,000 and a budget that they projected at $439,000 (Economic Empowerment Interface 1987).

And despite a fund-raising plan prepared and presented by the Secretary, fund-raising events planned for the year and an emergency appeal for funds the organization could never generate the necessary funds to sustain its operations on the scale it was intended to function. Even the reconstitution of the board of directors in April was not sufficient to generate the necessary funding, even through the crisis was at the center of this meeting in April (Baskerville, April 23, 1987).

In mid-1987, a survey was performed by the Secretary of NBLR in order to determine why the organizations involved were unable to fund the organization. The main finding was that part of the problem was related to the nature of the organizations, since most were relatively young organizations, with 23% being founded in the 1960s, 40% during the 1970s, and 6% since 1980. Also, 80% of the organizations were tax exempt nonprofit entities and 8% had applications pending, which meant that this category of organization generated little surplus funding that was not committed to projects. Another reality revealed by the survey was that while many organizations possessed the name "national," few of the organizations actually possessed the strength of national organizations, such as having budgets to sustain national operations and having field offices or requisite communications capacity or chapters in a significant number of states. Thus, the 20 percent sample surveyed revealed serious weaknesses in the general pool of organizations that the NBLR had attracted. This was important in that many of the older, better established and financed organizations were associated with the Black Leadership Forum, but other organizations with substantial financial capacity were not members of either group.

Thus, the following candid assessment of the state of the financial crisis was presented by staff:

> As originally conceived, the Roundtable was to be solely dependent on contributions of the Black Family. The board made the conscious decision not to seek a tax-exempt status for the organization so that its activities would be unhindered by government interference. Moreover, as late as its meeting of May 19, 1987, the board decided that NBLR would not compete for white corporate support but would instead rely heavily on support of Black organizations, individuals, and unions with substantial Black memberships. Unfortunately, the commitment from

national Black organizations to provide financial support to the Roundtable simply is not there; and so without a 501c (3) foundation [tax-exempt status], grants are next to impossible to attract, and basic fundraising activities are not as effective as they would be with tax write-off possibilities. ("Roundtable in Review" 1988)

Even though the staff had begun to apply for tax-exempt status for NBLR, it was clear from its political activities that its application would either be delayed or rejected, inasmuch as other such applications that Black organizations had filed were delayed by a conservative Republican–controlled IRS. Thus, the NBLR limped along for two years, having episodic meetings, but with Walter Fauntroy resigning from Congress in 1990 to run for mayor of the District of Columbia and financial support for staff inadequate, the organization slowly failed to operate by the end of 1991, even though Fauntroy felt that the 1991 conference was "clearly the most productive such conference that we have had since the one in 1985, when the network supported two successful measurable goals for collective action" ("The African American" 1991). Despite his confidence, at the end of 1991, the National Black Leadership Roundtable would become a footnote to African American political history.

CONCLUSION

The National Black Leadership Roundtable was a promising experience in the attempt to construct a principle of collective Black leadership at the national level that would also include state and local organizations in the process of influencing major policy institutions such as the White House and the Congress. Moreover, this vehicle came to be conceived, through the promulgation of the Black Leadership Family Plan, as an organization that would help to routinize the internal activity of community maintenance and mobilization through the formation and implementation of an ideology of leadership. Although the ideology of "family leadership" did not remain, the stylistic notion of "summitry," which incorporates some of the same elements, has grown to be quite popular. One example is the First Annual Statewide Black Economic Summit presented by an organization known as Unity Partnership in Columbus, Ohio, that was designed to "serve as a catalyst for the implementation of neighborhood revitalization and development projects and growth within our city." Sessions included such topics as "what works in community empowerment," grant funding, government and the social service contribution to economic development, starting daycare centers, the Community Reinvestment Act, how to start a Community Development

Corporation, church/bank lending efforts, and others (Glason-Thornton 1997:15A).

Because of the diversification of Black leadership organizations in the 1980s and 1990s, it was difficult during such flux to build a framework of leadership that would incorporate the many kinds of organizations and leaders emerging. And, of course, no similar formation has been attempted since the demise of the NBLR; ironically, it was a period when the challenges affecting the quality of life for the average African American have grown in the light of the truncation of both public and private resources.

The demise of the NBLR, nevertheless, is a painful object lesson in the dynamics of the intersection between the political objectives of such organizations and their ability to survive financially. With this case study one generalization suggests itself—apparently, the *less overtly political* the objectives of an organization, the better its opportunities to raise funds through the tax-exempt structure of granting institutions, which enhances the chances of the organization's survival. Conversely, the adoption of an organizational structure designed to maximize the political activities of an organization, which also has the dedicated ideological purpose of affecting its survival based on the financial resources provided by Black people, would appear to jeopardize the organization's survival.

It was assumed that this elementary lesson, learned from the experience of many of the movement-oriented Black organizations that existed in the 1960s, could be a framework. However, the structure of such national organizations was so weak that this base of support was also not directly dependent upon Black contributions, but rather upon the economic resources provided by foundations and government grants. This fundamental problem in the base of support of Black organizations—which is extended to the umbrella coalition that they support—will color the political viability of the coalition leadership structure.

With respect to the relationship between the structure of the NBLR and its success in implementing the agenda, one could say that it was only successful to a minor degree. The large projects such as the investment vehicle were not supported by the public, and the success at mobilizing the Action Alert Network was minimally successful in influencing major pieces of legislation, with the exception of the District of Columbia Home Rule Charter, the South Africa Apartheid Act, and the Martin Luther King Jr. Holiday bill, which it worked with other organizations to achieve. Perhaps the most important aspect of its success was symbolic, in that there existed a recognized leadership structure and a core ideology that was supported by most Black organizations, which had a process of meeting in order to lay on the table significant problems facing the Black community, and attempted to solve them in a collective way.

CHAPTER 9

Popular Black Struggle:
Mass Mobilization in the 1990s

The point of view is currently fashionable that Blacks do not need to exercise any popular pressure on the political system through mass demonstrations or other tactics; that it is possible in the 1980s and 1990s to work through institutions with leaders who are elected to seats of power and through regular civic mechanisms of access to these officials by such routine methods as meetings, writing letters, making phone calls, or even sending e-mail. Thus, the era of popular pressure is often thought to reside exclusively in the history of the 1960s, while the era of institutional approaches using professional system-oriented leadership tactics is hegemonic.

I would submit that the above view of the extent to which it is possible to "routinize" leadership strategies through institutional means is largely fallacious, because it does not comport with the necessity to mount the requisite pressure on the political system that would produce "large changes" sufficient to address the problems of most Black communities. This is likely since it has been frequently demonstrated that the normal mode of the outcomes from political institutions is either to enact measures that are unfavorable to Black interests or to dispense marginal resources in a style that is incremental (Smith 1996).

Therefore, it must be understood that since "the marching stopped" there have been few victories for Blacks in the national political arena that have come exclusively through the exercise of influence by institutional methods alone. If one considers major legislative initiatives mentioned earlier such as, the Martin Luther King Jr. Holiday, or the Anti-Apartheid Sanctions bill, which will be discussed later, this is certainly true. Perhaps the 1982 amendments to the Voting Rights Act and the Civil Rights Act of 1991 are exceptions; but then the failure of the Humphrey-Hawkins bill of the mid-1970s, in which Black leaders invested such enormous energy, is a stark confirmation of this assertion.

It is, therefore, worthwhile to examine the extent to which popular mobilization continues to constitute an important leadership tactic in Black politics both in local communities and on a national level. Perhaps it is in local communities where this lesson of power is most applicable, rather than at the national level. Here, I will briefly review the examples of local labor struggles in Los Angeles and Chicago, the Miami boycott of 1990, and the national Million Man March.

LOCAL BLACK MOBILIZATIONS

Miami: The Mandela Boycott

Nelson Mandela came to the United States in 1990 on a triumphal tour after his historic release from prison by the White minority regime of South Africa. In May of 1990, the African National Congress of South Africa (ANC) announced that one of the stops on his tour would be Miami, Flordia, to speak at the annual convention of the American Federation of State, County and Municipal Employees union. At this stop, Mandela was originally to have received the key to the city, but on June 21, in a television interview with Ted Koppel of ABC's *Night Line*, he announced his continuing respect for and solidarity with Fidel Castro, Moammar Gadhafi, and Yasser Arafat. Mandela had refused to separate himself from these world leaders, considered pariahs in the West, because they supported the ANC when many Western countries supported the White minority regime that controlled South Africa.

Mandela's statement of solidarity with Castro was of particular significance to the city of Miami because Mandela was planning a visit there shortly after his appearance on Koppel's show. Thus, anticipating his visit on June 22, a Dade County commissioner of Cuban extraction demanded that the proclamation that had been prepared for Mandela be withdrawn and a few days later, five Cuban mayors in Dade County signed a letter criticizing Mandela for his comments on Koppel's show (Fiedler and Goldfarb 1990:1A). Jewish leaders as well, very influential in Dade County, were also disturbed that Mandela continued his support for Yasser Arafat, whose activities to them were those of a "terrorist."

The reaction in the Black community to this initial snub of Mandela was swift, as the head of the local NAACP said that, "by rejecting Mandela, you reject us." Then, H. T. Smith, the then head of the National Conference of Black Lawyers, said that Blacks would call a boycott if Mandela was not given the planned key to the city.

Yet, when Mandela arrived in Miami on June 28, he was not accorded the traditional honor of visiting dignitaries, of being presented the key. Therefore, the National Bar Association, the nation's foremost Black legal organization, began the boycott by deciding on July 17, to rescind their decision to hold their 1993 convention in Miami. The first response of Mayor Xavier Suarez was bluster, responding to the boycott organizers by issuing his own statement, which demanded an apology from Smith, with several Blacks, Jewish, and Cuban leaders standing at his side. The business community, fearful of the loss of tourist revenue, issued a signed statement supporting the mayor's position. The response by Smith and others was to organize a coalition of organizations committed to the boycott called, "People United for Justice" that rejected Suarez's statement (Crockett and Fiedler 1990:1A). The only major organization to break ranks was the National Urban League, which held its convention in the city and because of the criticism it received from the coalition, defended itself by saying that it had already signed contracts that could not be broken on pain of financial penalties.

The coalition released a statement that was described by Johnnie McMillian, president of the Miami NAACP, as a "brilliant piece of strategy." It not only rejected the mayor's demands, but asserted that their action was not "merely symbolic"; that the snub of Mandela served to remind them of the arrogance and contempt with which they were treated, and as such, the boycott was "an expression of our own self-respect, our own dignity, and our own pride as Black people. Beyond that, it is a demand that others respect us as well" (ibid.). The statement linked this act of disrespect of Mandela to the fact that Blacks had been locked out of the mainstream of the local tourist-dominated economy, which set the stage for the attitude that the organizers would not merely settle for a statement expressing regret from the mayors.

By late December, the boycott had already cost Dade County $12 million, and apparently, understanding that a boycott was in process, Mayor Suarez softened his position with another statement expressing his pain that the actions of Dade County mayors had "affronted the dignity of our Black brothers"; however, inasmuch as Black leaders had expected a public apology, the boycott continued.

In any case a few weeks later, the coalition sought to test the mayors' sincerity and, in January of 1991, a proclamation was drafted in which they asked the mayors to sign and backdate and apologize to Mandela, but the mayors again refused to sign it. This was also a tactical gesture addressed to leaders in Miami's private sector, such as James K. Batten, head of the formidable Knight-Ridder chain of twenty-eight newspapers, including the *Miami Herald*. Batten counseled the coalition, in a keynote speech to a business luncheon in December 1990, to "move on" after the snub of Mandela, that it was an "unfortunate" act, that they may even suffer from White "backlash," and that they were hurting the "goodwill" of others (Fiedler 1990:28). But the failure of similar business leaders to respond positively to the proclamation idea with pressure on the city government only gave added impetus to the boycott, which continued until the Miami Beach government declared a separate proclamation of "Nelson Mandela Day" on April 27. The action taken by the city government of Miami Beach on April 27 satisfied the demand of the Black leadership that Nelson Mandela be recognized and on May 12, 1993, the boycott ended (ibid.).

Over the three years, the boycott had been in effect, it had canceled twenty-four meetings with 46,000 delegates, costing Miami-Dade County an estimated $20 million in tourist spending. However, as indicated, the position of Blacks was that the price of ending the boycott should go beyond the treatment of Mandela, to the economic development of the Black community, which formed the basis of the negotiating points to end the boycott.

The coalition constructed a twenty-point agenda that had to be negotiated with the major political and business leaders of the Miami-Dade area before they would attempt to bring Blacks back into the Miami tourist market. Items on the agenda included such things as investigating a July 1990 incident of police brutality against Haitian protestors; more Black representation in the tourist industry; single-member voting districts for seats on both the Miami-Dade County Commission and the school board; and scholarships for industry training and college attendance. Another major goal of the boycott was to establish a Black-owned convention hotel in Miami Beach (Pugh 1993:1A). This agreement was signed by city leaders and a new pact was created with Black leaders known as "Miami Partners for Progress" that would monitor the implementation of the agreement. And although Hispanic leaders, who had participated in the rejection of Mandela, opposed the agreement because they were not included, it went into force in any case.

The dynamism of the boycott spread to other areas of Florida, such as Tampa, where Black leaders also proposed a boycott when local Cuban leaders refused to agree to their "Agenda for Inclusion." Then, the activity in Miami and Tampa influenced Blacks in Ft. Lauderdale to begin a movement for economic progress that would result in the development of their own resort hotel coming to fruition by the fall of 1997.[1] This strategic move was led by the Ft. Lauderdale NAACP, which realized that Broward County had begun to aggressively court businesses and organizations that were avoiding the Dade County boycott, just over the county line. So, following the Dade County model, they began to negotiate for better jobs and a Black-owned resort hotel, in order that Blacks would be able to be employed in positions other than "making beds and doing dishes" (Hecker and McCarty 1990:1BR).

In support of the neighboring movement, H. T. Smith encouraged the adoption of the more aggressive stand, saying, "It is a model that can work for them, but they must have the courage and the determination to pull it off" (ibid.). In the spring of 1997, the Ft. Lauderdale movement was threatening to re-open the boycott because of the threat that the Broward County Commission would not approve their license to build and operate a Black-owned hotel.

Los Angeles: Rebuilding South Central

Following the beating of Rodney King and the not guilty verdict, masses of Black and Latino people in south-central Los Angeles took to the street in rebellion to express the depths of their anger and destitution. Few mainstream politicians wanted to deal with the underlying causes, except Congresswoman Maxine Waters, whose congressional district included south-central Los Angeles. She said:

> In LA, between 40 and 50 percent of African-American men are unemployed. The poverty rate is 32.9 percent. According to the most recent census, 40,000 teenagers—that is 20 percent of the city's 16- to 19-year-olds—are both out of school and unemployed. An estimated 40,000 additional jobs were just lost as a result of the civil unrest in the last two weeks. The LA Chamber of Commerce has said that at least 15,000 of these job losses will be permanent. This represents another 10 to 20 percent of south-central LA's entire workforce permanently unemployed. (Waters 1992:26)

It is obvious, that a major key to the rebuilding of south-central Los Angeles was the provision of employment to the residents of that area. Construction was occurring around this section of the city, however, little effort was made to hire Black workers and many of the construction projects were initiated without subcontracting with Black firms as well. Latino workers were often hired because they were more easily exploited by virtue of their immigration status and low levels of education, which make for compliant workers at the lowest wages. Blacks were somewhat more difficult to exploit because they have fostered a legacy of legal protection through civil rights laws, to which they often had access by virtue of their longer status as citizens. Furthermore, their socialization to American standards of living made them desire higher wages and adequate working conditions.

One of the strongest community organizations confronting this problem was the Brotherhood Crusade. A nonprofit organization, the Crusade is headed by Danny Bakewell, an aggressive leader who has developed a formidable organization that has broad community support. It has obtained social services for the community through both normal engagement with the system, as well as through protest. The group also has the capability of initiating development projects, one of the most visible of which is the building of a shopping center in south central with a supermarket, in the midst of the destruction of the riots.

Another example is related to the annual Rose Bowl parade. Each year, in conjunction with the Rose Bowl football game, there is the Tournament of Roses parade in Los Angeles that has become a veritable industry, yielding thousands of jobs and involving millions of dollars. In October 1993, Bakewell and other activists gathered on the steps of Tournament House in Pasadena, stating they would "bring the Tournament to its knees" if it did not provide opportunities for Blacks to participate in the organization's decision-making bodies. They demanded that two Blacks, two Latinos, and one Asian, five minorities altogether (one of whom must be a woman) be added to the Tournament of Roses board. The organization's executive board stated it was committed to diversity by virtue of the contingent of minorities previously added to the membership of the Tournament Committee. Bakewell in return replied that these were "foot-shuffling gestures" that did not address the core question of economic power. The objective of the protest was "to participate in the feast of the economic pie," and threats were made that Rev. Jesse Jackson might be brought in to lead a counterparade if the demands were not met.

After the protest, the Tournament Executive Committee issued a list of steps it would take to rectify the lack of diversity in its operation. This list included adding minorities to its membership, giving minorities input in the distribution of charitable funds from the event, integrating minorities throughout the event and accepting affirmative action in hiring (Newton 1993:3B).

In the flurry of rebuilding projects in the wake of the south central rebellion, a picture appeared in the *Los Angeles Times* of Danny Bakewell, standing on a bulldozer at the Gardena construction site. Together with members of his organization, he was holding up work until more Black workers were hired. In this case, as in many others, employers had also discriminated against Latinos and Blacks by hiring Anglos who lived in the Valley and other suburban areas for the most coveted jobs.

The Brotherhood Crusade launched protests at several of these construction sites for about one month and some success was achieved. For example, through negotiations that involved the Justice Department, the general contractor at the Gardena Shopping Center site agreed to hire thirty more Black construction workers. Bakewell said: "This is a real landmark agreement. We stand by our motto: If Black people don't work, nobody will work in this community." The agreement stated that African American workers would be given "maximum opportunity to participate in construction projects." Bakewell cited the "moral responsibility" for employers to hire more Black workers and promised more demonstrations against those who refused (ibid.).

The Brotherhood Crusade confronted another construction site managed by the Nagel Construction Company at Venice Boulevard and Western Avenue with a demonstration of nearly fifty people. As a result of this action, Bakewell's negotiations with the president of the firm secured both the addition of Black carpenters on site as well as the participation of Black subcontractors in the work. One of the carpenters, Mark Fletcher, who received a job said that "I think these kinds of protest are totally necessary" (ibid.). Many other job site actions were initiated with equal success and with a concomitant understanding by the recipients of the necessity for militant action to secure their rights to employment against the abject failure of more moderate means.

Chicago: Fighting for Construction Jobs

In the summer of 1994, a similar picture to that of Bakewell confronting a construction supervisor, appeared in the Chicago press featuring Eddie Reed, president of Chicago Black United Communities (CBUC), and members of his organization. Their objective was the same as the Brotherhood Crusade's and the protestors chanted similar slogans: "We want work!" "No Jobs, No Peace," "If we don't work, nobody works" (McCarron 1994:3).

Ten years earlier, the city of Chicago passed an ordinance that reserved half of all city public-works jobs for city residents. Since it was never enforced, by 1990, 53 percent of all city construction jobs were held by White suburbanites. Only 25 percent of the jobs reserved for Chicago residents were set aside for minorities. In the same ten-year period, the city had lost an estimated 9,000 jobs while 50,000 new jobs were being created in the suburbs. In the wake of White out-migration from Chicago of 2.8 million total city residents, Blacks amounted to 40 percent and Hispanics 18 percent of the population. Yet they both lagged far behind in the proportion of construction jobs (see table 9.1).

Blacks and Hispanics together account for 60 percent of the population, but occupy far less than 40 percent of the jobs in each of the skill trades categories in the city of Chicago. That is why CBUC considered the figure of 25 percent too low and demanded 40 percent of the jobs in the city and 70 percent of the jobs in the Black community alone.

The CBUC was founded in 1980 by Lou Palmer, a longtime Black community activist, who also serves as chairman. The organization is under the policy direction of a Council of Elders. This council is comprised of seasoned Black activists and respected individuals from many segments of the Chicago Black community. The council makes recommendations for the overall direction of CBUC and the various organizations represented in the council often participate in its actions. The goals

TABLE 9.1
Minority and Female Participation in the
Construction Trades in Chicago, 1994
(data in thousands)

	Carpenters		Electrical		Plumbers/ Pipe fitters		Painters		Metal workers	
	M	F	M	F	M	F	M	F	M	F
Total	10.1	0.2	5.5	0.1	3.3	0.03	6.1	0.4	594	0
Hispanic	2.2	0.03	739	0.03	0.4	0	1.5	0.2	77	0
Black	1.5	0.04	1.3	0.05	800	0.02	1.4	0.08	121	0

SOURCE: J. Linn Allen and Jerry Thomas, "Hammering Away at Prejudice," *Chicago Tribune*, September 4, 1994, section C, p. 1.

of CBUC, a coalition, have been, "to change the personal and community lives of Black people in terms of oppressive politicians and limited services, and to conduct programs that provide as much information, knowledge and clarity about the systems and processes which affect and impact our lives" (Chicago United Black Communities 1990). The organization has established goals in both the social and political arenas. Its affiliate members of the coalition, the Black Independent Organization (BIO), serves as its arm in the political system through which it initiates accountability projects. This recognizes the linkage between the behavior of community residents in the political system and the provision of services to Black community residents.

The CBUC launched its project aimed at increasing the share of jobs in the construction industry in 1993 because of its perception that Mayor Richard Daley Jr. was doing little to vigorously enforce affirmative action. The typical method used was that Eddie Reed would lead his task force to a construction site to confront the supervisor, as he did at 63rd and Wabash in the summer of 1994, where the Brothers Construction Co. was working with two White men and three Hispanics. The demand would be made, as it was in this case, to hire a skilled Black worker. Very often, the pressure of a potential total work stoppage provoked the desired response to the confrontation, when the supervisor placed an experienced Black worker in a job. In the 63rd and Wabash site, this tactic resulted in a Black acquiring a job operating a jackhammer, earning $20.15 per hour.

In June 1994, a dozen sites were visited with the same demands. Very often, when the protesters mounted the scaffolding at a construction project, they did so in a method they called "crackerjacking" where

they took up workers' tools and positions on the spot. As often, this provoked opposition from the foreman or other workers, which sometimes
escalated into physical assaults. In early July, after an arrest, Reed
vowed to step up action, as members of Operation Push joined his coalition on the construction sites. Reed and one hundred supporters confronted the Rossi Construction Company at 69th and Paxton Streets
with the slogan, "If we don't work, nobody works"; however, owner
Ron Rossi indicated that "the minority quotas have been met." The
action at this site alone resulted in Reed's third arrest, but the CBUC
persisted and eventually forced hiring of Blacks.

These events often resulted in charges of "intimidation" and violence by the construction management against CBUC, and as often,
Reed was arrested and briefly incarcerated. Such protests not only drew
loud and angry reaction from construction owners but equally negative
responses from the press. Opinion editorials indicated that this was the
wrong strategy to increase the Black share of construction jobs, and that
when force was used to shut down construction sites it constituted
"extortion." For example, the *Chicago Sun-Times* regularly suggested
that the demand for 40 and 70 percent of the construction jobs was
"unreasonable," while letters to the same paper often pronounced Eddie
Reed as a "hero." The Black press, on the other hand, asked the pertinent questions:

> Should literally millions of people permit their rights and dignity to be
> regularly and relentlessly trampled upon? Should they overlook the fact
> that their tax dollars are being used to create opportunities for others
> and not for the victims? Should they stand idly by hoping that the
> racists, or those who benefit from a bigoted system, will one day expe-
> rience a great spiritual awakening and change their ways? Should the
> victims wait generation after generation for the necessary changes and
> fairness to magically appear? No! Emphatically no! ("When Job Site"
> 1994:11)

The city government, meanwhile, temporized, indicating that it was
powerless to intervene, while its own standards designated that 30 percent of workers at a construction site be minority, and 16.9 percent of
city contracts be awarded to minority contractors and 4.5 percent to
females. In practice, however, groups in the city such as the Association
of Minority Contractors were regarded by some as "front" organizations for White construction owners. Thus, the fact that Blacks and others predisposed to equal hiring lacked effective political power in government since the Harold Washington administration, meant that Blacks
had also lost much of their protection in critical areas such as employment, in a city where politics and jobs have always been synonymous.

Over the course of the yearlong campaign by CBUC, nearly a hundred individuals were placed in jobs. Otherwise, where CBUC did not directly benefit from this campaign, other organizations did. For example, the Chicago branch of the National Urban League won a $500,000 contract from the city to monitor its workforce compliance on the city transit construction of the Green Line. While this step would appear to be positive, it was also evaluated by Professor Robert Starks as a possible "pacification" move to blunt the militant protest launched by CBUC.

NATIONAL BLACK MOBILIZATIONS

The Texaco Boycott

In 1994, six Black employees filed a racial discrimination complaint with the Equal Employment Opportunity Commission (EEOC) against the Texaco Oil Company and the EEOC launched an investigation, finding that the company did discriminate on the basis of race in promotions and did not meet the EEOC standards of employee evaluation. A statistical workforce analysis of the $35.6 billion company, the twelfth largest in the United States, revealed that although minorities made up 20 percent of all employees, they were promoted much slower and as a result, few reached the upper ranks of the corporation and none of the senior managers or top executives were Black (Eichenwald 1996:F3).

Indeed, information that reached the attorneys for the plaintiffs showed that Texaco corporate heads exhibited a hostile attitude toward minority employees, as indicated by a complaint filed by an accountant for the company, Ms. Devorce, in 1991. When the manager who received the complaint of Ms. Devorce checked with his supervisor as to the next course of action, the supervisor indicated that he would "fire her Black ass," and when the manager objected, his superior indicated, "I guess we treat niggers differently down here" (ibid.). In any case, on the basis of the EEOC findings, the Texaco employees filed a lawsuit in 1994, however, the treatment of employees was confirmed when in early November 1996, lawyers for the plaintiffs released tapes of conservations among Texaco executives that contained racists connotations. In press accounts of the transcripts, one manager was reported to have used the term "nigger," and there were other comments about "Aunt Jemima," "Orangutans," "Black Jelly beans," and "Porch monkies" ("Texaco" 1996:A22). Upon hearing the tapes, Texaco Chairman Peter Bijur expressed "shock and outrage" at the apparent comments; however, he also commissioned his own analysis of the tapes, later finding them not as offensive as he once thought (Walsh 1996a:A1).

Given the apparent intransigence of Texaco officials and the public outrage over the newly revealed remarks of their managers, Rev. Jesse Jackson, in a press conference with Rev. Al Sharpton on November 12, 1996, called for an immediate boycott of products sold by the corporation. Jackson, addressing reporters, said that, "It will be cheaper to settle this suit than to prolong it," and that, "I hope when you leave here and you'll need gas, you'll see a Texaco station and go right by" (Wheeler 1996:3).

Immediately, boycotts sprung up in several major cities such as New York, Philadelphia, and Chicago, supported by civil rights and labor organizations. For example, in New York City, William Taylor, head of the Oil Chemical and Atomic Workers Union Local 7-507 said: "I've added Texaco to my list of companies not to patronize. A boycott can be effective if it is properly organized. When enough people stop buying Texaco products the company will yield" (ibid.). Then, picket lines sprang up at many Texaco stations, such as those in Philadelphia, where the Coalition of African Americans for Justice Against Texaco, which involved the local NAACP, Nation of Islam, and other organizations, was active.

In fact, Jerome Mondesire, president of the Philadelphia chapter of the NAACP, called the boycott a "nationwide effort," and said, "the activities of a corporation are influenced most when you hit them in the pocketbook" (Muhammad 1996:6). This was a reference to the fact that the national president of the NAACP, Kweisi Mfume, had called for a stock divesture campaign against the Texaco Corporation if it did not negotiate in good faith with the complainants. Mfume said, "If a swift agreement is not reached and Texaco is unwilling to address the root causes of the problems there, we will work with our broad-based coalition to target Texaco's stock" (Brown 1996:C11).

Nevertheless, the threat of public pressure through a national boycott with the combination of factors such as the resulting negative corporate image, and the possible impact of this on a vulnerable stock position, the executives of Texaco reached a settlement that was announced on November 15 (Walsh 1996b:A1). The dramatic end to the case came with the Texaco chairman, Bijur, pledging, "I have committed myself—and the entire management team of this company—to the elimination of any trace of discrimination in Texaco," to achieve, "zero tolerance of bigotry and scrupulously fair treatment for every individual" (ibid.). The settlement awarded the class of Black employees involved in the case, potentially 1,400 people, $176 million in damages, and a retroactive 10 percent increase in pay together with a $26 million fund to administer pay increases over the succeeding five years. The company also agreed to create a task force of full-time employees to administer its fair employment practices plan, under court authority, for five years.

Both Reverend Jackson and Kweisi Mfume said that the Texaco response was a "good first step." Jackson indicated that he would commence talks with Bijur to stimulate economic development for those Blacks wishing to own Texaco stations, and Mfume indicated that if the "reconcilement" steps were not monitored and honored over time, his organization would reconsider its promised stock action.[2] Proof of the fact that this action by Texaco was addressed as much to its profitability as to the complaint lodged against it was the fact that its stock price increased by $2.75 a share after the announcement of the settlement.

THE MILLION MAN MARCH

All of the militant actions above have one thing in common: they are aggressive strategies designed to confront a perceived injustice on the part of elements of the majority community against the Black community and to enhance the resource position of the Black community by making effective demands. The mass mobilization of the Million Man March was also a militant strategy, however, it was not addressed to the majority, but to the internal community maintenance function of Black leadership. As such, it is a unique movement worth much greater consideration than it can be given here.

Minister Louis Farrakhan, who originated the idea of the Million Man March, began speaking at "men only" events in January 1993, recommending that they support the march that he was calling to be held in October 1995 (Muhammad 1994:8). By 1994, the causes of the march had been defined by Minister Farrakhan in terms that suggested it was addressed to the currents in the existing political culture. His statement began with the following:

> There is an increasingly conservative and hostile climate growing in America toward the aspirations of Black people and people of color for justice. The "Contract with America," proposed by the Republicans and thus far agreed to by the Congress is turning back the hands of time, depriving the Black community of many of the gains made through the suffering and sacrifice of our fellow advocates of change during the 50s and 60s. (Farrakhan 1995:A5)

The statement went on to point out the danger of recent Supreme Court decisions that would further restrict Black rights and the crime bill that would result in the incarceration of more Black males, the unchecked proliferation of drugs in the inner city, and the negative image of the

Black male portrayed in the media and in other aspects of the culture.

To this, he proposed that the march take place on October 16, 1995, and be declared a "Holy Day of Atonement and Reconciliation" in which Black males would reconcile themselves to their creator for the violation of the moral vision he represented and thereby recommit themselves to the perfection of their various roles as sons, husbands, fathers, leaders in the community and bread-winners for their families. This assemblage, therefore, was to be spiritual in tone and addressed to more than the individuals and groups represented and their internal roles within the Black community. Nevertheless, in August 1994, when asked the purpose of the march, he said that it would be, "To make demands on our government, and on ourselves" (Flagome 1994:3). So, his initial rendering of the march's purpose was inconsistent.

Minister Farrakhan attempted to develop support from the Black religious community, including especially Christians, and requested that they make their churches available for various support activities such as voter registration and worship. He also asked Black women to support the march by permitting the men to come alone and for them to sponsor various support activities to ensure its success.

As the October 1995 march date neared, the debate in the media concerning the role of Minister Farrakhan overshadowed the purpose for which it was being held and why it appeared that, although little systematic publicity had been observed, preparations for a substantial mobilization were being detected all over the country.[3] And although the debate raged on in the media about Farrakhan, who was generally considered "anti-Semitic" by the mainstream press, some reasons why the men were coming to Washington included statements such as those below:

- "Somewhere along the way we forgot what we should be about. The March isn't totally a stop sign, but it's a yield sign that says we should hold up."

- "We have to begin with ourselves. All the answers lie within ourselves."

- "We have to begin to take back our neighborhoods. We have to give the brothers who have fallen by the wayside a chance, but bring judgment against them if they continue in the error of their ways."

- "I don't see a representative of myself in the media. All the images in the media of Black men are negative."

- "We're working-class Black men working every day taking care of our families. I'm pro-Black but any man who doesn't take care of his family is worse than a dog."

- "Caucasian men fear Black men so they hire Black females."
- "Integration, that's where we got off the track."
- "Prisons—all these young Black men in prison—it's just a new form of slavery." (DeWitt 1995:22)

Some marchers even denied that racism was implicated as a motivation for the March, offering instead to emphasize the subjective responsibility of Black males. "This will revive the spirit of the African American male [and] be a catalyst to help him take his rightful place as a leader of his family, community and his church" (Peterson 1995:5D).

In any case, a systematic study of march participants also confirmed the emphasis of the marchers on basic personal, community, and some policy rationales for their participation in the mobilization, rather than their commitment to Minister Farrakhan (McCormick et al. 1995; McCormick 1997). For example, 88% of the men said that "Affirming moral values in the Black community" was important; 85% favored "building broad-based Black unity" as a motive; 78% approved of the fact that the leadership of Black men in the march was emphasized; 77% approved of the call for atonement and reconciliation; and 75% supported the call for Black economic progress (McCormick et al. 1995).

It should be recognized that this complex of rationales of both an anecdotal and systematic nature point directly to the overrriding presence of Black nationalism as the dominant philosophy of the march and its leader, even though most marchers did not identify with the leader. The classic aspects of Black nationalism such as a strong sense of self-determination, Black identity, Black group unity and responsibility, and strong opposition to racism are inescapable from the evidence above (Kinfe 1991). Yet few have characterized the largest march in American history as having been motivated by this philosophy. And yet, without characterizing it, the values inherent in Black nationalism have often had the power to mobilize millions of Blacks because they are the dominant values that define the core culture of African American people as a peoplehood in a way that integrationism, constitutionalism, and Americanism do not. What has more often separated most Blacks who support the values of Black nationalism from its public expression are not the inherent values but the militancy and radicalism that also alienates them from integrationists as well.

The most serious threat to the march was the issue of who would support it from among the established Black leaders, especially since there had been a conflict between them and Farrakhan over the 1993 March on Washington commemoration. In fact, Black Christian ministers had reacted to an early assertion of Farrakhan's that he would utilize the march to put forth a "Muslim Program," which suggested that the march was a possible effort to recruit Black men into the Muslim faith, a prospect that made some of the most powerful Christian leaders hostile to it.[4] One example is Rev. Henry Lyons, president of the National Baptist Convention, the 1.3 million member denomination, who opposed the march and who was openly challenged by many of its supporters because of his position.[5]

In any case, individuals with strong civil rights credentials and substantial followers such as Rev. Al Sharpton, Rev. Jesse Jackson, Rev. Calvin Butts, Rosa Parks, and Rev. Joseph Lowery, and others began to publicly endorse the march ("March" 1995:2). The gravitation of a significant number of traditional Black leaders toward support of the march was important, since Minister Farrakhan and the planning committee were not only strongly Muslim, but largely Black nationalists in nature, and the antipathy between these two segments of the Black leadership has been historically deep seated. Although for large movements, it has often been necessary for the two to come together, since they have also often had similar political objectives.[6] It was also important in building its general momentum, as a signal to other major organizations that began to voice their support, such as the National Bar Association, the National Black Police Officers Association, the Elks, the Progressive National Baptist Church, the National Association of Black Social Workers, Blacks in Government, and the National Political Congress of Black Women. Add to this group, the Black student organizations, Black nationalist organizations, and in the last few days before October 16, it was clear to the nation that a massive Black poplar mobilization was under way.

The program at the march included a wide range of speakers, who voiced an array of themes including the general theme of atonement and spiritual commitment to each other and community.[7] Nevertheless, the lack of policy and political themes projected as a strong rationale for the march concerned some observers and struck others as a contradiction that a gathering on the Mall behind the Capitol, one of the most political spaces in the country, would not project such messages as a major reason for coming to Washington, D.C.

The central speech of the march was that of Minister Farrakhan, which followed the themes as advertised with a strong moral tone to its presentation. Possibly the other major speech was that given by Rev. Jesse Jackson, who attempted to provide a political/policy rationale for the gathering, by asserting that the march had actually been organized by Newt Gingrich and the radical conservative political revolution that had threatened to cut off the resources coming from government to the Black community.

In fact, the more politically sensitive members of the March Planning Committee had attempted to assert an overt political purpose for the march, including challenges to policy-makers, all of which was either de-emphasized or ignored altogether. In any case, a statement was drafted by Dr. Maulana Karenga, representing the Executive Committee of the March Organizing Committee. The statement began with the familiar themes of atonement as the basis for reconciliation and a "challenge to ourselves" for the assumption of various kinds of "responsibility." However, it also included substantial sections challenging government and corporations, and suggesting follow-up strategies that would turn the major principles of the march into reality.[8]

After the march, there was a conflict over the number of marchers who had assembled on the Mall. The march organizers claimed that there had been between 1.2 and 2 million marchers and the official count provided by the National Park Service was 400,000. However, the Boston University Center for Remote Sensing reanalyzed the pictorial evidence and suggested that the figure was at least double the 400,000 estimate, probably over 800,000 and thus closer to the one million figure than previously thought (Associated Press 1995).

What is important here in this brief survey of the March was to present a summary description of the fact that the mobilization occurred and, secondly, what, if any consequences ensued?

THE MARCH: ONE YEAR LATER

It is important to note that as important as the Million Man March was as an example of mobilization and of popular struggle, the content of the struggle was largely directed toward the internal rehabilitation of the commitment of African American males to attend to their personal responsibilities and to the leadership of their communities. However, one of the most dramatic and positive features of the march was the pledge directed at the marchers by Minister Farrakhan that committed them to return home and initiate activities to rectify the conditions that promoted the march.

In the intervening year between the March and its first anniversary in 1996, in many locations throughout the country, activities were indeed initiated that constituted a pattern of personal and group commitment to the goals of the march (Harris 1996:C3). Local Organizing Committees (LOCs) in places like Baltimore; Buffalo, New York; New York City; Newark; Columbus, Ohio; San Diego; and Prince George's County, Maryland, sponsored citywide or countywide issue forums to disseminate the themes of the march as an agenda for action. In Richmond, Virginia, the forum took the theme of "Keeping the Spirit of the Million Man March Alive."[9] Sympathetic marches as a tactic to raise awareness of certain issues were held in Denver; Newark; and Trenton, New Jersey ("Black Families" 1996:B5). Issues such as education were confronted in Houston and Dallas. Local marches and workshops against drug use and sales were conducted and direct confrontations with drug dealers were orchestrated in New York and Detroit, and the LOC in Detroit aided police on "Devil's Night" (Halloween), where vandalism in Detroit dramatically decreased (Oguntoyinbo 1996a, 1996b).

Political activities were heightened in many cases because 1996 was a presidential election year. Thus, in Denver, the LOC endorsed a candidate for the congressional seat opened by the resignation of Pat Schroeder, by putting the Black agenda to both Republican and Democratic candidates. They eventually chose a White female Democrat, Diana DeGette, over the Black male Republican, Joe Rogers.[10] And there were many other such manifestations.

In San Diego, an active LOC had marches and demonstrations trying to defeat the California Civil Rights Initiative that was on the state ballot, and local voter registration drives were held. Also, students at Prince George's Community College, led by the LOC, sponsored voter registration drives (Gilmore 1996:B9).

In addition, the march stimulated support of other local organizations such as the NAACP, as the national office reported a substantial increase in membership after the march in many cities.[11] In fact, fifty-three-year-old Michael Motley, who said that he was inspired by the march, was elected chair of the Philadelphia Branch of the NAACP (Janco 1996:B2).

Perhaps the most anticipated political mobilization as a consequence of the march, however, did not materialize. Shortly after the march was held in Washington, D.C., a meeting to solidify the LOCs and provide an implementation structure was held under the aegis of the National African American Leadership Summit, an organization that had been created by Rev. Benjamin Chavis while he served as head of the NAACP to unify Black leadership. The LOCs, meeting on the campus of Howard University, November 16–18, 1995, was structured into nine committees, one of which was "Political Mobilization/Voter Registration."[12] The Political Mobilization Committee deliberated and arrived at a recommendation to hold a National Black Political Convention in 1996.[13]

As preparation for the projected convention, a "National Hearing on Issues and Public Policy" was held in Chicago on July 26, at which Minister Farrakhan spelled out his rationale for the convention. Declaring a "new day in politics," he noted that, "Democracy had run its course and had to be "cleaned up because it has destroyed human life." Continuing, he said that he "didn't join politics to be your average Negro flunky" but that we "joined this thing to take it over," not to take orders, but "we have orders to give" ("Minister Farrakhan" 1996:3). This aggressive stance was augmented by a fifty-six-page agenda of issues and upon its release, Rev. Chavis indicated, "We don't intend to give our vote away. No more back-door deals, hidden agendas, back-peddling or reacting to slick TV ads. This is a follow-up to the Million Man March" (ibid., 8).

The convention was held in late September of 1996 and the lead sentence in an editorial by the *St. Louis Post Dispatch* indicated: "Last weekend's Black political convention here was a disappointment from just about every perspective" ("Mr. Farrakhan's" 1996:6B). This harsh indictment of the convention was based on such factors as: mainline politicians such as the Black mayor of the city, Freeman Bosley Jr., the city's Black member of Congress, William Clay, and others were absent; the attendees, which numbered about 2,000, were far less than the 20,000 projected by the organizers; and the message of the keynote speech and that of other speakers appeared to be obsessed with letting Minister Farrakhan receive a $1 billion gift that had been hinted would be presented to him by Libyan President Moammar Gadhafi.

While the judgment of the *Dispatch* could be difficult to challenge on the merits, the meeting appears to have been even more of a failure because of the lack of substantive political strategy. In fact, Minister Farrakhan had confused some of the conventioneers by proposing that his followers stay at home after having vigorously supported voter registration activities previously and proposing to transform the political system to a "god-centered system" (Mannies 1996:7A).

While convening such a meeting was well intentioned, the message was inconsistent with the independent laden rhetoric of the leadership at the July 26 National Hearings on Issues and Public Policy Conference in Chicago. In fact, the political message of the convention leadership in St. Louis was muddled and the lack of a clear strategy coming from the meeting contributed to the fact that it played no significant role in the general strategy of Blacks in the 1996 elections.

The above conclusion is especially striking given the fact that Black males apparently turned out to vote in much greater numbers than in 1992. The analysis of the 1996 election by Curtis Gans of the Committee for the Study of the American Electorate found a striking 1.5 million increase in Black male voters over 1992, which was important in that there were also .5 million fewer votes of Black women (Bositis 1996:C1). Given the strong emphasis on voter mobilization of the Million Man March and the LOC activity afterward, as well as the general emphasis in the Black community at large on voter registration, it is reasonable to attribute the increase substantially to the march as perhaps its most important national manifestation, rather than to any strategic political role of the march leadership.

MILITANT LEADERSHIP: PRECIPITATING FACTORS

I will attempt to summarize, at this point, what factors were important in stimulating a militant approach to leadership. Indeed, one of the powerful rationales for the use of militant tactics and strategies is that they are oriented more directly toward economic and social objectives than is the case when political representation is utilized, because the latter is a process that has to be managed through complex institutions. In any case, it is instructive to determine what conditions made necessary the use of such leadership strategies in both the local and national political arenas.

Public Policy and the Status of Work

The pressure that we saw being placed on construction jobs in Chicago and Los Angeles is related to the national status of Black employment. A number of factors were important in explaining the fact that work was more difficult to obtain, such as the flight of jobs and the enhanced skill requirements and the elimination of job-training programs.

First, the policies of the Reagan administration in 1983 eliminated the Comprehensive Training and Employment Act (CETA) and shifted large segments of the social budget into military spending, and the result of this and other important factors was substantial increases in Black unemployment. For example, the Black unemployment rate rose from 14 percent in 1980 to 20 percent by 1993. In addition, those who earned low wages also increased as a Black high school graduate in 1987 was likely to earn as much as a Black high school dropout in 1973. The percentage of Black college graduates who earned low wages doubled in the same period from 8.3 to 16.7 percent. In this context, the death of the CETA program was particularly disastrous, since by 1980, it served nearly one million recipients who had income from this program. The change to the Job Training and Partnership Act (JPTA) by the Reagan administration was essentially the privatization of job training with far fewer minority enrollees and consequentially much less financial support to families.

Second, job flight was caused by a major shift of population from the Northeast and Midwest to the South and West from 1980 to 1985, which was critical because 70 percent of all manufacturing jobs were in the

Northeast and Midwest. Seventeen million jobs were created in the South, 11 million in the West, but just 7.5 million in the Midwest and 5 million in the Northeast. At the same time, the educational qualifications of those jobs rose and the dropout rate among minorities increased, from 7.6 percent in 1969 to 30 percent by 1985 (Kasarda 1988:149, 185).

In particular, Whites continued to move their residence from cities at a rapid rate in the 1970s and 1980s. Between 1975 and 1985 the Black inner-city population increased more than 5 percent. Together with the Hispanic share of city growth increasing as well, some cities increased their share of minorities between 10 and 20 percent (ibid., 157, 179). With the absence of jobs, the inner cities were increasingly becoming "labor reserves" competing for the available jobs left in construction with Whites even taking a large share of jobs in the cities where the economic scale of projects and the political connections of Whites still favor their dominance in the construction industry.

Third, the changes in the nature of the economy between the early 1970s and the early 1990s, from an industrial economy to a service-oriented one with an increased emphasis on high technology and financial services, made the skill requirements of jobs at the entry level much higher than before (Bluestone and Harrison 1982). This meant that a labor pool began to build up of individuals in the Black community whose industrial skills, with their emphasis on manual labor, were not competitive in the labor force. This was particularly true of Black males, whose average wage in 1989 ($14,182) was less than it was in 1979 ($14,619) and whereas in 1989, they earned 60 percent of the average White income by 1992 it was 58 percent. In the 1979–89 period, White males by comparison saw their income increase slightly, from $20,361 to $20,564 ("Trends" 1995:B3).

Fourth, increases in poverty have acted as an incentive to miliant actions. In a recent work on urban poverty, James Jenning cites the opinion of Marcia Bok that "only grass-roots protest and mass movements in the United States will elicit policies favorable to the well-being of the poor." He goes on to add an impressive array of other researchers who fundamentally agree, such as Curt Lamb, Joan Ecklein, Ann Withorn, Frances Fox Piven, Richard Cloward, Walda K. Fishman, Guida West and Rhoda Lois Blumber, Michael Katz, and Gary Delgado. Doubtless, they would also agree with the sentiment expressed by William Goldsmith and Edward Blakley: "We believe better policy to minimize poverty will result only from new political forces, which are most likely to be rooted in the poverty of the central city. We believe, that is, that an urban policy strategy is the most practical approach for attacking America's poverty problem" (Jennings 1994:134). The poverty that spurs the militancy of urban workers is important because poverty constitutes the only alternative, and the underground, illegal economy becomes the only recourse for income if other options are either closed or are few. In this sense, the Miami boycott and the construction protests are only symptons of a massive disease that affects all areas of urban life.

Immigration

The immigration effect has added considerable population to many of the cities where non-Hispanic Whites have moved from the reduced employment centers in the Northeast and the Midwest. For example, in the period between 1975 and 1985, one million Asians immigrated to the West, with the majority settling in California. This same period saw an increase of the Hispanic population by about the same amount, although in the following decade, Hispanic immigration had far outnumbered Asian. The effect of immigration has set up a competition for the jobs that are disappearing (entry-level jobs) in places like Los Angeles and Miami. In cities like New York and Chicago, the admixture of foreign-born residents increases the minority population of central cities seeking access to fewer jobs utilizing physical labor (see table 9.2) (Waldinger 1996).

The effect of the Miami boycott was important inasmuch as the conditions of Blacks in the urban centers of Flordia had been undergoing substantial pressures on their livelihood because of the demographics of migration from Latin America. Just at the point where they began to participate substantially in the political life of the state and its various locations, they were overrun by a more numerous population of Latinos who quickly gained both political and economic power, challenging and in many cases subduing Blacks who had been there far longer (Navarro

TABLE 9.2
Black and Hispanic Composition of the
Four Largest Norther Cities, 1970, 1980, 1990

	1970	*1980*	*1990*
New York	36%	48%	52%
Chicago	41	57	58
Philadelphia	36	43	45
Detroit	46	67	78

SOURCE: Michael G. H. McGeary and Laurance Lynn (eds.), *Urban Change and Poverty* (Washington, D.C.: National Academy Press, 1988), table 12, p. 179; also, 1990 Census data tables for Hispanic population by place.

1997:10). This situation, which expresses itself in many ways in other urban centers in the country, illustrates a major factor that has undermined the promise of more moderate methodologies of social change and, as such, constitutes a fundamental reason why more militant and aggressive strategies are often necessary.

Self-Determination Values

Many Blacks, especially in the low-income inner cities, who have wanted to exercise the values of responsibility by supporting their families and raising their children, have often experienced serious impediments to acquiring normal social and community services and access to legal employment. Of course, for those individuals there is the avenue of militant political action to create the opportunities that should have come from a fair distribution of resources, but the political structure is weighed against them.

Fundamentally, self-determination and empowerment can most decisively be felt by those who participate in mass mobilizations. For example, at the press conference when the statement was read initiating the Miami boycott, Bill Perry Jr., a well-known community activist, expressed his feelings by weeping, saying that, "[H. T.] Smith really caused me to fill with a sense of pride I've never felt since I've been in Miami. It's just so heartwarming to see the African-American professional community take their rightful place in our struggle for liberation" (Crockett and Fiedler 1990).

Those who desire that the local community have a sense of pride in itself, based on its own action in support of its development, find that the core value of self-determination is a currency in mobilizing people to take action. For example, Wayne County Commissioner Bernard Parker, who was also a member of the Detroit Million Man March Alumni Group, said that the idea of self-sufficiency "gives us a sense of worth and ownership" (Eversley 1997:3B). This article went on to explain that the ethic of self-help or self-sufficiency has a long historical existence within the Black community as the concept of "self-determination" preached by Marcus Garvey and other Black nationalists.

CONCLUSION

In the context of the popular struggles discussed in this chapter, the function of militant leadership is in lieu of the positive and proper functioning of the political system, which should distribute resources to areas of the country on an equitable basis. This action is in reaction to the existence of a "deficit" urban policy pursued by both Republicans and Democrats alike since 1980, a policy that has found "cities" out of fashion politically (Caraley 1992). In fact, "cities," because of their ethnic and racial composition, have largely become a euphemism for Black or minority populations and the negative and racist attitudes so prevalent toward these minorities have now been transposed into policies associated with "cities." This means that cities will continue to suffer from the stigma of race and crime and other associated social problems, until there is a crisis that again draws public attention to their plight.

The alternative vision is that these popular struggles are a manifestation of the resolve of Blacks and their leadership to exercise the degree of self-determination that it takes to reject exclusion, fight exploitation, and mobilize the human resources to participate in the process of developing their areas. These case studies also illustrate the fact that a substantial degree of leadership and organization is necessary to bring about the desired results.

In all of the urban cases and in the Million Man March as well, it was a combination of an urgent idea and the existence of charismatic leadership that made possible either large or significant mobilization over a period of time. The Texaco boycott, for example, sparked an urgent, spontaneous action that was triggered by the emotional outrage of Blacks who began to answer Reverend Jackson's call to boycott gas stations all over the country. And although it did not last very long, had the company not responded quickly and the boycott continued, it would also have required considerable organization to have kept going. It might, likewise, have required the organization of additional pressure through the promised stock action that the NAACP had committed itself to employ.

Another point worth noting is that in the case of the Miami boycott, the Chicago construction confrontations, the Texaco boycott, and the Million Man March, the existence of coalitions of Black organizations employed in an act of collective movement oriented toward the same goal was especially important to the result. This is the case where such movements required human power in order to make them effective protests or especially the dramatic gathering of more than a million Black men in Washington, D.C.

Finally, added evidence of the importance of such leadership is found in the responses to the Texaco boycott, where Blacks were consuming gasoline at some stations either ignorant of the boycott or in defiance of it. One reporter asked those Blacks at a Texaco station in Washington, D.C., near Howard University what they thought of the boycott, and the replies were as follows:

- One respondent said that she did not conceive of the local station as a Texaco station, but as the station of the local owner.

- Another expressed the same sympathy, saying, "I don't care what Jesse says, I buy here because the people here are all right with me. I can't hold these people responsible for what some Texaco executive said or did."
- Another said the owners (Pakistanis) were "people of color."
- "They are independent, franchised dealers who are trying to make a living like everybody else." (Brown 1996)

Such responses are often typical of social movements where, especially at the beginning, the issue of whether or not to commit personal resources is at stake. These responses illustrate the considerable odds against organizing a common political response, in such cases where people are not educated about the problem being confronted, and not socialized to the stakes of the intended action. In other words, these responses suggest that aggressive leadership is required for militant action, where it is not possible to rely on emotion for spontaneous action that leads to mobilization. This requirement also constitutes an important reason why militant action is not utilized as frequently as possible, for even considering that some of the most powerful returns are derived from such tactics or strategies, they are also the most difficult to employ.

CHAPTER 10

Serving the People:
Unity and Accountability

This chapter focuses on the analysis of those elements necessary for the unity and accountability of leadership as frequently expressed values within the community for building the power necessary to accomplish group objectives.[1] As such we will discuss leadership most often at the national level, since it is easier at that level to discuss abstract elements of leadership that might apply to leaders at all levels. However, I will attempt to relate both individual and collective leadership to a paradigm of "empowerment" that takes into consideration the representative functions of both with a primary focus on the objectives of the people at the community level.

This discussion is approached with the understanding that the current social, economic, and political context will probably change very little in the immediate future. I assume this because such factors as the structural properties of racial stratification in America, the conservative culture of political institutions and their policy output affecting rights, and the economic dynamics of income, globalization, and devolution that affect the opportunity structure are expected to govern the landscape of American politics for a considerable period of time to come.

PROBLEM OF WHO SPEAKS FOR BLACK AMERICA

The internal political problems of authoritative agency has been a consistent problem within the community because of the lack of a formal process of sanction across the leadership spectrum. To be sure, there is an internal process of the validation of leaders; however, it takes place within a given organization, where elections may, in fact, occur. The validity of the members of the leadership class, though, is legitimated by an informal process of recognition where processes of mutual recognition and selection, strategic recognition by mass audiences at formal events, and other social strategies are used to anoint individual internal leaders.

As such, the lack of a formal process of legitimation also means that there is no process of formal sanction for violation of group norms and, thus, informal sanction is used. Again, sanction may be located within each organization if there is a violation of the specific norms of an organization, but there is no mechanism that exists across the leadership spectrum for delegitimizing leaders, except for the informal process of social or political exclusion. In any case, one does not need to give the impression that such informal processes are ineffective. They are often very effective within the group; however, what occurs within the arena of the community may be challenged by the external process of leadership legitimation that is part and parcel of the internal process of recognition. It is the persistent threat of the external intervention that has made the unity and accountability of leaders such important values to the integrity of the function of the group.

The question of agency might be broadened by attention to what organizations or categories of organizations might be considered effective or viable. The organizational structure of the community has recognized the civil rights leaders and political leaders as the preeminent representatives of the group and the most legitimate carriers of its agenda. This occurs primarily because the arenas in which they operate are authoritative decision-makers for the entire nation, such that most other categories of leaders and their issues are serviced by these types of leaders. Below I will consider some systematic evidence for the prominence of certain individuals, organizations and types of leaders in a discussion of the values posed above.

Individual Leaders

There have been several analyses of leadership that have taken the form of polls on the popularity of various prominent individuals and polls on public opinion about the suitability of individuals for specific leadership roles.

The common heritage of the community is an important frame of reference for leadership as well as issue determination as illustrated in a poll taken by the Data Organization for *Ebony* magazine in August 1984 (*Ebony*, January 1985, 110–15). For example, the unmistakable importance of unemployment and the desire for jobs is seen in responses to questions suggesting it as "the most important problem," "the problem most worrisome," or even as the best method for reducing "Black on Black crime." At the same time, the survey leaves the impression that they are not members of organizations devoted to direct action for social change, since only 14 percent of respondents are members of civil rights organizations, although one can perceive other organizations as also performing such a function.

However, it was troubling that while a high percentage of respondents recognized Rev. Jesse Jackson to be the most influential Black leader, and admired him most of all, other leaders received so few responses that the study concluded that these "leaders are largely unknown to a large percent of the population." The base of those most admired or recognized as leaders is extremely narrow, consisting almost entirely of politicians, entertainers, or athletes—figures projected by the mass media rather than by themselves, such that other types of leaders like businesspersons, ministers, educators, academics, and others are entirely missing. This poll is highly revealing of the status of knowledge of leadership organizations and individuals who are presumed to be on the cutting edge of change and, therefore, gives to leadership a substantial task of organizational recruitment and an emphasis on solid achievements that project the goals, benefits, and personalities involved in making change.

Another such study of the attitudes of African Americans toward civil rights organizations was published by *The Detroit News and Free Press* in February 1992.[2] The results from this national study are reported in table 10.1. While the results of the poll validate the extent to which Americans still express overwhelming support for civil rights organizations, they also manifest the desire for substantial change in their style and substance. Contrary to many assertions in the media, many believe that civil rights organizations are still necessary and that they are legitimate to the extent that the federal government does pay attention to their demands. The desire for unity among leaders is manifested by the views of the survey respondents that, in the first instance, the job done so far has not been sufficient and (perhaps consequentially) that the influence of Whites constitutes an impediment, reflecting an equally important belief that accountability is the basic ingredient in leadership effectiveness. The evidence above also suggest those issues about which the respondents have high expectations for effective action by civil rights organizations, such as education, unemployment, crime, and poverty.

The study is concerned with a narrow category of leadership and the relative lack of attention to other categories might be explained by my view of the dynamic character of the activities in which civil rights leaders engage.

In one sense, the question of "who" might be addressed by assessing individuals. To that extent, a Gallup Poll taken in the summer of 1994, of a national sample of respondents asked the question, "Who was the most influential leader?" The survey found that Rev. Jesse Jackson, a political as well as a civil rights leader, was considered, by far, to be the most influential national Black leader in a survey of national opinion ("Civil Rights" 1993; "Few Blacks" 1994) (see table 10.2).

TABLE 10.1
"Who Speaks for Black America?"
Selected Results

Question	Percent Agree
White people have too much influence on the policies of the NAACP, the National Urban League, SCLC, and CORE.	55%
Federal and local governments pay attention to what the NAACP, the National Urban League, SCLC, and CORE have to say.	57%
The NAACP, the National Urban League, SCLC, and CORE are useful to us.	86%
The overall situation of Americans can be improved only if every person works hard to get ahead on his/her own.	78%
What type of job are the NAACP, the National Urban League, SCLC, and CORE doing in building unity in the community?	55% say "poor"

How important to you is the involvement of the civil rights organizations in the following issues (% very important):

Education	Crime	Poor	Unemployment	Affirmative Action
89%	84%	84%	82%	73%

SOURCE: "Who Speaks for America," *The Detroit News and Free Press*, p. 9.

TABLE 10.2
Combined Poll: 1993 Most Influential Leaders,
1994 Leader Who Represents People's Views Well

Leader	Blacks*	Whites*	1994†
Jesse Jackson	39%	35%	76%
Colin Powell	3	4	46
Clarence Thomas	0	1	40
Benjamin Chavis	3	1	32
Ron Brown	1	1	
Louis Farrakhan	3	0	33
Douglas Wilder	1	1	
Carol Moseley-Braun	1	0	

*CNN/USA Today, Gallup Poll, August 1993.
† CNN/USA Today, Gallup Poll, August 1994.

The polls cited in table 10.2 are important in two respects. First, they confirm other surveys of the status of Reverend Jackson's leadership prominence among both Blacks and Whites in general in the post civil rights era. Perhaps the basis of Reverend Jackson's support is that his activities have involved elements of both civil rights and political leadership in his rise to national prominence. Therefore, his acknowledged charisma has been utilized in the general field of American politics, defined by two dynamic sectors of mobilization, that is, civil rights and presidential politics.

Here, it is important to note that other civil rights leaders have made a transition to electoral politics such as Andrew Young and John Lewis, who were both close associates of Martin Luther King Jr. and served in the U.S. House of Representatives, but within an institution and in a role that, to the public, is more characteristic of administration than political mobilization. As a consequence, neither are as well known as Jackson nationally, nor have they acquired the opprobrium that is also characteristic of leaders who challenge the prevailing authority or practices of the majority.

A February 1996 survey by the Joint Center for Political and Economic Studies also supports the above results. In this survey, respondents were asked to what extent they felt favorable toward several national leaders in order to exact a statistical rating. The study confirms that according to respondents, Reverend Jackson ranks ahead among leaders. However, while Jackson scores far less well with the general population, Colin Powell ranks nearly equally well with both groups, being second to Jackson. Given the nature of the leaders selected for this survey, however, one must draw attention to the fact that the responses presuppose an evaluation of who the respondent might conceive to be a valid presidential contender. Undoubtedly, this is the reason why they chose President Clinton first (see table 10.3).

Secondly, with respect to what kind of leader, the CNN/USA Today Gallup Poll survey referred to in table 10.2 also contains the views of the respondents concerning the category of leaders they considered to be *very influential or most influential.* Here the survey also confirmed the finding in the *Detroit News* survey reflecting the strong loyalty of the public to traditional civil rights organizations as "very influential."

However, the poll also found that, *as a category,* the respondents viewed athletes and entertainers to be the "most influential" leaders (see table 10.4). This result might substantiate the widely held view that "public regardingness" is critical to the evaluation of what constitutes a most serious indication of the development of a public conception of leadership within the community that is more sharply defined. On the other hand, the lesser value for civil rights organizations might also be

TABLE 10.3
Favorable Ratings by Whites and Blacks of Selected Leaders by Percent*

Leader	Blacks	Whites
Clinton	88%	58%
Dole	31	49
Jackson	76	34
Powell	68	70
Gingrich	15	30
Farrahkan	34	8
Thomas	33	31
Perot	37	37

SOURCE: Joint Center for Political and Economic Studies' 1996 National Opinion Poll: Political Attitudes, David A. Bositis, Joint Center for Political and Economic Studies, February 1996.

*Unfavorable ratings are not given to enhance the comparison between the categories of responses.

TABLE 10.4
Most Influential Category of Leaders

Category	Percent Saying Most Influential
Members of Congress	45
Mayors	45
Businesspeople	44
Ministers and Clergy	50
Athletes	64
Entertainers	53

SOURCE: CNN/USA Today, Gallup Poll, August 1993.

explained by respondents' assessments, in the *Detroit Free Press* survey, that civil rights organizations were still viable, but that they were not effective on priority issues.

Leaders for Different Purposes

Finally, it is important to note that the respondents' views in various surveys about the individuals listed must not be conceptualized one-dimensionally. That is to say, Jackson, Powell, and Farrahkan have all received high marks in various surveys depending upon the nature of the context constructed for the evaluation by the question.[3]

Jackson.   As indicated in table 10.4, in polls where the respondent is asked to name the most prominent or influential leaders, Jackson will generally poll the highest. And he will be far less attractive to Whites than Colin Powell. This is so, as suggested, because Jackson most often appears to the public, including Blacks, as an archetypal leader, someone who is seen exhorting Blacks or others to do something (vote, boycott, etc.) to increase their power, influence, participation, or access in the political and social system. And he is also seen meeting with those who hold power on behalf of dispossessed groups to challenge them to deliver power resources in various arenas. Thus, their perception of him as a "leader" is warranted by the frequency, potency, and symbolism of his role.

Of course, Jackson also has serious detractors, many of whom believe that he is most often a patron of his own cause. However, this charge is difficult to substantiate on the strength of his public visibility alone, when the *content* of that visibility is consistently on the side of the dispossessed. Moreover, it is easier to see the tangible results of the advocacy of official leaders, since their advocacy is tied to the possession and use of official power to produce results. Leaders, especially in the field of civil rights, do not have direct ties to the power necessary to produce results by virtue of their unofficial positions as challengers. Their linkage has been more indirect through their ability to put pressure on public officials that, then, may produce results.

In Jackson's case, for example, he rarely receives credit for having played a role in the peace settlement in the Middle East, even though he strongly advocated and attempted to bring about such dialogue between Arabs and Israelis in the face of an intransigent U.S. government that supported a "no talk" policy (see Stanford 1997). Put another way, if a president wants to claim credit for something he was forced or advised to do, what is there to stop him? So, generally presidents and other official decision-makers have been given credit for policies they were forced to produce, even in cases where they were originally opposed, as we have seen above.

One source of the criticism of Jackson is found in the conflict between his own perception of his leadership and others' perception of it. For while most of America sees him as a "race leader," in the traditional posture of a "leader," Jackson does not. In fact, with his two presidential campaigns, he transcended the role of a traditional "leader" by developing a base, however small, within the White community at large, among other non-White groups and with White women. He has, therefore, had difficulty, even in the midst of his widely acknowledged primacy within the community and among leaders, taking on the mantle of a "leader" and organizing the leadership class. And one might argue that to the extent that he has not, others less able have a stronger role as "leaders" while Jackson has been less effective as an "American leader" because of the strong opposition to his progressive positions rooted in the conservative temper of the times.

Colin Powell.   As early as March of 1995, it was clear that Gen. Colin Powell was popular with Americans. A Business Week/Harris Poll indicated that Powell had a 74% approval rating with Americans in general, Bill Clinton was second with 54%, and Jesse Jackson was third with 46%. It was even more striking that the "disapproval rate" showed Powell at only 14%, but Clinton at 42% and Jackson at 48%, Clinton and Jackson's negatives being roughly the norm of the list of leaders, with House Democratic leader Dick Gephardt's being the lowest (33%) in a long listing of prospective presidential candidates ("Portrait" 1995). Polls taken from the fall of 1995 through early 1996, asking who would make the best president of the United States, consistently showed Powell in the lead. This position continued into the fall 1996 elections and even into the spring of 1997.

This historic response was material to the elevation of Powell as an "American leader" and in that role, he has generally been supported far more by Whites than by Blacks. For example, in the spring of 1996, while 54% of Whites said they would vote for Powell, only 25% of Blacks supported him (Scales 1996:3). And even though Powell proved to be a moderate Republican as defined by his support of affirmative action, his ties to that party, as well as his military role in the Gulf War and the Granada and Panama invasions under Ronald Reagan, as well as his generally White middle-class demeanor, described as "un-Negro" by one writer, made Blacks reticent to support him (Walters 1995:A3). Of course, the comparisons to Jesse Jackson were inevitable and in a wide-ranging interview with Powell, Professor Henry Louis Gates described the difference. "Powell talks like a schoolmaster, Jackson talks like the Holy Ghost." Then, quoting others, he continued: "When Jesse walks into a room, white people hear some sad-eyed Negro spiritual; when Powell walks in, they hear 'The Star-Spangled Banner' and 'God Bless America'" (Gates 1995:70).

At the same time, it should be noted that Powell rejected being perceived as a "leader" in no uncertain terms: "I am not a leader. I am not trying to be a leader" ("Powell Defeats Dole" 1995:A2). So the issue of Powell's leadership perception is fascinating because of the tendency for Whites to accord race leadership status to almost any prominent person regardless of his or her profession. Whether Powell will acquire the currency of legitimacy and become a Black leader or remain an American leader will depend upon whether or not he accepts racial roles and how well he performs them.

Farrakhan.   Polls taken at the time of the Million Man March in October 1995 through January 1996 clearly indicated that the public was willing to credit Minister Farrahkan for having led such a signally important event in the history of the community and in the nation. However, respondents were as clearly not willing to legitimize him to the same degree as either Jackson or Powell as a national leader. Although he polled well (44%) with the audience that participated in the march, as "an important leader" in the national population,[4] his support is similar to that of Clarence Thomas, Benjamin Chavis, or Colin Powell among Blacks. Moreover, the fact that Johnny Cochran (O. J. Simpson's defense attorney) and Coretta Scott King were also placed high at 35% and 34% respectively among marchers is a strong indication that the respondents were communicating current choices of individuals who were not necessary "leaders" but popular personalities.

Minister Farrakhan is a classic nationalist leader with the strongest legitimacy within the community of any other nationalist leader. Predictably, such leaders have enjoyed low levels of support within the White community, as he has, and even attract fear and hostility. Nevertheless, there is also no little awe expressed by journalists and others, both Black and White, at the stability and strength of his support within the community and concern that his influence may grow within the community and perhaps in the mainstream as well. Thus, there has been a singular focus upon his attitude as a Muslim toward Jews as a serious limitation upon his acquisition of greater mainstream support among Whites and upon his ability to radicalize the racial attitudes and ideology among Blacks to the point that the leadership of moderate, coalition-oriented leaders is diminished.

More recently, there has been grudging acknowledgment of his popularity with the masses of Blacks, which has found political expression in such incidents as that which found the mayor of Philadelphia, Edward Rendell, who is Jewish, willingly—and with great criticism from Jews—sharing the podium with Farrakhan at a demonstration and rally in that city. In February of 1997, a group of White men in Philadelphia attacked a Black woman, her son, and nephew and a month later, in the same neighborhood, in the course of robbing a store, two Black men shot a White teenager (Janofsky 1997:A19). Sensing the possibility of serious racial conflict, Rendell invited Farrakhan to join him at a rally, rather than leading a protest demonstration through the White working-class section of the city where the shooting occurred.

Despite his attempt to bring about greater understanding of himself and his organization in the mainstream, by attending editorial board meetings of major newspapers and welcoming television interviews, Minister Farrakhan's rhetoric about Jews forestalls any reconciliation with them and as such complicates and often alienates his relationship with other Black leaders.[5]

Then, his direct attack on other Black leaders only adds to this problem. For example, in his speech to the National Leadership Summit in June of 1994, he appeared hurt that "a litmus test has been placed on leadership . . . that someone came before us and between us." He threatened to "march on your corporations" and "wage war on Negro leaders who won't unite. . . . Pull them out, let them lay down with the slave master whom they love more than freedom." However, it was as clear that he valued the overture of the NAACP under Chavis' leadership, saying, "If we can put our differences aside, then we can help and hope can be kept alive" for collective leadership.

Given the vital role of nationalism in the mobilization of Blacks for many types of causes, and as an internal antidote to White racism, Minister Farrakhan's role within the leadership structure would have to be created if it did not exist. The criticism of Jewish leaders that Black leaders should separate themselves from Minister Farrakhan is actually one of the sources of his continuing support among Blacks. It feeds upon the resentment among Blacks at being told who is a legitimate leader or not, an emotion that transcends the nationalist sector of the community and gives Farrakhan some respectability among many who would otherwise not desire to associate with him or the Nation of Islam.

Jackson, Powell, and Farrakhan constitute a paradigm of leadership for America, one whose legitimacy is largely within the White community, another whose support is totally within the Black community, and a third whose support is almost totally within the Black community, but with some support among Whites. It would be rare if it were possible for such individuals to function within the context of a collective leadership structure, however loose, given the powerful determinants of legitimacy for leadership that exist outside of the community.

THE NEW STRUGGLE FOR
COLLECTIVE LEADERSHIP

The legacy of the practice of collective leadership has proven that it has a powerful instrumental character and that unity and accountability are necessary ingredients in defining the integrity of the collectivity, or the way in which leaders interact in order to achieve important tasks. In fact, it might be asserted as a principle that because of the low power quotient of Blacks, the more important the task is, the more necessary collective leadership has become.

The Desire for Collective Leadership

The year 1993 is important in a modern history of Black leadership, inasmuch as the Rev. Benjamin Chavis, former head of the Commission for Racial Justice of the United Church of Christ and a longtime civil rights activist, became the new president of the NAACP.[6] Immediately, Chavis adopted a strongly activist posture in which he not only sponsored gang summits of inner-city youths in an attempt to stop urban violence, but he also alienated other leaders of the NAACP when it was discovered that he had used organizational funds to pay legal fees to protect himself from a former female assistant who had charged him with sexual harassment; and for the use of the organization's finances in this manner he was removed from his post in 1994.[7]

Chavis' removal from the leadership of the NAACP would result in an even closer association between him and Minister Louis Farrahkan, partly because, shortly after his appointment as NAACP head, Chavis had sought to develop a structure for collective leadership by the creation of the National African American Leadership Summit that included all of the major recognized leaders, including Minister Farrakhan.

The first meeting of the summit was in Baltimore, Maryland, in June 1993 and at this meeting, Chavis' determination to have an all-inclusive leadership meeting was tested by his insistence that Minister Farrakhan be included. Also tested was the response to his invitation by other leaders who were sensitive to the position of some of their Jewish allies who objected to Chavis' attempt to legitimize Farrahkan as a part of the leadership family.

The tension was heightened by a catalytic event that occurred when Minister Farrahkan was disinvited by the March on Washington Commemoration Executive Committee as a speaker at the event in August 1993. Originally, Minister Farrakhan was invited but he was later disinvited as a result of protests from Jewish leaders. A confidential letter to march organizers from Rabbi David Sapperstein of the Religious Action Center of Reform Judaism was made public and threatened to withdraw Jewish physical and financial support from the march unless Minister Farrakhan was disinvited. He said, in part:

> During the 20th and 25th anniversary marches, I was fully in the loop in the development of the platform and program. I am exceedingly disappointed, considering how closely I have worked with all of you over the years and how strongly you must have known the Jewish community would react to these decisions, that these decisions were not only made without my participation and ability to share my community's concern, but without even the courtesy of prior consultation. This feels like a major breach of good faith.[8]

Nevertheless, Chavis continued to attempt to bring Farrakhan closer into an alliance of major leaders. An opportunity presented itself the following month when, as part of the annual series of weeklong events sponsored by the Congressional Black Caucus (CBC), on September 16, there was a National Town Hall Meeting entitled, "Race in America: The Political Perspective," which featured such speakers as the then Congressman Kweisi Mfume, chair of the CBC; Rev. Benjamin Chavis; Minister Farrakhan; Congresswoman Maxine Waters; and the Rev. Jesse Jackson. The session is considered to be important, because it featured the most representative, well-known political leaders; because of the drama evoked by the tension among the leaders; but also because their collective presentations surfaced many of the critical problems of leadership in Black America today (Kinch 1993:1).

This forum was an attempt by the Congressional Black Caucus to refocus the general crisis of the African American community upon the issue of racism as the major impediment to its forward progress and to reaffirm the responsibilities of race leaders. Thus, the assembled group of leaders addressed first and foremost the issue of unity and the question of whether or not the relationship among leaders should take precedence over challenges from outside of the community.

Chavis, striking an ecumenical note, said that the decision to disinvite Farrahkan to the 1993 march had been wrong and he vowed to work together with the Nation of Islam in the future in an "alliance." Likewise, Representative Mfume said that the CBC would make a "covenant" with the Nation of Islam on issues of most importance to the community. Reverend Jackson, however, called for "unity without uniformity"—a slogan devised in the 1960s by Amiri Baraka, which had become the standard formula for operational unity among various segments of the leadership, but which also was meant to preserve the autonomy of groups within a unified structure. What was meant by an "alliance" was more definite, implying a close working relationship. However, the meaning of the "covenant" was not made explicit, and with this lack of momentary clarification they pledged to define it in subsequent private meetings. However, no subsequent meeting was held to define the terms of the relationship, since Mfume was rebuked by his own colleagues in the CBC for having entered into an "alliance" without their agreement (see Merida 1994:A16).

The sensitivity between the more radical members of the leadership and the elected leaders illustrates the difficulty of unity. Mfume retracted the notion of alliance as a result of what was described by The Washington Post as a "testy" meeting of the caucus where some members challenged him, saying that they had never given him the authority to enter into a "covenant" with Farrakhan. (Such members included former Black Panther Bobby L. Rush from Chicago.) Mfume's subsequent formulation of this relationship made it clear that individual member of the caucus were free to engage in projects sponsored by the Nation of Islam at their will. Major Owens from New York City, who also expressed concern about the so-called "covenant" said, "Responsible African American leaders should *cease* [my emphasis] the pursuit of total unity within the community. We must leave the 10 percent who advocate hatred and violence and let them march off to their own destruction" (ibid.).

Nevertheless, among the two thousand in attendance at the CBC Forum, the venue itself acted as an instrument of accountability since Minister Farrahkan asked directly to whom leaders would be accountable. Then the strongly positive response to Congresswoman Waters' call for self-determination, was based on her notion of individual accountability, and her recognition of the view that unified and accountable leadership begins with some positive commitment and action by individuals. This thought reaffirmed the fact that whatever the problems of people, their basic responsibility for it marks them as the dominant aspect of the solution. This view is supportive of the principle often enunciated by Reverend Jackson that although Blacks may not have been responsible historically for getting knocked down, it is still their responsibility—even as the victim—to get up.

There appeared to be a rough audience consensus among all concerned about the comments of Minister Farrahkan that unity among leaders was possible so long as there was no *intervention from forces outside the community.*[9] Therefore, running through the dialogue and response from the audience was a deep alienation and sensitivity to the influence of outsiders upon leaders, as indicated in the data above and in the *Detroit Free Press* survey.[10]

Any formulation of pure autonomy, however, is a difficult criteria to operationalize, since some of the largest and most effective organizations exist substantially on the resources provided by non-Blacks and logically this gives the providers of such resources the presumptive right to intervene through such organizations in critical decisions affecting Blacks. Indeed, part of the tension surrounding the attempt to legitimize Minister Farrahkan within the leadership collective is the acceptance of his view of accountability, one that, if accepted by some leaders and their organizations, would exclude the traditional participation of Whites and Jews, in particular, in the structure of some organizations.

Proof of the difficulty of this criteria is the fact that the leaders present at the CBC Forum were reticent to discuss publicly problems, for example, that had divided Minister Farrakhan and Rev. Jesse Jackson in the past, for fear that a full discussion of the implications would open up the issue of accountability in a way that would be exploited by the media.[11]

The issue of accountability raises the question of whether there does exists—or should exist—a zone of autonomy as an important factor in maintaining the legitimacy not only of leadership but also the legitimacy of a common cultural ethos of the community in general. In short, it questions the nature of the "weness" of leadership in relation to the structure of its accountability. Many otherwise "Black" organizations in terms of their membership and leadership have also adopted overt integrationist positions that negate the value of their autonomy for all but symbolically cultural purposes. Yet the irony here is that many of the symbolically "Black" organizations have also performed more valuable services in support of the survival of people than those that consider themselves ideologically "nationalist." This irony has to do with the essentially reformist context of the political culture within which politics operates, which is reflected in leadership strategies.

The dependence of Black organizations on the resources of non-Black institutions, however, is more a function of the subordinate status of Blacks and their lack of major resources, rather than any other structural element. In any case, strong support of organizations by Blacks would lessen the reliance of their organizations upon resources outside of the community and limit the degree of intervention by those who seek to control their decision-making. However, one might retort that the positions organizations take on issues and the vigor with which they seek to cultivate support bears directly upon their success in obtaining additional resources, thus creating a series of interactive problems and a cycle of limited effectiveness that must eventually be broken, if the expectations of those who are represented by these organizations are to be maximized and an enhanced level of unity and accountability is to occur.

In any case, the cycle has not been broken. Therefore, it can safely be concluded that the case study of the head of the NAACP, the most important civil rights organization in the United States, attempting to forge a concept of pure leadership unity was watched closely by both Blacks and Whites. The fascination of the experiment was lodged in the knowledge that Chavis' attempts to bring about a collective leadership that included individuals abhorrent to Whites, especially to Jewish leaders, such as Minister Farrakhan was all but doomed to failure, but that if it succeeded, it would constitute a monumental change in the character of leadership if the organizations involved were willing to pay the price.

The Practice of Interactive Leadership

As important as the instrumental objectives of unity and accountability are considered to be and as complex as these values are to achieve in practice, there are successful examples of the practice among leaders of different categories.

A common corollary to the popular notion of the primacy of elected and appointed office that has arisen is the presumption that, by definition, membership in a major political institution is more powerful than an extra-institutional role in community leadership. However, *this is a questionable assumption.* In fact, two case studies of public policy in the mid-1980s, signed into law by a president hostile to them, indicate that it was the combination of citizen mobilization and public policy actors that was responsible for these victories. Then, a third case of interaction between public policy actors and a mass demonstration may have contributed to the issue accountability of the CBC even though the results were not as spectacular as the previous cases. These three cases will be discussed below.

First, the 1986 Anti-Apartheid Act, which cut off American investment and trade in South Africa, was a product of massive demonstrations at the South African embassy and its consulates around the country and the fortunate presence of Black legislators who managed the policy process in the House of Representatives (Walters 1987:65–82). The presence of Black legislators in the House of Representatives alone was not enough, since they had previously proposed legislation to cut off U.S. economic relations with South Africa, but it was not passed until the action of Blacks ignited a national protest involving people representing all kinds of American organizations opposed to apartheid, which was so large that even though President Reagan vetoed the Anti-Apartheid Act Congress would override the veto (ibid.).

Second, a similar scenario was present in the case of the Martin Luther King Jr. Holiday bill. For several years, Congressman John Conyers had proposed such legislation, but it was not until it became a popular national cause through high visibility, annual demonstrations on the Mall in Washington, D.C., beginning in 1978, involving individuals such as Stevie Wonder, who popularized the cause through the writing of a song, "Happy Birthday to You." As the demand for a holiday in honor of Martin Luther King Jr. became more visible and the objections by Republican President Reagan became more transparent, it was addressed seriously when the Democrats regained control of the Congress in 1984 and the president signed it into law in 1985.

A third case, mentioned above, involved the massive demonstration on August 17, 1993, which was developed to commemorate the 1963 March on Washington for "Jobs, Peace, and Justice." The 1993 march/demonstration was widely held to have been less effective than the 1963 march because it took place outside the context of any wider mobilization of the Black community and because its message was unfocused, largely because of an attempt to attract the largest supportive and diverse set of compatible policy interests and social groups.

Yet as contentious as the problems of its sponsorship appeared, perhaps overlooked was the fact that the effectiveness of the CBC in the wake of this demonstration might have been enhanced. The CBC, its numbers and institutional power enhanced by the 1990 census, was active in the budget negotiations of the new President Bill Clinton, and Kweisi Mfume, head of the CBC, later asserted that the mobilization may have helped them to obtain $10 billion in the Clinton budget package. For example, the CBC had an acknowledged influence on keeping in the Budget Act the $3.5 billion for "empowerment zones" (commonly known as enterprise zones); expanding the Earned Income Tax Credit from $17 billion; keeping $2.5 billion in food stamps that were phased out in the Senate version; and securing $1 billion for family preservation ("Role of the CBC" 1993). Without a mobilization, they perhaps would not have been as successful with the stimulus package, which contained $17 billion of economic resources much of which was directed at the cities, since it passed the House of Representatives by only six votes, eventually being killed in a Senate filibuster.

Perhaps the 1993 march had only marginal effect, but the fact that it served as a stage for policy pressure for the CBC, where speakers made demands for political reciprocity with the Democratic Party, may have helped the CBC proposals to gain a successful hearing with the Clinton administration. For despite the early tensions created by the CBC's rejection of an overture by President Clinton to meet with them in the wake of his withdrawal of Professor Lani Guinier's nomination as Assistant Attorney General for Civil Rights, a meeting subsequently occurred. Also administration officials were not only present at the events surrounding the 1993 march, but Attorney General Janet Reno marched in the demonstration itself. Thus, it was inevitable that administration officials were socialized to the demands of the march and may have responded to the demands as the politics of accountability.

The above cases are illustrative of the exercise of political influence in a way that is applicable at all levels of government. The methodology is the union between citizens and elected officials in a given action which acknowledges that *with an aware, mobilized constituency, elected officials often have the leverage to accomplish far more than through the singular power of their office alone.* Therefore, if the policy stakes are significant it would be logical that Black leaders would be challenged to not only share their responsibilities, but also their status with other leaders by devising common forums and strategies of action. The essential reason is that the combination of various kinds of organizations and individual leaders represents the combination of power necessary to confront intractable problems.

The Growing Complexity of Ideological Unity

From the previous discussion, the issue of leadership divisiveness often turns around the question of which individual or which leadership style is most effective in reflecting the interests of the Black community. One of the most divisive aspects of Black leadership has been the growing ideological conflict since the early 1980s. In fact, such conflict has been promoted by opinion leaders, politicians, and others external to the Black community who have been uncomfortable with the liberal cast of thought as the dominant ideology of the Black leadership group.

In order to affect a change in the liberal ideology of the Black community leadership, a meeting was held in San Francisco in December 1980. Arranged by Dr. Thomas Sowell, a conservative Black Hoover Institute economist, the meeting was funded by a foundation associated with Ronald Reagan's attorney general, Edwin Meese. After two days of discussion by various Black intellectuals and politicians, Meese characterized the meeting's objective as the promoting of, in his words "a new corps of trans-ethnic political leaders. . . . You also talked about the diversification of Black leadership. I think it is tremendously important for people who come from similar backgrounds to be able to have different ideas about how to solve their problems" (*Fairmont Papers* 1981:160).

This initiative was followed by President Ronald Reagan's rejection of meetings between his administration and Black civil rights and elected leaders with traditional constituencies and his attempt to put far more conservative Black leaders forward as spokespersons for the national Black community. When liberal leaders were invited to the White House on issues of importance to the Black community, conservative Blacks were also invited; when Black leaders representing hundreds of thousands of people were invited to appear on media fora, conservative spokespersons representing a narrow category of interests were invited to oppose them. The attempt was to delegitimize mainstream Black leadership, fostering the illusion, created by such staged conflict, that the major Black leaders were "out of touch" with their followers and that their followers actually desired a far more conservative approach to public policy.[12]

Although it is clear that there exists a set of traditionally conservative attitudes within the Black community, they have not extended to the rejection of the role of government or to the deprecation of measures designed to advance Blacks within the American opportunity structure.[13]

In any case, the issue here is whether or not the views of the masses of Blacks differ significantly from those of Black leaders as alleged by analysts from the ideological right.[14] An HBO/Joint Center for Political and Economic Studies survey attempted to address this issue directly by collecting data from Black party delegates and comparing them to the views of Blacks in the general public (table 10.5).[15]

In four of the six issues listed the views of Black Democratic Party leaders were not far from those of general Black Democratic identifiers, the outstanding exceptions being the issues of term limits and abortion. And while this survey is suggestive of the point that on most issues the views of Black leaders are not far from those of the Black mass public, the data also indicated that the strength of this generalization depends upon the kind of issues involved. Other studies have revealed similar substantial differences between Black leaders and followers with respect to the issues of school prayer, the death penalty, and gay rights (Hamilton 1982; Seltzer and Smith 1985; Smith and Seltzer 1992: chaps. 3–4). However, much more remains to be done on this subject.

The issue of the death penalty, however, reveals a substantial problem in the assertion that the views of Black leaders are often not synonymous with those of their followers, since when it is revealed that the death penalty is administered in a racially discriminatory way, the views of Blacks often change in the direction of their leaders. In any case, there are times when the views of leaders should not be the same as those of the followers because of the differential base of information often available to leaders, the difference in the arenas within which they must operate and the nature of their responsibility to often take advanced or otherwise different positions on some issues.

TABLE 10.5
Black Democratic Elites Compared to
Black Mass Public Attitudes on Selected Policy Issues

Issues	Black Mass Public	Democratic Delegates
Favor term limits	73.8%	37.5%
Pro-Choice	34.2	90.5
Support affirmative action	83.3	93.1
Favor school choice	32.3	25.9
Support government health programs	93.3	85.5
Cut defense spending	85.6	83.8

SOURCE: Data from a survey on Democratic and Republican delegates, 1992, The Party Elite Study and the HBO/Joint Center Survey in David A. Bositis, "McClosky Revisited: Issue Conflict and Consensus among African-American Party Leaders and Followers," Joint Center for Political and Economic Studies, Washington, D.C. Paper presented to the 1993 Annual Meeting of the American Political Science Association, September 2–5, 1993, Washington, D.C.

Although the effort to delegitimize traditional Black leaders has been largely unsuccessful, the residue of this strategy has been rationalized in the name of tolerating "diversity" of ideas within the Black community, a liberal idea. Cultural diversity is a fact of existence for any large group; however, when that group engages in competition within the political system as a group to attain its basic objectives, the *utmost political unity* is required. Unity, then, is a primary political resource for success, among others, for a subordinate racial minority.

EMPOWERMENT: THE PRIMACY
OF COMMUNITY POWER

The above discussion has illustrated the challenges that Black leadership faces in the process of representing the interests of the Black community. At this point, we may be in a position to make some deductive comments about the role of leadership in that regard. It must be recognized that since Black leadership, like all leadership, is set within a political system, it is necessary to allude to its basic processes.

Leadership is intrinsic to the comprehensive process of group empowerment as an instrument to acquire and manage influence, and its unity and accountability are essential to the effective representation of Black interests. James Jennings has addressed this concept directly:

> Black empowerment activists distinguish between "access" to the powerful and actual "power"; they believe that only the latter can make a difference in social and economic conditions for the majority of Blacks. Black empowerment suggests that power relations between Blacks and whites must change before the economic conditions facing Blacks can be improved. (Jennings 1992:34)

Jenning's distinction between the goals of access and power acquisition defines the goals of Black leadership that are addressed to the external power acquisition and projection functions. However, Black leaders accumulate community power resources, not only for the purpose of *external power projection-acquisition* in the major political arena but also more fundamentally for the sociocultural organization of community life itself. These individuals operate, as we have suggested, in two modes, first as individuals, such that the primary function of religious leaders is religious; economic leaders, business; governmental leaders, public policy. But to the extent that some individuals from each of these categories cohere into a leadership class for certain purposes, it is to direct community affairs by participation in the agenda-setting and decision-making process. In any case, the leadership style or strategy should not overshadow the objective: the community is the primary level in the process of empowerment since it is the origin of the legitimacy of its leaders and the recipient of their efforts in a reciprocal flow of power, legitimacy, and authority.

Power

To begin with, all objective discussions of power involve the ability of an individual or group to utilize resources in a manner that makes it possible to achieve certain objectives in a given situation. James Mac-Gregor Burns says that in the variety of definitions about leadership, one of the most compelling reasons why people submit to the authority of certain other individuals or groups to lead them is the overriding issue of the *purpose* involved for coming together in an organized form (Burns 1978:19). He suggests that "power and leadership are measured by the degree of production of intended effects" (ibid., 22). Since leaders use the support provided them by others as a power resource with which to achieve certain ends (produce intended effects), ultimately the discussion of leadership is about the rationale for that support, its magnitude, and the responsible use of the legitimacy it provides.

The local and national Black community are, then, the reference point for the determination of interests to be represented within the political system and the source of the consent to use the power that leaders acquire. This primacy of the community or the Black collective is the basis of the internal democratic system of the Black community and the ultimate basis too of the unity and accountability that are the source of its integrity.

Legitimacy

Leadership/organization resources are important because they determine the extent to which objectives might be achieved and external intervention into the organizational affairs of the Black community is possible and, therefore, whether the "zone of autonomy" that the leaders attempt to construct is actually possible.[16] Thus, leaders will often have different roles based on the origin of their resources, but they will also have such differences based on the nature of the organizations they lead, whether religious or secular, political or economic, national or local, and so on.

As such, leadership derives its authority and legitimacy from the community from which it emerges, and the African American community, like all coherent cultural groups, seeks to develop and control community resources and external resources in a way that creates the influence that enables the achievement of both collective and individual objectives. This suggests a logical model comprised of several factors that can be utilized to discuss the broad issue of the challenges of Black leadership in the process of empowerment.

One outgrowth of the differences that have emerged within the Black community, as was illustrated by the CBC forum discussed above, is that there are still important residual conflicts among Black leaders that have little to do with differences about the issues. Very often the source of such differences relates to role differentiation and leadership, and this relates to the origin of leadership resources. Table 10.6 might be useful in illustrating the source of role conflict. It asserts that political legitimacy of a leader is based upon the origin of his or her resources and that this is a major factor of, if not the decisive key to his or her political behavior.

The typology in table 10.6 is meant to suggest that the *consensus leader* is effective at acquiring resources both within and outside of the Black community and as such is in a maximum position to exercise leadership. The leader who has *internal* legitimacy/resources from the Black community alone can be very effective in leading it, but has limitations with respect to the extension of the influence of the community into the dominant political system. The leader who primarily utilizes *external* resources/legitimacy can be most effective outside the Black community and often is called upon to represent it within that arena. However, there will always be a question of legitimacy raised from within the Black community in this regard. Finally, the individual who has no significant sanction either within the Black community or externally is *autoselected* and can usually be only marginally effective in very limited leadership situations, since his or her resource base does not permit legitimate representation.

Therefore, in terms of the above discussion, it would appear that depending upon the survey, both Jesse Jackson and Colin Powell are candidates for "consensus" leaders in the Black community, Minister

TABLE 10.6
Leadership Legitimacy

Black Community Legitimacy	*White Community Legitimacy*	*Leadership Behavior*
Yes	Yes	Consensus
Yes	No	Community
No	Yes	External
No	No	Autoselected

Farrakhan is a "community" leader, Clarence Thomas is an "external" leader, and any individual might be regarded as "autoselected" with low legitimacy ratings in both communities.

Authority

The concept of Black "empowerment" often begins with a recognition that effective access to various official political arenas, such as legislatures, is important. However, access per se in the form of having won seats on city councils or in state, county, or national legislatures, is not, in itself, empowerment. If anything, elected or appointed office is a form of potential "instrumental power," depending upon how it is utilized. Empowerment entails utilizing these assets to actually obtain the items that enable the community to perform at an optimum level for its members.

Thus, it is possible to say that the process of "empowerment" enables the community, through the exercise of its instrumental resources (elected and appointed officials, community leaders, financial and political power, demonstrations, etc.) to acquire and manage the requisite influence (have more power) that would facilitate its ability to obtain the items necessary to its survival and development.

The Role of Leadership Coalitions

As Black leaders and their organizations have come to depend upon resources outside of their own community, they have underscored this by an overt philosophy of coalition-building, joining with other groups that are engaged in similar struggles. Such coalitions have been necessary on both the local and national level and here, I will briefly refer to the Leadership Conference on Civil Rights as the national example, and a local case of environmental racism.

The Leadership Conference on Civil Rights was started in 1950 by A. Phillip Randolph, Roy Wilkins, the then head of the NAACP, and Arnold Aronson, leader of the National Jewish Community Relations Advisory Council, with a mission to implement the report of the Commission on Civil Rights established by President Harry Truman in his speech, "To Secure These Rights." The meeting that established the conference, which in many ways crowned the Black-Jewish coalition as well, was held on January 15, 1950, in Washington, D.C., to lobby for fair employment practices. It drew 4,000 people, associated with 60 organizations, including 350 delegates from the B'nai B'rith, 185 from the American Jewish Council, 386 from the C.I.O., and 119 from the A.F.L. (Wilkins and Matthews 1982:208–9). Of these organizations, thirty became the basis of the Leadership Conference. In order to be eligible for membership, an organization had to be national in scope and have an ongoing civil rights program. The autonomy of each organization was protected in that the policies of the conference were not binding upon members and the organization was managed by a national board and an executive committee. It began the push for civil rights legislation with the passage of the Civil Rights Acts of 1957 and 1960, and although it played a role in all of the subsequent bills they were carried to conclusion largely by the momentum of the movement.

In the 1970s and 1980s, the conference broadened its concern with civil rights to include other groups, which made it possible for it to advocate for women, labor, the elderly, the disabled, gays and lesbians, and other civil liberties and human rights causes. Perhaps the most important of the recent Leadership Conference efforts was the Civil Rights Act of 1991, on which women took the lead, and a similar strategy was followed in the fight against Proposition 209—the California measure that invalidated affirmative action programs in state-sponsored institutions.

In the 1990s, the Leadership Conference has grown to more than 150 members, and there are times when, as with any large coalition, there are clashes of interest within the structure.[17] Thus, one might imagine that when Reverend Chavis was head of the NAACP and had sponsored the entry of Minister Louis Farrakhan into the Black leadership group, the apprehension extended into the heart of the coalition, which had always maintained strong Jewish support.

In 1991, the fledgling movement against "environmental racism" took shape with a three-day conference in Washington, D.C., sponsored by the Commission for Racial Justice of which Rev. Chavis was then the leader and which drew Black, Hispanic, and Native American leaders. In the five years before this meeting, local activists had begun to discover a pattern of the disproportionate placement of environmental hazards such as landfills, toxic waste dumps, water-polluting industrial facilities, and others near Black communities. This conference and other events stimulated national concern over the issue as thirty-two Black members of the Louisiana legislature gathered in December of 1993 in the small town of St. Gabriel on the banks of the Mississippi River to investigate charges of pollution of Black areas. Their concern was raised because a newly proposed plant would be the eleventh in the tiny town that was 65 percent Black (Bronstein 1993:A1).

This issue was raised to a national level when it was discovered that Black communities throughout the South were affected, causing officials at the Environmental Equity Fund to say that, "These communities bear a disproportionate share of the nation's air-water-and-waste-contaminant problems" ("EPA Official" 1994:A7). Fighting the problem involved establishing coalitions between civil rights group, legal organizations, and the affected leadership of the small Black towns, and by 1996 victories began to appear in places such as Carville, Louisiana, "Cancer Alley," where the governor, Edwin Edwards, prohibited the building of a hazardous water-treatment facility based on a Louisiana Supreme Court decision requiring equity in siting (Smith 1994:A3).

These instances of coalition politics often require that Blacks cede some autonomy of action in exchange for the acquisition of the necessary resources to achieve their objectives, such as legal assistance or expertise and financing for a campaign to establish favorable public policy and media attention in order to compete with highly financed, well-organized, and politically connected opponents. Moreover, the success of coalitions may also establish long-term dependency relationships, but if such costs are benign, it may be preferable, as a methodology of leadership, to bear them, until cost-free methods might be established. On the other hand, we remember the point made above that some organizations consider the cost of integrated coalitions itself a civic value in which they participate for its own sake as well. Otherwise, the costs and benefits of absolute self-determination strategies in such circumstances must be considered.

CONCLUSION

The issues of unity and accountability are also questions pertinent to the cultural coherence of Black people, which is threatened by modern economic and political forces that enhance the growth of class division. This is a substantial challenge to the Black middle class, which has historically borne the brunt of the leadership responsibility. One understands the strains and tensions of those who pursue the opportunity rightfully won by their own persistent struggle and sacrifice to move into new areas of residential and professional life, and the countervailing direction in that their efforts must also be directed toward shoring up the old places that gave and still give meaning to that opportunity. This is perhaps one of the greatest of all questions, whether or not the Black middle class will still see this task of reconstructing the Black community as its primary responsibility or that of someone else. In other words, will it begin to operate out of its own class interest or continue the tradition of fostering active leadership directed toward the preservation of the race?

The implications of the growth and diversification of the Black middle class for leadership are important, since (with the exception of militant Black nationalists such as Marcus Garvey and Malcolm X), they have predominantly formed the class of individuals that has ascended to the head of the organizational structure in virtually all Black organizations, including nationalist ones such as the Black Panther Party. Much of the desire for a "leaderless" Black community or for a "diverse" leadership is a rejection of the idea of community itself and emanates from the expanding privileges available to the Black middle class today, to such an extent that it has begun to weaken the support for traditional organizations and inhibit new Black civic organizational formation.[18]

Finally, as argued here, the common objective of all leadership is a democratic process of empowerment and to the extent that representative leadership is formed through a process of consent that flows from the masses to legitimatize and thereby create authoritative organizations and individuals, it involves all classes. And here, the struggle to obtain a consent that is not distorted by the disabilities of Black life, many of which emanate from decisions made by the majority, is the greatest challenge. The ability of the majority, as indicated in chapter 6, to establish the context for leadership and to reinterpret the terms of debates over racial access to national resources is a constant problem, which establishes a constant confrontation to which Black leaders must respond. In the management of consent, unified and accountable leadership is important and for the success of "operational unity," an appreciation of the different roles leaders play according to the source of their legitimacy is necessary both for leaders and followers alike, for the success of "operational unity." An appreciation of the different roles leaders play according to the source of their legitimacy is necessary both for leaders and followers alike.

Therefore, given the magnitude and complexity of the problems, a major question is how to maintain the consistency that is the underlying ingredient that builds faith in leadership and defines what is a responsible act of leadership? Authentic leaders must be grounded enough in the history and culture of their people to know, or to know how to find, the answers to such questions.

CHAPTER 11

Leadership toward What Ends?

It should be obvious, from the analysis in the previous chapters, that the primary function of Black leadership is to provide the strategic assistance in strengthening the common frame of reference and the common resource base in the Black community in order to help individuals and the group to achieve objectives perceived to be of value. In performing these tasks, leaders must interact in an effective way with followers in a community maintenance function in the first instance, and in arenas outside of the Black community in the second.

Black Leadership and Democratic Values

However, for most of this work, just as we have posited the fact that the dominant role of Black leadership has emanated from the functions expressed above, it is important at this point to suggest that a great many tasks of Black leadership are not postured toward the majority as only an oppositional, resource-providing social system, but are also directed toward conveying a sense that the Black community wants to exist within a democratic framework of harmonious social relationships and, as such, desires to be united with the rest of the country in the maintenance and furtherance of democratic processes and values.

In this sense, the politics of Black leadership has been conducted within the frame of reference of the democratic values to which the country aspires in its most important documents, such as the Declaration of Independence, the Constitution, the Bill of Rights, and other basic expressions of the high humanitarian calling of this society to liberate individuals from all sorts of tyranny by the rule of *democratic* law. Thus, the unique contribution and function of Black leadership has been to remind the nation occasionally through its own politics, that it is this allegiance to *democratic* law that is the source of its moral content, not merely the rule of law.

Thus, when the *Dred Scott* decision was issued by the Supreme Court in 1854, Frederick Douglass denounced it and rejected allegiance to it, since, as he said, it was merely the opinion of the "slave-holding wing of the Court" and thereby did not live up to the higher moral law of God that made slavery immoral and, as such, untenable. Similarly,

Martin Luther King Jr. denounced the laws of segregation as unjust and immoral and thus not worthy of Black allegiance, holding them to the standard of a higher moral law. Therefore, because at least in theory, the moral wrongness of the subordination of human beings is a widely shared value within the Judeo-Christian culture, its invocation by King challenged the moral conscience of Americans and ultimately provided the basis for their recruitment into the struggle for civil rights for Blacks.

The expression of these values by Black leaders has not been devoted to the liberation of Blacks from various forms of oppression only to enter into a corrupt social system, it has been to attempt to enrich the entire democratic legacy of the nation, and to use this legacy as a standard with which to measure the treatment of Black citizens whom they represent. Moveover, they have also pursued these values in an attempt to indicate that no modern democracy would be sustainable unless a course of racial reconciliation was at its center. Raising the issue of social inequality that affects many different groups has been a signal contribution to the continued search for a democratic construction for the entire nation, and among the various causes for inequality, racism has represented and continues to represent the Achilles heel of the promise of American democracy. Thus, the various projects of social change aimed at eliminating racism and constructing a regime of fairness have broadened the scope of democracy not only for Blacks but for others as well.

The more radical sector of the leadership of the Black community, however, has rejected the possibility of achieving real democracy, within the current context of racism and capitalism, as naive, and, thus, they have perceived the purest form of democracy to be possible only under conditions where racism and capitalism have been eliminated. This has given the radical leadership a continuing critical and, at times, oppositional stance to the mainstream leadership of both the Black and the White communities. Black radicals and nationalists have often expressed the desire to experience democracy, but within the framework of Black autonomy and control, even tolerating aspects of capitalism as long as it was within the goal structure established by Blacks themselves.[1] Black Marxists have likewise wanted socialist democracy that clearly subordinated capitalism to the interests of the working class and the enhancement of its socioeconomic status. The problem here, however, is that they have not been able to solve the dilemma of racism between the Black and White working classes to achieve it.

At all ends, it should be apparent that in a situation where there is a goal conflict that is inherent in the Black community, there can be no true consensus on the efficacy of leadership. Nevertheless, what gives some sense of coherence to Black leadership is the overwhelming preference for certain values expressed within the community that tend toward the accommodationist model, with Blacks seeking a level of social harmony with Whites while attempting to eliminate the impediments to enjoying the same rights and responsibilities of citizenship.[2]

Strategies

The characterization of most of the leadership strategies that Blacks have employed are, therefore, moderately change-oriented traditionally, as they would be for any group seeking entry into full membership in society. Thus, a strategy of change is dominated by *opposition* to forms of racist oppression whether from political, economic, technological, environmental, or other sources in the social system. It must be noted that the most radical oppositionist organizations (the Student Non-Violent Coordinating Committee, the Black Panther Party, the Revolutionary Action Movement, the All African People's Revolutionary Party, and many others) have all but disappeared. This occurred because, in contrast to more moderate system-oriented organizations, they were more aggressive targets of official surveillance and disruption, they were not supported in a sustained fashion by private or public financial resources, and they never had much active support among either Blacks or Whites.[3]

Another group of strategies is oriented toward a pattern of *incorporation* or integration into the system that, in some cases, may also be interpreted as change-oriented. If Blacks were to achieve positions in society where there were none before, that constitutes a physical change, such as the fact that a Black person served as head of one of the largest foundations in America, the Ford Foundation. There is some evidence of significant Black integration in this instance, the symbolic importance, however, of this lay in the fact that it is now known that an individual Black person may realistically aspire to such a position. Yet, as an objective observation, the symbolic value of Blacks in such positions is outweighed by the meager evidence that such persons' tenure have much impact on the quality of life in any measurable sector of the Black community. However, a more substantive test of change is whether or not the content of the institutional outcome changes as a result of the incorporation of Blacks.

Another example is broad-based incorporation. Here, the media is an example of where significant numbers of Blacks have been incorporated or integrated into the industry, but where there is little evidence that they have collectively affected the nature of the press coverage given to racial issues.

From our discussion above, it is clear that there are some dominant patterns of practice being utilized by the Black leadership class that distribute their activities into three broad areas: the growth of system-oriented leadership, collective leadership, and militant mass mobilization.

Expansion of Bureaucratic Leadership

It is difficult to find systematic data on the actual expansion of the Black presence in bureaucratic positions. However, both in the public and private sectors, Blacks have made impressive individual gains in the Clinton cabinet, for example. For a comparison of cabinet officials, see table 11.1.

In the beginning of the first Clinton administration there were five Black cabinet secretaries plus Surgeon General Joycelyn Elders, a noncabinet official. However, by the end of Clinton's term only two were left, Hazel O'Leary and Jesse Brown. In the second Clinton term, there were three Black cabinet secretaries, plus Frank Raines, director of the Office of Management and Budget and Dr. David Satcher, Surgeon General.

The most tension and conflict was over Alexis Herman, who was initially opposed by organized labor, although the AFL-CIO eventually supported her. However, her appointment was held hostage by Republicans attempting to gain leverage over President Clinton to cooperate with the investigation of the Democratic Party fund-raising scandal in his presidential campaign. A wide range of Black political leaders such as Jesse Jackson, C. Delores Tucker, and others fought for Herman's nomination, which played a role in her eventual confirmation. On the other hand, Rodney Slater, director of the National Highway Transportation Safety Board and a longtime Clinton political operative in Arkansas, with no hint of scandal, was assured of elevation to the top spot in Transportation to succeed Frederico Pena. Pena was placed at Energy, placating Hispanics who demanded that their strong showing

TABLE 11.1
African American Representation in the Clinton Cabinets,
First and Second Administrations

	Clinton I	*Clinton II*
Agriculture	Mike Espy*	Dan Glickman
Commerce	Ron Brown*	William Daley
Drug Czar	Lee Brown*	Barry McCaffrey
Energy	Hazel O'Leary*	Frederico Pena
Labor	Robert Reich	Alexis Herman*
Transportation	Frederico Pena	Rodney Slater*
Veterans	Jesse Brown*	Togo West*
Surgeon General	Joycelyn Elders*	David Slatcher*

*Black Americans

for Clinton be rewarded. The other Hispanic in the administration is Bill Richardson, former congressman from New Mexico who was appointed U.S. Ambassador to the United Nations.

Unlike Blacks, who no doubt have felt that their representation in the Clinton administration was sufficient at the cabinet level, Hispanics spoke out consistently that they were not well represented in the administration. However, even in the first Clinton administration there was a paucity of Blacks at the White House executive and policy-making level. In a letter written by Reverend Jackson to President Clinton in June 1977, he pointed to the criticism of Christopher Edley Jr., former presidential assistant, who said that: "For all the great success the Clinton administration has had in achieving racial diversity in the cabinet, the subcabinet, and the judiciary, the situation has been lame when it comes to the President's own White House staff" (Edley 1996). Edley continued to note that in the office of the National Economic Council, the Domestic Policy Council, the National Security Council, the Office of Management and Budget, the Office of Science and Technology Policy, and the Council on Environmental Quality there were nearly 750 staffers and not one of these appointees was an African American or Hispanic, and only one was Asian American (Jackson 1997:2).

A great deal of political energy is normally expended in getting Blacks into strategic positions during an administration and it would appear that this objective was met since the highest number of Blacks served in the cabinet in history during the Clinton era. Still, the fact that Clinton signed the welfare reform bill, eliminated the largest minority set-aside program in the federal government, and has "downsized" more Blacks from government than any other president in history means that far more important than individual positions is the right policy direction coming from the White House. The logic of this is that although positions are important, far more political leverage should be expanded in achieving policy leverage since *positions* may also be used as political currency to substitute for real *policy outcomes*.

Militant Mass Mobilization

What we have suggested in chapter 9 is that despite the wide perception that mass mobilization ended with the 1960s, it continues at both the local and national levels. Mass demonstrations continue to be conducted, as the brief case studies in chapter 9 show, with respect to the demand for Black employment in both Los Angeles and Chicago, the Miami boycott, and the Million Man March. Other cases of recent demonstrations have occurred with respect to such issues as police brutality in Pittsburgh and against racist violence in Philadelphia. Perhaps the strategy of mass mobilization is more widespread than suspected, because more dramatic and visible mass demonstrations in various localities may have given way to boycotts, characterized by the kind of passive collective behavior that withdraws support and financial resources but is nonetheless very effective as the Florida and Texaco cases show.

However, mass mobilization appears to have been utilized in numerous instances where issues of education, environmental racism, housing, or other issues are involved. In short, where a condition exists that threatens the interest of Blacks, and system-oriented strategies do not produce results, mass action exists as a powerful resource with which to intervene in order to produce results.

Does the phenomenal success of the Million Man March signal another strategy shift to a more Black-nationalistic form of militant mass mobilization in response to a current political culture dominated by a conservative ideology? Perhaps. But this will likewise depend upon the nature of the specific challenges. The confrontation of the Brotherhood Crusade discussed in chapter 9 occurred in the wake of the Los Angeles rebellion sparked by the Rodney King verdict. Such a spark is impossible to predict with any accuracy, although it is probable that if the punishing attitude toward Blacks that is so apparent in the conservative ideology and mood continues, there will be an inevitable series of sparks created.

Integrated Leadership Strategies

From the cases mentioned and discussed above, it is evident that the most promising outcomes may be produced when dynamic forms of leadership are joined; where bureaucratic and mass movement leadership work together in an integrated system of political action. As suggested in the case study on the National Black Leadership Roundtable, however, the Congressional Black Caucus is now without a dedicated arm such as the roundtable organizations. Nevertheless, even without the roundtable, the selection of strategic legislative targets by the CBC should encompass the kind of political strategies that could be mounted outside of the Congress and that would raise the profile of legislative struggles within the body. This is a standard tactic of other effective groups that now plan policy campaigns to support various issues as professionally as they do electoral campaigns.

FEMALE LEADERSHIP

Women leaders are part of the expansion of leadership into business, government managerial positions, and political arenas in a pronounced fashion. A substantial cadre of Black women have gained prominence as leaders in a public sense and, as with men, their involvement in civil rights gives them special prominence. Here, one still thinks of Coretta Scott King, the widow of Martin Luther King Jr. and Myrlie Evers-Williams, the widow of Medgar Evers and former chair of the NAACP board, and Betty Shabazz, the deceased widow of Malcolm X. Other women, such as C. Delores Tucker, have achieved public status in the field of civil rights outside of the mainline organizations. Tucker gained recognition for her controversial fight against gangster rap lyrics with the record companies. However, she has also headed the National Political Congress of Black Women, which has been forceful in recommending Black women for positions in government. In fact, she and Dorothy Height, head of the National Council of Negro Women (NCNW), led a coalition of women in the fight for Alexis Herman to be the secretary of labor.

Dorothy Height—a quiet but influential woman of eighty-three (in 1997), has been president of the NCNW for thirty-eight years, following its founder, Mary McLeod Bethune—has perhaps the most national esteem among Black women leaders in symbolizing the role of Black women in the civil rights movement and in building an edifice in Washington, D.C., representing Black women's contributions to and their continuing role in Black community development. Its stated goal is "to advance opportunities and the quality of life for African American women, their families and communities."[4] This is accomplished through community service programs, advocacy, research, and education in the United States and Africa.

Height, whose leadership as the only woman in the pantheon of 1960s Black civil rights leaders, was very influential through the entire period of the civil rights movement and has remained so in the 1990s, as she became president of the Leadership Conference on Civil Rights. However, in the 1990s, she effected a shift in the NCNW that she said was "underscored by the lack of interest that many politicians now had toward civil rights." She continued: "The conditions facing our people today are such that we need to develop national strategies to produce grassroots results" (Trescott 1996:C1).

In 1986, the NCNW initiated the National Black Family Reunion, which originated as a three-day summer festival of family-oriented music, recreational, educational, and service tents set up on the Mall in Washington, D.C., which featured workshops by nationally known figures in many fields. The idea also spread to other cities and in the late 1990s, it involved some 6 million people in several cities. Its drawing power is vested in fact that valuable information is distributed involving families, but there is also the attractive theme of pride in the Black family and what one participant described as its "positivity" (Powell 1996:B3).

The council is unique in its role as a coalition of thirty-four affiliated Black women's organizations that comprise 250 sections or chapters in local communities around the nation, which includes major Black organizations in health services and education, as well as trade union women's groups, church women's groups, sororities, and others. It currently has sixty thousand members who are focused on programs, one of which is the Dorothy I. Height Leadership Institute designed to train college-educated young women in leadership skills, and another is the National Centers for African American Women, which serves as a center for information on critical issues of importance to women and families. The NCNW has also reached out to African women in various program areas.

One of the major driving ideas of NCNW is that although women have been the fuel of many Black organizations, they have seldom been promoted as leaders. In this respect, Height said:

> I think it is important for African American women to get credit for what we do, and to acknowledge that we are doing it well, and to see ourselves as victorious, and not forget women like (civil rights activist) Fannie Lou Hamer and (newspaper publisher) Ida B. Well. Any entity, [even] the political bodies and the churches, that is oppressive to women, we should withdraw our support from. (Trescott 1996)

Two of the most prominent Black women in politics are members of Congress, Maxine Waters of south-central Los Angeles, chair of the CBC (1996–98) and Congresswoman Eleanor Holmes Norton of Washington, D.C., who is known nationally from her public appearances and her former role in the Carter administration as head of the Equal Employment Opportunity Commission. In the Congressional Black Caucus, women play a significant role, as in the 105th Congress, the third woman to head the organization, Maxine Waters, was elected chair and also elected was a group of officers dominated by women: the second vice chair, Eddie Bernice Johnson of Texas; the secretary, Corrine Brown (Florida); and Whip Sheila Jackson Lee (also of Texas) are all women, and only one male, Earl Hillard (Alabama), vice president, is in the caucus leadership.

In addition, women sometimes express their political views differently than men with respect to gender-oriented issues. For instance, in the 103rd Congress, the vote on the Hyde Amendment, which prohibited federal funding for abortions, was unanimously opposed by the CBC; however, over half of the women in the CBC felt so strongly about the inclusion of the Hyde Amendment in the Labor, HHS and Education Appropriations bill that they voted against the main bill, but only three men did so in a vote where the bill was passed 305–124 (Bositis 1993:21).

Overall, as the number of Black elected officials has reached over

8,500, Black females at every level of government have still been growing to the point that they had achieved a 1:3 ratio to Black males in the
mid-1990s, with the rate of growth in numbers of both male and females
falling off. This treatment of women in leadership positions was not
meant to be exhaustive, but to raise the issue as posed by Smith in part I
of whether there is substantial difference between Black female and male
leadership as a serious question for further research.

LEADERSHIP ORGANIZATION

One agrees with a sentiment previously expressed by both this writer
and Robert Smith that one factor that explains the judgment that Black
leaders and their organizations have accomplished less than they are
capable of is because they are supported by a relatively anemic institutional base. As such, there is the necessity for the rehabilitation of the
Black organizational structure as an ongoing project in order to achieve
a more formidable support base for Black leadership that includes individual leaders and followers as well (Smith 1996:122).

The Rehabilitation of Black Organizations

As there is comparatively little emphasis on Black leadership, there is, as
pointed out in part I, even less systematic information on the nature of
Black organizations, and again, such information that exists does so in
the form of studies of individual Black organizations.

This observation is grounded in the reality that effective leadership
cannot be developed simply from the availability of a stable of fine individual leaders or even a collection of organization heads involved in a
loose organizational structure. It must have an infrastructure comprised
of instruments that give leaders the ability to better understand where
the nation and their community stand in time and in the space of global
events. It must give to the strategies and positions taken by leaders some
concrete, substantive direction that is drawn from an authentic wellspring of analysis rooted in the history, culture, and data of the group
and its requirements for progress. And as surely as it must focus on economic and political topics of local, national, and international significance, it must also adopt a more effective methodology for communicating ideas. A brief comment follows on each of these tasks.

Agenda-Building Resources

The management of a national agenda requires a competent political
infrastructure. Therefore, more political institutions controlled by
Blacks must come into existence at local, state, and national levels to

supplement the individual organizations of political leaders. Political organizations should exist that capitalize upon the substantial voting power of the Black community and turn it into a leverage force for economic and social objectives. The campaigns of Rev. Jesse Jackson for president, for example, have shown the obvious value in having an independent political organization that can compete for all votes, but that organizes the Black vote into a power bloc that is able to elect party and public officials. The formation of an independent institution that is able to field candidates for office, provide technical assistance and funds, and provide a structure for projecting policy issues and keeping officials accountable is a logical direction of political development. It is especially urgent, moreover, considering both the growing negative signals by leaders in the Democratic Party and the continuing hostility of the Republican Party to Black interests and political participation.

Also, it is obvious that there needs to be established a more effective lobbying apparatus controlled by Blacks. The demise of the NBLR with its Action Alert Network, the demise of the various political action committees, and the lack of strength of the existing Black policy organizations has left the civil rights organizations and the Congressional Black Caucus as the most effective lobbying complex. There has been the irony that one of the most effective Black lobbying organizations is TransAfrica, headed by Randall Robinson, which worked on issues regarding Africa and the Caribbean and was largely responsible for the Anti-Apartheid Act of 1986. The aggressiveness and mobilization techniques of TransAfrica should have been duplicated with greater skill in the domestic sector of the Black agenda.

As such, there needs to be an enhanced policy focus on social programming by various organizations, but there should also be some place where *priorities* are decided and where part of the resources of each organization are devoted to these urgent social needs. For example, when the policies of the Reagan administration began to take away the "social safety net" from the Black community and affected the ability of some Black youth to obtain college loans, a national network of Black churches was organized and began to attempt to provide supplements to needy students in 1982 and 1983. This project, which, in part, led to the creation of the National Congress of Black Churches was a commendable example of what should be done, but it was not as effective as possible because of the inability of the leadership to get a large number of church and other organizations involved through an informal decision network.

Framework for Collaborative Leadership

What would greatly facilitate decision-making of national development institutions in the political, social, and economic fields is the parallel development of Black leadership organization networks with formal structures that cut across interest lines. Obviously, without glorifying segregation, one of its advantages was that Blacks in various capacities were forced to *commune* together, and to a great extent the presence of so many different skills, social classes, and other resources has been vital to the success of the Black church as a multipurpose institution in the Black community. But the cohesiveness of the institutional parameters of the community have been weakened by the forces we cited above, so one great task, without which reconstruction is impossible, is recreating the *sense* of community through reclamation of the ability of Blacks to commune together at the leadership level for the purpose of local and national community development.

One of the more interesting projects was that sponsored by Rev. Tom Skinner and his wife Barbara Skinner (a former executive director of the Congressional Black Caucus), who annually held retreats for a network of top heads of Black organizations. These "off-the-record" retreats were sponsored with the assumption that if Black leaders could come together and get to know each other on an informal level, that trust and communication among them would be enhanced and a process of leadership activity would follow as a natural consequence. The sessions also acknowledged the need for spiritual communication and refreshment in light of the considerable burdens shared by each member of the group.

Methodologies. Such methodologies as that mentioned above enhance the initiation of frequent dialogue about goals and strategies for achieving them. However, such enrichment must increasingly be accomplished as a dedicated activity through the use of modern technology. A variety of techniques are developing with rapidity such as employing low-power television stations or cable in Black neighborhoods, purchasing time for public affairs programming on music-oriented radio stations, and the sponsorship of more issue discussions by mainline civil rights groups and religious institutions, discussions modeled on the Black Entertainment Television Issue forums held monthly in Washington, D.C.

Also, the development of networks facilitates the creation of a national computer network that could link the headquarters of national Black organizations. At the very least, more creative use could be made of telephone conferences and joint "planning dialogues" to supplement many of the traditional annual "information-sharing" conferences that feature big-name speakers, dinners, and ultimately little of lasting substance. Organizational budgets might emphasize increased allocation for more collective planning over a series of meetings, rather than large one-shot affairs. Some of this is occurring with the natural growth of web sites, where individuals and groups "discover" each other in cyberspace. However, these incidental occurrances need to give way to structured electronic information sharing.

Beyond the methodology of collective leadership, there is the question of the skill at acquiring the resources to work through its problematics. In many local communities, for instance, Black leaders are engaged in building linkages to local and national funding organizations such as foundations, banks, and state government in an effort to conduct local development initiatives. The information revolution has placed greater demands upon the technical skills in response to the new necessity to achieve some level of competence in the use of the information technology. However, once mastered, it opens up vast informational resources that can be placed at the disposal of leaders. In short, whereas the leadership tools of the 1960s were a megaphone, telephone, typewriter, and xerox machine, along with intelligence and the energy to organize door-to-door, today intelligence is still required but the application of it has changed considerably to the use of faxes, computers, cell phones, power books, and an array of other sophisticated means of contacting and organizing people; in addition to the "tried and true" method of going door-to-door and talking to people face-to-face.

Finally, there should be a more robust polling and survey capacity in order to systematically assess the opinions and attitudes of the Black masses with regard to leadership and organization on a more frequent basis than is currently the case. At present, the socioeconomic status data on the Black community is produced by the decennial Census and current population estimates are produced in the interim. Other surveys are administered by major survey organizations for various media. These surveys only occasionally oversample the Black population segment of their national surveys in order to extract valid Black opinion data sets on major issues of the day. The National Program of Research on Black Americans at the University of Michigan has been mostly concerned with the behavioral manifestations of Black community life in their surveys, the exceptions being the 1984 and 1988 National Black Election Surveys and their participation in the design of the *Detroit Free Press* study. Finally, the Joint Center for Political and Economic Studies has produced surveys generally tied to the electoral cycle, the depth of which have been of limited utility. None of these surveys addresses the nature of Black leadership and organization beyond the popularity assessments of individual Black leaders.

Leadership Training.   Given the importance of local leadership in the entire process of empowerment that allows national leaders to represent important interests, leadership training is important. Many local leaders in the larger cities are connected to the national leadership by their chapter relationship and by the necessity for national politicians to raise funds for their campaigns outside of their political jurisdictions. On the other hand, local leaders need to gain legitimacy and substantial resources for their projects from local, state, and national sources. As such, leaders in these communities are often able to call upon the mainline civil rights, political, and economic leaders to come into their community to give exposure to important causes.

However, the domain of local leadership in many smaller Black communities is often unconnected to this system and, therefore, such leaders are more dependent upon skills and other resources from a variety of sources. They, therefore, need the training to be able to successfully access leadership resources, especially in an environment where many social services are being withdrawn at the national level and resources are being "devolved" to state governments, 60 percent of which are now dominated by Republican governors and conservative lawmakers whose interests are often inhospitable to those of inner-city Blacks, who are mostly Democrats. In light of the possibility that there will be added pressures on localities by the loss of government economic support, local residents will suffer if their leaders are not creative and resourceful.

Finally, efforts should be directed toward creating an independent student and youth leadership formation. SNCC was critically important in the civil rights movement in terms of bringing to the fore new ideas, tactics, and strategies, and generally serving as the movement's frontline "shock troops" (see Dittmer 1995; Payne 1995). Such an organization is needed in the post–civil rights era as part of a comprehensive structure of leadership. For a time the Black Student Leadership Network (BSLN) played this role. BSLN operated from 1991 to 1996 under the umbrella of the Black Community Crusade for Children, whose parent organization was the Children's Defense Fund, headed by Marion Wright Edelman. Through the Ella Baker Child Policy Institute, the BSLN trained hundreds of young adults between the ages of eighteen and thirty in community-organizing tactics, teaching methodology, and advocacy approaches "by linking community service with advocacy" (Franklin 1998). However, due to a variety of internal and external factors, the BSLN was only able to sustain itself for a short period of time (ibid.).

Ultimately, it is the accountability to national problems under conditions where issues have systemic effects at local levels, which gives national decision-making maximum credibility, as the leadership of every truly national organization knows. So, an obvious challenge would be to build a collective structure of national leadership that not only has the ability to pursue horizontal collaboration, but the capability to implement local servicing of national projects.

THE LEADERSHIP CONCEPT IN SOCIAL SCIENCE

I have not sought in this section of the book, which was fundamentally concerned with praxis, to consider where the practice of Black leadership fits within the existing studies in the general field of leadership. This field itself is currently on an uncertain footing as a subdiscipline of political science; however, there is important work being done to determine what contribution leadership studies might make to the discipline and to the furtherance of the goals of a democratic society.[5] And considering that studies of Black Leadership, as indicated by Smith in part I, also have not attracted many serious students and as such, have largely disappeared, my goal was to address the empirical elements of Black leadership from the ground up, as an exercise in providing raw data for subsequent analysis of many of the issues raised herein. Nevertheless, I will entertain in a preliminary fashion some of the issues I consider to be most relevant at this stage, issues drawn from the literature of political leadership.

Content.   The concept of Black leadership, considering the socio-economic status of the community it reflects, must by definition be change-oriented as it confronts the dominant culture, because Black leaders must secure the resources and the necessities that regulate the achievement of the vision of ultimate inclusion. The issue of "system change" requires some definition in light of our previous point about the finding in a 1997 Gallup survey that Blacks exhibit less support for system-change strategies than for change in their individual behavior. The project of "system-change," then, in order to attract the support of Black followers, must be targeted to changes in elements of the system, such as racial disadvantage, rather than to radical changes in the nature of the system itself.

The nature of Black leadership, oriented as it has been toward the exercise of power in an effort to mount projects directed toward changing the status of Blacks in America, would appear to conform to the description of *Transforming* leadership, offered by James MacGregor Burns. He says, "*Transforming* leadership while more complex is more potent [than Transactional leadership]" (Burns 1978:4). Burns continues that the acquisition and manipulation of power and influence in order to enact transforming objectives in the political system is a feature of leadership, and as such agrees with Matthew Holden and others that "the transforming leader recognized and exploits a potential need or demand of a potential follower. But beyond that, the transforming leader looks for potential motives in followers, seeks to satisfy higher needs, and engages the full person of the follower. The result of transforming leadership is a relationship of mutual stimulation and elevation that converts followers into leaders and may convert leaders into moral agents" (ibid.; see also Holden 1975: chap. 2).

In his concern with moral leadership, Burns defines the source of the power of the civil rights movement and the moral authority of its ideology fashioned by religious practitioners such as Dr. Martin Luther King Jr. It was not only that such leaders promoted Christian religious dogma, but King was exceedingly valuable in his ability to translate biblical teachings into the civil context of social movement and also to utilize it to analyze modern-day socioeconomic problems.[6]

Before leaving this topic, however, it should not be assumed that the writer feels that all Black leadership is Transforming. In fact, with the growth and dispersal of the Black middle class into a variety of professional pursuits, Transactional leadership also has expanded. Nevertheless, even Transactional issues may possess a different flavor for Black professionals than for Whites because of the pervasive role of race and culture. Indeed, the growth of Transactional leadership may have outstripped Transformational concerns within the Black community to such an extent that it may have become a barrier to the further emergence of Black progressive political leadership.[7]

Context.   As we have seen throughout in all of the cases, and as we have seen above in the concern with the cultural basis of leadership, context is very important. In fact, as Aaron Wildavsky says, "Context is crucial." Following this thought, he cited the view of John Miller on the lack of a correlation between leader behavior and organizational outcomes, which he answered by asserting that "leadership is a function of regime." Continuing to build a cultural interpretation of the problem, he says, "how leaders function . . . depends more on the social relationships that they are trying to justify than on whatever is inherent in the situations with which they are faced" (Wildavsky 1989:97). Wildavsky goes on to describe models of various regimes using two criteria, parsimony and persuasiveness, asking about group identity, group boundaries, and group objectives; in short, variables that describe the political culture or system within which the group operates and thus within which there is an interactive relationship (ibid., 99). This is a striking comment and it raises the question of the fit between organizational style and the requirements of the issue faced. At one point in the late 1950s, for example, the NAACP did not use direct action tactics, even though the system of racial segregation clearly required such a confrontation (Walters, forthcoming). One could say that by actively rejecting direct action, initially, they were behaving within Wildavsky's theory of justifying their stylistic strategies by their social goals.

Andrew McFarland also helps us to conceptualize the contextual variable with his advice that in order to understand the limits of a leader's action, we mentally extract the person out of the political environment and then think of what might have happened if the leader had not been there (cited in Wildavsky 1989). To this extent, Fred Greenstein defines what should happen with the thought that: "The impact of an individual's action varies with (1) the degree to which the actions take place in an environment which admits of restructuring, (2) the location of the actor in that environment, and (3) the actor's peculiar strength or weaknesses" (Greenstein 1967).

This discussion would appear to suggest that both the political culture of Blacks and the larger circumstance within which they find themselves have the most powerful shaping influences upon leadership. In fact, Wildavsky says something to that effect: "How strong or weak each culture is relative to the other cultures that operate in the same arena exercises a crucial influence over its behavior" (Wildavsky 1989:107). And while one might agree with the general thrust of this assertion, there is the problem of the balance among these variables, or the question of whether or not the cohesiveness of the group is more powerful a determinant of political outcomes, in a given situation, than contextual factors. I am sure that Wildavsky would say, "It depends."

Legitimacy.   In Wildavsky's work cited here there is included a statement from Benjamin Barber about the importance of values to leadership, that brings to mind the discussion in Burns about moral leadership and his assertion of its power in Black politics. However, I do not assert that the moral power of Black politics, which is based on a societal recognition of past injustices toward Blacks, is either the only power resource or the most stable since in order to be effective it requires the agreement of the majority in any given era. One finds in this era that the White majority has institutionally reinterpreted the moral content of the laws produced by the civil rights movement to be immoral as it affects them and feel injured by them.[8] Thus, even values are, to use Miller's term, "situationally dependent." In any case, Barber says: "Our dilemma is not an absence of leaders, but a paucity of values that might sustain leaders, not a failure of leadership but a failure of followership, a failure of popular will from which leadership might draw strength" (Wildavsky 1989:96). What this seems to say is that, in my concern with the nature of consent as the basis of leadership accountability and follower empowerment, followers have more to do with the legitimacy of leadership by virtue of the consent they provide and, by inference, the process by which it is provided. Bryan Jones has given us in table 11.2 a classification of values where he cross-classifies "the extent of influence on leaders of economic circumstance (structure vs. agency) and of followers (democratic accountability)" (Jones 1989:6).

Therefore, the problem of the basis of legitimacy might be posed as one of values based on the consent of followers, as Jones and I have suggested, with a strong emphasis on economic influences as an underlying resource variable.[9] And while my own designations are slightly different than those in table 11.2, there is also a high prospect for rationalizing it with Jones' model. For example, the "agent" might have legitimacy from followers only within the African American community, constituting the "community" leader; the "delegate/trustee" might have legitimacy in both Black and White communities to various degrees, as the "consensus" or "external" leader, and the "lackey/entrepreneur," lacking accountability, would be the equivalent of my "autoselected" leader. Finally, what Jones regards as the value basis of his model I suggest results in structural considerations that greatly influence leader behavior as does he.

Followership. Followers are obviously necessary to leadership, but whether or not they make leaders or simply provide a passive landscape against the leader's acts is a source of great debate. In a sense, this continues the concern with the issue of legitimacy, because it is not always possible to determine, with respect to any given leader, whether or not that he or she speaks with the authority of followers, since one of the qualities of leadership is that such individuals have effective opportunities to represent groups as though they were speaking with their authority. In any case, this problem is solved to some extent by Burns, whose view is that "leadership" exists as a function of "followership," in a never-ending set of transactions that determine the legitimacy, the content of the direction of leadership, and many other elements (Burns 1978:18–19). Such is the case, we suggest, with respect to Black leaders and followers, with an important caveat that I would pose.

Therefore, one must distinguish between the type of impact of followers upon leaders that creates leadership as "agency," or whether

TABLE 11.2
A Structure of Leadership Accountability

Structure	*Accountable*	*Unaccountable*
Agent	Delegate/Trustee	Lackey/Entrepreneur

SOURCE: Bryan D. Jones, "Causation, Constraint, and Political Leadership," in Bryan D. Jones (ed.), *Leadership and Politics: New Perspectives in Political Science* (Lawrence: University of Kansas Press, 1989), 7, table 1.1.

leadership means departing in some fundamental ways from the role of pure agent in order to operationalize unexpected strategies to achieve the ultimate goals of the group in any case. Leaders, then, are often focused on the long-term goals of the group, while followers are often focused on the short-term crises and thus, the leader, with just as valid a motivation, might depart from the short-term direction of the follower in order to attain long-term goals.

Since neither the Burns volume nor other leadership studies are very instructive about the nature of followership in transformational settings,[10] I conclude that, at the moment, the most informative studies of this subject are by sociologists who have been concerned with the process of recruitment in social movements. Zald and Ash in particular discuss the process of mass membership recruitment as a transference of interests and commitment between the leader and the followers (Zald and Ash 1970). They spend considerable time examining the situational factors that process recruits into and out of movements in a stable cycle of allegiance to the cause for which the movement has been mounted.

Therefore, cause-sensitive followership has characterized the adherence of Black masses to various organizations. The causes of civil rights, social justice, fair employment, equal education, and the like have probably (an assertion without any systematic verification to the contrary) regulated the flow of recruitment into and out of the various organizations that have attempted to represent an effective approach to confronting the issues for which the cause has been joined. In any case, this raises an intriguing question about the relevance of Miller's above observation in its application to Transactional or Transformational leadership.

Crisis. James MacGregor Burns begins his volume on leadership with the assertion of a "crisis in leadership" that was defined by the hunger among people all over the world for creative leadership in various situations and the lack of the institutionalization of leadership study and analysis as a major field of intellectual inquiry. This gap, for him, defined the crisis. Wildavsky's conception of this gap is defined by his term "(Anti)leadership," a notion which he describes as follows: "The greater the gap between demand and support, the larger the leadership problem" (Wildavsky 1989:104).

These concepts bring to mind the views of those within the Black community who, as we have seen above, have high expectations for leadership, given the relative weight of their circumstances to other groups in society and often low performance of leaders. Thus the concepts above would appear to provide an analytic model for Black alienation from their leadership that is similar to the relative deprivation model sociologists use to describe the alienation of Blacks and other dis-possessed groups in relation to society in general. One indication that the dysfunctionality of Black leadership is not as great as theorized by some is the lack of disruptive expressions of alienation from Black lead-ership by their followers. The cause of this may, however, mask a more interesting set of phenomena that might be unearthed by more rigorous analysis.[11]

As might be easily noted, I have taken the balance of my concepts in this section from the works of James MacGregor Burns and Aaron Wil-davsky. In my engagement with the evolving literature on leadership and its appropriateness for framing problems associated with the Black com-munity, I believe that there is far more to be considered in the works of Burns and its relevance to African American or Black leadership than I have attempted to address here. In addition, I have also found Wil-davsky's use of political culture, as the basis of his own contributions, to be a persuasive foundation for accurate observations and study of this subject.[12] Because I am concerned here with Black political leadership and its substantial focus on change, perhaps in further studies of system-oriented leadership, other aspects of the prevailing literature will be found to be more relevant in their explanatory power.

We Have No Leaders, Bad Leaders . . .

What appears to underlay the strong criticisms of the performance of Black leaders as indicated in the *Detroit Free Press* study mentioned in chapter 6 is the fundamental fact that Blacks, in general, continue to have strong expectations of them. This constitutes an objective affirma-tion that leadership is a natural part of any cohesive group and seriously vitiates the notion of a "leaderless" people. The logic of this view is that the process of Black incorporation into the general society is complete and thus Blacks can discard the old group/cultural leadership, especially the official national leadership, as their only valid or necessary form. Of course, there are many signs that the incorporation process is not only incomplete, but has stalled. One of the salient issues is the continuing evidence of the practice of Black exclusion from many arenas of Ameri-can life and active marginalization in most of those areas where they have been incorporated. This is reflected in the persistence of many Black organizations of an amazing variety; in the extent to which local and national Black leaders continue to sponsor "summits" and attempt to develop and implement "Black agendas" in their field of expertise; and in the empirical evidence pointed to above that illustrates the views of respondents that there is a necessity for leaders to overcome negative conditions by the use of power.

Thus, the conclusion that Blacks are leaderless or that their leadership is useless because of its incorporation into the mainstream must be tempered with the notion that Black leadership has always been incorporated to some degree on both a formal and informal level. This came to be true of the incorporation of Frederick Douglass, Booker T. Washington, the NAACP and the National Urban League, the Black cabinet of Franklin D. Roosevelt, and even the civil rights movement. While challenging racism in the South from outside of the political system, the civil rights movement utilized not only direct-action protest demonstrations, but the instrumentalities of the federal government. In fact, one could argue that the process of political collaboration between them itself facilitated the incorporation of Blacks into the political system. The same can be said of those who utilized the legal system to successfully challenge the legal infrastructure of racial subordination on many fronts.

One dilemma of the incorporationist stance is its increased dependence upon dominant majority institutions in a way that might also incorporate Blacks into the deprecative schemes and activities of that group. For once having legitimized that system and the system has adopted a strident ideological rejection of the use of race in the process of fostering changes in the status of Blacks and other oppressed non-Whites, incorporated Blacks are now, at the end of the 1990s, at its mercy. Thus, the critical dilemma of Black and other non-White leadership is whether to follow the incorporationalist theme and become part of the new ideology and system of renewed exclusion and resubordination, or to "fight from within" or intensify the fight from without.

The judgment might also be made that some of the most significant contributions to important changes in lives of Blacks have come about by leadership that was not incorporated because it could successfully mount mobilizations or otherwise challenge the existing racist practices from outside of the control of the political system. This, of course, is true of such challengers as W. E. B. DuBois, Paul Robeson, A. Philip Randolph, Malcolm X, and the Black Panther Party and others. And while some, such as Randolph, were successful in using the threat of political mobilization to derive concrete outcomes from the political system in the form of executive orders and the like, others in the listing were important in that they stimulated the public to pay attention to the issues at hand, which were often taken up by more moderate, establishment-oriented leaders. In this sense, we have referred above to the anti-apartheid movement in Southern Africa; other instances include police brutality and the right to self-defense, reparations, nationhood and the dignity of Black civilization, community control, and others.

Nevertheless, it is patently the case that, more often than not, Black leaders have not lived up to the expectations of the Black masses and skilled observers, as indicated in the surveys cited above. Seldom taken into sufficient consideration in this regard is the fact, as suggested, that a leadership reflects its people, their history, their personal and collective socioeconomic status, and their exposure to leadership resources such as technology and above all their funding base. To put it another way, an autonomous status of Black people in the United States would warrant an autonomous leadership class and structure similar to that enjoyed by White Americans. However, this posture for the group was clearly impossible and thus, the Black leadership in the nineteenth century was caught on the horns of a dilemma as the most effective strategy of the expression of Black autonomy was remission back to Africa, and yet the consensus was to remain in the United States. This contradiction and the consensus that emerged led to the establishment of a highly integrative posture as the dominant political objective of the Black community, which the leadership tends to reflect in their practice, seeking "upward elevation" and successful entry into the mainstream of American society. As such, the continuing acceptance of the integrative ideology—even in the face of its substantial rejection by the majority in practice—defines the Black leadership crucible and its class as being involved in the persistent pursuit of contentious goals. The nature of its political strategies must constantly take into consideration the etiquette of incorporation, a large element of which is the sensibilities and positions of the majority since it is their control over institutions and the political decisions within them that must be influenced to effectuate change. Such contradictions, at both the level of goal and strategy, have the endemic quality of reflecting the condition of the Black community in America, and thus, the wellspring of disapproval and approval of its leadership. For this reason, as one observer stated: "The tradition of internal dissension and criticism of black leadership was as old as racial uplift ideology itself" (Gaines 1996:246).

Thus, the radical solutions—and those who prefer them, because they have challenged both the notion and the etiquette of incorporation—have always been avoided, even deprecated by the mainstream leadership class. This is the source of their antipathy with Black nationalist, Marxist revolutionary, and other radical prescriptions for change. Nevertheless, with a substantially lessened concern for this etiquette, one might argue that strategies could be bolder and more flexible, but then, the leadership resource base would have to change to match the size and content of their ideas. Indeed, the fact that there are historically the inevitable explosions of Black militant nationalism may lie in the inadequacy of the accommodationist, incorporationlist, racial-uplift ideology that, as Kevin Gaines has suggested, left intact the racist logic of Black pathology, in the post–civil rights era, because it either left the racial integrity ideologies to the designs of the Black nationalists or, as I would observe, often reaffirmed the integrity of Black nationhood from a weak or defensive posture.

Some of the strongest critiques of Black leadership have been made by Black scholars, inevitably holding them up to high standards of performance. This, however, is the origin of the political antipathy between many intellectuals and a Black leadership class that often views the perspective of scholars as "unrealistic" and divorced from the context of the daily realities they face.[13] This is a reason why Black scholars may be invited to make presentations at the various annual conferences of the major Black organizations, but they do not generally function informally as a source of advice and information for the Black leadership, with, of course, a few historical exceptions.

Effective Leadership: A Constant Pursuit

Despite the modern tolerance of diversity, individualism, and the emerging variety of African American cultures, what Martin Luther King Jr. said in 1967 is still as important today: "Our nettlesome task is to discover how to organize our strength into compelling power so that government cannot elude our demands" (King 1967:137). However, it is even more urgent that the focus of effective leadership continue to be addressed, not only to government but more emphatically directly to the local African American communities, as we saw in the case of the Million Man March. There the critical issues that emerge necessitate the development of action strategies employing to a maximum degree the energy and skills of trained and dedicated leaders and followers.

Perhaps at this point it is necessary to enumerate a set of principles from the discussion above that may parsimoniously suggest those minimal issues that might facilitate the achievement of an effective unity among Black leaders both operationally and structurally. Effectiveness is presumed to be the ability of the leadership class to coalesce their resources in order to direct them to initiatives that result in the empowerment of the Black community. Therefore, regardless of the legitimacy of the resource base, there is the cross-cutting need for national organizations to:

1. Define and elaborate a style of leadership consultation that allows for both problem-solving and accountability to the wider Black community.

2. Give mutual respect to the diversity of roles among Black leaders and the individual requirement of their organizations, but to place the primacy of the maintenance of collective leadership among Blacks above external commitments.

3. Achieve a technical capability that would allow them to both service national memberships effectively and communicate with each other, such as the enhancement of managerial skills and use of telecommunications for rapid information sharing and issue mobilization.

4. Be responsive to the main currents of Black opinion, but seek to enrich it with creative and diverse ideas, tactics, and strategies.

5. Provide accurate analytical information to the public on the condition of the Black community and the aspirations of its people.

6. Be aggressive in the process of agenda-building in light of the considerable odds generally weighted against Black leadership in whatever forum.

With respect to leadership of both an individual and collective character, therefore, the observation made by Matthew Holden is still valid in addressing the condition of Blacks in whatever age: "The problem of current black strategy, therefore, is to save the future. Saving the future implies giving consideration to two other important problems: (*a*) the relationship of blacks to whites, and the ways in which that should affect black action; and (*b*) the development of a stronger objective capacity for action by the black 'nation'" (Holden 1973:144).

PART III

Conclusion

CHAPTER 12

Black Leadership: Toward a Twenty-First Century Perspective

In concluding this work, we return to a fundamental premise, which is that Black leadership emanates from the Black community in the sense that the individuals who present themselves for leadership have their origin in that community and its culture and that they should reflect the needs and aspirations of that community.

We interpret community in an "essentialist" fashion. That is, to us it is self-evident that there is a Black community; a historically constructed community of shared history and memory; with distinctive cultural, political, and economic interests; and with a geographic or spatial anchor in the nation's urban centers and the heavily populated Black belt counties of the rural South. We are concerned in this book with the actual behavior of men and women, as leaders, who attempt to mobilize power resources in pursuit of that community's interests.[1] To assume otherwise—that the idea of the Black community and a Black leader is itself problematic—would be to engage in a project of theoretical fantasy that ignores facts and evidence in pursuit of the researcher's vision of reality rather than the reality envisioned by Blacks themselves.[2] And while our major objectives in this volume were to summarize the existing research on Black leadership, make a critical analysis of the theory and practice of leadership, and thereby contribute to the parameters of the field of study, an underlying premise is the legitimacy and integrity of the post–civil rights era Black community.

THE STABILITY OF BLACK LEADERSHIP

When one considers the breath of the research on Black leadership over the last sixty years, one is struck by the degree of stability of the issues raised over time and by the continued usefulness of the analytical categories used to describe this complex phenomenon. While the studies published in the last decade do not make explicit use of these categories,

249

we note that the analytic categories developed in part I—power structure, social background, organization, and leadership styles—find consistent support over time.

Community Power and Its Structure

With respect to community power, we reconfirm our view that the community, either local or national, is not only the wellspring for Black leadership but the most critical element of its outcome-based performance. Therefore, the view of the community with respect to the performance outcomes of its leadership is the most legitimate source of evaluation. However, this legitimacy will always be contested by forces internal to the community and by forces in the dominant society.

This has much to do with the relative power of the Black community in relation to the dominant society. The ideas advanced in part II of clientage linkages between the Black power structure and the dominant White community is crucial to understanding Black leadership behavior. It posits a vertical set of relations in which Black leaders interact and connect with Whites and a set of horizontal structures and activities that connects Black leaders with other Blacks. In other words, Black leadership is characterized by a dynamic internal conflict over values, resources, and legitimacy as well as a simultaneous conflict with the dominant community, a dominant community that is frequently involved in a patron-client relationship with leadership factions within the community.

Social Background

While Black leaders are still drawn disproportionately from the middle class, we believe that the color of Black leaders, as a reflection of proximity to Whites, is less of a problem today than in earlier times. This is in part because the focus on "Blackness" as an ideology of group culture and pride has helped to lessen, though not to obliterate, such distinctions altogether. What we see today is the residual effects of the earlier "mulatto aristocracy" written about Myrdal, E. Franklin Frazier, and others: that is, the persistence of Blacks with lighter skins in positions of leadership through the consistency of familial ties, as well as the emergence of new formations of multiracial families among middle-class Blacks and Whites who have access to each other within elite social situations.

Otherwise, it is a matter of our subjective impressions that the mediation of opportunities available to Blacks has generally not occurred with respect to the color hierarchy, since the opening of access to institutions of higher education have been afforded to most Blacks, thus persons of all colors are able to assume positions of leadership. It is also our subjective impression—supported by some evidence—that skin color does not affect leadership ideologies or styles (Seltzer and Smith 1991).

Organization

As noted in part I, since the 1930s there has been remarkable stability in the structure of Black organizations, at the local level in particular, which is of course important to any community's leadership. These organizations, whether civil rights, civic, religious, or professional, have traditionally contributed to the leadership class of the Black community at the local level. Moreover, the national organizational structure has been remarkably stable, with a core group of civil rights, religious, political, and professional groups.

In the first instance our task is to understand what has been responsible for this consistency, and then account for changes in growth or decay of this structure. And although we have not attempted in this work to do more than outline a suggestive agenda of research, it is clearly one of the more important tasks that lay ahead in Black leadership studies. Clearly one direction to explore is that which suggests that the condition of the Black middle class is important to organizational growth. In sociological terms, it is the knowledge that resource mobilization is facilitated by the strength or weakness of this class.

This brings into relief the necessity to consider those factors responsible for the viability and health of community organizations, such as the opportunities for middle-class Blacks to exercise social mobility by moving into the broader environment of organizations. It would be logical to suggest that factors such as the withdrawal of economic resources by business, government and the philanthropic community from urban areas during the last two decades has caused a weakening of community life and therefore of its institutions and organizations. In addition, factors such as the outward migration of the middle class from cities and the upsurge in crime and social disorganization have exacerbated the problem. How have these factors affected organizational health, especially those agenda-setting and community-activism groups at the local level? Is there a reflection of growth or decay of these organizations at the national level?

A second challenge is to understand what factors are responsible for the cycle of growth and decay of organizations that arise on the stage of history in response to a given crisis, only to wither away not long after the crisis has receded. Thus, if one examines the 1960s in terms of the civil rights movement, the popular uprisings in the ghettos, and the Black power and Pan African movements that followed, a diverse array of organizations came into existence but they lasted only for a decade or less. Did the relevant factors have to do with the waning of the crisis, the weakness of the organizations, the maladaptation of leadership strategies and tactics, the inadequacy of organizational recruitment, or simply the process of struggle itself?

These issues are important, but we will not be able to answer them except to suggest that the acknowledged decline in the membership of organizations such as the NAACP may be due more fundamentally to the factors we cite, rather than to the lack of programmatic effectiveness. Or perhaps it is some combination of these factors.

Leadership Styles

Black community objectives are defined by a diffuse and often very abstract or generalized set of ideas such as "freedom," "justice," and "equality." These abstractions are then elaborated by more concrete policy objectives such as affirmative action, education reform, welfare reform, or employment policies. These policy objectives are then mediated by different styles of leadership behavior. Do we then confuse the various style differences with the objectives or their policy manifestations? The question suggests that there is a systemic relationship between the policy demands, the arenas in which the demands are processed, and leadership styles.

Thus, while it is relatively unimportant to determine stylistic manifestations of leaders with respect to the abstract objectives, it is critically important to understand leadership styles in terms of concrete policy issues. Obviously, in the situations described in chapter 9 dealing with mass protest mobilization, we have a style of leadership fitted to levying pressure for change in employment practices and contracting. However, how are we to evaluate the leadership style of Congressional Black Caucus Chair Maxine Waters when in December 1997 she organized a mass mobilization to protest a House subcommitttee hearing intended to pass legislation eliminating affirmative action (the hearing was successfully disrupted and forced to adjourn)? And how are we to evaluate Rev. Jesse Jackson's opening an office on Wall Street, meeting with the nation's economic policy-makers and financial leaders and the use of tactics such as buying stock in fifty major corporations in order to have access to stockholder meetings to press the case for equity? And what is the style involved in the NAACP's Kwesi Mfume's negotiation of what he described as a "Reciprocal Economic Empowerment Initiative," to encourage and monitor selective buying by Blacks at hotels with poor records of employing and contracting with Blacks? All of these tactical stylistic thrusts are contrary to the post–civil rights era presumption that large complex institutions no longer respond to mass protests, and as such Black leaders must abandon those styles of leadership.

Perhaps what is meant by this presumption is that far more influence can now be exercised by Blacks when they act as managers of economic development, bank executives, corporate board members, or others who have the ability to directly influence the allocation of economic resources. However, realism requires evaluation first of the extent to which Blacks in such positions will have the range of capabilities to allocate such resources toward the Black community. And second, to what extent might reinforcing styles of internal influence along with external pressures constitute a more effective strategic formulation.

Historical Transformations in Leadership Styles

In part I it was noted that the 1930s marked the advent of modern Black leadership. It was also noted that much of the contemporary research lacks an appreciation of the historiography of the emergence of the modern Black leadership class and how it has been transformed in the last several decades. Powerful social and demographic forces have played important roles in these transformations. For example, the consolidation of the Black urban leadership class in the 1930s in the North and West was a direct response to Black migration out of the South during this period. Leadership arose in the process of the adjustments of Black populations to the challenges of becoming socialized to new conditions, whether in the industrial cities of the Northeast and Midwest or in the rough terrain of the West, where Blacks built new settlements or contributed to existing settlements such as those in Texas and California.

The issue of class, however, must be seen as a major force in the early diversification of the Black leadership group from its base among preachers, teachers, and small businesspeople. One of the most important manifestations of this diversification was the Harlem Renaissance (which existed in other cities as well), which foretold the emergence of a new post-Reconstruction intellectual class. The growth of this class, fueled by such institutional factors as Black colleges and universities, Black churches, and White philanthropy, was an important factor in the aggressive mobilizations that would start in the 1940s and reach their peak in the 1960s.

The class factor has had the most important impact on the nature of Black leadership during the 1980s and 1990s, in that the continued growth and diversification of the Black middle class has resulted in its occupying new, elite positions in government, business, the academy, and the nonprofit sector, thus increasingly complicating what one means by "Black leader."

The historical transformations of the Black middle class and its impact on the changing character of Black leadership may be related to the problem of "strategy shifts" from one historical period to another. Black leadership has the onerous task of accurately determining, within any given historical context, what problems with what strategies can be addressed that give promise of positive outcomes. While this task of historical assessment is important, it should not result in the complete elimination of any set of strategies but rather experimentation with the entire arsenal of approaches that historically have demonstrated viability. The basis of this suggestion is that minority groups and their leaders possess relatively fewer power resources and therefore need to be alert to the use of strategies that may not, at first glance, appear likely to be successful. Such is the historical logic of the Selma to Montgomery March in 1965, the anti-apartheid demonstrations in the 1980s, or the marches and rallies that helped to mobilize support for the Martin Luther King Jr. Holiday Act.

REFLECTIONS ON LEADERSHIP PRAXIS

Having commented on some of the more salient features of the studies on leadership with an emphasis on their theoretical aspects, we turn our attention to some summary comments on the nature of changes in leadership practice. These issues of practice compliment those raised in part I but include other factors such as leadership beliefs (ideologies), gender, unity and diversity, and protest and accommodation.

Ideology, we think, is a dynamic determinant in both the historical development of leadership and a problem in leadership unity. Although the belief system within the Black community is diverse, the range of critical policy differences is relatively small. So, for example, while most members of the Congressional Black Caucus are liberal in public policy preferences, these ideological labels may mean different things within the Black community because these ideological constructs are defined by the dominant group.

For example, in the last decade of the twentieth century what might be considered "moderate" policies may be defined by Blacks as radical conservatism to the extent that they detrimentally alter the structures of opportunity. Accordingly, Blacks who are defined as liberal should be understood to be so only in respect to dominant group attitudes on issues of race and social justice. In the larger framework of Black politics, however, dominant group liberalism has been in tension with self-determination as was illustrated by its conflict with the Black power movement of the 1960s.[3]

These differences notwithstanding, the belief system within the Black community is extraordinarily diverse encompassing various varieties of Black nationalism, liberal and conservative integrationists, as well as radical Marxists and democratic socialists (Smith 1992). However, as we suggested above there is a relatively clear set of consensus positions on a number of issues that constitute a "Black mainstream." Nevertheless, some differences in policy preferences are so critical as to be internally and publicly divisive, and this allows for the exploitation of the collective power of the group.

An important example of this is the role of Black conservative leaders. With regard to the internal politics of the Black community, the NAACP is a relatively conservative organization that is squarely within—in fact, helps to define—the mainstream of Black politics. Black conservatives, while within the dominant group mainstream, are clearly outside of the Black mainstream. What Black conservatism therefore represents is the dynamic tension between the Black perspective and the attempt by Whites to impose the dominant group perspective on the minority.

Black and White conservatives share a consistency of views on such issues as the values of patriotism, Christianity, the traditional family, school prayer, the death penalty, public school choice, and relatively lower taxes and spending on social programs. And of course they share in the negation of mainstream Black leadership.

While mainstream Black leaders and Black mass opinion share conservative values on some of these issues, the fault line for Black conservatives in the Black community is their deference to White conservatism's narrow view of race, which renders them, in the eyes of the Black majority, a minority without autonomy or legitimacy. However, since the dominant group accords them extraordinary visibility, they appear to have legitimacy and thus they are a source of disunity.

Unity and Diversity

Obviously, the changing nature of the community and its historical diversification creates new challenges to unity. The emergence of Black conservatives as a putative leadership group in the wake of the election of Ronald Reagan is an obvious example. However, the collective response of Black leaders to the Texaco case is also revealing. The National Urban League was consciously absent in this response. The rationale for the league's absence was explained by its president, Hugh Price, in an interview with *Emerge* magazine.

> PRICE. Not every organization can do the same thing; you don't do that. If every organization does the same thing, then when you've accomplished

that [and] you've got to do the next things that follows from it, you don't have an organization there that can do that. You have no victory. You've won, but you don't have the ability to deliver on it.

We are bridge-builders. We maintain the bridges between corporate America and the African American community, between the media and the African American community. It is our strategic niche to say we'll be in the advocacy mode, but we'll work with these companies to try to create those hiring policies that bring young people into the contracting policies, etc.

EMERGE. But, what if these corporations don't do as they promise, in terms of minority hiring, and refuse to work with you? What do you do? Do you boycott them?

PRICE. Other organizations can do that. I mean, that's again, why you have to have in a civil rights movement, different kinds of organization that play different roles. We had breakfast meetings, we had midnight conference calls. And we were all of the same mind about what Texaco had to do. And we were all supportive of the direct action that was taken even though not all of us engaged in direct action. You have to have a variety of people who play different roles at different points of time. ("Price Fixing" 1986:38)

These sentiments by Price show the further complexity of the quest for unity. Even when there is basic belief system agreement and unity of objectives, Black organizations because of their role perceptions and differential linkages to dominant group powers may have less leverage to engage in strategies of protest.

A final example is the relationship between Black nationalist Minister Louis Farrakhan and the Rev. Jesse Jackson. Putting aside basic differences in belief systems, when Minister Farrakhan returned to the United States from a fifty-two nation world tour in February of 1998, he strongly criticized Reverend Jackson—on moral grounds—for Jackson's silence in the face of President Clinton's preparations for war with Iraq (Fletcher 1998:A9). This suggests that while on some issues—the basis of group identity and legitimacy—there may be room for agreement, on others there may be inevitable conflict. A critical factor in this particular incident is that Jackson was at the time a presidential envoy to Africa and thus his ability to exercise independent leverage in the Iraq crisis was constrained, while Farrakhan was free to behave as he wished.

Perhaps, then, a realistic view of the issue of unity among Black leaders must take into consideration the diversification of Black leadership roles in the post–civil rights era, a situation that creates both opportunities and constraints. When there exists leaders such as Reverend Jackson, Minister Farrakhan, General Powell, as well as others, who command large followings in separate and overlapping domains and have access to powerful dominant group leaders, national and international (although, paradoxically, they are often excluded from other power centers and often treated as "Negroes" in the most debased meaning of that term), the prospects for unity inevitably ebbs and flows. For these leaders must react to issues and circumstances contingent on the legitimate needs of the Black community as well as the legitimacy of dominant group communities. So, unity of action is not always an option.

Gender

The most important social fact that will influence the composition of Black leadership in the future is the changing role of Black women. Women have been a part of the struggle for freedom since the abolitionist movement (Richardson 1987). Nevertheless, the growing predominance of Black females in colleges and universities suggests that Black women will play increasingly important leadership roles. This too may create problems for unity, to the extent that men refuse to yield power and status. A larger proportion of Black women relatively to Black men are graduating from college, obtaining graduate and professional training, and moving into professional, executive, and managerial positions, as well as elective office (40% of all Blacks in state legislatures are women).

Protest or Accommodation

Protest has ebbed as a major strategy of Black leadership, as more moderate approaches have come to dominate in the post–civil rights era. This strategic shift toward accommodation is in part a result of the incorporation of middle-class Blacks into mainstream institutions and civic organizations. The argument might be advanced that since in the past protest politics produced more then accommodation, the relatively small degree of incorporation into mainstream institutions and processes and its accommodationist imperatives is not warranted given the distance Blacks have to go to achieve equality in the United States. So, while in part II a case is made for the persistence of protest mobilization, it should be clear that this case is usually not persuasive to mainstream leaders.

Here, it is tempting to suggest that a new era of accommodationist politics is here to stay, driven not as much as in the 1950s and 1960s by the ties of religious leaders to the White power structure of localities, but by the rise of the new middle class and the reluctance of the leaders of that class, in each of the institutional arenas in which they operate, to put those relationships at risk for more radical strategies of Black advancement.[4] Whether one assesses the leadership of the new class of Black mayors in Cleveland or Detroit, the lack of protest or dissent by

Black cabinet and subcabinet officials to the punitive public policies of the last decade (including the Clinton welfare reform legislation) or by the overall lack of demand from the middle-class Black intelligentsia for a more aggressive politics; accommodation is paramount. However, if the status of the Black community continues to deteriorate, then accommodation may turn on itself, leading to increasing alienation of ordinary Blacks from mainstream leadership. This would make it difficult for this leadership to use protest when it might seem strategically efficacious, or to lead a spontaneous popular mobilization when such mobilizations occur in the twenty-first century.

NOTES

PREFACE

1. Helen Astin and Alexander Astin, *A Social Change Model of Leadership Development Guidebook* (Los Angeles: Higher Education Research Institute, University of California, Los Angeles, version III, January 1996).
2. See *The Urban League Review*, tenth anniversary edition, 9.1 (Summer 1985).
3. Robert C. Smith, *Black Leadership: A Survey of Theory and Research*, research monograph (Washington, D.C.: Institute of Urban Affairs and Research, Howard University, 1983).
4. The last chapter of the monograph is not included in this volume because it dealt largely with the strategic implications for Black leadership of the election in 1980 of Ronald Reagan to the presidency.
5. For example, chapter 7 combines and revises two articles that were originally published as "The Challenge of Black Leadership: An Analysis of the Problem of Strategy Shift," *Urban League Review* 5.1 (Summer 1980): 77–88; and "The Imperatives of Black Leadership: Policy Mobilization and Community Development," *Urban League Review* 9.1 (Summer 1985): 20–41. Chapter 9 on militant Black leadership was based on "The Imperative of Popular Struggle: Three Examples from Miami, Los Angeles and Chicago," *The Black Scholar* 24.4 (Fall 1994): 32–38. Chapter 10, "Unity and Accountability," originally appeared as "Serving the People: African American Leadership and the Challenge of Empowerment," in *The State of Black America 1994* (New York: National Urban League, January 1994), 163–70. Finally the framework of chapter 6 is based on "Black Politics and Democratic Theory: The Tension between Two Strivings," in Niara Sudarkasa and Levi A. Nwachuku (eds.), *Exploring the African-American Experience*, 2nd ed. (Lincoln, Pa.: Lincoln University Press, 1996), 195–206.

PART I

We should like to thank Professors David Covin, Joseph McCormick, Charles Henry, Mack Jones, and Hanes Walton Jr. for their comments on and contributions to the postscript.

2. THE NEGRO LEADERSHIP LITERATURE

1. In addition to this leadership typology, Myrdal (1944, 1962:781) also developed a classification of Negro ideologies or what he calls "Negro popular

theories." The following Negro "thought types" were identified: (1) Courting the "Best People" Among the Whites, (2) The Doctrine of Labor Solidarity, (3) Equity Within Segregation, (4) Boosting Negro Business (Black capitalism), (5) Back-to-Africa, and (6) miscellaneous ideologies such as the Forty-Ninth State advocates and the movement for self-determination in the southern Black belt.

2. Wilson also identified three "functional" leadership types: the prestige leader, the token leader, and the organizer (1960a:256). He also notes that some logically possible types appear to have no counterpart in Chicago—for instance, the mass agitator or a counterpart to New York's Adam Clayton Powell.

3. E. Franklin Frazier in his brief treatise on the Black church writes that "as a result of the elimination of Negroes from the political life of the American community, the Negro church became the arena of their political activities. The church was the main area of social life in which Negroes could aspire to become leaders of men. It was the area of social life where ambitious individuals could achieve distinction and the symbols of status. The church was the arena in which the struggle for power and thirst for power could be satisfied" (1964:43).

3. FROM NEGRO TO BLACK LEADERSHIP

1. The classification of persons who are nationalist or Marxist in ideological rather than positional terms is a methodological device designed to display the presence/absence of these ideologies in the leadership stratum. Of course, nationalists and Marxists are also writers, publishers, preachers, and so forth, and they theoretically could be elected officials and leaders of civil rights organization, although empirically they tend not to be. Specifically, in 1963 and 1975 the nationalists in the *Ebony* leadership group were ministers. In 1975, the nationalists included a minister, a writer, the director of CORE; the Marxists included an educator and two officials of the Black Panther Party. Persons are classified as nationalist or Marxist on the basis of their self-designation and analysis of their speeches and writings.

4. THE BLACK LEADERSHIP LITERATURE

1. It should be noted that Hunter's 1980 study, unlike his 1953 work, is much less systematic and methodologically rigorous. Rather, it is more anecdotal and belletristic, and some of the findings lack technical reliability and may lack validity.

2. I was an observer-participant at the 1980 Philadelphia Convention.

3. Walters in his writings and activities has been flexible in discussing the party's ideology and constituency base. He argues only that it should be "nationalist," by which he means "all people or groups which can be said to have adopted a serious program to better the material and spiritual conditions of black life" (1973:16). But Manning Marable, another leading academic-activist in the party, is much more sectarian. He argues that the party should be "a genuine, anti-capitalist party, which rejects fundamental compromise and

class collaboration with the Democratic Party" (1978:318), and that the established liberal integrationist Black leaders should be excluded from the party because they "express tendencies toward class collaboration with the State" (1978:373). This divergence in view between two leading members of the party's intelligentsia on the basic questions of party ideology and constituency is illustrative of the historic sectarian factionalism that has bedeviled all previous efforts at building a unified Black community political structure.

4. The question of cultural nationalism is inextricably bound to the question of the status of Black culture, an extraordinarily difficult and complex phenomenon for the political scientist. The basic problem in terms of the question of Black culture is whether Blacks in the United States constitute a separate and distinct culture grouping (in terms of patterns in symbols and action) or whether they basically share the symbolic and action patterns of the "American" culture. To some extent one's position on this question of the status of Black culture depends upon: (1) one's definition of culture (Kroeber and Kluchhohn [1952] were able to list 164 distinct definitions of the concept by authorities in the field); and (2) what attributes of Black people's behavior and symbols are distinguishable from the behavior and symbols of other Americans. For analysis and research on this problem, see Huggins 1971; Hannerz 1969; Baraka 1969; Valentine 1968; Rainwater 1973; Cruse 1968; Levine 1978; and Patterson 1972.

5. In his contribution to the National Urban League's 1982 annual *State of Black America* report "Measuring Black Conservatism," Hamilton indicates that the pertinent data show that Blacks agree with conservative thought only on homosexuality, legalization of drugs, pre- and extramarital sex, and stricter law enforcement.

6. Cole (1976) also compared the ideological self-placement of this political elite with the self-placement of a random sample of the population, finding that both elites—but especially Blacks—were to the left of their respective mass. For example, while 16 percent of the Black elected officials labeled themselves radical and none conservative, only 5 percent of the Black population described itself as radical but 26 percent as conservative (1979:94). The nonrestrictive, open-ended nature of the self-placement scale makes this finding difficult to interpret precisely, given the Nie, Verba, and Petrocik (1976) findings regarding the absence of conservatism in the Black population. But it is likely here that the Black masses are expressing a conservatism on crime and cultural issues—such as sex and drugs—that may not be shared by the Black leadership.

7. In informal conversation I have heard the same evaluation from local and national officials of the NAACP and the Urban League.

8. Conyers and Wallace (1976:31) report the following data on the attitudes of Black and White elected officials toward aspects of socialism and capitalism (percentage agreement):

	Black Elected Officials	White Elected Officals
The country is moving dangerously close to socialism	42%	66%
The country is moving dangerously close to fascism	36	18

	Black Elected Officials	White Elected Officals
True democracy is limited by business privilege	70	26
The first responsibility of society is to protect property rights	37	50

The data suggest support for capitalism among Black elected officials, but considerably less support than among their White counterparts.

9. On the limitations of protest, see also Fox Piven and Cloward 1977; Garrow 1978; Lipsky 1968; and Wilson 1961.

10. Walters (1981:85–86) argues that these limitations might be overcome if, as a result of worsening economic conditions, the masses develop some perspective on the limitations of system-oriented electoral politics. Walters argues further that these limitations might be overcome if the leadership has the "honesty and integrity" to admit "openly that it cannot effect the necessary social change for blacks totally from within American institutions, and again support system-challenging strategies as a balanced plan of attack for the long run." The result of one or both of these developments would be the emergence of a system challenging Black leadership based upon a "balanced strategy" involving electoral politics and protest. Walters notes, however, that such a balanced system challenging strategy is only viable if the "pragmatic new black middle class" is willing to operate on such nonrational ingredients as "belief" and "faith."

11. Hamilton (1972:71–77) estimates that there are more than 57,000 Black churches in the United States with a membership in excess of 16 million and a clergy constituted by more than 50,000 persons.

12. Marx (1967:100–101) reports findings from national opinion survey data that show "irrespective of the dimension of religiosity considered, the greater the religiosity, the lower percentage militant. Militancy increases consistently from a low of 22 percent among those who said religion was 'extremely important' to a high of 62 percent among those who indicated that religion was 'not at all important' to them. For those high in orthodoxy (having no doubt about the existence of God, the devil or an afterlife), only 20 percent were militant, while for those totally rejecting these ideas 57 percent indicated concern over civil rights." Militancy also was found to be inversely related to church attendance.

It should be clear that, while the church may not have realized its potential as a political force in the Black community, it probably effectively serves the spiritual needs of the community, facilitates its cultural continuity, and contributes to its moral uplift. The clergy are also leaders of their congregations and communities in terms of other matters that focus on intracommunity issues that are not explicitly political (Nelsen, Yokley, and Nelsen 1971).

13. At the end of the Reagan administration, the number of senior level Black appointees was about 5 percent.

14. An exception to this generalization and others regarding Blacks in city politics is Los Angeles. See Halley, Acock, and Greene 1976; Hahn, Klingman, and Pachon 1976; and Pettigrew 1972.

15. Not only have academics noted the limits of Black mayoral power, Kenneth Gibson (1978) has written of the dependency of Newark and other cities upon federal and state policies if the fundamental problems of the city, especially its poor, are to be resolved. Carl Stokes (1973) described his tenure as mayor of Cleveland as the "promise of power" rather than its reality.

16. In the face of Gary's continued social and economic deterioration, Mayor Hatcher in 1987 was defeated after twenty years in office by Thomas Barnes, an African American. And in 1995 Gary made history by becoming the first African American–majority city to elect a White mayor, Scott King. Also Kenneth Gibson, the first Black mayor of Newark, was defeated (by an African American) in 1986 after four terms.

17. [Author's note] In 1986 Jack Greenberg, the White director of the NAACP Legal Defense Fund, resigned. He was succeeded by Julius Chambers, a Black attorney, and since then the fund has always been lead by an African American.

5. LEADERSHIP IN NEGRO AND BLACK

1. In an important insight into the Negro movement, Walker (1963:36) argued that "as long as broad agreement exists on ultimate goals of equality and an end to racial discrimination, some disunity over proper methods of social action may be positively desirable."

2. It may be of some interest to students of the sociology of knowledge to note that most of the studies in Negro leadership were conducted by Whites, while much of the Black leadership research has been conducted by Blacks.

3. On the theoretical limitations of the ethnic analogy, see McLemore 1972. The ethnic analogy has been discredited for purposes of theory in Black politics, most scholars agreeing with Pettigrew (1970:30) that it is "dangerously misleading." But the ethnic analogy is still primly applied by at least one prominent student (Eisinger 1980, 1978b) in his study of the transition to Black governance in the American city. The ethnic analogy is also employed by Sowell (1975 and 1981) in his studies.

4. While Jones' race-dominance framework is adequate to explain developments in Atlanta's Black politics prior to the advent of the administration of former Mayor Maynard Jackson, the framework is less satisfactory in accounting for Black politics in Atlanta since Jackson's election. This is so because in cities where Blacks are in power the research evidence indicates that their limited impact on the life chances of their Black constituents, especially the poor, is as much a function of the limitations on the authority of municipal governments and the oligarchical organization of the economy as it is of racial domination. On this latter point, Hunter's Atlanta case study (1980) is more theoretically relevant, suggesting that in the present era, race analysis must be joined with class analysis if satisfactory explanatory propositions are to be advanced.

POSTSCRIPT

1. In addition to the social science literature, there are several useful historical and biographical profiles of nineteenth- and twentieth-century Black

leaders. See Franklin and Meier 1982; Rabinowitz 1982; Litwack and Meier 1988; White 1990; and Williams 1996. See also Elliot's (1986) series of in-depth interviews with twenty-four prominent African American leaders, including five members of Congress, four high-ranking cabinet or subcabinet members, three persons in the judicial branch, five leaders of civil rights organizations, and seven state and local government officials.

2. *Shaw et al. v. Reno*, 509 U.S. (1993).

3. On African American women in Congress, see Gill's (1997) study of each of the fifteen Black women who have served in the Congress since the election of Shirley Chisholm in 1968.

4. There is little work on differential styles of Black leadership in Congress, comparing and contrasting, for example, such diverse Black congressman as Augustus Hawkins, Charles Diggs, John Conyers, Walter Fauntroy, Ronald Dellums, William Gray, Shirley Chisholm, Barbara Jordan, Gus Savage, or Bill Gray. An early example of such work comparing William Dawson and Adam Clayton Powell is Wilson's (1960b) study.

5. Professor Michael Preston edited the symposium where these case studies appeared in volume 2 of the *National Political Science Review*.

6. The concept of deracialization was initially developed in a 1973 essay by Charles Hamilton as a strategy to develop a coalition to enact full-employment legislation. On his reflections on this new use of the concept, see Hamilton 1992. Hamilton and Hamilton (1997) show that Black leaders and organizations have at least since the New Deal embraced a deracialized or what they call a "dual agenda" of race-specific civil rights reform as well as broad issues of employment and social welfare.

7. The formation in 1984 of the National Political Caucus of Black Women suggests that African American women are seeking a more active, distinct, and perhaps gendered role in leadership.

8. In 1995 the National Conference of Black Political Scientists initiated a special project involving evaluation by its members of the leadership, organization, and effectiveness of local NAACP chapters. Several studies have been completed and it is anticipated that in the next several years a couple of dozen local chapters from all parts of the country might be studied, which would permit the development of some empirically based analytic generalizations.

9. The Bush-edited collection focuses on the mobilization of mass support for the Harold Washington 1983 mayoral campaign and the Jesse Jackson 1984 presidential campaign; the mobilization of support for Mel King's Boston mayoral campaigns in 1979 and 1983; the election of the Marxist activist Ken Cockrel to the Detroit City Council in 1977; and the organization of mass activism in Oakland by the Peace and Justice Project to protest Reagan administration social and economic policies. Jenning's work focuses on grassroots activism in Boston and several other cities. And Covin's work focuses on community mobilization around the 1991 redistricting of the Sacramento City Council.

10. Both Barker and Walters were active participants in the 1984 campaign. Barker served as a Jackson convention delegate from Missouri and subsequently wrote a memoir about his experiences (Barker 1988), and Walters was

a deputy campaign manager and subsequently wrote a book on strategies of Black participation in the presidential selection process (Walters 1988).

11. See Henry 1996 for a collection of Bunche's papers, including several of his critiques of New Deal–era Black leadership.

12. Covin also found that California's African American legislators did not have "fully developed constituencies"—constituencies that are as fully mobilized as those of White legislators. Therefore, Black communities are unable to consistently apply any kind of pressure on White legislators. Moreover, this leaves African American legislators relatively free to develop and pursue their own agendas, without regard to the priorities of their electorates (1993:29).

13. African American mass opinion does exhibit a conservative tendency on many social-moral issues (abortion, gay rights, and traditional views on the role of women and family, crime, the death penalty, and school prayer). However, on economic issues, the welfare state, and civil rights Black opinion is near homogeneously liberal. And it is economic and civil rights issues rather than social-moral ones that determine Black partisanship and voting behavior (see Smith and Seltzer 1992).

14. The conservative African American economist Glenn Loury has been a consistent advocate of this point of view. See Loury 1984, 1985.

15. Robert Woodson, an African American conservative spokesperson and head of an organization founded in 1981 called the National Center for Neighborhood Enterprise, reportedly advised congressional Republicans on the design of the welfare reform legislation. On the role of the Reagan administration in helping to confer leadership status on Woodson, see Jones 1987:29 and Smith 1996:135.

16. In his second term, Clinton's major initiative on race was to launch a so-called dialogue on race rather than new programs or policies.

17. It would be useful to have biographies and memoirs of such important modern leaders as Mayors Richard Hatcher, Kenneth Gibson, Thomas Bradley, and Harold Washington; Congressmen John Conyers, William Dawson, Augustus Hawkins, Bill Gray, and Charles Diggs; and executive branch officials such as Robert Weaver, Andrew Brimmer, Patricia Roberts Harris, Samuel Pierce, and Ronald Brown. Work might also be done on such important community leaders as Lu Palmer in Chicago, Mel King in Boston, Danny Bakewell in Los Angeles, and Ken Cockrel in Detroit. Full-length biographies of Dorothy Height, the longtime president of the National Council of Negro Women, and Stokely Carmichael, the SNCC leader and architect of Black power, would also be valuable.

18. The historian V. P. Franklin used biography to good effect in his *Living Our Stories, Telling Our Truths: Autobiography and the Making of the African American Intellectual Tradition* (1995). See also Child's (1989) historical study comparing the leadership styles of Booker Washington, W. E. B. DuBois, Arturo Schomberg, George Ellis, and Elijah Muhammad, and James' (1997) historiography of the "talented" tenth, femininism, and civil rights leadership.

19. It is also striking that almost without exception the literature of the past decade on Black leadership has been produced by Black scholars, in con-

trast to the research of the earlier periods. This transition in the racial characteristics of the students of Black leadership began in the late 1960s and by the 1980s was virtually complete.

PART II

6. THE PRACTICE OF BLACK LEADERSHIP

1. Daniel Patrick Moynihan, now senator from New York, originator of the report: "The Negro Family: A Case for National Action" (1965).

2. Illustrative of such opinions is Tom Wicker's chapter, "The End of Integration," in his *Tragic Failure: Racial Integration in America* (New York: William Morrow, 1996): 1–13.

3. A more comprehensive and striking discussion of this assertion, as well as other aspects of Black politics that are influenced by contextual variables, may be found in an important study by Hanes Walton Jr., *African American Power and Politics: The Political Variable Context* (New York: Columbia University Press 1997).

4. See an early article, Roger W. Cobb and Charles D. Elder, "The Politics of Agenda-Building: An Alternative Perspective for Modern Democratic Theory," *Journal of Politics*, 33 (1971): 893–915. Also, by the same authors, *Participation in American Politics: The Dynamics of Agenda-Building*, 2nd ed. (Baltimore, Md.: Johns Hopkins University Press 1983).

5. There has been little improvement of the original insights of Matthew Holden in his description of the basis of Black politics in the development of the informal governmental structure of leadership. See Matthew Holden, *The Politics of the Black Nation* (New York: Chandler, 1973): 1–41.

6. The chief consideration of this meeting was whether to approve of emigration to Canada or to stay. "The Pioneer National Negro Convention," in Herbert Apthekek (ed.), *A Documentary History of the Negro People in the United States* (New York: Citadel Press, 1967), 1:102.

7. There are a number of case studies of the work of organizers from the Black community and others in the 1960s. Movements such as Jesse Gray's rent strike in Harlem, and others are well known. Also, Sam Yette's description of the Community Action Agency program that funded community organizers in the mid-1960s as a "pacification program" aimed at the Black liberation struggle was confirmed when the funding was eliminated when the movement for citizen involvement in city government actually began to reap some results. See Fred M. Cox, John L. Erlich, Jack Rothman, and John E. Tropman (eds.), *Strategies of Community Organization: A Book of Readings* (Itasca, Ill.: F. E. Peacock Publishers, 1974). Also, Samuel Yette, *The Choice: The Issue of Black Survival in America* (New York: G. P. Putnam's Sons, 1971), 39–40.

8. Common Cause web site, feature on Joe L. Reed; *Black Elected Officials: A National Roster*, 1994, Joint Center for Political Studies Press. This writer interviewed Joe Reed and the majority of the Black Caucus of the

Alabama State Legislature in 1989 in connection with the legal case on Black higher education, *Knight v. Alabama*. Reed, the caucus, and other elected officials have developed an effective interaction that has led to real influence on state politics where the Black community is concerned, especially in the area of education policy.

7. THE PROBLEM OF STRATEGY SHIFT

1. This sentiment is strong in areas governed by desegregation consent decrees of long standing where, as citizens in Prince George's County, Md., and San Francisco, Calif., argued, the original goals of desegregation have either been met or are unattainable because of continued out-migration by Whites, but the goals of quality education have not been attained for minorities. Rex Bossert, "Wider Desegregation Action South," *Daily Journal* (Oakland, Calif.: March 9, 1993), p. 1.

2. These comments were heard frequently by the author. The first comment was associated with Congressman Walter Fauntroy, the second with Eddie Williams, president of the Joint Center for Political and Economic Studies, and the third with Ossie Davis at the inaugural dinner of the Congressional Black Caucus in 1970.

3. See any of the recent annual surveys of the top 100 Black businesses published by *Black Enterprise* magazine.

4. Typical of such studies, see Charles Hamilton, "Blacks and Electoral Politics," *Social Policy*, May/June 1978, 21–27.

5. In this regard, the Rainbow Coalition is illustrative and interesting in that it purports to test the thesis of temporary coalitions rather with a permanent one.

6. A "large change" conceptually would be a radical increase in funding for an existing program, or a new program or policy, that would render service delivery in the Black community at a level that greatly improves the quality of life.

7. While many protest demonstrations are policy-relevant in specific terms, there is no guarantee that they will result in such an outcome, and they are often so alienated from the policy system that relations are not established with most useful institutional actors.

8. NATIONAL BLACK LEADERSHIP ROUNDTABLE

1. The author was a member of the CBC Political Participation Brain Trust (out of which NBLR developed) from its inception and this chapter is constructed from his notes.

2. Memorandum, Walter Fauntroy to Congressman's Home Rule Cadre, September 10, 1973. See also "Whip List," September 24, 1973.

3. Memorandum, Walter Fauntroy to National Black Leadership Summit, December 8, 1977. The Advisory Committee that structured the roundtable con-

sisted of: Walter E. Fauntroy, Kent Amos, James Brown, Eleanor Farrar, Norman Hill, James Gibson, Clifton Smith, Ron Walters, Wesley Young, and Joan Riggs (for Bill Pollard of the AFL-CIO civil rights office).

4. Letter, Fauntroy to mailing list, July 18, 1977, my emphasis. Fauntroy also used the theme, "Arithmetic of Black Political Power" for the Caucus Weekend Seminar on Voter Participation and Network Development, in September 1980.

5.. Memorandum, "Black Leadership Group," Parren J. Mitchell, chairman, June 22, 1978; Memorandum, "Black Leadership," Parren J. Mitchell, June 25, 1978; National Black Leadership Roundtable Meeting, Agenda, Saturday, July 15, 1978, Congressional Black Caucus.

6. I had been present because I expressed a sense of the implementation council in a letter to Rev. Joseph Lowery, chairman of the Black Leadership Forum: that the vital decision on the People's Platform and the issue of a Black presidential candidacy to be made at the April 30 meeting, should be made with as broad a support base as possible. Letter, Walters to Lowery, April 20, 1983.

7. The forum was held on May 28, 1983, on the campus of Howard University and featured: Francesca Farmer, Rev. David Eaton, Dr. Robert Smith, E. Livonia Allison, and Dr. Ronald Walters.

9. POPULAR BLACK STRUGGLE

1. Interview with head of Reddick Legal Society, Ft. Lauderdale, one of the organizers of the new hotel, May 2, 1997.

2. Indeed, a wider group of civil rights leaders including Rev. Joseph Lowery met to review Texaco's terms, and once satisfied pronounced the boycott ended. Kurt Eichenwald, "Texaco Plans Wide Program for Minorities, Rights Leaders Praise Deal and Drop Boycott," *The New York Times*, December 19, p. D1.

3. Ronald Walters, "This One's Not for Followers," *The Washington Post*, September 30, 1995 p. A23. This was written in reply to highly critical September 19 article by *Washington Post* writer Richard Cohen, who wondered why individuals such as myself, Philadelphia Mayor Ed Rendell, and otherwise legitimate groups of individuals, would be supporting Minister Farrakhan. My article labored to suggest that Minister Farrakhan was not the reason why most Black men were coming to Washington. This emphasis is clearly from *The Washington Post*, October 15, 1996 issue that contains front-page articles on the marchers, asking whether the march direction is "Unifying or Divisive," and another front-page article on Minister Farrakhan.

4. The reference to a "Muslim Program" is found in an article by Donald Muhammad, "A Brief History of Civil Rights Marches."

5. One example of this was a front-page article by a Ft. Lauderdale attorney, Charles W. Cherry, II, "Baptist Leader Refuses to March with Farrakhan While Black People Are Suffering," *Palm Beach Gazette*, October 12, 1995, p. 1.

6. In this regard, see James H. Cone, *Martin & Malcolm & America: A Dream or a Nightmare?* (New York: Maryknoll, N.Y.: 1991). Also, Herbert H.

Haines, *Black Radicals and the Civil Rights Mainstream, 1954–1970* (Knoxville: University of Tennessee Press, 1988), 1–76.

7. Hanes Walton, "Public Policy Responses to the Million Man March," *The Black Scholar* 25.4 (Fall 1995): 17. Walton explains that it has historically been characteristic of nationalist leaders who have harbored conservative and populism that the March "would not—nor could it—generate a list of public policy demands and wishes for policy-makers in the federal government," p. 19. He goes on to cite the efforts of individuals on the planning committee such as Professors Maulana Karenga and Robert Starks' attempts to give some public policy substance to the march through the development of a "manifesto."

8. Memorandum from Dr. Maulana Karenga to National Million Man March and Day of Absence Organizing Committee, Executive Council, "The Million Man March: Day of Atonement, Reconciliation and Responsibility, Day of Absence, Final Draft Mission Statement," October 7, 1995. For a compilation of the speeches, position papers, and other documents and commentaries on the march, see Haki Madhubuti and Mauluna Karenga (eds.), *Million Man March: Day of Absence* (Chicago: Third World Press, 1996).

9. "MMM Events in City to Mark Anniversary," *The Richmond Free Press*, October 10–12, 1996, p. 2. Mobilizing meeting were also held in Richmond as early as February 16 that year, where the agenda reveals a concern with such problems as: moral/spiritual renewal, family parenting, education, health, crime/violence prevention, children and youth activities, politics and voter registration, jobs and economic development and welfare reform. A comparison of this agenda to that of the LOC in Wichita, Kansas, also held sometime in 1996, reveals a strikingly similar set of issues addressed.

10. As important as the decision of the march leadership on the candidate, Diana DeGette, was the method they utilized of drafting a Black agenda and determining which of the candidates would support it. Tilie Fong, "DeGette Wins Million Man March Support over Rogers," *Rocky Mountain News*, October 5, p. 21A.

11. "LOCs Fulfilled MMM Promise," *The Washington Afro-American*, November 18, 1995, p. A13. This article describes activity in cities such as: Minneapolis, Minnesota; Detroit, Michigan; Kansas City, Mo.; Raleigh, N.C.; Buffalo, N.Y.; Chicago; and New York City.

12. The other committees were: Economic Development, Moral and Spiritual Renewal, Youth and Community Empowerment, Education, Health/Environment, Communication/Media, Human Rights, Law and Justice/Prisoners, and International Affairs. "NAALS," Conference Agenda.

13. "The Report of the Political Mobilization Committee," co-chairs, Ben Chavis, Ron Walters, Bob Starks, Ron Daniels, and Mark Thompson.

10. SERVING THE PEOPLE

1. The theme of Black unity and accountability appeared prominently as a strong motivation for the Million Man March in the Wellington Group/Howard University Survey of march participants. For example, they sup-

ported "building broad-based Black unity (85.1%) and self-determination by the Black community (85%) and atonement and reconciliation among Blacks (77%)—a form of accountability. Moreover, it was relatively explicit in the rhetoric of Minister Farrakhan and others with respect to Black leadership: "The unity of the Congressional Black Caucus forged a new relationship with President Clinton, they are giving a new meaning to race. The President knew he had to make some kind of a deal with the Congressional Black Caucus to get his legislative agenda through. That's power, that's unity. The Congressional Black Caucus must not break that unity and we in leadership must establish that unity." Louis Farrakhan, "Giving New Meaning to Race," *The Final Call*, October 13, p. 19.

2. This poll was conducted by the Gordon S. Black Corporation, from a survey questionnaire designed by Dr. James Jackson, director of the National Program of Research on Black Americans in the Survey Research Center at the University of Michigan. The survey contained a sample of 1,211 Black adults and was conducted in the winter of 1991–92, and contained a 2.8 percent margin of error. Janice Hayes and Ellyn Ferguson, "Who Speaks for Black America?" *The Detroit News and Free Press*, February 21, 1992, p. A9.

3. A revealing article confirms the essential popularity of Jackson, Powell, and Farrakhan and the rank unpopularity of Clarence Thomas, and the largely positive view of the NAACP and the Congressional Black Caucus in a number of surveys taken about Black leadership in 1995 by various organizations stimulated by the Million Man March. For example, a Princeton Survey Research poll for *Newsweek* in mid-October had the following response to the question of favorability of Black leaders, with Blacks responding that: Rev. Jesse Jackson (80% favorable; 15% unfavorable), Colin Powell (57% favorable; 16% unfavorable), Louis Farrakhan (41% favorable; 41 unfavorable), Clarence Thomas (25% favorable; 46% unfavorable). The article continued to point out that a Yankelovich Partners poll in the same time period of the Million Man March, with an open-ended question about "the most important Black leader" that had the following result: Farrakhan 21%; Jackson 17%; and Powell 11%. Finally, a *NBC News/Wall Street Journal* poll taken a few weeks later asked respondents who was the most important Black leader, given only three choices with the following result: Jackson 38%; Powell 30%, and Farrakhan 20%. Kathryn Bowman, "How African-Americans Size Up Their Political Leaders and Institutions," *Roll Call*, December 4, 1995, 21.

4. Minister Farrakhan received the highest rating (44%) among the individuals such as Johnny Cochran (35%) and Coretta Scott King (34%). See the survey conducted by the Wellington Group/Howard University Team, p. 6.

5. This comment broaches upon the much wider topic of Black-Jewish relations, which Abraham Foxman, head of the Anti-Defamation League, called "a dialogue of disagreement," is integrally related to this aspects of the problem of Black leadership, but it suggests a much more detailed treatment of the subject that is outside of the scope of this work. Foxman's comments were made in the midst of Ben Chavis' attempt to defend Minister Farrakhan from further attacks by Jewish leaders. See Lynne Duke, "A Continuing 'Dialogue of Disagreement'," *The Washington Post*, March 28, p. 1.

6. The process of leadership transition in Black organizations itself is

strikingly important and deserves a substantial amount of analysis by serious students of leadership and organizational behavior that we will not be able to give here. However, Chavis came to be elected in a field that included a dynamic woman, Jewel Jackson McCabe, and Rev. Jesse Jackson. Thus Chavis was chosen by a conservative board of directors who, it was widely perceived, was prepared to accept neither a female president, nor Rev. Jackson, whom they feared to be largely uncontrollable.

7. After Chavis was fired, strong majorities of Black respondents in a USA Today/CNN Gallup Poll favored strengthening Black unity by reaching out to Black conservatives (71%) and Black nationalists alike (62%). And while a significant group (38%) of largely young people approved of moving the NAACP in a more radical direction, the consensus supported the organization staying moderate (50%) and rejected reaching out to gang members (64%) and rap artists (66%). Maria Puente, "Blacks Like Chavis' Goals, Not His Focus on Rap, Gangs," *USA Today*, August 26, 1994, p. 5A.

8. A letter of complaint from Rabbi David Saperstein of the Religious Action Center of Reform Judasm to the major sponsors of the march, chiding them for not consulting Jewish leaders, indicating that if Minister Farrakhan spoke, they would not participate. See *The Washington Afro-American*, September 6, 1993, p. 1. Also Ron Daniels, "Vantage Point," *The Challenger* (Buffalo, N.Y.), September 15, 1993, p. 17.

9. It is difficult to use the author's notes of this meeting with much accuracy regarding the validity of the sentiments expressed, since even observing the scene as a participant in the meeting did not afford a perspective on what proportion of the audience were members of the Nation of Islam.

10. Indeed, a few days later, a *New York Times* editorial charged that Congressman Mfume, who had thus far made a creditable showing in his leadership of the CBC, had been "had" with his pledge of an alliance with Minister Farrakhan. "The Black Caucus Gets Mugged," *The New York Times*, September 25, 1993, p. A22.

11. Minister Farrakhan supported Reverend Jackson in his electoral campaign of 1984 and shortly after the campaign opened, Minister Farrakhan made the remarks widely reputed to him that Hitler was "great" and that "Judaism was a gutter religion." Those who heard the original remarks claim Minister Farrakhan had said that Hitler was "*wickedly* great" and that, with respect to the massacres of Palestinians in Shatila and Sabra refugee camps in Lebanon, any group that had done that in the name of religion was practicing a dirty religion. Nevertheless, press accounts distorted his remarks and the Jackson campaign became defensive of its association with Minister Farrakhan, which increased in the light of the remarks made by Reverend Jackson to a *Washington Post* reporter, Milton Coleman, characterizing Jews as "Hymies" and New York City as "Hymietown." Reverend Jackson's attempt to atone for these remarks to the Jewish community in various ways only deepened the estrangement between him and Minister Farrakhan.

12. The press has long appeared to be interested in the possibility that the liberal interests represented by Black leaders in politics and public policy were not congruent with the views of Black people generally. See, for example, "Black

Leaders Out of Step with Their People?" *U.S. News and World Report*, April 7, 1980, pp. 68–73.

13. A survey containing one of the largest samples of Blacks by the Gallup organization indicated that Blacks and Whites disagree, for example, that government's role should be to improve conditions for minorities (Blacks –53%). Whites, on the other hand, believe that government should not make any special effort to help Blacks, that they should help themselves (59%), and that affirmative action should be kept the same (29%) or decreased (37%). "Black/White Relations in the United States," Executive Summary, The Gallup Organization, Princeton, N.J., June 1997. Another survey that reveals the liberal ideological preferences of Blacks shows that 62% prefer a federal government that provides more services even if it costs more in taxes while 62% of Whites prefer a federal government that taxes less and provides fewer services. See *The Four Americas: Government and Social Policy through the Eyes of America's Multi-Racial and Multi-Ethnic Society*, a report of the Washington Post/Kaiser Family Foundation/Harvard Survey Project, December 1995, p. 25.

14. An example is Linda Lichter, "Who Speaks for Black America," *Public Opinion*, August–September 1985, pp. 41–44, 58.

15. The sample size was 750 Democrats and Republicans and the survey was conducted June 22–30, 1990 by Omnifacts, Inc. of Philadelphia, for the Joint Center for Political and Economic Studies, Washington, D.C.

16. For example, with respect to the issue of unity pledged by leaders at the CBC forum with Minister Farrakhan, in addition to *The New York Times* editorial that denounced this action as a mistake Congressman Mfume responded to a series of requests for meetings by prominent Jewish organizations. In the statement issued after one meeting with the Jewish leadership on September 28, Mfume indicated in effect that the CBC had to be allowed to work with anyone in their communities who could help bring progress and that, in that process, there would be some respectful disagreement with others of their allies, but that they should understand that it should not be a barrier to their mutual support of other mutual interests. Some members of the CBC were critical of the announcement of an "alliance" with Minister Farrakhan as well.

17. On the clash of interests within the Leadership Conference, see Dianne Pinderhughes, "Divisions in the Civil Rights Movement," *PS* 25 (1992): 485–87, and her "Black Interest Groups and the Extension of the Voting Rights Act," in Huey Perry and Wayne Parent (eds.), *Blacks and the American Political System* (Gainesville, Fla.: University of Florida Press, 1995).

18. This suggestion is not informed by any empirical data, since the growth and death cycle of Black organizations is yet another subject that deserves but has not yet attracted serious study by scholars of Black leadership. Yet this writer has the distinct impression from rough observations, that the new generation that has recently come to maturity has not created a new set of organizations to any substantial degree nor has it begun to energize the older organizations. Some notable exceptions are such organizations as the National Association of Black Masters of Business Administration, 100 Black Men and 100 Black Women, Concerned Black Men, and other professional male and female civic organizations. In the political realm, as the number of Black elected

officials has grown, so has the membership of the organizations that serve them. Although this is promising evidence of some growth, one senses from the *Detroit Free Press* survey that the vast majority of Blacks are not connected to any of the existing civil rights organizations by membership or activity.

11. LEADERSHIP TOWARD WHAT ENDS?

1. Many have made the observation that the strategies of radical political leaders are too narrow and insufficient to bridge the chasm of race and class, but see also Burman's analysis, which says that the Black leadership constitutes a "comprador class" existing as a buffer class that has taken on the work of defending the existing system of social relations. He says further that this class has initiated social movements in the past where the White majority has been uncompromising and that it would do so again, if the position of the business class was equally oppositional. There is, he continues, enough "play" in the system to give it entrance into critical sectors, although in ways that continue to comport with the social status of Blacks. The bargain, then, that the Black leadership has struck, he says, "is the willingness to administers its own community in exchange for the maximum obtainable progress under the prevailing social system." He considers the emergence of this class to be an indication of an accommodation strategy (or incorporation, as we have discussed here) that has, "accomplished the remarkable feat of turning the Black challenge around so that ultimately, the stability of the class system [and racial order] has been reinforced rather than undermined." Stephen Burman, *The Black Progress Question: Explaining the African American Predicament* (Thousand Oaks, Calif.: Sage, 1995), 205–6.

2. This view is supported by a 1997 Gallup survey of 1,000 Black and 2,000 White respondents that found that although there are substantive differences between Blacks and Whites, Black respondents wanted to focus more on changing themselves (54%) than on changing the system (31%). Moreover, they expressed a set of values that affirmed their positive attitude toward integration in that 75% of Blacks said they had close friends who were White; 83% of Blacks wanted to live in a neighborhood that was racially mixed; 88% of Blacks would rather work alongside Whites; 77% approve of interracial marriage between Blacks and Whites. See, "Black/White Relations in the United States," The Gallup Organization, Princeton, N.J., June 1997.

3. The COINTELPRO program of the Justice Department surreptitiously surveilled all of the major Black organizations in the late 1960s and early 1970s. However, it targeted for disruption and elimination the more radical of these, formulating the BLACKPRO program for Black militants in particular. See Kenneth O'Reilly, *"Racial Matters:" The FBI's Secret File on Black America, 1960–1972* (New York: Macmillan/The Free Press, 1989).

4. Fact Sheet, National Council of Negro Women, www.ncnw.com..

5. Here, one might mention the Kellogg Foundation National Leadership Scholars Network headed by Dr. James MacGregor Burns of the Academy of Leadership at the University of Maryland, College Park. This project is nearing the end of a four-year cycle of funding, and its deliberations are yielding some

interesting observations on the theory of the practice of leadership. This writer has attended some of the sessions, the results of which will be published featuring the wor¹· of its working groups, one of which is devoted to assessing problems of leadership for the twenty-first century.

6. For a thorough and insightful analysis of Dr. King's leadership roles, especially his sophisticated use of the media to create moral dilemmas and dramas, see Glenda Suber, "Thoreauvian Theater Impacting American Politics: Martin Luther King's Use of the Media and His Leadership," *National Political Science Review* 7 (1998): forthcoming.

7. Progressive, social change–oriented leaders also need followers, albeit more enthusiastic and committed followers, and there is some evidence in the cynicism about those change-oriented leaders on the scene that either they are not adequate to the current period or that change-oriented leadership is losing its support as a category of leadership.

8. There has appeared a veritable flood of philosophical writings in the past decade arguing the principles that underlay the project of justice and fairness prompted by the challenge of the conservative movement to the civil rights laws passed in the 1960s. One example, which tangentially addresses our argument, is from Michael Rosenfeld, *Affirmative Action and Justice: A Philosophical and Constitutional Inquiry* (New Haven: Yale University Press, 1991), 152. Rosenfeld argues that the principle of "anti-discrimination" is not value-neutral or colorblind, that it has consequences for both minority and majority.

9. See my matrix in chapter 6.

10. The Burns discussion (pp. 129–37) about the creation of followers is a balanced discussion of the process, such that we do not get even in his later discussion about revolutionary China a good view of the process by which change-oriented followers adhere to leaders, the interaction between charisma and such followers, and other such perspectives.

11. One might begin with the view that intelligent followers perceive that if they overthrow their own leaders, as a subordinate group, they could be left at the mercy of even less sympathetic and more hostile leaders and, as such, withdrawal would not be a winning move.

12. Wildavsky is not alone in his use of the cultural model of politics. Katznelson, for example, has pointed to the fact that the process of legitimacy that we discussed above is ultimately a product of culture. See Ira Katznelson, *City Trenches: Urban Politics and the Patterning of Class in the United States* (Chicago: University of Chicago Press, 1982).

13. Here one thinks of the withering criticisms made by such scholars as Harold Cruse, Ralph Bunche, and E. Franklin Frazier and the sensitive response of the Black leadership class to their critiques.

12. BLACK LEADERSHIP

1. See Harold Cruse's discussion of the concept of a plural society in relationship to the idea of Black community in *Plural but Equal: A Critical Study of Blacks and Minorities in America's Plural Society* (New York: William Morrow, 1987).

2. For a radically erroneous, idiosyncratic example of this phenomenon, see Orlando Patterson, *The Ordeal of Integration: Progress and Resentment in America's "Racial" Crisis* (Washington, D.C.: Civitas/Counterpoint, 1997).

3. For a thoroughgoing philosophical inquiry into the built-in tensions between liberalism and the Black quest for community, see David Cochran, *The Color of Freedom: Race and Contemporary Liberalism* (Albany: State University of New York Press, forthcoming).

4. Michael Lind argues that in exchange for affirmative action and other meliorative benefits Black leaders have made a "tacit agreement" with the elites of the dominant society not to disrupt the status quo, a status quo that benefits them. See his *The Next American Nation: The New Nationalism and the Fourth American Revolution* (New York: The Free Press, 1993), as quoted in Norman Kelly, "Disappearing Act: The Decline of Black Leadership," *Bedford-Stuyvesant Current*, Winter 1997, p. 4.

BIBLIOGRAPHY

"A Report of the First Congressional Black Caucus Southern Regional Forum." June 1979. Congressional Black Caucus, Carl Green, director of Network Development.

Aberbach, J., and J. Walker. 1970. "The Meaning of Black Power: A Comparison of White and Black Interpretations of a Political Slogan." *American Political Science Review* 64:1119–1219.

"The African American New World Order Agenda with Measurable Goals for 1991." 1991. African American Action Alert Communications Network. March 14.

Allen, B. 1997. "A Re-articulation of Black Female Community Leadership: Processes, Networks and a Culture of Resistence." *African American Research Perspectives* 7: 61–67.

Allen, R. 1969. *Black Awakening in Capitalist America.* Garden City, N.Y.: Doubleday.

Almond, G., and G. Powell. *Comparative Politics.* Boston: Little, Brown.

Altshuler, A. 1970. *Community Control: The Black Demand for Participation in Large American Cities.* New York: Pegasus.

"America's First National Minority Venture Capital Fund." 1985. Parren J. Mitchell, September 28.

"Anti-Allen Protest Plan Adjusted by Rights Group." 1997. *Richmond Free Press,* April 24–26, p. 1.

Ardey, S. 1994. "The Political Behavior of Black Women: Contextual, Structural and Psychological Factors." In H. Walton (ed.), *Black Politics and Black Political Behavior.* Westport, Conn.: Praeger.

Associated Press. 1995. Washington, D.C., October 19.

Axelrod, R. 1972. "Where the Vote Comes From: An Analysis of Electoral Coalitions, 1952–68." *American Political Science Review* 66: 11–20.

———. 1982. "Communications." *American Political Science Review* 76: 393–96.

Babchuck, N. and R. Thompson. 1962. "The Voluntary Association of Negroes." *American Sociological Review* 27: 647–55.

Bailey, H. 1968. "Negro Interest Group Strategies." *Urban Affairs Quarterly* 4: 27–38.

Bailis, L. 1974. *Bread or Justice: Grassroots Organizing in the Welfare Rights Movement.* Lexington, Mass.: Lexington Books.

Banfield, E., and J. Wilson. 1963. *City Politics.* New York: Vintage.

Baraka, I. A. 1969. "A Black Value System." *Black Scholar* 1:54–60.

———. 1972. "Toward the Creation of Political Institutions for All African Peoples." *Black World,* October, 54–78.

——. 1975. "Why I Changed My Ideology: Black Nationalism and Socialist Revolution." *Black World*, July, 30–42.

Bardolph, R. (ed.). 1970. *The Civil Rights Record: Black Americans and the Law, 1849–1970*. New York: Thomas Y. Crowell.

Barker, L. 1988. *Our Time Has Come: A Delegate's Diary of Jesse Jackson's 1984 Campaign*. Urbana: University of Illinois Press.

——, and R. Walters (eds.). 1989. *Jesse Jackson's 1984 Presidential Campaign*. Urbana: University of Illinois Press.

Barnett, M. 1975. "The Congressional Black Caucus." In H. Mansfield (ed.), *Congress against the President*. New York: Praeger.

——. 1976. "A Theoretical Perspective on American Racial Public Policy." In M. Barnett and J. Hefner (eds.), *Public Policy for the Black Community*. Port Washington, N.Y.: Alfred.

——. 1977. "The Congressional Black Caucus: Symbol, Myth, and Reality." *Black Scholar* 9: 17–26.

——. 1982. "The Congressional Black Caucus: Illusions and Realities of Power." In M. Preston, L. Henderson, and P. Puryear (eds.), *The New Black Politics*. New York: Longmans.

Barth, E., and B. Abu-Laban. 1959. "Power Structure in the Negro Subcommunity." *American Sociological Review* 24: 69–76.

Baskerville, L. 1987, April 23. Memorandum. Executive director, National Black Leadership Roundtable.

——. 1987, Sept. 26. "Roundtable CBC Meeting in Review." Executive director, National Black Leadership Roundtable.

Bell, H. 1957. "National Negro Conventions of the Middle 1840s: Moral Suasion vs. Political Action." *Journal of Negro History* 22: 247–60.

Bendick, M., C. W. Jackson, and V. A. Reinoso. 1997. "Measuring Employment Discrimination through Controlled Experiments." In James Stewart (ed.), *African Americans and Post-Industrial Labor Markets*. New Brunswick, N.J.: Transaction Publishers.

Bennett, L. 1964. "The Black Establishment." In *The Negro Mood and Other Essays*. New York: Ballantine Books.

Berenson, W., K. Elifson, and T. Tollerson. 1976. "Preachers in Politics: A Study of Political Activism among the Black Ministry." *Journal of Black Studies* 6: 373–92.

Berg, J. 1987. "The Congressional Black Caucus Budget and the Representation of Black Interests." Paper prepared for presentation at the 1987 Annual Meeting of the American Political Science Association, Chicago.

——. 1994. *Unequal Struggle: Class, Gender, Race, and Power in the U.S. Congress*. Boulder, Colo.: Westview Press.

Berube, M. 1995. "Public Academy," *The New Yorker*. January 9, 73–80.

Billingsley, A. 1992. *Climbing Jacob's Ladder: The Enduring Legacy of African American Families*. New York: Simon & Schuster.

"Biracial Blueprint for Change Boycott Ends with Pact, Promises." 1993. *The Miami Herald*, May 13, 1993, p. 1A.

"Black Families Join in Trenton March." 1996. Photo caption. *The New York Times*, March 7, p. B5.

"Black Leadership Family Plan Released to Mark Black History Month." 1982. Press release. The Congressional Black Caucus, February 1.

Black Professional Interface. 1985. Resolution. "Establishing 'Mentor' or 'Role Model' Programs for Our Youth/Community Services." No. II, A, NBLR Conference, March 16.

Bluestone, B., and B. Harrison. 1982. *The DeIndustrialization of America: Plant Closing, Community Abandonment and the Dismantling of America.* New York: Basic Books.

Bolce, L., and S. Gray. 1979. "Blacks, Whites and Race Politics." *The Public Interest* (Winter): 61–76.

Bositis, D. 1994. *The Congressional Black Caucus in the 103rd Congress.* Washington, D.C.: Joint Center for Political and Economic Studies.

———. 1996. "The Farrakhan Factor: Behind the Big Increase in Black Men Voting." *The Washington Post*, December 8, p. C1.

Bowman, K. 1995. "How African Americans Size Up Their Political Leaders and Institutions." *Roll Call*, December 4.

Bracey, J., A. Meier, and E. Rudwick, E. 1970. *Black Nationalism in America.* Indianapolis: Bobbs-Merrill.

Braxton, G. 1994. "African American Women and Politics: Research Trends and Directions." *National Political Science Review* 4: 281–96.

Brink, W., and L. Harris. 1963. *The Negro Revolution.* New York: Simon & Schuster.

Bronstein, S. 1993. "Environmental Racism Targeted." *Atlanta Constitution*, December 7, p. A1.

Brown, R., and M. Wolford. 1994. "Religious Resources and African American Political Action." *National Political Science Review* 4: 30–48.

Brown, W. 1996. "So Far, No Slump at the Pump, District Texaco Franchise Owner's Customers Ignoring Boycott Calls." *The Washington Post*, November 15, p. C11.

Browning, R., D. Marshall, and D. Tabb. 1984. *Protest Is Not Enough.* Berkeley: University of California Press.

———. (eds.). 1990. *Racial Politics in American Cities.* White Plains, N.Y.: Longman.

———. 1997. *Racial Politics in American Cities,* 2nd ed. New York: Longman.

"BUIRG Study—Hourly Wages and Annual Earnings." Table, Men = Education: High School Diploma or Less—Greater Boston Labor Market—1993–1994. Analysis of Greater Boston Social Survey, University of Massachusetts, Boston.

Bullock, C. 1975. "The Election of Blacks in the South: Preconditions and Consequences." *American Journal of Political Science* 10: 727–39.

Bunche, R. 1939. "The Programs of Organizations Devoted to the Improvement of the Status of the Negro." *Journal of Negro Education* 8: 539–50.

———. 1973. *The Political Status of the Negro in the Age of FDR.* Chicago: University of Chicago Press, Documents in American History Series.

Burgess, M. 1962. *Negro Leadership in a Southern City.* Chapel Hill: University of North Carolina Press.

Burman, S. 1995. *The Black Progress Question: Explaining the African America Predicament.* Newbury Park, Calif.: Sage.

Burns, J. 1978. *Leadership*. New York: Harper & Row.

Bush, R. (ed.). 1984. *The New Black Vote: Politics and Power in Four American Cities*. San Francisco: Synthesis Publications.

Button, J. 1980. *Black Violence: Political Impact of the 1960s Riots*. Princeton: Princeton University Press.

Campbell, A. 1970. *White Attitudes toward Black People*. Ann Arbor: University of Michigan, Institute for Social Research.

———. 1971. *Racial Attitudes in Fifteen American Cities*. Ann Arbor: University of Michigan, Institute for Social Research.

Campbell, D., and J. Feagin. 1975. "Black Politics in the South: A Descriptive Analysis." *Journal of Politics* 37: 129–62.

Caralay, D. 1992. "Washington Abandons the City." *Political Science Quarterly* 107: 9–27.

Carmichael, S. 1969. "Pan-Africanism: Land and Power." *Black Scholar* 1: 36–54.

———, and C. Hamilton. 1992 [1967]. *Black Power*. New York: Vintage Books.

Carson, C. 1981. *In Struggle: SNCC and the Black Awakening of the 1960s*. Cambridge, Mass.: Harvard University Press.

Cavanaugh, T., and L. Foster. 1984. *Jesse Jackson's Campaign: The Primaries and Caucuses*. Washington, D.C.: Joint Center for Political Studies.

Cavanaugh, T. and D. Stockton. 1982. *Characteristics of Black Elected Officials*. Washington, D.C.: Joint Center for Political Studies.

CBC Fact Sheet. 1983. "Questions and Answers on the Community Renewal Employment Act, H.R. 1036." September.

"CBC Staff Operations—Summary of Key Activities." January–March 1978, Congressional Black Caucus.

Center for Budget Priorities. 1984. *Falling Behind: A Report on How Blacks Fared Under Reagan Policies*. Washington, D.C.

Champagne, R., and L. Rieselbach. 1995. "The Evolving Congressional Black Caucus: The Reagan and Bush Years." In H. Perry, and W. Parent (eds.), *Blacks and the American Political System*. Tallahasse: University Press of Florida.

Childs, J. 1989. *Leadership, Conflict, and Cooperation in Afro-American Social Thought*. Philadelphia: Temple University Press.

"Civil Rights and Gender." 1993. CNN/USA Today, Gallup Poll, August 23–25, p. 6.

Clark, K. 1967. *Dark Ghetto*. New York: Harper & Row.

———. 1982. "The Civil Rights Movement: Momentum and Organization." Cited in D. McAdam, *Political Process and the Development of Black Insurgency*. Chicago: University of Chicago Press.

———, and M. Clark. 1980. "What Do Blacks Think of Themselves?" *Ebony Magazine*, November, 176–82.

Clay, W. 1972. "Emerging New Black Politics." *Black World*, October, 32–39.

———. 1992. *Just Permanent Interests*. New York: Amsitad Press.

CNN/Today. 1993. "Civil Rights and Gender." Gallup Poll, August 23–25.

Cobb, R., and C. Elder. 1971. "The Politics of Agenda Building: An Alternative Perspective for Modern Democratic Theory." *Journal of Politics* 33: 893–915.

——. 1983. *Participation in American Politics*. Baltimore: Johns Hopkins University Press.

Cole, L. 1976. *Blacks In Power: A Comparative Study of Black and White Elected Officials*. Princeton: Princeton University Press.

Collins, S. 1986. *The Rainbow Challenge: The Jesse Jackson Campaign and the Future of U.S. Politics*. New York: Monthly Review Press.

Colton, E. 1989. *The Jesse Jackson Phenomenon: The Man, the Power, the Message*. Garden City, N.Y.: Doubleday.

Commemorative Booklet, Annual Conference. 1990. Chicago United Black Communities.

Committee on Education and Labor. 1975. Print, H. R. 50, Full Employment and Balanced Growth Act, Summary and Section-by-Section Analysis. U.S. House of Representatives, Washington, D.C., March 20.

Cone, J. 1991. *Martin & Malcolm and America: A Dream or Nightmare?* Maryknoll, N.Y.: Orbit Books.

Congressional Black Caucus. 1971. "Congressional Black Caucus Recommendations to President Nixon. 92nd Congress, 1st session." *Congressional Record*, March 30, 1971.

——. 1982. *The Black Leadership Family Program for the Survival and Progress of the Black Nation*. Washington: Congressional Black Caucus.

"Congressional Black Caucus Plans Extensive Follow-up to Full Employment Hearing." 1975. Press Release, Friday, May 23.

Conti, J., and B. Stetson. 1989. *Challenging the Civil Rights Establishment: Profiles of A New Black Vanguard*. Westport, Conn.: Praeger.

Conyers, J., and W. Wallace. 1976. *Black Elected Officials*. New York: Russell Sage.

Cooper, K. 1994. "Black Caucus Tries to Cushion the Fall from Its Height." *Washington Post*, December 16, p. A21.

Cose, E. 1996. "The Realities of Black and White: Jim Crow is Long Dead, But the Promise of Integration Remains Unfulfilled." *Newsweek*, April 29, p. 26.

Covin, D. 1993. "Reflections on the Dilemmas of African American Leadership." In G. Persons (ed.), *Dilemmas of Black Politics: Issues of Leadership and Strategy*. New York: HarperCollins.

——. 1997. "Social Movement Theory in the Examination of Mobilization in a Black Community: The 1991 Sacramento Redistricting Project." *National Political Science Review* 6: 94–109.

Cox, F. et al. (eds.). 1974. *Strategies of Community Organization*. Itasia, Ill.: F. E. Peacock.

Cox, O. 1965. "Leadership among Negroes in the United States." In A. Gouldner (ed.), *Studies in Leadership*. New York: Harper & Row.

Crawford, V., et al. 1990. *Women in The Civil Rights Movement: Trailblazers and Torchbearers, 1941–1965*. Brooklyn, N.Y.: Carlson Publishing.

Crockett, K., and T. Fiedler. 1990. "Coalition Rejects Suarez Statement, Offers Proposal for Boycott Talks." *Miami Herald*, December 21, p. 1A

Cruse, H. 1967. *The Crisis of the Negro Intellectual*. New York: William Morrow.

——. 1968. *Rebellion or Revolution*. New York: William Morrow.

———. 1987. *Plural But Equal: Blacks and Minorities in America's Plural Society*. New York: William Morrow.

Dahl, R. 1961. *Who Governs?* New Haven, Conn.: Yale University Press.

———. 1972. *Democracy in the United States*. Chicago: Rand McNally.

Darcy, R., and C. Hadley. 1988. "Black Women in Politics: The Puzzle of Success." *Social Science Quarterly* 69: 629–45.

Darity, W. A. Jr., and S. L. Myers Jr. 1992. "Racial Earnings Inequality into the 21st Century." *The State of Black America, 1992*. New York: National Urban League.

Davis, A. 1974. *Angela Davis: An Autobiography*. New York: Random House.

Dawson, M., R. Brown, and R. Allen. 1990. "Racial Belief System, Religious Guidance, and African American Political Participation." *National Political Science Review* 2: 22–44.

Delaney, P. 1978. "Middle Class Gains Create Tension in Black Community." *The New York Times*, February 28, A1.

Dellums, R. V. 1993. "Black Leadership." In W. E. Rosenbach and R. L. Taylor (eds.), *Contemporary Issues in Leadership*, 3rd ed. Boulder, Colo.: Westview Press.

"Democratic Leaders Pushing Jobs Bill." 1983. *The Washington Post*, September 15, p. A4.

Denzin, N. 1989. *Interpretative Biography*. Sage University Series on Qualitative Research Methods, Vol. 17. Thousand Oaks, Calif.: Sage.

Devine, D. 1972. *The Political Culture of the United States*. Boston: Little, Brown.

DeWitt, K. 1995. "Black Men Say the March in Washington Is About Them, Not Farrakhan." *The New York Times*, October 15, p. 22.

Dittmer, J. 1995. *Local People: The Struggle for Civil Rights in Mississippi*. Urbana: University of Illinois Press.

Dollard, J. 1957. *Caste and Class in a Southern Town*. Garden City, N.J.: Doubleday.

Dorfman, D. 1980. "More Riots Likely if Black Unemployment Was at Fault in Miami." *The Washington Post*, May 25, H3.

Douglass, F. 1962. *The Life and Times of Frederick Douglass*. New York: Collier Books.

Drake, S., and H. Cayton. 1945. *Black Metropolis*. New York: Harcourt Brace.

Dye, T. 1972. *Understanding Public Policy*. Englewood Cliffs, N.J.: Prentice-Hall.

———. 1976. *Who's Running America*. Englewood Cliffs, N.J.: Prentice Hall.

———, and J. Strickland. 1982. "Women at the Top." *Social Science Quarterly* 63: 309–31.

Ebony. 1963. "100 Most Influential Black Americans." September, 228–32.

———. 1971. "100 Most Influential Black Americans." April, 33–40.

———. 1975. "100 Most Influential Black Americans." May, 45–52.

———. 1980. "100 Most Influential Black Americans." May, 63–72.

———. 1996. "100 +: America's Most Influential Blacks." May, 119–47.

Economy Empowerment Interface. 1987. Resolutions. NBLR Summit.

Edds, M. 1990. *Claiming the Dream: The Victorious Campaign of Douglas Wilder*. Chapel Hill, N.C.: Algonquin Books.

Edelman, P. 1997. "The Worst Thing That Clinton Has Done." *Atlantic Monthly*, May.

Edley, C. 1996. *Not All Black and White*. New York: Farrar Strauss Books.

Eichenwald, K. 1996. "The Two Faces of Texaco." *The New York Times*, November 10, p. F3.

Eisinger, P. 1974. "Racial Differences in Protest Participation." *American Political Science Review* 68: 592–607.

———. 1978a. "The Community Action Program and the Development of Black Leadership." Paper presented to the American Political Science Association, New York.

———. 1978b. "Ethnic Political Transition in Boston, 1884–1933: Some Lessons for Contemporary Cities." *Political Science Quarterly* 93: 217–39.

———. 1980. *The Politics of Displacement: Racial and Ethnic Transition in Three American Cities*. New York: Academic Press.

Elliot, J. 1986. *Black Voices in American Politics*. New York: Harcourt Brace Jovanovich.

Ellis, W. 1969. *White Ethics and Black Power: The Emergence of the Westside Organization*. Chicago: Aldine.

Ellison, R. 1973. "An American Dilemma." In J. Ladner (ed.), *The Death of White Sociology*. New York: Random House.

Engstrom, R., and M. McDonald. 1981. "Black City Council Representation: Clarifying the Impact of Electoral Arrangements on the Seats-Population Relationship." *American Political Science Review* 75: 344–54.

"EPA Official: U.S. Government Condoned 'Environmental Racism' Policy." 1994. *San Francisco Examiner*, February 21, p. A7.

Eversley, M. 1997. "Groups Call for Self-Help: The Idea of Self-Sufficiency Has a Long History among Black People in America." *Detroit Free Press*, February 10, p. 3B.

Fairmount Papers: Black Alternatives Conference. 1981. San Francisco: Institute for Contemporary Studies.

Farrakhan, L. 1980. *The Final Call*. Chicago: Nation of Islam.

———. 1995. "The Vision for the Million Man March." *The Washington Afro-American*, September 30, p. A5.

Fauntroy, W. 1979. Letter to mailing list, April 4.

———. 1983. Letter to Mayor Ernest N. Morial. New Orleans, La., May 5.

———. 1983a. Memorandum to the National Black Leadership Roundtable, "Proposal for a Formal Relationship between the National Black Leadership Roundtable and the Black Leadership Forum."

———. 1983b. "Statement from Black Leadership Consultation Meeting in Chicago." Saturday, April 30.

———. 1985. Memorandum to the NBLR board members. February 15.

Faw, B., and N. Skelton. 1986. *Thunder in America: The Improbable Presidential Campaign of Jesse Jackson*. Austin, Tex.: Monthly Press.

Feagin, J. 1988. "A Slavery Unwilling to Die." *Journal of Black Studies* 18 (1988): 451–69.

———, and H. Vera. 1995. *White Racism*. New York: Routledge.

Fendrich, J. 1993. *Ideal Citizens: The Legacy of the Civil Rights Movement.* Albany: State University of New York Press.

"Few Blacks Disapprove of NAACP's Dismissal of Chavis." 1994. *USA Today,* August 26, p. 5A.

Fiedler, T. 1990. "Boycott Leaders Urged to 'Move On'." *Miami Herald,* December 5, p. 28.

———, and C. Goldfarb. 1990. "Suarez Offers Olive Branch Expresses Regret over Handling of Mandela Visit." *Miami Herald,* December 21, p. 1A.

Fix, M., and R. Struk (eds.). 1990. *Clear and Convincing Evidence: Measurement of Discrimination in America.* Washington: Urban Institute Press.

Flagome, C. 1994. "Farrakhan Stirs Debate among Black Leaders with Plan for a March." *The Christian Science Monitor,* August 17, p. 3.

Fletcher, M. 1998. "Farrakhan Sees Big Economic Conspiracy." *The Washington Post,* February 23, p. A9.

"For the People." 1979. *Newsletter* 4.1, First/Second Quarter Legislative Report. Congressional Black Caucus.

———. 1980. *The Congressional Black Caucus 1980 Communications Action Alert Report* 5.7 (November).

Forsythe, D. 1972. "A Functional Definition of Black Leadership." *Black Scholar* 3: 18–26.

Fox Piven, F., and R. Cloward. 1970. "The Great Society as Political Strategy." *Columbia Forum* (Summer): 271–77.

———. 1977. *Poor People's Movements: Why They Succeed and Why They Fail.* New York: Random House.

Franklin, J. II. 1967. *From Slavery to Freedom.* New York: Alfred Knopf.

———, and A. Meier. 1982. *Black Leaders of the Twentieth Century.* Urbana: University of Illinois.

Franklin, S. 1998. "Black Organizational Development and the Black Student Leadership Network." Paper prepared for presentation at the Annual Meeting of the National Conference of Black Political Scientists, Atlanta, Ga., April 8–11.

Franklin, V. P. 1984. *Black Self-Determination.* Westport, Conn.: Lawrence Hill.

———. 1995. *Living Our Stories, Telling Our Truths: Autobiography and the Making of the African American Intellectual Tradition.* New York: Oxford University Press.

Frazier, E. F. 1964. *The Negro Church in America.* New York: Schocken Books.

Frederickson, G. 1981. *White Supremacy: A Comparative Study in American and South African History.* New York: Oxford University Press.

Freeman, R. 1977. *The Black Elite.* New York: McGraw-Hill.

Froman, P. 1948. "The Theory of Case Studies." *Social Forces* 26: 408–19.

Frye, H. 1980. *Black Parties and Political Power: A Case Study.* Boston: G. K. Hall.

———. 1986. *Jesse Jackson and the Rainbow Coalition: Conflict, the Democratic Party and the Black Community.* Oakland: Third World Organizing Committee.

Futuregram. 1985. Brochure. "Minorities Expand Their Inroads into the Economic Mainstream."

Gaines, K. 1996. *Uplifting the Race: Black Leadership, Politics, and Culture in the Twentieth Century*. Chapel Hill: University of North Carolina Press.

Gardell, M. 1996. *In the Name of Elijah Muhammad: Louis Farrakhan and the Nation of Islam*. Durham, N.C.: Duke University Press.

Garrow, D. 1978. *Protest at Selma: Martin Luther King, Jr. and the Voting Rights Act of 1965*. New Haven, Conn.: Yale University Press.

Gates, H. L. 1994. "The Black Leadership Myth." *The New Yorker*. August, 8–13.

———. 1995. "Powell and the Black Elite." *New Yorker*, September 25.

———, and C. West. 1996. *The Future of the Race*. New York: Knopf.

Geschwender, J. 1977. *Cass, Race and Worker Insurgency: The League of Revolutionary Black Workers*. Cambridge: Cambridge University Press.

Gibbs, C. 1950. "Leadership." *International Encylopedia of the Social Sciences*. New York: Macmillan.

Gibson, K. 1978. "A Case For Equity in Federal-Local Relations." *The Annals* 439: 135–46.

Giles, C. 1988. "Building in Many Places: Multiple Commitments in Black Women's Community Work." In Ann Bookman, and S. Morgan (eds.), *Women and the Politics of Empowerment*. Philadelphia: Temple University Press.

Gill, L. 1997. *African American Women in Congress: Forming and Transforming History*. New Brunswick, N.J.: Rutgers University Press.

Gilmore, G. 1996. "Area Students Join MMM Voter Registration Drive." *The Washington Afro-American*, September 21, p. B9.

Glasgow, D. 1980. *The Black Underclass*. San Francisco: Jossey-Bass.

Glason-Thornton, P. 1997. "Summit Provides Insight on Economic Development." *The Columbus Post*, April 24–30, p. 15A.

Glazer, N., and D. P. Moynihan. 1963, 1970. *Beyond The Melting Pot*. Cambridge: MIT Press.

Goren, A. 1970. *New York Jews and the Quest for Community*. New York: Columbia University Press.

Gosnell, H. 1967 [1935]. *Negro Politicians: The Rise of Negro Politics in Chicago*. Chicago: University of Chicago Press.

"Grassroots Questions Mayor Masiello on Issues Facing Inner-City Neighborhoods." 1977. *The Challenger* (Buffalo, N.Y.), April 16, p. 3.

Greenberg, S. 1980. *Race and State in Capitalist Development*. New Haven, Conn.: Yale University Press.

Greenstein, F. 1967. "The Impact of Personality on Politics." *American Political Science Review* 61: 629–41.

Gregory, J. M. 1971. *Frederick Douglass: The Orator*. Chicago: Apollo Editions.

Gross, B. 1966. "The First National Negro Convention." *Journal of Negro History* 31: 435–43.

Hacker, A. 1995. *Two Nations: Black and White, Separate, Hostile Unequal*. New York: Ballentine.

Hadden, J., L. Massotti, and V. Thiessen. 1968. "The Making of Negro Mayors. *Transaction*, January-February, 21–30.

Hahn, H., D. Klingman, and H. Pachon. 1976. "Cleavages, Coalitions and the Black Candidates: The Los Angeles Mayoralty Elections of 1969 and 1973." *Western Political Quarterly* 29: 507–20.

Haines, H. 1988. *Black Radicals and the Civil Rights Movement*. Knoxville: University of Tennessee Press.

Hall, W., W. Cross, and R. Freedle. 1972. "Stages in the Development of Black Awareness: An Exploratory Investigation." In R. L. Jones (ed.), *Black Psychology*. New York: Harper & Row.

Halley, R., A. Acock, and T. Greene. 1976. "Ethnicity and Social Class: Voting in the 1973 Municipal Election." *Western Political Quarterly* 29: 521–30.

Hamilton, C. 1972. *The Black Preacher in America*. New York: William Morrow.

———. 1973a. *The Black Experience in American Politics*. New York: G. P. Putnam.

———. 1973b. "Full Employment as a Viable Issue." In *When the Marching Stopped: An Analysis of Black Issues in the '70s*. New York: National Urban League.

———. 1976. "Public Policy and Some Political Consequences." In M. Barnett and J. Hefner (eds.), *Public Policy for the Black Community*. Port Washington, N.Y.: Alfred.

———. 1978. "Blacks and Electoral Politics." *Social Policy* 9: 21–27.

———. 1981. "The Status of Black Leadership." *New Directions*, April, 7–9.

———. 1982. "Measuring Black Conservatism." In *The State of Black America*. New York: National Urban League.

———. 1992. "The Politics of Deracialization in the 1990s." *National Political Science Review* 3: 175–78.

———, and D. Hamilton. 1997. *The Dual Agenda: Race and Social Welfare Policies of Civil Rights Organizations*. New York: Columbia University Press.

Hanks, L. 1987. *The Struggle for Black Power in Three Georgia Counties*. Knoxville: University of Tennessee Press.

Hanley, R. 1997. "New Jersey Will Not Force High School's Desegregation." *The New York Times*, February 7, p. B4.

Hannerz, U. 1968. "The Rhetoric of Soul: Identification in Negro Society." *Race* 9 (Summer): 453–65.

———. 1969. *Soulside: Studies in Ghetto Culture and Community*. New York: Columbia University Press.

Harmon-Martin, S. 1994. "Black Women in Politics: A Research Note." In H. Walton (ed.), *Black Politics and Black Political Behavior*. Westport, Conn.: Praeger.

Harrigan, J. 1971. "Militancy as a Criterion for Analyzing Black Leadership." Paper presented to the Northeast Political Science Association, Saratoga Springs, New York.

Harris, D. 1994. "On Symbolic and Material Caucus Power: The Congressional Black Caucus, 92nd–103rd Congress." Paper prepared for presentation at the 1994 Annual Meeting of the American Political Science Association, New York.

Harris, F. 1994. "Something Within: Religion as a Mobilizer of African American Political Activism." *Journal of Politics* 56: 48–65.

Harris, H. R. 1996. "A Look at the Legacy of the Million Man March: So Far, Brothers, It Isn't Far Enough, We Need to Be Marching Every Day." *The Washington Post*, October 13, p. C3.

Hayes, J., and E. Ferguson. 1992. "Who Speaks for Black America." *Detroit News and Free Press*, February 21, p. A1.

Hechter, M. 1972. "Toward a Theory of Ethnic Change." *Politics and Society* 2: 21–45.

Hecker, C. E., and J. F. McCarty. 1990. "Boycott Stirs Broward's Discontent." *Miami Herald*, December 9, p. 1.

Henderson, L. 1978a. "Administrative Advocacy and Black Urban Administrators." *The Annals* 439: 68–79.

———. 1978b. *Administrative Advocacy: Black Administrators in Urban Bureaucracies*. Palo Alto, Calif.: R. E. Research Associates.

Henderson, W., and L. Lewdebur. 1972. *Economic Disparity: Problems and Strategies for Black America*. New York: The Free Press/Macmillan.

Henry, C. 1977. "Legitimizing Race in Congressional Politics." *American Politics Quarterly* 5: 149–76.

———. 1981. "Ebony's Elite: America's Most Influential Blacks." *Phylon* 42: 120–32.

———. 1991. *Jesse Jackson: The Search for Common Ground*. Oakland, Calif.: Black Scholar Press.

———. 1995. *Ralph J. Bunche: Selected Speeches & Writings*. Ann Arbor: University of Michigan Press.

Hertzke, A. 1993. *Echoes of Discontent: Jesse Jackson, Pat Robertson and the Resurgence of Populism*. Washington, D.C.: CQ Press.

Higham, J. 1978. *Ethnic Leadership in America*. Baltimore: Johns Hopkins University Press.

Hill, R. 1996. "The New Custodians of the Black Experience: A Critique of Black Public Intellectuals." Paper prepared for presentation at the 19th Annual Olive-Harvey Black Studies Conference, Chicago.

Holden, M. 1973. *The Politics of the Black "Nation."* New York: Chandler.

Hraba, J., and G. Grant. 1970. "Black Is Beautiful: A Reexamination of Racial Preference and Identification." *Journal of Personality and Social Psychology* 16: 398–402.

Huggins, N. 1971. "Afro-American History: Myths, Heroes, and Reality." In M. Kilson, D. Fox, and N. Huggins, *Key Issues in the Afro-American Experience*. New York: Harcourt Brace Jovanovich.

———. 1978. "Afro-Americans." In J. Higham (ed.), *Ethnic Leadership in America*. Baltimore: Johns Hopkins University Press.

Hunter, F. 1953. *Community Power Structure*. Chapel Hill: University of North Carolina Press.

———. 1980. *Community Power Succession: Atlanta's Policy Makers Revisited*. Chapel Hill: University of North Carolina Press.

Jackson, B. 1990. "Black Political Power in Los Angeles: An Analysis of Tom Bradley's Electoral Success." *National Political Science Review* 2: 169–75.

Jackson, E. 1977. "Social Backgrounds of Black Federal Judges." *Journal of Political Repression* 1: 52–58.

Jackson, J. (ed.). 1991. *Life in Black America.* Newbury Park, Calif.: Sage.

Jackson, Jesse. 1997. Letter to President William Jefferson Clinton, May 29, p. 2.

James, J. 1997. *Transcending the Talented Tenth: Black Leaders and American Intellectuals.* New York: Routledge.

Janco, M. A. 1996. "Momentum Leads to NAACP Post, Michael Motley Was Inspired by the Million Man March. He Was Elected Branch President." *The Philadelphia Inquirer,* November 19, p. B2.

Janofsky M. 1997. "Philadelphia Mayor Joins Farrakhan to Calm Ethnic Tensions." *The New York Times,* April 15, p. A19.

Jennings, J. 1990. "The Politics of Black Empowerment in Urban America." In J. Klug and P. Posner (eds.), *Dilemmas of Activism.* Philadelphia: Temple University Press.

———. 1992. *The Politics of Black Empowerment: The Transformation of Activism in Urban America.* Detroit: Wayne State University Press.

———. 1994. *Understanding the Nature of Urban Poverty in Urban America.* Westport, Conn.: Praeger.

"Jobs, Peace, and Justice." 1993. *Coordinators' Guide.* Washington, D.C.: The New Coalition of Conscience, 3.

Joint Center for Political and Economic Studies. 1983. *A Policy Framework for Racial Justice.* Washington, D.C.

Joint Center for Political Studies. 1978. *Roster of Black Elected Officials, 1978.* Washington, D.C.

Jones, B. (ed.). 1989. *Leadership and Politics: New Perspectives in Political Science.* Lawrence: University of Kansas Press.

———. 1989. "Causation, Constraints and Political Leadership." In Bryan Jones (ed.), *Leadership and Politics: New Perspectives in Political Science.* Lawrence: University of Kansas Press.

Jones, C. 1987. "An Overview of the Congressional Black Caucus, 1970–1985." In F. Jones, et al. (eds.), *Readings in American Politics.* Dubuque, Iowa: Kendall/Hunt.

———, and M. Clemons. 1993. "A Model of Racial Crossover Voting: An Assessment of the Wilder Victory." In G. Persons (ed.), *Dilemmas of Black Politics: Issues of Leadership and Strategy.* New York: HarperCollins.

Jones, M. 1972. "A Frame of Reference for Black Politics." In L. Henderson (ed.), *Black Political Life in the United States.* New York: Chandler.

———. 1976. "Black Office Holding and Political Development in the Rural South." *Review of Black Political Economy* 7 (Summer): 375–407.

———. 1978. "Black Political Empowerment in Atlanta: Myth and Reality." *The Annals* 439: 90–117.

———. 1981. "The Increasing Irrelevance of Black Leadership." Paper presented to the National Conference of Black Political Scientists, Baltimore, Md.

———. 1987. "The Political Thought of the New Black Conservatives." In F. Jones, et al. (eds.), *Readings in American Politics.* Dubuque, Iowa: Kendall/Hunt.

King, M. L. Jr. 1967. *Where Do We Go from Here: Chaos or Community?* Boston: Beacon Press.

Kluger, R. 1975. *Simple Justice: The History of Brown v. Board of Education.* New York: Random House.

Kroeber, A., and C. Kluckhohn. 1952. *Culture: A Critical Review of Concepts and Definitions.* New York: Vintage Books.

Ladd, E. 1966. *Negro Political Leadership.* Ithaca, N.Y.: Cornell University Press.

Lane, E. 1962. *Political Ideology: Why the American Common Man Believes What He Does.* New York: The Free Press.

Latimer, M. 1979. "Black Political Representation in Southern Cites." *Urban Affairs Quarterly* 15: 65–86.

"Leadership Summit to Be Held at Drew/Freeman." 1997. *The Prince George's Post,* May 1–7, p. A6.

Levine, C. 1974. "The Black Mayoral Leadership Dilemma." Paper presented at the American Political Science Association, Chicago.

———. 1976. *Racial Conflict and the American Mayor.* Lexington, Mass.: D.C. Heath.

Levine, L. 1978. *Black Culture and Black Consciousness: Afro-American Folk Thought from Slavery to Freedom.* New York: Oxford University Press.

Levy, A., and S. Stoudinger. 1976. "Sources of Voting Cues for the Congressional Black Caucus." *Journal of Black Studies* 7: 29–46.

———. 1978. "The Black Caucus in the 92nd Congress: Gauging Its Success." *Phylon* 39 (January): 322–33.

Lichter, L. 1985. "Who Speaks for Black America?" *Public Opinion,* August–September, pp. 41–44, 58.

Lincoln, C. 1994 [1968]. *The Black Muslims in America.* 3rd ed. Lawrenceville, N.J.: Africa World Press.

———, and L. Mamiya. 1990. *The Black Church and the African American Experience.* Durham, N.C.: Duke University Press.

Lipsky, M. 1968. "Protest as a Political Resource." *American Political Science Review* 62: 1144–58.

Litwack, L., and A. Meier. 1988. *Black Leaders of the Nineteenth Century.* Urbana: University of Illinois Press.

Lomax, L. 1970. "The Demand for Dynamic Leadership." In L. Fishel and B. Quartes (eds.), *The Black American.* Glenview, Ill.:Scott Foresman.

Loury, G. 1984. "The Need for Moral Leadership in the Black Community." *New Perspectives* 16: 14–19.

———. 1985. "The Moral Quandary of the Black Community." *The Public Interest* 79: 9–22.

Marable, C. 1994. *African Americans at the Crossroads: The Restructuring of Black Leadership and the 1992 Election.* Boston: South End Press.

McDonald, A. 1975. "Black Power." *Journal of Negro Education* 44: 547–54.

Madhubuti, H., and M. Karenga (eds.). 1996. *Million Man March: Day of Absence.* Chicago: Third World Press.

Magida, A. 1996. *A Prophet of Rage: Louis Farrakhan and His Nation of Islam.* New York: HarperCollins.

———. 1990. "Black Mayoral Leadership in Atlanta." *National Pc ence Review* 2: 138–47.

———. 1994. "Black Leadership and the Continuing Struggle for tice." In L. Barker, and M. Jones, *African Americans and the Ame ical System*. Englewood Cliffs, N.J.: Prentice-Hall.

Kaplan, D. 1993. "Constitutional Doubt Is Thrown on Bizarre-S tricts." *Congressional Quarterly*, July 3, p. 1762.

Karenga, R. 1977. "Kawaida and its Critics: A Socio-historical Anal *nal of Black Studies* 8: 125–48.

Karnig, A. 1976. "Black Representation on City Councils: The Im trict Elections and Socioeconomic Factors." *Urban Affairs Q* 223–56.

———, and S. Welch. 1981. *Black Representation and Urban Poli* University of Chicago Press.

Kasarda, J. 1988. "Jobs, Migration and Emerging Urban Misi M. G. H. McGeary and L. E. Lynn Jr. (eds.), *Urban Change* Washington, D.C.: National Academy Press.

Katznelson, I. 1971. "Power in the Reformulation of Race Res Orleans and W. Ellis (eds.), *Race, Change and Urban Society*. Calif.: Sage.

———. 1973. *Black Men, White Cities*. New York: Oxford Unive

———. 1982. *City Trenches: Urban Politics and the Patterning c United States*. Chicago: University of Chicago Press.

Kaufman, H. 1958. "The Next Step in Case Studies." *Public A Review* 18 (Winter): 52–95.

Keech, W. 1968. *The Impact of the Negro Vote*. Chicago: Rand

Keller, E. 1978. "The Impact of Black Mayors on Urban Policy 439: 40–52.

———. 1979. "Electoral Politics in Gary: Mayoral Performance cal Economy of the Black Vote." *Urban Affairs Quarterly* 15

Kerlinger, F. 1964. *Foundations of Behavioral Research*. New Yc hart and Winston.

Killan, L. 1968. *The Impossible Revolution? Black Power and Dream*. New York: Random House.

———, and C. Smith. 1960. "Negro Protest Leaders in a Sou nity." *Social Forces* 38 (March): 253–57.

Kilson, M. 1971. "Political Change in the Negro Ghetto, 190 Huggins, M. Kilson, and D. Fox (eds.), *Key Issues in the Experience*. New York: Harcourt Brace, Jovanovich.

———. 1993. "Anatomy of Black Conservatism." *Transition* 5

———. 1994. "Anatomy of the Black Political Class." Paper p sentation at the National Conference on Conflict and C Minorities, Wellesley College, April 9–11.

Kinch, D. L. 1993. "March Leaders Seek Unity with Farrakhan *ton Afro-American*, September 25, p. 1.

Kinfe, A. 1991. *Politics of Black Nationalism: From Harlem ton*, N.J.: Africa World Press.

Mamiya, L. 1982. "From Black Muslim to Bialian: The Evolution of a Movement." *Journal for the Scientific Study of Religion* 21: 139–57.

Mannies, J. 1996. "Summit Agenda Outlines a Better Life: Blacks Want Share of Prosperity." *The St. Louis Post Dispatch*, September 29, p. 7A.

Marable, M. 1978. "Anatomy of Black Politics." *Review of Black Political Economy* (Summer): 68–83.

———. 1980. "Black Nationalism in the 1970s: Through the Prism of Race and Class." *Socialist Review* (Fall): 68–83.

"March on Washington! Jackson, Sharpton, Are the Latest to Endorse Historic Million Man March." *The Challenger*, September 27, p. 2.

Martin, J. 1979. *Civil Rights and the Crisis of Liberalism: The Democratic Party 1945–76*. Boulder, Colo.: Westview Press.

Martin, L. 1978. "Fact Sheets." Assistant to the president for minority affairs, the White House, January.

Marx, G. 1967. *Protest and Prejudice: A Study of Belief in the Black Community*. New York: Harper Torchbooks.

Matthews, D. 1954. *The Social Backgrounds of Decision Makers*. Garden City, N.J.: Doubleday.

———, and J. Protho. 1966. *Negroes and the New Southern Politics*. New York: Harcourt Brace and World.

McAdams, D. 1982. *Political Process and the Development of Black Insurgency*. Chicago: University of Chicago Press.

McCarron, J. 1994. "Minority Job Push Can Be Constructive." *Chicago Tribune*, June 12, p. 3.

McClain, P. 1996. "Black Politics at the Crossroads: Or in the Cross-Hairs." *American Political Science Review* 90: 867–73.

———, and J. Garcia. 1993. "Expanding Disciplinary Boundaries: Black, Latino, and Racial Minority Group Politics." In A. Finifter (ed.), *Political Science: The State of the Discipline, II*. Washington, D.C.: American Political Science Association.

McCormack, D. 1973. "Stokely Carmichael and Pan-Africanism: Back to Black Power." *Journal of Politics* 35: 386–409.

McCormick, J. 1979. "The Continuing Significance of Race: Racial Change and Electoral Politics in Cleveland, Ohio (1961–1977)." Paper presented at the American Political Science Association, Washington, D.C.

———, and C. Jones. 1993. "The Conceptualization of Deracialization." In G. Persons (ed.), *Dilemmas of Black Politics: Issues of Leadership and Strategy*. New York: HarperCollins.

——— et al. 1995. "Preliminary Report on the Survey of Million Man March." Washington: Howard University, Department of Political Science, manuscript.

———. 1997. "The Message and the Messenger: Opinions from the Million Men Who Marched." *National Political Science Review* 6: 142–64.

McLemore, L. 1972. "Toward a Theory of Black Politics: The Black and Ethnic Models Revisited." *Journal of Black Studies* 1: 323–31.

Meier, A. 1965. "On the Role of Martin Luther King." *New Politics* (Winter): 52–59.

———. 1968. *Negro Thought in America, 1880–1915.* Ann Arbor: University of Michigan Press.

———, and E. Rudwick. 1973. *CORE: A Study in the Civil Rights Movement 1942–68.* New York: Oxford University Press.

Merida, K. 1994. "Black Caucus Says It Has No Official Working Ties with Nation of Islam." *The Washington Post,* February 3, p. A16.

"Million Man March." 1995. *The Black Scholar,* special issue, 25.4 (Fall).

"Minister Farrakhan Announces 'A New Day' in Politics." 1996. *The Final Call,* August 6, p. 3.

Mock, J. 1981. "The Black Political Executive and Black Political Interests: 1961–80." Ph.D. dissertation, University of Tennessee.

———. 1982. "The Black Vote Output: Black Political Executives 1961–1980." Paper presented at the Midwest Political Science Association, Milwaukee.

Monohan, T., and E. Monohan. 1956. "Some Characteristics of Negro Leaders." *American Sociological Review* 21: 589–96.

Morris, A. 1984. *Origins of the Civil Rights Movement.* New York: Free Press.

Morris, L. (ed.). 1990. *The Social and Political Implications of the 1984 Jesse Jackson Presidential Campaign.* Westport, Conn.: Praeger.

Morris, M. 1975. *The Politics of Black America.* New York: Harper & Row.

Morrison, M. 1987. *Black Political Mobilization: Leadership, Power, and Mass Behavior.* Albany: State University of New York Press.

Moynihan, D. 1969. *Maximum Feasible Misunderstanding.* New York: The Free Press.

"Mr. Farrakhan's Convention." 1996. *St. Louis Post Dispatch,* October 2, p. 6B.

Muhammad, D. 1994. "A Brief History of Civil Rights Marches." *The Final Call,* December 14, p. 8.

Muhammad, M. Z. 1996. "Philly Drops Texaco Stock." *The Final Call,* December 3, p. 6.

Muhammad, W. 1980. *As the Light Shineth from the East.* Chicago: WDM Publishing.

Mullings, L. 1986. "Anthropological Perspectives on the Afro-American Family." *The American Journal of Social Psychiatry* 6.1(Winter): 15.

Murray, R., and A. Vedlitz. 1974. "Political Organization in Deprived Communities: Black Electoral Groups in Houston, Dallas, and New Orleans." Paper presented at the American Political Science Association, Chicago.

———. 1978. "Racial Voting Patterns in the South." *The Annals* 439: 29–39.

Myrdal, G. 1962 [1944]. *An American Dilemma: The Negro Problem and Modern Democracy.* New York: Harper & Row.

National Black Leadership Roundtable. 1985/86. *The Roundtable Record* 1.2 (Winter): 10.

National Conference of Christians and Jews. 1978. *A Study of Attitudes toward Racial and Religious Minorities.* New York: National Conference of Christians and Jews.

National Urban League. 1973. *When the Marching Stopped: An Analysis of Black Issues in the 70s.* New York: National Urban League.

Navarro, M. 1997. "Many Florida Blacks, Tossed by Population Shifts, Say They Feel 'Left Out.'" *The New York Times,* February 17, p. 10.

Nelsen, H., R. Yokley, and A. Nelsen. 1971. *The Black Church in America*. New York: Basic Books.

Nelson, W. 1972. *Black Politics in Gary: Problems and Prospects*. Washington, D.C.: Joint Center for Political Studies.

————. 1977. "Institutionalizing Black Control: Black Machine Politics in Cleveland." Paper presented at the Midwest Political Science Association, Chicago.

————. 1978. "Black Mayors as Urban Managers." *The Annals* 439: 53–67.

————. 1990. "Black Mayoral Leadership: A Twenty-Year Perspective." *National Political Science Review* 2: 188–95.

————, and P. Meranto. 1977. *Electing Black Mayors: Political Action in the Black Community*. Columbus: Ohio State University Press.

Newton, E. 1993. "Protesters Threaten to Block Rose Parade." *Los Angeles Times*, October 15, p. 3B.

Nie, N., S. Verba, and J. Petrocik. 1976. *The Changing American Voter*. Cambridge: Harvard University Press.

Obadele, O. 1971. "The Republic of New Africa—An Independent Black Nation." *Black World*, May, 81–89.

Ofari, E. 1972. "Marxist-Leninism—The Key to Black Liberation." *Black Scholar* 4: 35–46.

Oguntoyinbo, L. 1996a. "City Tries to Get Ahead of Devil's Night Arson." *Detroit Free Press*, September 24, p. 3B.

————. 1996b. "Neighbors Join the Battle against Drugs." *Detroit Free Press*, December 31, p. 8A.

"Ohio Legislative Black Caucus Appoints New Executive Director." 1997. *The Columbus Post*, May 22–28, p. 1.

Olsen, M. 1970. "Social and Political Participation of Blacks." *American Sociological Review* 34: 674–88.

O'Reilly, K. 1989. *"Racial Matters": The FBI's Secret File on Black America*. New York: Macmillan/Free Press.

Orum, M. 1966. "A Reappraisal of the Social and Political Participation of Blacks." *American Journal of Sociology* 62: 32–46.

Paige, G. 1977. *The Scientific Study of Leadership*. New York: The Free Press.

Parenti, M. 1966. "The Black Muslims: From Revolution to Institution." *Social Research* 31: 175–94.

Patterson, E. 1974. *Black City Politics*. New York: Dodd, Mead.

Patterson, O. 1977. *Ethnic Chauvinism: The Reactionary Impulse*. New York: Stein & Day.

Payne, C. 1995. *I've Got the Light of the Freedom: The Organizing Tradition and the Mississippi Freedom Struggle*. Berkeley: University of California Press.

Perry, H., (ed.). 1990a. "Black Electoral Success in 1989." *PS* 23: 141–62.

————. 1990b. "Black Political and Mayoral Leadership in Birmingham and New Orleans." *National Political Science Review* 2: 154–60.

————. 1991. "Deracialization as an Analytic Construct." *Urban Affairs Quarterly* 27: 181–91.

Persons, G. 1985. "Reflections on Mayoral Leadership." *Phylon* 46: 205–18.

———. 1987. "The Philadelphia Move Incident as an Anomaly in Models of Mayoral Leadership." *Phylon* 48: 249–60.

———. 1993. *Dilemmas of Black Leadership: Issues of Leadership and Strategy.* New York: HarperCollins.

———, and L. Henderson. 1990. "Mayor of the Colony: Effective Leadership As a Matter of Perception." *National Political Science Review* 2: 145–53.

Peterson, K. 1995. "A Million Men, A Single Message: Black Dads Hope to Restore Spirit of African-American Male." *USA Today*, October 13, p. 5D.

Peterson, P. 1979. "Organizational Imperatives and Ideological Change: The Case of Black Power." *Urban Affairs Quarterly* 14: 465–84.

———, and D. Greenstone. 1979. "Racial Change and Citizen Participation: The Mobilization of Low Income Communities through Community Action." In R. Haveman (ed.), *A Decade of Federal Antipoverty Programs.* New York: Academic Press.

Pettigrew, T. 1970. "Ethnicity in American Life: A Social Psychological Perspective." In O. Fainstein (ed.), *Ethnic Groups in the City.* Lexington, Mass.: D. C. Heath.

———. 1971. *Racially Separate or Together?* New York: McGraw-Hill.

———. 1972. "When Black Candidates Run for Mayor: Race and Voting Behavior." In H. Hahan (ed.), *People and Politics in Urban Society.* Beverly Hills, Calif.: Sage.

Pfautz, H. 1962. "The Power Structure of the Negro Subcommunity: A Case Study and Comparative View." *Phylon* 21: 156–66.

Pinderhughes, D. 1979. "The President, the Congress and the Black Community, or Logic and Collective Politics." Paper presented at the Midwest Political Science Association, Chicago.

———. 1980. "Racial Interest Groups and Incremental Politics." Unpublished manuscript, Dartmouth College.

———. 1992. "Divisions in the Civil Rights Community." *PS* 25: 485–87.

———. 1995. "Black Interest Groups and the 1982 Extension of the Voting Rights Act." In H. Perry and W. Parent (eds.), *Blacks and the American Political System.* Tallahasse: University Press of Florida.

Poinsett, A. 1973. "Class Patterns in Black Politics." *Ebony Magazine*, August, 36–40.

Political Participation Brain Trust Summary Report, CBC. 1977. July 18.

Polsby, N. 1963. *Community Power and Political Theory.* New Haven, Conn.: Yale University Press.

"Portrait of an Anxious Public." 1995. *Business Week*, March 13.

"Powell Defeats Dole in New Hampshire Poll." 1995. *San Francisco Chronicle*, October 19, p. A2.

Powell, M. 1996. "Reunion Transforms Soggy Mall: Thousands Attend Black Family Event." *The Washington Post*, September 8, p. B3.

Pressman, J. 1972. "Preconditions of Mayoral Leadership." *American Political Science Review* 66.

Prestage, J. 1987. "Black Women Judges: An Examination of Their Socio-Economic, Educational, and Political Backgrounds and Judicial Placement." In F. Jones, et al. (eds.), *Readings in American Politics.* Dubuque, Iowa: Kendall/Hunt.

———. 1991. "In Quest of African American Political Woman." *Annals of the American Academy of Political and Social Science* 515: 88–103.

Preston, M. 1976. "Limitations of Black Urban Power: The Case of Black Mayors." In L. Massotti and R. Lineberry (eds.), *The New Urban Politics*. Cambridge, Mass.: Ballinger.

———. 1990. "Introduction, Symposium on Big City Black Mayors," and "Big City Black Mayors: An Overview." *National Political Science Review* 2: 129–30, 131–37.

"Preview of CBC Dinner Weekend Activities." 1976. *Newsletter*, Congressional Black Caucus, Washington, D.C.

"Price Fixing." 1986. *Emerge*, December/January, p. 38.

Pugh, T. 1993. "A Biracial Blueprint for Change, Boycott Ends with Pact, Promises." *Miami Herald*, May 13, p. 1A.

Rabinowitz, H. 1982. *Southern Black Leaders of the Reconstruction Era*. Urbana: University of Illinois Press.

Rainbow Coalition. 1984. "Summary of Campaign Results." Washington, D.C., Unpublished report, November.

Rainwater, L. 1973. *Black Experience: Soul*. New Brunswick, N.J.: Transaction Books.

Ransom, B. 1990. "Mayor W. Wilson Goode: The Technocrat." *National Political Science Review* 2: 183–87.

Rapoport, A. 1958. "Varieties of Political Theory." *American Political Science Review* 52: 972–88.

Raspberry, W. 1982. "12 Rules for Black Progress." *The Washington Post*, February 5, p. 11.

Reed, A. 1986. *The Jesse Jackson Phenomenon*. New Haven: Yale University Press.

———. 1988. "The Black Urban Regime: Structural Origins and Constraints." In M. Smith (ed.), *Power, Community, and the City* New Brunswick, N.J.: Transaction.

———. 1995. "Demobilization in the New Black Political Regime: Ideological Capitulation in the Post Segregation Era." In M. Smith and Joe R. Feagin (eds.), *The Bubbling Cauldron: Race, Ethnicity, and the Urban Crisis*. Minneapolis: University of Minnesota Press.

Reese, L., and R. Brown. 1995. "The Effects of Religious Messages on Racial Identity and System Blame among African Americans." *Journal of Politics* 57: 24–39.

Rich, W. 1990. "The Politics of Detroit: A Look Ahead." *National Political Science Review* 2: 176–82.

———. 1996. *Black Mayors and School Politics: The Failure of Reform in Detroit, Gary, and Newark*. New York: Garland.

Richardson, M. 1987. *Maria Stewart: America's First Black Woman Political Writer*. Bloomington: Indiana University Press..

Robeck, B. 1974. "The Congressional Black Caucus and Black Representation." Paper presented at the American Political Science Association, Chicago.

Robnet, B. 1997. *How Long? How Long?: African American Women in the Struggle for Civil Rights*. New York: Oxford University Press.

Rogers, H. 1981. "Civil Rights: Another Myth of Popular Sovereignty." *Journal of Black Studies* 12: 53–70.

"Role of the CBC in the Budget Reconciliation." 1993. Press conference. Congressional Black Caucus. August.

Roster of Black Elected Officials. 1981. Washington, D.C.: Joint Center for Political Studies.

Roucek, J. 1956. "Minority-Majority Relations in Their Power Aspects." *Phylon* 15: 24–30.

"Roundtable in Review: 1985–1989." 1988. Executive director, National Black Leadership Roundtable.

"Roundup of Elections '86." 1986. Walter Fauntroy, president, National Black Leadership Roundtable, November 6.

Rustin, B. 1965. "From Protest to Politics: The Future of the Civil Rights Movement." *Commentary* 39 (February): 25–31.

———. 1971. *Down the Line: Collected Writings* Chicago: Quadrangle.

Sack, Karin. 1988. "Gender and Grassroots Leadership." In A. Bookman and S. Morgan (eds.), *Women and the Politics of Empowerment.* Philadelphia: Temple University Press.

Salamon, L. 1973. "Leadership and Modernization: The Emerging Black Political Elite in the American South." *Journal of Politics* 35: 615–46.

Saloma, J. 1984. *Ominous Politics: The New Conservative Labyrinth.* New York: Hill and Wang.

Scales, A. 1996. "Race, Politics and Perception." *Boston Globe,* April 12, p. 3.

Scammon, R., and B. Wattenberg. 1973. "Black Progress and Liberal Rhetoric." *Commentary,* April, 35–44.

Schlozman, K., and S. Verba. 1979. *Injury to Insult: Unemployment, Class and Political Response.* Cambridge, Mass.: Harvard University Press.

Scoble, H. 1968. "The Effects of the Riots on Negro Leadership." In L. Massoti and D. Bowen (eds.), *Riots and Rebellion: Civil Violence in the Urban Community.* Beverly Hills, Calif.: Sage.

Seligman, L. 1950. "The Study of Political Leadership." *American Political Science Review* 44: 904–15.

Seltzer, R., and R. C. Smith. 1985. "Race and Ideology: Measuring Liberalism and Conservatism." *Phylon* 46: 98–105.

———. 1991. "Skin Color Differences in the Afro-American Community and the Differences They Make." *Journal of Black Studies* 21 (March): 279–86.

Sheppard, N. 1973. "The Congressional Black Caucus in Search of A Role." *Race Relations Reporter,* March, 18–21.

Shingles, R. 1981. "Black Consciousness and Political Participation." *American Political Science Review* 75: 76–91.

Singer, J. 1981. "With a Friend in the White House, Black Conservatives Are Speaking Out." *National Journal* 75: 8–12.

Singh, R. 1997. *The Farrakhan Phenomenon: Race, Reaction and the Paranoid Style in American Politics.* Washington, D.C.: George Washington University Press.

———. 1998. *The Congressional Black Caucus: Racial Politics in the U.S. Congress.* Thousand Oaks, Calif.: Sage Publications.

Smith, M. 1994. "Around the South: Region in Brief." *Atlanta Journal and Constitution*, January 25, p. A3.

Smith, R. 1976. "Black Elites and Black Groups in the Federal Policy Process: A Study in Interest Articulation." Ph.D. dissertation, Howard University.

———. 1978a. "The Changing Shape of Urban Black Politics, 1960–70." *The Annals* 439: 16–28.

———. 1978b. "Interaction and Cooperation among National Level Black Elites: An Exploration of the Black Quasi-Government Theory." Paper presented at the National Conference of Black Political Scientists, Jackson, Mississippi.

———. 1981a. "Black Appointed Officials: A Neglected Category of Political Participation Research." Paper presented at the National Conference of Black Political Scientists, Baltimore, Md. Subsequently published in the *Journal of Black Studies* 14: 369–88.

———. 1981b. "The Black Congressional Delegation." *Western Political Quarterly* 34: 203–21.

———. 1981c. "Black Power and the Transformation from Protest to Politics." *Political Science Quarterly* 96: 431–45.

———. 1981d. "The Role of the Congressional Black Caucus in the American Political System." Paper presented at the Northeast Political Science Association, Newark, N.J.

———. 1996. *We Have No Leaders: African Americans in the Post–Civil Rights Era*. Albany: State University of New York Press.

———, and J. McCormick. 1985. "The Challenge of a Black Presidential Candidacy: An Assessment." *New Directions* 12 (April–July): 24–31, 22–25.

———. 1990a. "From Insurgency toward Inclusion: The Jackson Campaigns of 1984 and 1988." In L. Morris (ed.), *The Social and Political Implications of the 1984 Jesse Jackson Campaign*. New York: Greenwood.

———. 1990b. "Recent Elections and Black Politics: The Maturation or Death of Black Politics." *PS* 2: 160–62.

———, and R. Seltzer. 1992. *Race, Class, and Culture: A Study in Afro-American Mass Opinion*. Albany: State University of New York Press.

———. 1992. "Ideology as the Enduring Dilemma of Black Politics." In G. Persons (ed.), *Dilemmas of Black Politics*. New York: Harper Collins.

———, and H. Walton. 1994. "U-Turn: Martin Kilson and Black Conservatism." *Transition* 62: 209–16.

———. 1995. *Racism in the Post Civil Rights Era: Now You See It, Now You Don't*. Albany: State University of New York Press.

Sowell, T. 1975. *Race and Economics*. New York: Longmans. .

———. 1981. *Ethnic America: A History*. New York: Basic Books.

Stanford, K. 1997. *Beyond the Boundaries: Jesse Jackson in International Affairs*. Albany: State University of New York Press.

Starks, R. 1991. "A Commentary and Response to Exploring the Meaning and Implications of Deracialization." *Urban Affairs Quarterly* 27: 216–22.

———, and M. Preston. 1990. "The Political Legacy of Harold Washington, 1983–87." *National Political Science Review* 2: 161–68.

Stinchcombe, A. 1968. *Constructing Social Theories.* New York: Harcourt, Brace & World.

Stokes, C. 1973. *Promises of Power: A Political Biography.* New York: Simon & Schuster.

Stone, C. 1968. *Black Political Power in America.* New York: Dell.

———, D. Imbrosio, and M. Orr. 1991. "The Reshaping of Urban Leadership in U.S. Cities: A Regime Analysis." In M. Gottdiener and C. Pickvance (eds.), *Urban Life in Transition*, vol. 39, *Urban Affairs Annual Review.* Thousand Oaks, Calif.: Sage.

Stone, P. 1978. "Social Bias in the Recruitment of Black Elected Officials in the United States." *Review of Black Political Economy* 9 (Summer): 384–404.

———. 1980. "Ambition Theory and the Black Politician." *Western Political Quarterly* 32: 94–107.

Strickland, W. 1972. "The Gary Convention and the Crisis of American Politics." *Black World*, October, 18–26.

Suber, G. 1998. "Thoreauvian Theater Impacting American Politics: Martin Luther King's Use of the Media and His Leadership." *National Political Science Review* 7 (forthcoming).

"Suggested Strategies for Local Action to Oppose Proposed Budget Cuts." 1979. Congressional Black Caucus, March 21.

Sussman, B., and H. Denton. 1981. "Lingering Racial Stereotypes Damage Blacks." *The Washington Post*, March 26.

Swain, C. 1993. *Black Faces, Black Interests: The Representation of African American Interests in Congress.* Cambridge: Harvard University Press.

Swinton, D. 1990. "The Economic Status of Black Americans during the 1980s: A Decade of Limited Progress." *The State of Black America, 1990.* New York: National Urban League, 1990, 25–71.

Tate, K. 1992. "The Impact of Jackson's Presidential Bid on Blacks and the Democratic Party." *National Political Science Review* 3: 184–97.

Taylor, C. 1994. *The Black Churches of Brooklyn.* New York: Columbia University Press.

"Texaco and the Tapes." 1996. *The Washington Post*, November 13, p. A22.

"The 1982 Black Convention." Columbus, Ohio, July 9–11.

Thompson, D. 1963. *The Negro Leadership Class.* Englewood Cliffs, N.J.: Prentice Hall.

Thornton, A. 1983. "Alternative Budgets of the Congressional Black Caucus: Participation of an Ideological Minority in the Budget Process." Paper prepared for presentation at the 1983 Annual Meeting of the National Conference of Black Political Scientists, Houston, Tex.

Timoner, R. 1996. "Ready or Not: An Assessment of Low Income Advocacy." Working Paper Series, Oakland, Calif.: Applied Research Center.

"Trends Watch Demographics." 1995. *The Atlanta Constitution*, June 1, p. B3.

Trescott, J. 1996. "An Affirmative Action: Black Women's Group Invests in Its Future." *The Washington Post*, September 8, p. C1.

Truman, D. 1951. *The Governmental Process.* New York: Knopf.

Tucker, D. 1983. Letter to Ronald Walters, July 27.

"21 Outstanding Young Black Men Represent Hope and Inspiration for the Future." *The Challenger* (Buffalo, N.Y.), April 16, p. 1.

"UPDATE." 1983. *Newsletter*, The Black Issues Convention, vol. 1, no. 2 (July).

U.S. Bureau of the Census. 1973.*Voting and Registration in the Election of November 1972*, Population Characteristics, Current Population reports. Washington, D.C.: U.S. Bureau of the Census, p. 27.

———. 1975. *The Social and Economic Status of the Black Population.* Washington, D.C.: U.S. Bureau of the Census.

———. 1978. *The Social and Economic Status of the Black Population—An Historical Overview.* Washington, D.C.: U.S. Bureau of the Census.

———. 1980. "Families, by Total Money Income: Race and Spanish Origin of Householder, 1947–1980." Series p-60, *1980 Census of Population.*

———. 1980. *Social Indicators III.* Washington, D.C.: U.S. Department of Commerce, Bureau of the Census, p. 483.

U.S. Senate. 1976. *Supplementary Detailed Staff Reports on Intelligence Activities and the Rights of Americans, Book III, Final Report of the Select Committee to Study Government Operations with Respect to Intelligence Activities.* Washington, D.C.: 94th Congress, 2nd Session.

Valentine, C. 1968. *Culture and Poverty.* Chicago: University of Chicago Press.

Waldinger, R. 1996. *Still the Promised Land: New Immigrants and African Americans in Post-Industrial New York.* Cambridge: Harvard University Press.

Walker, J. 1963. "The Function of Disunity: Negro Leadership in a Southern City." *Journal of Negro Education* 32: 227–36.

Walsh, S. 1996a. "Tape Analysis Disproves Racial Slurs, Texaco Says, Company Calls 'Tone, Context' Unacceptable." November 12, p. A1.

———. 1996b. "Texaco Settles Bias Suit, $176 Million Payment Is Largest Ever, Diversity Promised." *The Washington Post*, November 16, p. A1.

Walters, R. 1972. "The New Black Political Culture." *Black World*, October, 4–17.

———. 1973. "African-American Nationalism." *Black World*, October, 9–27.

———. 1975. "Strategy for 1976: A Black Political Party." *Black Scholar* 7: 7–20.

———. 1980. "Black Presidential Politics 1980: Bargaining or Begging?" *Black Scholar* 11: 22–31.

———. 1981. "The Challenge of Black Leadership: An Analysis of the Problem of Strategy Shift." *Urban League Review* 5 (Summer): 77–88.

———. 1983. "Black Candidacy in '84 Is No Joke." *Lost Angeles Times,* June 12, part IV, p. 5.

———. 1985. "Reaction to Black Activism is a Key Component of the Conservative 'White Consensus,'" *Baltimore Sun*, January 6, p. 5J.

———. 1987. "African American Influence on U.S. Foreign Policy toward South Africa." In Mohammad Ahrari (ed.), *Ethnic Groups and U.S. Foreign Policy.* New York: Greenwood Press.

———. 1988. *Black Presidential Politics in America: A Strategic Approach.* Albany: State University of New York Press.

———. 1992. "Two Political Traditions: Black Politics in the 1990s." *National Political Science Review* 3: 198–208.

———. 1995. "Colin Powell: Patriot, Icon, Enigma." *San Francisco Chronicle*, July 21, p. A23.

———. Forthcoming. "The Mid-Western Sit-In Movement, 1958–1960." In William Tuttle (ed.), *The Civil Rights Movement in the Midwest*. New York: New York University Press.

Walton, H. 1969. *The Negro in Third Party Politics*. Philadelphia: Dorrance.

———. 1972. *Black Politics: A Theoretical and Structural Analysis*. Philadelphia: J. B. Lippincott.

———. 1994a. "Black Female Presidential Candidates: Bass, Mitchell, Chisholm, Wright, Reid, Davis, and Fulanni." In Walton (ed.), *Black Politics and Black Political Behavior*. Westport, Conn.: Praeger.

———. 1994b. "The Gender Linkages." In Walton (ed.), *Black Politics and Black Political Behavior*. Westport, Conn.: Praeger.

———. 1995a. "Public Policy Responses to the Million Man March." *Black Scholar* 25 (Fall): 17–26.

———. 1995b. *Black Women at the United Nations*. San Bernardino, Calif.: Borgo Press.

Washington, J. (ed.). 1992. *A Testament of Hope: The Essential Writings of Martin Luther King, Jr.* New York: Harper & Row.

Waters, M. 1992. Testimony before the Senate Banking Committee, May 14, 1992. *Inside the L.A. Riots*. New York: Institute for Alternative Journalism, 26.

Watson, D. 1980. "Do Mayors Matter? The Role of Black Leadership in Urban Policy." Paper presented at the American Political Science Association, Washington, D.C.

Watt, J. "Can A Hybrid Pot Call A Mulatto Kettle Black?: On Tom Sowell and His Critics." Unpublished Manuscript, Department of Political Science, Yale University.

Weisbord, B. A. (ed.). 1965. *The Economics of Poverty: An American Paradox*. Englewood Cliffs, N.J.: Prentice Hall, 111.

Wheeler, T. 1996. "Texaco Boycott Targets Big Oil Racism." *People's Weekly World*, November 16, p. 3.

"When Job Site Protests Are Necessary." 1994. *Chicago Defender*, June 23, p. 11.

Whitby, K. 1997. *The Color of Representation: Congressional Behavior and Black Interests*. Ann Arbor: University of Michigan Press.

White, J. 1990. *Black Leaderships in America: From Booker T. Washington to Jesse Jackson*. New York: Longman.

Wildavsky, A. 1989. "A Cultural Theory of Leadership." In Bryan Jones (ed.), *Leadership and Politics: New Perspectives in Political Science*. Lawrence: University of Kansas Press.

Wilkins, R., and T. Matthews. 1982. *Standing Fast: The Autobiography of Roy Wilkins*. New York: Viking Press, pp. 208–9.

Williams, E. 1982. "Black Political Progress in the 1970s: The Electoral Arena." In M. Preston, L. Henderson, and P. Puryear (eds.), *The New Black Politics*. New York: Longmans.

Williams, L. 1996. *Servants of the People: The 1960s Legacy of African American Leadership*. New York: St. Martin's Press.

Willingham, A. 1981. "The Place of the New Black Conservatives in Black Social Thought: Groundwork for the Full Critique." Paper presented at the Association for the Study of Afro-American Life and History, Philadelphia.

Wilson, J. 1960a. *Negro Politics: The Search for Leadership*. New York: The Free Press.

———. 1960b. "Two Negro Politicians: An Interpretation." *Midwest Journal of Political Science* 12: 365–69.

———. 1961. "The Strategy of Protest." *Journal of Conflict Resolution* 3: 291–303.

———. 1966. "The Negro in American Politics: The Present." *The American Negro Reference Book*. Englewood Cliffs, N.J.: Prentice Hall.

———. 1973. *Political Organizations*. New York: Basic Books.

Wilson, W. 1972a. "Black Demands and American Government Response." *Journal of Black Studies* 1: 7–28.

———. 1972b. *The Declining Significance of Race*. Chicago: University of Chicago Press.

Wittner, L. 1968. "The National Negro Congress: A Reassessment." *American Quarterly* 22: 883–90.

Wolfinger, R. 1976. *The Politics of Progress*. Englewood Cliffs, N.J.: Prentice Hall.

Wolman, H., and N. Thomas. 1970. "Black Interests, Black Groups, and Black Influence in the Federal Policy Process: The Cases of Housing and Education." *Journal of Politics* 32: 875–97.

"Working the Plan." 1979. Walter E. Fauntroy, chairman, Congressional Black Caucus Voter Participation and Network Development Brain Trust, National Newspaper Publishers Association Annual Conference, August 8.

Yankelovich, D. 1974. *The New Morality: A Profile of American Youth in the 70s*. New York: McGraw-Hill.

Yette, S. 1971. *The Choice: The Issue of Black Survival in America*. New York: G. P. Putnam Sons.

"Youth Recognition: Youth Achievements Given Spotlight at Ninth Annual MYRA Ceremony." *The Columbus Post*, April 24–30, p. 7-A.

Zald, M., and R. Ash. 1970. "Social Movement Organizations: Growth, Decay and Change." In Joseph Gusfeld (ed.), *Protest, Reform and Revolt*. New York: John Wiley & Sons.

Zinn, H. 1964. *SNCC: The New Abolitionists*. Boston: Beacon Press.

INDEX